everything's an argument

Third Edition

EVERYTHING'S AN argument

Andrea A. Lunsford
Stanford University

John J. Ruszkiewicz
University of Texas at Austin

BEDFORD/ST. MARTIN'S
BOSTON ■ NEW YORK

For Bedford/St. Martin's

Developmental Editor: Stephanie Carpenter
Production Editor: Bernard Onken
Senior Production Supervisor: Nancy Myers
Art Director: Lucy Krikorian
Text Design: Anna George
Copy Editor: Alice Vigliani
Indexer: Riofrancos & Co. Indexes
Photo Research: Alice Lundoff
Cover Design: Lucy Krikorian
Cover Photos: Barbie doll: the first Barbie doll produced in 1959, Barbie Doll
    Museum, Palo Alto. Photo © Frederic Neema /CORBIS; Seal of the President/
    United States. Photo Joseph Sohm/Photo Researchers. White Dove: Photo ©
    Roger Tidman/CORBIS; 4×4 on Road: Photo Getty Images/Antonio M. Rosario.
Composition: Monotype Composition Company, Inc.
Printing and Binding: Haddon Craftsmen, Inc., an R.R. Donnelley & Sons Company

President: Joan E. Feinberg
Editorial Director: Denise B. Wydra
Editor in Chief: Nancy Perry
Director of Marketing: Karen Melton Soeltz
Director of Editing, Design, and Production: Marcia Cohen
Managing Editor: Erica T. Appel

Library of Congress Control Number: 2003107544

Manufactured in the United States of America.
9 8 7 6 5 4
f e d c b

For information, write:
Bedford/St. Martin's
75 Arlington Street
Boston, MA 02116   (617-399-4000)

ISBN: 0-312-40716-5

ACKNOWLEDGMENTS

*Acknowledgments and copyrights appear at the back of the book on pages 465–466, which con-
stitute an extension of the copyright page.*

PREFACE

In this third edition, *Everything's an Argument* remains a labor of love for us, a lively introduction to rhetoric drawn directly from our experiences teaching persuasive writing. The chapters still practically write themselves, and we take special pleasure in discovering fresh new arguments or provocative visual images that illuminate the ways we all use language to assert our presence in the world. Apparently, the book continues to strike a chord with many students and instructors who have made *Everything's an Argument* a best-seller in its field since its debut. We offer now a third edition, thoroughly revised to reach even more writers and instructors and to account for changes we see in the way arguments are framed and circulated throughout the world.

The purposefully controversial title of this text sums up two key assumptions we share. First, language provides the most powerful means of understanding the world and of using that understanding to help shape lives. Second, all language—including the language of visual images or of symbol systems other than writing—is persuasive, pointing in a direction and asking for response. From the morning news to the presidential seal, from the American flag to the Mercedes three-pointed star, from the latest hip-hop hit to the brand identity of Pepsi, texts everywhere beckon for response. People walk, talk, and breathe persuasion very much as they breathe the air: *everything* is a potential argument.

So our purpose in *Everything's an Argument* is to present argument as something that's as natural and everyday as an old pair of jeans, as something we do almost from the moment we are born (in fact, an infant's first cry is as poignant a claim as we can imagine), and—because of its ever-present nature—as something worthy of careful attention and practice. In pursuing this goal, we try to use ordinary language whenever possible and to keep our use of specialized terminology to a minimum. But we also see argument, and want students to see it, as a craft both delicate and powerful. So we have designed *Everything's an Argument* to be itself an argument for argument, with a voice that aims to appeal to readers cordially but that doesn't hesitate to make demands on them when appropriate.

We also aim to balance attention to the critical *reading* of arguments (analysis) with attention to the writing of arguments (production). Moreover, we have tried to demonstrate both activities with lively — and realistic — examples, on the principle that the best way to appreciate an argument may be to see it in action. Indeed, we have worked hard to enhance the power of the examples selected for this third edition, expanding the range of texts we present and including works more deliberately oriented toward the concerns of college students in all their diversity.

In the previous edition, we broadened the context of argument to include visual media and the public spaces and electronic environments that students now inhabit so much of the time. We've intensified that effort in this latest edition, with every chapter presenting new images and fresh argumentative situations. We also offer more about that remarkably useful ancient way of approaching arguments called "stasis theory," integrating its principles across several key chapters. In addition, this third edition offers more advice about rhetorical analysis and then goes on to show students how to write an analysis of their own, since such assignments are increasingly common in courses on argument. Based on advice from teachers and students using this text and from reviewers, we have expanded both our general chapter on logical arguments (Chapter 7) and our more specialized chapter on Toulmin reasoning (Chapter 8) so that writers can choose what sort of approach to take toward reasoning. As a result, the Toulmin chapter not only includes more helpful explanations and diagrams, but also shows how Toulmin's concepts operate in extended arguments, illustrating the point by focusing on a lively essay by Alan M. Dershowitz. To help students better understand the increasingly complicated world of intellectual property and to show them how to avoid plagiarism, we've expanded Chapter 20 on intellectual property to offer more examples of situations familiar to students. We've also carefully revised the prose throughout *Everything's an Argument* to make our discussions livelier and clearer. We use fewer abstract subjects, fewer passive verbs, more lively images, and many more examples in some chapters. We hope the new book is even more engaging to read than the first two editions.

Key Features

- A fresh and winning approach, going beyond pro/con assumptions to show that argument is everywhere—in essays, news articles, scholarly writing, poems, advertisements, cartoons, posters, bumper stickers, billboards, Web sites, Web logs, and other electronic environments.

- Student-friendly explanations in simple, everyday language, many brief examples, and a minimum of technical terminology.

- Eleven sample essays, including six by student writers, annotated to show rhetorical features. Most of these readings are new to the third edition.

- Unique, full chapters on visual argument, argument in electronic environments, spoken argument, and humor in argument.

- Extensive coverage of the use of sources in argument, with full chapters on assessing and using sources, documenting sources in up-to-date MLA and APA styles, and intellectual property.

New to this Edition

- Expanded coverage of analyzing arguments in Chapter 2 to improve students' critical thinking and help them form their own arguments. Analyses of both a visual and a written text demonstrate this process for students.

- Greater integration of visual arguments in every chapter throughout the book so that students can recognize and respond to a more diverse range of arguments.

- An expanded intellectual property chapter, within a trio of chapters on using sources, that helps students understand the larger issues surrounding intellectual property and addresses the concerns about avoiding plagiarism that students face daily in their college courses.

- More help in understanding Toulmin argument through a sample Toulmin analysis of a full argument and more diagrams to explain the relationships among claims, reasons, warrants, and qualifiers. These additional aids help students analyze arguments and develop and test their own ideas.

- Additional extended examples of how to use the stasis questions during invention to show students how this ancient theory can help them in their own writing.
- Livelier prose and a greater range of examples to make the third edition more engaging than ever.

Acknowledgments

We owe a debt of gratitude to many people for making *Everything's an Argument* possible. Our first thanks must go to the students we have taught in our writing courses for more than two decades, particularly first-year students at The Ohio State University, Stanford University, and the University of Texas at Austin. Almost every chapter in this book has been informed by a classroom encounter with a student whose shrewd observation or perceptive question sent an ambitious lesson plan spiraling to the ground. (Anyone who has tried to teach claims and warrants on the fly to skeptical first-year students will surely appreciate why we have qualified our claims in the Toulmin chapter so carefully.) But students have also provided the motive for writing this book. More than ever, students need to know how to read and write arguments effectively if they are to secure a place in a world growing ever smaller and more rhetorically challenging.

We are grateful to our editors at Bedford/St. Martin's who contributed their talents to our book, beginning with Joan Feinberg and Nancy Perry, who have enthusiastically supported the project and provided us with the resources and feedback needed to keep us on track. Most of the day-to-day work on the project has been handled by the remarkably patient and perceptive Stephanie Carpenter. She prevented more than a few lapses of judgment yet understands the spirit of this book—which involves, occasionally, taking risks to make a memorable point. We have appreciated, too, her advice about pop culture issues, which begin to escape us, and her uncanny ability to focus our attention where it mattered.

We are similarly grateful to others at Bedford/St. Martin's who contributed their talents to our book: Bernard Onken, Nicholas Wolven, Alice Lundoff, Lucy Krikorian, Nancy Myers, Nick Carbone, and especially Anna George, whose design contributes so much to the book's appeal and accessibility. Thanks also to Karen Melton Soeltz and Brian Wheel for their superb marketing.

We'd also like to thank the astute instructors and students who reviewed the third edition: Petia Dimitrova Alexieva, University of South Carolina; Darlene Anderson, University of South Carolina; Cathryn Best, Grand Rapids Community College; Joyce Brownell, Ferris State University; Thomas Bonfiglio, Arizona State University; Terri-Ann Burack, Iowa State University; Jennifer R. Bush, Pennsylvania State University; Alison Cable, North Carolina State University; Patrick Clauss, Butler University; Michelle Comstock, University of South Alabama; Lauren Coulter, University of Tennessee–Chattanooga; Jane Fife, University of Tennessee–Chattanooga; Kenneth Hawley, University of Kentucky; Mary Hocks, Georgia State University; Janice Hudley, U.S. Military Academy–West Point; Priscilla Kanet, Clemson University; Lindsay Lightner, Pennsylvania State University; Amy Lister, Louisiana State University; Rachel Lutwick-Deaner, North Carolina State University; Aimee Mapes, Louisiana State University; Kristine V. Nakutis, United States Military Academy–West Point; Richard Ogle, University of Tennessee–Chattanooga; Darrel Jesse Peters, University of North Carolina–Pembroke; Malea Powell, University of Nebraska–Lincoln; Catherine E. Ross, The University of Texas at Tyler; Stephen Schneider, Pennsylvania State University; Carol Severino, University of Iowa; Lee S. Tesdell, Iowa State University; Alex Vuilleumier, Oregon State University; Anne Wiegard, SUNY–Cortland; the excellent group of teaching assistants at The University of Texas who shared their ideas early in the revision; and the students of Cassie Armstrong's English 141 class at the University of Colorado–Colorado Springs.

Thanks, too, to Ben Feigert, who wrote some of the original exercises for *Everything's an Argument,* and to John Kinkade, who has prepared the instructor's guide for this third edition. Finally, we are grateful to the students whose fine argumentative essays appear in our chapters.

We hope that *Everything's an Argument* responds to what students and instructors have said they want and need. And we hope readers of this text will let us know how we've done: please share your opinions and suggestions with us at bedfordstmartins.com/everythingsanargument.

Andrea A. Lunsford
John J. Ruszkiewicz

CONTENTS

PART 5   CONVENTIONS OF ARGUMENT   365

PART 1

INTRODUCING
argument

chapter one

Everything Is an Argument

"Best Breakfast Anywhere!" proclaims a sign in the window of a diner.

A professor interrupts a lecture to urge her students to spend less time on Instant Messaging and more in the company of thick, old books.

A senator tells a C-SPAN caller that recent legislation, such as the Homeland Security Bill, does not reduce citizens' constitutional rights or their privacy.

A nurse assures a youngster eyeing an approaching needle, "This won't hurt one bit."

A sports columnist blasts a football coach for passing on fourth down and two in a close game—even though the play produces a touchdown.

Sign found on a teenager's bedroom door:

Bumper sticker sighted in November 2002:

A thousand points of light,
and we got the dim one.
www.votescount2002.com

"Please let me make it through this chem exam!" a student silently prays.

■ ■ ■

These visual and verbal messages all contain arguments. In fact, it's hard to go more than a few minutes without encountering some form of argument in our culture. From the clothes you wear to the foods you choose to eat to the groups you decide to join—all of these everyday activities make nuanced, sometimes implicit, arguments about who you are and what you value. Thus an argument can be any text—whether written, spoken, or visual—that expresses a point of view. Sometimes arguments can be aggressive, composed deliberately to change what readers believe, think, or do. At other times your goals may be more subtle, and your writing may be designed to convince yourself or others that specific facts are reliable or that certain views should be considered or at least tolerated.

In fact, some theorists claim that language is itself inherently persuasive (even when you say "hi, how's it going?" for instance, you are in one sense arguing that your hello deserves a response) and hence *every* text is also an argument, designed to influence readers. For example, a poem that observes what little girls do in church may indirectly critique the role religion plays in women's lives, for good or ill:

I worry for the girls.
I once had braids,
and wore lace that made me suffer.

> I had not yet done the things
> that would need forgiving.
> –Kathleen Norris, "Little Girls in Church"

To take another example, observations about family life among the poor in India may suddenly illuminate the writer's life and the reader's experience, forcing comparisons that quietly argue for change:

> I have learned from Jagat and his family a kind of commitment, a form of friendship that is not always available in the West, where we have become cynical and instrumental in so many of our relationships to others.
>
> –Jeremy Seabrook, "Family Values"

Even humor makes an argument when it causes readers to become aware—through bursts of laughter or just a faint smile—of the way things are and how they might be different. Take a look, for example, at an excerpt from the introduction to Dave Barry's latest book, *Dave Barry Hits Below the Beltway,* along with its cover, which also makes a humorous argument:

> To do even a halfway decent book on a subject as complex as the United States government, you have to spend a lot of time in Washington, D.C. So the first thing I decided, when I was getting ready to write this book, was that it would not be even halfway decent.

FIGURE 1.1 DAVE BARRY'S HUMOROUS ARGUMENT BEGINS ON HIS BOOK'S COVER.

More obvious as arguments are those that make a claim and present evidence to support it. Such writing often moves readers to recognize problems and to consider solutions. Suasion of this kind is usually easy to recognize:

> **Discrimination against Hispanics, or any other group, should be fought and there are laws and a massive apparatus to do so. But the way to eliminate such discrimination is not to classify all Hispanics as victims.**
>
> –Linda Chavez, "Towards a New Politics of Hispanic Assimilation"

> **[W]omen unhappy in their marriages often enter full-time employment as an escape. But although a woman's entrance into the workplace does tend to increase the stability of her marriage, it does not increase her happiness.**
>
> –The Popular Research Institute, Penn State University

> **Resistance to science is born of fear. Fear, in turn, is bred by ignorance. And it is ignorance that is our deepest malady.**
>
> –J. Michael Bishop, "Enemies of Promise"

ARGUMENT ISN'T JUST ABOUT WINNING

If in some ways all language has an argumentative edge that aims to make a point, not all language use aims to win out over others. In contrast to the traditional Western concept of argument as being about fighting or combat, communication theorists such as Sonja Foss, Cindy Griffin, and Josina Makau describe an *invitational* argument, which aims not to win over another person or group but to invite others to enter a space of mutual regard and exploration. In fact, as you'll see, writers and speakers have as many purposes for arguing as for using language, including—in addition to winning—to inform, to convince, to explore, to make decisions, even to meditate or pray.

Of course, many arguments *are* aimed at winning. Such is the traditional purpose of much writing and speaking in the political arena, in the business world, and in the law courts. Two candidates for office, for example, try to win out over each other in appealing for votes; the makers of one soft drink try to outsell their competitors by appealing to public tastes; and two lawyers try to defeat each other in pleading to a judge and jury. In your college writing, you may also be called on to make an argument that appeals to a "judge" and/or "jury" (your instructor and classmates). You might, for instance, argue that peer-to-peer file-sharing is protected under the doctrine of fair use. In doing so, you may need to defeat your unseen opponents—those who oppose such file-sharing.

At this point, it may be helpful to acknowledge a common academic distinction between argument and persuasion. In this view, the point of argument is to discover some version of the truth, using evidence and reasons. Argument of this sort leads audiences toward conviction, an agreement that a claim is true or reasonable, or that a course of action is desirable. The aim of persuasion is to change a point of view or to move others from conviction to action. In other words, writers or speakers argue to find some truth; they persuade when they think they already know it.

Argument (discover a truth) ⟶ conviction

Persuasion (know a truth) ⟶ action

In practice, this distinction between argument and persuasion can be hard to sustain. It is unnatural for writers or readers to imagine their minds divided between a part that pursues truth and a part that seeks to persuade. And yet, you may want to reserve the term *persuasion* for writing that is aggressively designed to change opinions through the use of both reason and other appropriate techniques. For writing that sets out to persuade at all costs, abandoning reason, fairness, and truth altogether, the term *propaganda,* with all its negative connotations, seems to fit. Some would suggest that *advertising* often works just as well.

But, as we have already suggested, arguing isn't always about winning or even about changing others' views. In addition to invitational argument, another school of argument—called Rogerian argument, after the psychotherapist Carl Rogers—is based on finding common ground and establishing trust among those who disagree about issues, and on approaching audiences in nonthreatening ways. Writers who follow Rogerian approaches seek to understand the perspectives of those with whom they disagree, looking for "both/and" or "win/win" solutions (rather than "either/or" or "win/lose" ones) whenever possible. Much successful argument today follows such principles, consciously or not.

Some other purposes or goals of argument are worth considering in more detail.

Arguments to Inform

You may want or need to argue with friends or colleagues over the merits of different academic majors. But your purpose in doing so may well be to inform and to be informed, for only in such detailed arguments can you come to the best choice. Consider how Joan Didion uses argument to inform readers about the artist Georgia O'Keeffe:

> This is a woman who in 1939 could advise her admirers that they were missing her point, that their appreciation of her famous flowers was merely sentimental. "When I paint a red hill," she observed coolly in the catalogue for an exhibition that year, "you say it is too bad that I don't always paint flowers. A flower touches almost everyone's heart. A red hill doesn't touch everyone's heart."
>
> —Joan Didion, "Georgia O'Keeffe"

By giving specific information about O'Keeffe and her own ideas about her art, Didion in this passage argues that readers should pay closer attention to the work of this artist.

Less subtle and more common as informative arguments are political posters featuring the smiling faces of candidates and the offices they are

FIGURE 1.2   GEORGIA O'KEEFFE'S *WHITE FLOWER ON RED EARTH, #1* (1943)

seeking: "Honda in 2002," "Lujan for Mayor." Of course, these visual texts are usually also aimed at winning out over an unmentioned opponent. But on the surface at least, they announce who is running for a specific office.

Arguments to Convince

If you are writing a report that attempts to identify the causes of changes in global temperatures, you would likely be trying not to conquer opponents but to satisfy readers that you've thoroughly examined those causes and that they merit serious attention. As a form of writing, reports typically aim to persuade readers rather than win out over opponents. Yet the presence of those who might disagree is always implied, and it shapes a writer's strategies. In the following passage, for example, Paul Osterman argues to convince readers of the urgency surrounding jobs for all citizens:

> Among employed 19- to 31-year-old high school graduates who did not go to college, more than 30 percent had not been in their position for even a year. Another 12 percent had only one year of tenure. The pattern was much the same for women who had remained in the labor force for the four years prior to the survey. These are adults who, for a variety of reasons—a lack of skills, training, or disposition— have not managed to secure "adult" jobs.
>
> –Paul Osterman, "Getting Started"

Osterman uses facts to report a seemingly objective conclusion about the stability of employment among certain groups, but he is also arguing against those who find that the current job situation is tolerable and not worthy of concern or action.

Arguments to Explore

Many important subjects call for arguments that take the form of exploration, either on your own or with others. If there's an "opponent" in such a situation at all (often there is not), it is likely the status quo or a current trend that—for one reason or another—is puzzling. Exploratory arguments may be deeply personal, such as E. B. White's often-reprinted essay "Once More to the Lake." Or the exploration may be aimed at addressing serious problems in society. James Fallows opens such an argument by explaining the process of exploration he went through:

> Over the past few months I interviewed several dozen people about what could be expected in Iraq after the United States dislodged

Saddam Hussein. . . . The people I asked were spies, Arabists, oil-company officials, diplomats, scholars, policy experts, and many active-duty and retired soldiers. They were from the United States, Europe, and the Middle East. Some firmly supported a pre-emptive war against Iraq; more were opposed. As of late summer, before the serious domestic debate had begun, most of the people I spoke with expected a war to occur.

                                    —James Fallows, "The Fifty-First State?"

Perhaps the essential argument in any such piece is the writer's assertion that a problem exists (in this case, whether or not to go to war with Iraq) and that the writer or reader needs to solve it. Some exploratory pieces present and defend solutions. Others remain more open-ended, as is the case with Fallows's essay, which concludes with a form of meditation:

> It has become a cliché in popular writing about the natural world that small disturbances to complex systems can have unpredictably large effects. The world of nations is perhaps not quite as intricate as the natural world, but it certainly holds the potential for great surprise. Merely itemizing the foreseeable effects of a war with Iraq suggests reverberations that would be felt for decades. If we can judge from past wars, the effects we can't imagine when the fighting begins will prove to be the ones that matter most.

Arguments to Make Decisions

Closely allied to argument that explores is that which aims at making good, sound decisions. In fact, the result of many exploratory arguments may be to argue for a particular decision, whether that decision relates to the best computer for you to buy or to the "right" person for you to choose as your life partner. For college students, choosing a major is a major decision, and one way to go about making that decision is to argue your way through several alternatives. By the time you have examined the pros and cons of each alternative, you should be at least one step closer to a good decision. In the following paragraphs, history major Jessica Cohen reasons her way toward a momentous decision, asking should she, or should she not, become an egg donor for a wealthy couple:

> Early in the spring of last year a classified ad ran for two weeks in the *Yale Daily News:* "EGG DONOR NEEDED." The couple [Michelle and David] that placed the ad was picky, and for that reason was offering $25,000 for an egg from the right donor. . . .

I kept dreaming about all the things I could do with $25,000. I had gone into the correspondence [with David and Michelle] on a whim. But soon, despite David's casual tone and the optimistic attitude of all the classifieds and information I read, I decided that this process was something I didn't want to be part of. I understand the desire for a child who will resemble and fit in with the family. But once a couple starts choosing a few characteristics, shooting for perfection is too easy—especially if they can afford it. The money might have changed my life for a while, but it would have led to the creation of a child encumbered with too many expectations.

–Jessica Cohen, "Grade A: The Market for a Yale Woman's Eggs"

Arguments to Meditate or Pray

Sometimes arguments can take the form of intense meditations on a theme, or of prayer. In such cases, the writer or speaker is most often hoping to transform something in him- or herself or to reach a state of equilibrium or peace of mind. If you know a familiar prayer or mantra, think for a moment of what it "argues" for and of how it uses quiet meditation to accomplish that goal. Such meditations do not have to be formal prayers, however. Look, for example, at the ways in which Michael Lassell's poetry uses a kind of meditative language to reach understanding for himself and to evoke meditative thought in others:

Feel how it feels to
hold a man in your arms
whose arms are used to holding men.
Offer God anything to bring your brother back.
Know you have nothing God could possibly want.
Curse God, but do not
abandon Him.

–Michael Lassell, "How to Watch Your Brother Die"

Another sort of meditative argument can be found in the stained-glass windows of churches and other public buildings. Dazzled by a spectacle of light, people pause to consider a window's message longer than they might were the same idea conveyed on paper. The window engages viewers with a power not unlike that of poetry. (See Figure 1.3.)

As these examples suggest, the effectiveness of argument depends not only on the purposes of the writer but also on the context surrounding the plea and the people it seeks most directly to reach. Though we'll examine arguments of all types in this book, we'll focus chiefly on the kinds made in professional and academic situations.

FIGURE 1.3 STAINED-GLASS WINDOW PORTRAYING THE PRODIGAL SON LEAVING HIS
FATHER'S HOUSE

OCCASIONS FOR ARGUMENT

Another way of thinking about arguments is to consider the public occasions that call for them. In an ancient textbook of rhetoric, or the art of persuasion, the philosopher Aristotle provides an elegant scheme for classifying the purposes of arguments, one based on issues of time—past, future, and present. His formula is easy to remember and helpful in suggesting strategies for making convincing cases. But because all classifications overlap with others to a certain extent, don't be surprised to encounter many arguments that span more than one category—arguments about the past with implications for the future, arguments about the future with bearings on the present, and so on.

Arguments about the Past

Debates about what has happened in the past are called forensic arguments; such controversies are common in business, government, and academia. For example, in many criminal and civil cases, lawyers interrogate witnesses to establish exactly what happened at an earlier time: *Did the defendant sexually harass her employee? Did the company deliberately ignore evidence that its product was deficient? Was the contract properly enforced?* The contentious nature of some forensic arguments is evident in this brief excerpt from a letter to the editor of *The Atlantic Monthly:*

> Kenneth Brower's review of "Ansel Adams at 100," in your July/August issue, is misguided and inaccurate. . . . [In fact, Adams] worked seven days a week, never taking vacations, until he was eighty. It is impossible to imagine such activity in a person of "compromised health." Ditto for the notion of "delicate since childhood."
> —William A. Turnage

In replying to this letter, the author of the review, Kenneth Brower, disputes Turnage's statements, introducing more evidence in support of his original claim. Obviously, then, forensic arguments rely on evidence and testimony to re-create what can be known about events that have already occurred.

Forensic arguments also rely heavily on precedents—actions or decisions in the past that influence policies or decisions in the present—and on analyses of cause and effect. Consider the ongoing controversy over Christopher Columbus: Are his expeditions to the Americas events worth celebrating, or are they unhappy chapters in human history? No simple exchange of evidence will suffice to still this debate; the effects of Columbus's actions beginning in 1492 may be studied and debated for the next five hundred years. As you might suspect from this example, arguments about history are typically forensic.

Forensic cases may also be arguments about character, such as when someone's reputation is studied in a historical context to enrich current perspectives on the person. Allusions to the past can make present arguments more vivid, as in the following text about Ward Connerly, head of an organization that aims to dismantle affirmative action programs:

> Despite the fact that Connerly's message seems clearly opposed to the Civil Rights Movement, some people are fond of pointing out that the man is black. But as far as politics goes, that is irrelevant. Before black suffrage, there were African Americans who publicly argued against their own right to vote.
> —Carl Villarreal, "Connerly Is an Enemy of Civil Rights"

Such writing can be exploratory and open-ended, the point of argument being to enhance and sharpen knowledge, not just to generate heat or score points.

Arguments about the Future

Debates about the future are a form of deliberative argument. Legisla-tures, congresses, and parliaments are called deliberative bodies because they establish policies for the future: *Should Social Security be privatized? Should the United States build a defense against ballistic missiles?*

Because what has happened in the past influences the future, deliber-ative judgments often rely on prior forensic arguments. Thus, deliberative arguments often draw on evidence and testimony, as in this passage:

> The labor market is sending a clear signal. While the American way of moving youngsters from high school to the labor market may be imperfect, the chief problem is that, for many, even getting a job no longer guarantees a decent standard of living. More than ever, getting ahead, or even keeping up, means staying in school longer.
> —Paul Osterman, "Getting Started"

But since no one has a blueprint for what is to come, deliberative argu-ments also advance by means of projections, extrapolations, and rea-soned guesses — *if X is true, Y may be true; if X happens, so may Y; if X continues, then Y may occur:*

> In 2000, according to a World Health Organization assessment, 1.1 bil-lion people worldwide had no regular access to safe drinking water, and 2.4 billion had no regular access to sanitation systems. Lack of access to clean water leads to four billion cases of diarrhea each year. Peter Gleick, an expert on global freshwater resources, reveals that even if we reach the United Nations' stated goal of halving the num-ber of people without access to safe drinking water by 2015, as many as 76 million people will die from water-borne diseases before 2020.
> —Pacific Institute for Studies in Development, Environment, and Security

Arguments about the Present

Arguments about the present are often arguments about contemporary values — the ethical premises and assumptions that are widely held (or contested) within a society. Sometimes called epideictic arguments or cer-emonial arguments because they tend to be heard at public occasions, they include inaugural addresses, sermons, eulogies, graduation speeches, and civic remarks of all kinds. Ceremonial arguments can be passionate and eloquent, rich in anecdotes and examples. Martin Luther King Jr. was a master of ceremonial discourse, and he was particularly adept at find-ing affirmation in the depths of despair:

> Three nights later, our home was bombed. Strangely enough, I
> accepted the word of the bombing calmly. My experience with God
> had given me a new strength and trust. I know now that God is able to
> give us the interior resources to face the storms and problems of life.
> —Martin Luther King Jr., "Our God Is Able"

King argues here that the arbiter of good and evil in society is, ultimately,
God. But not all ceremonial arguments reach quite so far.

More typical are values arguments that explore contemporary culture,
praising what is admirable and blaming what is not. Andrew Sullivan,
for example, examines what he considers a national craving for often-
unjustified self-esteem. Yet he concludes by arguing that achieving a
strong self-image is still "surely worth the effort":

> Self-esteem isn't all that it's cracked up to be. In fact . . . it can be a
> huge part of the problem. New research has found that self-esteem
> can be just as high among D students, drunk drivers and former Pres-
> idents from Arkansas as it is among Nobel laureates, nuns and New
> York City fire fighters. In fact, according to research performed by Brad
> Bushman of Iowa State University and Roy Baumeister of Case West-
> ern Reserve University, people with high self-esteem can engage in far
> more antisocial behavior than those with low self-worth. . . . Racists,
> street thugs and school bullies all polled high on the self-esteem
> charts. And you can see why. If you think you're God's gift, you're par-
> ticularly offended if other people don't treat you that way. So you lash
> out or commit crimes or cut ethical corners to reassert your preemi-
> nence. After all, who are your moral inferiors to suggest that you could
> be doing something, er, wrong? What do they know? . . . Of course, in
> these therapized days, reality can be a touchy subject. It's hard to
> accept that we may not be the best at something or that we genuinely
> screwed up or that low self-esteem can sometimes be fully justified.
> But maintaining a robust self-image while being able to absorb diffi-
> cult criticism is surely worth the effort.
> —Andrew Sullivan, "Lacking in Self-Esteem: Good for You!"

As in many ceremonial arguments, Sullivan here reinforces common values of modesty and fair play.

KINDS OF ARGUMENT

Yet another way of categorizing arguments is to consider their status or
stasis—that is, the kinds of issues they address. This categorization system is called stasis theory. In ancient Greek and Roman civilizations,

rhetoricians defined a series of questions by which to examine legal cases. The questions would be posed in sequence, because each depended on the question(s) preceding it. Together, the questions helped determine the point of contention in an argument, the place where disputants could focus their energy and hence what kind of an argument to make. A modern version of those questions might look like the following:

- Did something happen?
- What is its nature?
- What is its quality?
- What actions should be taken?

Here's how the questions might be used to explore a "crime."

Did Something Happen?

Yes. A young man kissed a young woman against her will. The act was witnessed by a teacher and friends and acquaintances of both parties. The facts suggest clearly that something happened. If you were going to write an argument about this event, this first stasis question proves not very helpful, since there's no debate about whether the act occurred. If the event were debatable, however, you could develop an argument of fact.

What Is Its Nature?

The act might be construed as "sexual harassment," defined as the imposition of unwanted or unsolicited sexual attention or activity on a person. The young man kissed the young woman on the lips. Kissing people who aren't relatives on the lips is generally considered a sexual activity. The young woman did not want to be kissed and complained to her teacher. The young man's act meets the definition of "sexual harassment." Careful analysis of this stasis question could lead to an argument of definition.

What Is Its Quality?

Both the young man and young woman involved in the action are six years old. They were playing in a schoolyard. The boy didn't realize that kissing girls against their will was a violation of school policy; school sexual harassment policies had not in the past been enforced against first-graders. Most people don't regard six-year-olds as sexually culpable. Moreover, the girl wants to play with the boy again and apparently doesn't resent his action. Were you to decide on this focus, you would be developing an argument of evaluation.

What Actions Should Be Taken?

The case has raised a ruckus among parents, the general public, and some feminists and anti-feminists. The consensus seems to be that the school overreacted in seeking to brand the boy a sexual harasser. Yet it is important that the issue of sexual harassment not be dismissed as trivial. Consequently, the boy should be warned not to kiss girls against their will. The teachers should be warned not to make federal cases out of schoolyard spats. And with this stasis question as your focus, you would be developing a proposal argument.

As you can see, each of the stasis questions explores different aspects of a problem and uses different evidence or techniques to reach conclusions. You can use stasis theory to help you explore the aspects of any topic you are considering. In addition, studying the results of your exploration of the stasis questions can help you determine the major point you want to make and thus identify the type of argument that will be most effective.

Arguments of Fact — Did Something Happen?

An argument of fact usually involves a statement that can be proved or disproved with specific evidence or testimony. Although relatively simple to define, such arguments are often quite subtle, involving layers of complexity not apparent when the question is initially posed.

For example, the question of pollution of our oceans—Is it really occurring?—would seem relatively easy to settle. Either scientific data prove that the oceans are being polluted as a result of human activity, or they don't. But to settle the matter, writers and readers would first have to agree on a number of points, each of which would have to be examined and debated: *What constitutes pollution? How will such pollution be measured? Over what period of time? Are any current deviations in water quality unprecedented? How can one be certain that deviations are attributable to human action?*

Nevertheless, questions of this sort can be disputed primarily on the facts, complicated and contentious as they may be. But should you choose to develop an argument of fact, be aware of how difficult it can sometimes be to establish "facts." (For more on arguments based on facts, see Chapter 7.)

Arguments of Definition — What Is the Nature of the Thing?

Just as contentious as arguments based on facts are questions of definition. An argument of definition often involves determining whether one known object or action belongs in a second — and more highly contested — category. One of the most hotly debated issues in American life today involves a question of definition: *Is a human fetus a human being?* If one argues that it is, then a second issue of definition arises: *Is abortion murder?* As you can see, issues of definition can have mighty consequences — and decades of debate may leave the matter unresolved.

Writer Jan Morris defines a condition, homesickness, she assumes is familiar to almost everyone, but she works with shades of meaning to explain what homesickness is for her:

> Homesickness is the most delicious form of nostalgia, if only because, generally speaking, it really can be gratified. We cannot return to the past, but we can go home again. In my case homesickness is related to something the Welsh language calls *hiraeth*. This over-worked word (the Welsh are big on emotions) means literally "longing," "nostalgia," or sometimes plain "grief." It has come to signify, however, something even less exact: longing, yes, but for nothing definite; nostalgia, but for an indeterminate past; grief without cause or explanation. *Hiraeth!* — an insidious summation of all that is most poetical, most musical, most regretful, most opaque, most evasive, most extinguishable, in the character of Wales.
>
> —Jan Morris, "Home Thoughts from Abroad"

Bob Costas, eulogizing Mickey Mantle, a great baseball player who had many universally human faults, advances his assessment by means of an important definitional distinction:

> In the last year, Mickey Mantle, always so hard upon himself, finally came to accept and appreciate the distinction between a role model and a hero. The first he often was not, the second he always will be.
>
> —Bob Costas, "Eulogy for Mickey Mantle"

But arguments of definition can be less weighty than these, though still hotly contested: *Is video game playing a sport? Is Madonna an artist? Is ketchup a vegetable?* To argue such cases, one would first have to put forth definitions, and then those definitions would have to become the foci of debates themselves. (For more about arguments of definition, see Chapter 9.)

Arguments of Evaluation — What Is the Quality of the Thing?

Arguments of definition lead naturally into arguments of quality — that is, to questions about quality. Most auto enthusiasts, for example, would not be content merely to inquire whether the Corvette is a sports car. They'd prefer to argue whether it is a *good* sports car or a better sports car than, say, the Viper. Or they might wish to assert that it is the best sports car in the world, perhaps qualifying their claim with the caveat *for the price*. Arguments of evaluation are so common that writers sometimes take them for granted, ignoring their complexity and importance in establishing people's values and priorities. The stasis question "what is the quality of the thing" is at the heart of attempts to understand the nuclear capability of North Korea. Those working to develop U.S. policy toward North Korea need to use this stasis question to develop a compelling argument of evaluation.

Consider how Rosa Parks assesses Martin Luther King Jr. in the following passage. Though she seems to be defining the concept of "leader," she is measuring King against criteria she has set for "*true* leader," an important distinction:

> **Dr. King was a true leader. I never sensed fear in him. I just felt he knew what had to be done and took the leading role without regard to consequences. I knew he was destined to do great things. He had an elegance about him and a speaking style that let you know where you stood and inspired you to do the best you could. He truly is a role model for us all. The sacrifice of his life should never be forgotten, and his dream must live on.**
>
> **—Rosa Parks, "Role Models"**

Parks's comments represent a type of informal evaluation that is common in ceremonial arguments; because King is so well known, she doesn't have to burnish every claim with specific evidence. (See p. 14 for more on ceremonial arguments.) In contrast, Molly Ivins in praising Barbara Jordan makes quite explicit the connections between her claim and the evidence:

> **Barbara Jordan, whose name was so often preceded by the words "the first black woman to . . ." that they seemed like a permanent title, died Wednesday in Austin. A great spirit is gone.**
>
> **The first black woman to serve in the Texas Senate, the first black woman in Congress (she and Yvonne Brathwaite Burke of California were both elected in 1972, but Jordan had no Republican opposition), the first black elected to Congress from the South since Reconstruction, the first black woman to sit on major corporate boards, and so on. Were it not for the disease that slowly crippled her, she probably**

would have been the first black woman on the Supreme Court—it is known that Jimmy Carter had her on his short list.

And long before she became "the first and only black woman to . . ." there was that astounding string of achievements going back to high school valedictorian, honors at Texas Southern University, law degree from Boston University. Both her famous diction and her enormous dignity were present from the beginning, her high school teachers recalled. Her precise enunciation was a legacy from her father, a Baptist minister, and characteristic of educated blacks of his day. Her great baritone voice was so impressive that her colleagues in the Legislature used to joke that if Hollywood ever needed someone to be the voice of the Lord Almighty, only Jordan would do.

—Molly Ivins, "Barbara Jordan: A Great Spirit"

An argument of evaluation advances by presenting criteria and then measuring individual people, ideas, or things against those standards. Both the standards and the measurement can be explored argumentatively. And that's an important way to think of arguments—as ways to expand what is known, not just to settle differences. (For more about arguments of evaluation, see Chapter 10.)

Proposal Arguments — What Actions Should Be Taken?

Arguments may lead to proposals for action when writers have succeeded in presenting problems in such a compelling way that readers ask: *What can we do?* A proposal argument often begins with the presentation of research to document existing conditions. Thus if you are developing an argument about rising tuition costs at your college, you could use all of the stasis questions to explore the issue and to establish that costs are indeed rising. But the last question—"What actions should be taken?"— will probably be the most important, since it will lead you to develop concrete proposals to address the rise in fees. Knowing and explaining the status quo enable writers to explore appropriate and viable alternatives and then to recommend one preferable course of action. In examining a nationwide move to eliminate remedial education in colleges, John Cloud considers one possible proposal to avoid such action:

Students age 22 and over account for 43% of those in remedial classrooms, according to the National Center for Developmental Education. [. . . But] 55% of those needing remediation must take just one course. Is it too much to ask them to pay extra for that class or take it at a community college?

—John Cloud, "Who's Ready for College?"

Where a need is already obvious, writers may spend most of their energies describing and defending the solution. John Henry Newman, for example, assumes the need for strong higher learning in proposing a new form of liberal education in the nineteenth century. Here, he enumerates the benefits his preferred solution will bring to society:

> [A] university education is the great ordinary means to a great but ordinary end; it aims at raising the intellectual tone of society, at cultivating the public mind, at purifying the national taste, at supplying true principles to popular enthusiasm and fixed aims to popular aspiration, at giving enlargement and sobriety to the ideas of the age, at facilitating the exercise of political power, and refining the intercourse of private life.
> —John Henry Newman, "The Idea of a University"

Americans in particular tend to see the world in terms of problems and solutions; indeed, many Americans expect that any difficulty can be overcome by the proper infusion of technology and money. So proposal arguments seem especially appealing, even when quick-fix attitudes may themselves constitute a problem. (For more about proposal arguments, see Chapter 12.)

CULTURAL CONTEXTS FOR ARGUMENT

If you want to communicate effectively with people across cultures, then you need to try to learn something about the norms in those cultures—and to be aware of the norms guiding your own behavior.

- Be aware of the assumptions that guide your own customary ways of arguing a point. Remember that most of us tend to see our own way as the "normal" or "right" way to do things. Such assumptions guide your thinking and your judgments about what counts—and what "works"—in an argument.

- Keep in mind that if your own ways seem inherently right, then even without thinking about it you may assume that other ways are somehow less than right. Such thinking makes it hard to communicate effectively across cultures.

- Remember that ways of arguing are influenced by cultural contexts and that they differ widely across cultures. Pay attention to the ways people from cultures other than your own argue, and be flexible and open to the many ways of thinking you will no doubt encounter.

(continued)

- Respect the differences among individuals within a given culture; don't expect that every member of a community behaves — or argues — in just the same way.

The best advice, then, might be *don't assume.* Just because you think wearing a navy blazer and a knee-length skirt "argues" that you should be taken seriously as a job candidate at a multinational corporation, such dress may be perceived differently in other settings. And if in an interview a candidate does not look you in the eye, don't assume that this reflects any lack of confidence or respect; he or she may intend it as a sign of politeness.

STASIS QUESTIONS AT WORK

Suppose you have an opportunity to speak at a student conference on the issue of global warming, which has been a particularly hot topic on your campus. The Campus Young Republicans are sponsoring the conference, but they have made a point of inviting students with varying perspectives to speak. You are concerned about global warming and are tentatively in favor of making changes to industrial pollution standards aimed at reducing global warming trends. You decide that you'd like to learn a lot more by investigating the issue more fully and preparing to speak on it. You use the stasis questions to get started.

- **Did something happen?** Does global warming exist? The Bush administration, on the one hand, is skeptical, so much so that the President refused to sign an international agreement aimed at reducing global warming. Environmentalists, on the other hand, argue that the phenomenon does exist, that it has reached very serious proportions, and that it must be addressed as soon as possible. In coming to your own conclusion about global warming, you will weigh the factual evidence very carefully, making sure that you can support your answers to the question "Does it exist?" and that you can point out problems associated with counterarguments.
- **What is the nature of the thing?** Looking for definitions of global warming also reveals great disagreement. The Bush administration defines the phenomenon as naturally occurring, while environmentalists base their definition on industry-related causes. Thus you begin to consider competing definitions very carefully: How do the

(continued)

definitions they choose to use foster the goals of each group? Who gets to say what definition is acceptable? What is at stake for industry in promoting its definition of global warming? What is at stake for environmentalists in putting forth their definition? Exploring this stasis question will help you understand how the context of an argument shapes the claims that the argument makes.

- **What is the quality of the thing?** This question will lead you to examine claims that global warming is — or is not — harming our environment. Again, you quickly find that these charges are hotly contested. The pro-industry stance of the Bush administration shapes its analysis, leading to a dismissal of claims that the phenomenon is causing great environmental harm. Exploring these arguments will allow you to ask who or what entities are providing evidence in support of their claim and who stands to gain in this analysis. Turning to the environmentalist arguments, you ask the same questions: Where does evidence for the dangers of global warming come from? Who stands to gain if the dangers are accepted as real and present, and who stands to lose if they are not?

- **What actions should be taken?** In this case as well, you find wide disagreement. If global warming is a naturally occurring phenomenon, then it is at least arguable that nothing needs to be done, that the problem will correct itself in time. Or perhaps those in the administration who have made these arguments will decide to recommend a new study of global warming, in an effort to prove once and for all that their understanding of global warming and its effects is the correct one. If, on the other hand, global warming is a clear and present threat to the quality of the atmosphere, as the environmentalists argue, then they are bound to recommend implementing appropriate and effective responses to such danger (although not everyone agrees on precisely what such responses should be). You quickly discover that the goals and definitions being used directly shape the actions that each side recommends. As you investigate the proposals being made and the reasons that underlie them, you come closer and closer to developing your own argument.

Using the stasis questions as a way to get into the topic of global warming adds up to a crash course on the subject. As you sort through the claims and counterclaims associated with each of the questions, you move toward identifying your own stance on global warming — and toward the claim you want to make about it for the student con-

(continued)

ference. You come to the conclusion that global warming does exist and that it does present a serious danger. Yet given the audience for the conference, you know that you still have quite a bit of work to do. Since many will not agree with your conclusion, you begin to gather the most fair and evenhanded research available to make your case, and you begin working to establish your own credibility and to consider how best you can present your case to your specific audience.

IS EVERYTHING AN ARGUMENT?

In a world where argument is as abundant as fast food, everyone has a role to play in shaping and responding to arguments. Debate and discussion are, after all, key components of the never-ending conversation about our lives and the world that is sometimes called academic inquiry. Its standards are rigorous: Take no claim at face value, examine all evidence thoroughly, and study the implications of your own and others' beliefs. Developing an inquiring turn of mind like this can serve you well now and into the future. It might even lead you to wonder, with healthy suspicion, whether *everything* really is an argument.

RESPOND●

1. Can an argument really be any text that expresses a point of view? What kinds of arguments—if any—might be made by the following items?

   the embossed leather cover of a prayer book

   a Web site's home page

   a New York Yankees cap

   the label on a best-selling rap CD

   the health warning on a bag of no-fat potato chips

   a belated birthday card

   the nutrition label on a can of soup

   the cover of a science fiction novel

   a colored ribbon pinned to a shirt lapel

   a Rolex watch

2. Decide whether each of the following items is an example of *argument,*
    persuasion, or *propaganda.* You'll likely have a variety of responses
    among your classmates, so be prepared to explain your categor-
    ization.

    a proof in a calculus textbook

    a banner proclaiming "Halt Globalization Now!" at a World Trade
    Organization protest

    a U.S. president's State of the Union address

    a lawyer's opening statement at a jury trial

    a movie by American film director Martin Scorsese

    the television show *Jackass*

    a lecture on race in an anthropology class

    a marriage proposal

    an environmental ad by a chemical company

3. Write short paragraphs describing times in the recent past when
    you've used language to inform, to convince, to explore, to make deci-
    sions, and to meditate or pray. Be sure to write at least one paragraph
    for each of these purposes. Then decide whether each paragraph
    describes an act of argument, persuasion, or both, and offer some rea-
    sons in defense of your decisions.

    In class, trade paragraphs with a partner, and decide whether his
    or her descriptions accurately fit the categories to which they've been
    assigned. If they do not, work with your partner to figure out why. Is
    the problem with the descriptions? The categories? Both? Neither?

4. In a recent newspaper or periodical, find three editorials—one that
    makes a ceremonial argument, one a deliberative argument, and one
    a forensic argument. Analyze the arguments by asking these ques-
    tions: Who is arguing? What purposes are the writers trying to
    achieve? To whom are they directing their arguments?

    Then consider whether the arguments' purposes have been
    achieved in each case. If they have, offer some reasons for the argu-
    ments' success.

5. If everything really is an argument, then one should be able to read
    poetry through the same lens, and with the same methods, as one
    reads more obviously argumentative writing. This means considering
    the occasions, purposes, and stasis of the poem—a process that may
    seem odd but that might reveal some interesting results.

    Find a poem that you like and that seems completely *nonargumen-*
    tative (you might even pick one that you have written). Then read it as a
    rhetorician, paying attention to the issues in this chapter, searching for

claims, thinking about audience, and imagining occasions and purposes. Write a few paragraphs explaining why the poem is an argument.

Next, for balance (and to make this a good argument), write a paragraph or two explaining why the poem is not an argument. Make sure you give good reasons for your position. Which of the two positions is more persuasive? Is there a middle ground—that is, a way of thinking about the poem that enables it both to be an argument and not to be an argument?

6. Work with one or two other members of your class to examine the front and back covers of this textbook. What arguments do you find being made there? How do these arguments shape your understanding of this text's purposes? What other kinds of images or words might have been used to achieve this purpose more effectively?

chapter two

Reading
and Writing
Arguments

Do you love your sport utility vehicle? Unless you live in
New York City, you or someone you know likely owns one
of these tall, rugged-looking, luggage-toting, off-road-
capable (for the most part) trucks—maybe a Tahoe or a
Liberty or full-dress Excursion almost nineteen feet long.
They load it up with stuff, crank up the stereo, and hit
the highway, head and shoulders above more mundane
traffic, two tons or more of metal and plastic cushioning
them from other drivers.

Well, Keith Bradsher, for one, doesn't love SUVs, and
he's not shy about staking his claim:

> [T]he proliferation of SUVs has created huge prob-
> lems. Their safe image is an illusion. They roll over
> too easily, killing and injuring occupants at an

alarming rate, and they are dangerous to other road users, inflicting catastrophic damage to cars that they hit and posing a lethal threat to pedestrians. Their "green" image is also a mirage, because they contribute far more than cars to smog and global warming. Their gas-guzzling designs increase American dependence on imported oil at a time when anti-American sentiment is prevalent in the Middle East.

—Keith Bradsher, *High and Mighty: SUVs—The World's Most Dangerous Vehicles and How They Got That Way*

FIGURE 2.1   CRITICS CLAIM THAT 95% OF SUVS NEVER VENTURE OFF ROAD.

Bradsher wants the government to make gasoline taxes so high that people couldn't afford to drive SUVs or to legislate them out of existence by instituting tough new standards for fuel economy or exhaust emission. He argues his case in a nearly 500-page book thick with statistics and footnotes. You may agree with Bradsher, a reporter for the *New York Times*, or you may be handcuffing yourself to your Explorer, daring Hillary Clinton and Tom Daschle to take it away. But an argument has been made, a claim advanced, and the national machinery of deliberation is rolling on this and a thousand other matters, big and small, that affect your life in one way or another.

The fact is that there are people out there—good, well-intentioned, soft-spoken, well-organized citizens—ready to defend a woman's right to an abortion or to fight for the life of the unborn. There are people out there who want marijuana to be as legal as Coors beer, and others who argue passionately that the American League should dump the designated hitter. Some want the government to run the health care industry; others think the government should abandon the postal business. Still others want reparations paid to African Americans for centuries of slavery. Lots of Americans argue over the way college football chooses its national champion, and a few wonder whether we should keep the electoral college to choose presidents. Do you think adults age eighteen to twenty who can sign contracts and defend their country should also be able to drink alcohol legally? You'd better prepare to defend this because others aren't so sure. Do you like burgers and fries? Groups are gearing up to make them as politically incorrect as cigarettes.

You can, of course, kick back and pretend you don't care. After all, you're just one person and one vote. But so is Keith Bradsher, and *he's* gunning for your SUV. Sooner or later—and more than likely this week—you will be affected by an argument someone is making. Maybe it's a classmate pressuring a professor for an extension on a research project. Maybe it's a faculty committee arguing for an increase in student parking fees or a student group choosing campus speakers for next term. Maybe it's a secretary of defense wondering whether it's time to revive the draft. You need to be involved, ready to make and defend claims on your own. To do that, you need a sense of how to make an argument.

But given the variety of arguments (see Chapter 1) and all the different readers and occasions they serve, we can't outline a simple process for writing a convincing argument. Nor can we offer you simple formulas because there aren't many. But in this chapter we can draw your attention to six key issues that readers and writers routinely face when dealing with arguments:

- connecting as a reader or writer (Chapter 3)
- understanding lines of argument (Chapters 4–7)
- making a claim (Chapter 8)
- giving an argument shape (Chapters 9–13)
- giving an argument style (Chapters 14–17)
- managing the conventions of argument (Chapters 18–22)

As this list indicates, each of these matters is discussed in one or more chapters in this book. But because you'll be called upon to read and write arguments before you've finished the entire book, it's a good idea to get an overview of what's involved. In effect, this chapter provides a short lesson on strategies of argument and a quick look at dozens of topics you'll meet in more detail later on.

CONNECTING AS READER OR WRITER

Just as "know thyself" is the philosopher's touchstone, "know thy *audience*" has long been the watchword among people who are interested in persuasion. If you use Amazon.com, you know the company records what you browse and buy on the site so that it can offer you recommendations for your next purchases. Advertisers and TV producers also use demographic studies to target their customers, studying their consumers' likely ages, preferences, and habits. Stores even survey the way their customers shop so that they can create sales environments that make people eager to empty their wallets. Fortunately, understanding audiences isn't just a matter of discovering the age, income levels, reading preferences, and favorite colors of those whom you expect to reach. Connecting entails far more, whether you are a reader or a writer.

You won't be shocked to learn that American society is divided by markers of race, gender, ethnicity, class, intelligence, religion, age, sexuality, ability, and so on. To some extent, who we are and where we come from—culturally, socially, even geographically—determine what and how we'll write. We make assumptions, too, about the people who will read our arguments, slotting them into categories based on our own life experiences and, sometimes, the stereotypes we've developed. But our guesses are often wrong. Life would be much less interesting if they weren't.

In fact, relationships between readers and writers shift like clouds in a blustery wind. As you read, you'll likely notice when a writer who doesn't share your race, gender, or credit card limit sees the world differently than you do. When you write a particular piece, your own religion, sexual orientation, or age—alone or in combination with other factors—may play a part in how you present an idea. Even subjects that seem relatively neutral to some readers do not to others. What, for example, could SUVs have to do with gender or class? More than you suspect, maybe.

In short, as you read or write arguments, you must be aware of points of contact between readers and writers—some friendly, others more troubled. And, of course, any writer or reader exploring a new subject should be willing to learn that territory. Readers should ask what motivates writers to make a case—what credentials or experiences they bring to the table. And writers must consider how (and whether) to tell readers who they are. Consider how Catherine Crier, a former lawyer turned judge and then TV host, opens her book-length attack on the legal profession by introducing herself to readers:

From the time I was a little girl, I wanted to be a lawyer. I was obsessed by the notion of justice. Like the boy who became a marine biologist after witnessing his goldfish being flushed down the toilet, I had my reasons. My heroes were the great trial lawyers of our time, like Clarence Darrow, as portrayed by Spencer Tracy in *Inherit the Wind*, and Atticus Finch, as portrayed by Gregory Peck in *To Kill a Mockingbird*. Those were the characters who convinced me I wanted a career in the law. Now, if you'd asked my mother, she'd tell you I'd argue with a post and had to find a profession that would pay me to do that. Nevertheless, I like my story, and I'm sticking to it.

–Catherine Crier, *The Case Against Lawyers*

Connecting means learning to identify with a writer or a reader, imagining yourself in someone else's shoes or helping others to slip into yours. Writers who fail to see much beyond their own noses—who haven't considered alternative views and opinions—may seem unyielding and bigoted. If you're reading an argument that strikes you as narrow, you might ask yourself: *What is the writer missing? Who is he or she excluding from the audience, deliberately or not?*

As a writer, you may sometimes want to connect with readers who share your own concerns. It's natural to look for allies. For example, Anthony Brandt, an author who wonders whether nonreligious parents like himself should provide religious training for their children, aims his deliberative argument directly at parents in his own situation, addressing them familiarly as *us* and *we:*

For those of us without faith it's not so easy. Do we send our kids to Sunday school when we ourselves never go to church? Do we have them baptized even though we have no intention of raising them as religious?

–Anthony Brandt, "Do Kids Need Religion?"

Brandt's technique illustrated here is just one of many ways to build an author-reader relationship. Yet some readers might find his appeal too overt or aimed more at self-justification than at connecting with an audience. As we said, there are no formulas.

Another bond between readers and writers involves building trust. In reading arguments, you should look for signals that writers are sharing accurate, honest information. You may find such reassurance in careful documentation of facts, in relevant statistics, or in a style that is moderate, balanced, and civil. Also look for indications of a writer's experience with the subject. For example, if you read comic books devotedly, you'd probably want to be sure that someone writing a serious book about them really knew what he was talking about. Chances are you'd trust an author who introduced his study of popular culture this way:

> **Superhero comic books do strange and wonderful things when exposed to literary and psychoanalytic theory. No kidding. For years I read poetry and poetic theory in school, and I read superhero comics for fun. After a while I started having a hard time separating the two activities. This book is what I learned from that juxtaposition.**
> —Geoff Klock, *How to Read Superhero Comics and Why*

After all, before you agree with an argument, you want to be sure its author knows what he or she is talking about. And, as a writer of arguments, you have to pay attention to the very same issues — and do it right from the start of the writing process.

In short, connecting to an audience also means gaining authority over your subject matter — earning the right to write and be read. (For more about connecting, see Chapter 3.)

UNDERSTANDING LINES OF ARGUMENT

When you encounter an argument, you should immediately ask questions: *What is this piece up to? On what assumptions is it based? How good is its evidence? Am I being manipulated?* Likewise, when you write an argument, you must find strategies of your own to build a case. Consider these four tried and true appeals, or lines of argument:

- arguments from the heart
- arguments based on values
- arguments based on character
- arguments based on facts and reason

Discovering appeals that will work is called a process of *invention*. Aristotle described it as finding "all the available means of persuasion." You can return to the following four sections whenever you're given an argumentative assignment, asking yourself as you consider each of them which sort of appeals — to the heart, values, character, or reason — might make your case especially persuasive and powerful. People making arguments too often settle on the first or second idea that comes to mind, or they approach an issue from one direction only. These sections, like the four points of a compass, will help you navigate all the terrain your subject encompasses and give your arguments depth and perspective.

Finding Arguments from the Heart

Arguments from the heart appeal to readers' emotions and feelings. You've probably been told to watch out for emotions because they can lead to bad judgments. And indeed, some emotional appeals are, in fact, just ploys to win you over with a pretty face.

But emotions can also make readers think more carefully about what they do. So you need to consider which emotional appeals legitimately support a claim you want to make. For example, persuading people not to drink and drive by making them fear death, injury, or arrest seems like a fair use of an emotional appeal. That's exactly what the Texas Department of Transportation did in 2002 when it created a memorable ad campaign (see Figure 2.2) featuring the image of a formerly beautiful young woman horribly scarred in a fiery accident caused by an SUV driver who had too much to drink. The headline above the gut-wrenching image was simple: "Not everyone who gets hit by a drunk driver dies."

An argument you are developing may not require quite so powerful an appeal, but you should ask yourself what legitimate emotions might serve your cause: anger? sympathy? fear? happiness? envy? love? For instance, you might find strong scientific reasons for restricting logging in certain areas of the Northwest, but reminders of nature's beauty and fragility might also persuade a general audience. And, of course, the two appeals can work together. Or, if you wanted the argument to move the other way, you might make an audience resent government intrusions onto their land, provoking in them feelings of anger or fear.

In analyzing an argument that is heavy on emotional appeals, you'll always want to question exactly how the emotions generated support the claims a writer makes. Is there even a connection between the claim and the emotional appeal? Sometimes there isn't. Most readers have seen advertisements that promise an exciting life and attractive friends if only they drink the right beer or wear the best clothes. Few are fooled when they think about such ads. But emotional appeals often distract people from thinking just long enough to make a bad choice—and that's precisely the danger.

Finally, though people may not always realize it, humor, satire, and parody are potent forms of emotional argument that can make ideas or individuals seem foolish or laughable. (For more about emotional arguments, see Chapter 4.)

FIGURE 2.2 IMAGES AND WORDS COMBINE TO CREATE AN UNFORGETTABLE EMOTIONAL APPEAL.

Jacqueline Saburido was 20 years old when the car she was riding in was hit by a drunk driver. Today, at 24, she is still working to put her life back together.

Learn more at www.TexasDWI.org

DON'T DRINK & DRIVE   Save a Life

Texas Department of Public Safety • Texas Alcoholic Beverage Commission • Texas Standing Tall • Partnership for a Drug-Free Texas • Texas Commission on Alcohol and Drug Abuse
© 2003 Texas Department of Transportation

Finding Arguments Based on Values

Arguments that appeal to core values resemble emotional appeals, but they work chiefly within specific groups of people — groups as small as families or as large as nations. In such appeals, writers usually either (1) ask others to live up to higher principles, respected traditions, or even new values, or (2) complain that they have not done so. Here, for example, is social critic Michael Moore, famous for his anti-GM documentary *Roger and Me,* decrying the outcome of the 2000 presidential election, portraying it as an assault on fundamental American values and the resulting Bush administration as a *junta,* an illegitimate government:

> We are now finally no better than a backwater banana republic. We are asking ourselves why any of us should bother to get up in the morning to work our asses off to produce goods and services that only serve to make the junta and its cohorts in Corporate America (a separate, autonomous fiefdom within the United States that has been allowed to run on its own for some time) even richer. Why should we pay our taxes to finance their coup? Can we ever send our sons off into battle to give their lives defending "our way of life"—when all that really means is the lifestyle of the gray old men holed up in the headquarters they have seized by the Potomac?
>
> —Michael Moore, *Stupid White Men . . . And Other Sorry Excuses for the State of the Nation*

Moore's argument will succeed or fail depending on how readers react to his charge that the events that put Bush in the White House were, in fact, an assault on core American principles.

Appeals based on values take many forms—from the Nike swoosh on a pair of basketball shoes to the peal of a trumpet playing taps at a military funeral. Such appeals can support various kinds of claims, especially ceremonial arguments, which, in fact, define or celebrate the ideals of a society (see Chapter 1). Writers hoping to argue effectively need a keen sense of the values operating within the communities they are addressing.

As you consider making an argument, you should ask yourself who you want to persuade and what values that audience claims. Without compromising the beliefs you have or the claims you intend to make, you need to consider how to align your arguments with the values your readers likely hold. Consider, for instance, how difficult it might be to persuade many college students that reducing the drinking age to eighteen would be a bad idea. What values could you appeal to in this audience to accept such an argument? You might not find many, but even such a conclusion would be useful as you develop your case: you realize that you'll have to rely on other appeals to overcome a significant difference in values between you and your readers. (For more on arguments based on values, see Chapter 5.)

Finding Arguments Based on Character

Character matters when you read arguments, even when you don't know who the authors are. Readers tend to believe writers who seem honest, wise, and trustworthy. In examining an argument, you should look for evidence of these traits. Does the writer have authority to write on this subject? Are all claims qualified reasonably? Is evidence presented in full, not tailored to the writer's agenda? Are important objections to the author's position acknowledged and addressed? Are sources documented?

As a writer of arguments, expect readers to make the same demands of you. Realize, too, that everything you do in an argument sends signals to readers. Language that is hot and extreme (such as Michael Moore's in the preceding section) can mark you as either passionate or loony. Organization that is tight and orderly can suggest that you are in control. Confusing or imprecise language can make you seem incompetent; technical terms and abstract phrases can characterize you as either knowledgeable or pompous.

Yet arguments based on character reach well beyond the shape and structure of a piece itself. Readers respond powerfully to the people behind arguments, to the experience and power they bring to their work. Listen to the late Edward Abbey, novelist and environmentalist, introducing a collection of his work, explaining what it means to be a writer in a troubled world:

> **In such a world, why write? How justify this mad itch for scribbling? Speaking for myself, I write to entertain my friends and exasperate our enemies. I write to record the truth of our time, as best I can see it. To investigate the comedy and tragedy of human relationships. To resist and sabotage the contemporary drift toward a technocratic, militaristic totalitarianism, whatever its ideological coloration. To oppose injustice, defy the powerful, and speak for the voiceless.**
> **—Edward Abbey, *The Best of Edward Abbey***

Of course, not everyone can write with Abbey's hubris. But neither can writers ignore the power their own voices may have within an argument. (For more about arguments based on character, see Chapter 6.)

Where an argument appears also has a bearing on how seriously it is received. Not every such judgment will be fair, but it is hard to deny that a writer who is published in the *New Yorker* or *Commentary* or even *Newsweek* will be more respected than one who writes for a local paper or a supermarket tabloid. An argument that appears in a scholarly book thick with footnotes and appendices may seem more estimable than one that is offered in a photocopied newsletter handed out on the street corner. Likewise, facts and figures borrowed from the congressional Web site Thomas <thomas.loc.gov> will carry more weight than statistics from Jason's Gonzo Home Page.

Finding Arguments Based on Facts and Reason

In judging most arguments, you'll have to decide whether a writer has made a plausible claim and offered good reasons for you to believe it. You'll also need to examine links between the claim and any supporting reasons.

Claim	Federal income taxes should be cut . . .
Reason	. . . because the economy is growing too slowly.
Links	Tax cuts will stimulate the economy.
	A slow-growing economy is unhealthy.

Then you'll have to assess the evidence presented to support each part of the argument. In this case, you'd probably expect proof that the economy is, in fact, growing too slowly for the good of the country, as well as evidence from history that tax cuts do stimulate economic growth. In other words, you should always read arguments critically, testing every assumption, claim, fact, and source. (For more on arguments based on facts and reason, see Chapter 7.)

When you compose an argument, you should write with an equally skeptical reader in mind (think of the most demanding teacher you have ever had). Offer logical arguments backed with the best evidence, testimony, and authority you can find. To find potential logical arguments, nothing beats a good brainstorming session. Just list every argument, however implausible, that might support your case; jot down, too, any types of evidence that would really help your case if you could find them. Don't be too critical at this stage. You just want ideas to work with. Even those you eventually discard might help you anticipate objections to your stronger arguments. (For more about logical arguments, see Chapter 8.)

Many logical appeals rely heavily on data and information from reliable sources. Knowing how to judge the quality of sources is more important now than ever because the electronic pathways where increasing numbers of writers find their information are clogged with junk. The computer terminal may have become the equivalent of a library reference room in certain ways, but the sources available on-screen vary much more widely in quality. As a consequence, both readers and writers of arguments today must know the difference between reliable, firsthand, or fully documented sources and those that don't meet such standards. (For more on using and documenting sources, see Chapters 21 and 22.)

MAKING A CLAIM

Not every argument you read will package its claim in a neat sentence or thesis. A writer may tell a story from which you have to infer the claim: think of the way many films make a social or political statement by dramatizing an issue, whether it be political corruption, government censorship, or economic injustice. But in conventional arguments, the kind you might find on the editorial page of a newspaper, arguments may be as plain as nails. Writers stake out a claim and then offer the reasons you should buy it. Here are two such examples. The first is a feisty opening paragraph previewing the contents of an entire book; the second occurs nearer the conclusion of a lengthy article defending the car against its many snobbish critics:

> Political "debate" in this country is insufferable. Whether conducted in Congress, on the political talk shows, or played out at dinners and cocktail parties, politics is a nasty sport. At the risk of giving away the ending: It's all liberals' fault.
> —Ann H. Coulter, *Slander: Liberal Lies about the American Right*

> But even if we do all the things that can be done to limit the social costs of cars, the campaign against them will not stop. It will not stop because so many of the critics dislike everything the car stands for and everything society constructs to serve the needs of its occupants.
> —James Q. Wilson, "Cars and Their Enemies"

Think of claims as vortices of energy in an argument—little dust devils stirring up trouble. You need to decide on a claim early on in writing an argument. You'll spend the remainder of your time testing and refining that claim or thesis.

A lengthy essay may contain a series of claims, each developed to support an even larger point. Indeed, every paragraph in an argument may develop a specific claim. In reading arguments you need to keep track of all these separate propositions and the relationships among them. Likewise, in drafting an argument you must be sure that readers always know how to get from one point to another. Treat transitional words and phrases as guideposts to mark the trail you are building.

Yet a claim itself is not really an argument until it is attached to the reasons that support it and the premises that uphold it. Consider this claim from an article by Lynne Cheney, former head of the National Endowment for the Arts, who is writing about undergraduate education:

There are many reasons to be silent rather than to speak out on campuses today.

—Lynne Cheney, *Telling the Truth*

The sentence makes a point, but it doesn't offer an argument yet. That comes when the claim is backed by reasons that the author will then have to support. To show the connection, we've inserted a *because* between the two sentences Cheney actually wrote:

There are many reasons to be silent rather than to speak out on campuses today. [because] Undergraduates have to worry not only about the power of professors to determine grades, but also about faculty members' ability to make the classroom a miserable place for the dissenting student.

Now the author has a case she can set out to prove and a reader can test. When you read an argument, you'll always want to look for such claims and reasons, perhaps underlining them or marking them in some other way. Then you can weigh the argument against its claims—*Is the case based on reasonable assumptions and values readers would share? Does the writer provide sufficient evidence to prove the claim?*

When you are the one writing, you may find it necessary to change a claim you like but can't defend with good reasons or evidence. That process is called *education*. (For more on making and developing claims, see Chapter 8.)

GIVING AN ARGUMENT SHAPE

Most arguments have a logical structure. Aristotle carved the structure of argument to its bare bones when he observed that it had only two parts:

- statement
- proof

You could do worse, in reading an argument, than just to make sure that every claim a writer makes is backed by sufficient evidence. When you can do so, underline every major statement in an article and then look for the data offered to support it. Weigh those various claims, too, against the conclusion of the essay to determine whether the entire essay makes sense.

Most arguments you read and write will, however, be more than mere statements followed by proofs. Writers will typically offer some background information for readers who may not know precisely what's at stake. They'll qualify the arguments they make, too, so they don't bite off more than they can chew. Smart writers will even admit that other points of view are plausible, though they might spend more than a few paragraphs undercutting them.

Arguments may also contain various kinds of evidence. Some may open with anecdotes or incorporate whole narratives that, in fact, constitute the argument itself. Or the claim may be buttressed with charts, tables of statistics, diagrams, or photographs. Even sounds and short movies can now be incorporated into arguments when they appear on the World Wide Web, thanks to the capacity of computers to handle many types of media.

In any argument you write, all these elements must be connected in ways readers find logical and compelling. (For more about structuring arguments, see Chapters 8–13.)

GIVING AN ARGUMENT STYLE

Even a well-shaped and coherent argument flush with evidence may not connect with readers if it is dull, inappropriate, or offensive. You probably judge the credibility of writers yourself in part by how stylishly they make their cases — though you might not know exactly what *style* is. Consider how these simple, blunt sentences from the opening of an argument shape your image of the author and probably determine whether you are willing to continue to read the whole piece:

> **We are young, urban and professional. We are literate, respectable, intelligent and charming. But foremost and above all, we know what it's like to be unemployed.**
>
> –Julia Carlisle, "Young, Privileged and Unemployed"

Now consider how you would approach an argument that begins like the following, responding to a botched primary election in Florida following the electoral disaster of 2000:

> **The question you're asking yourself is: Does South Florida contain the highest concentration of morons in the entire world? Or just in the United States?**
>
> **The reason you're asking this, of course, is South Florida's performance in Tuesday's election. This election was critical to our image, because of our performance in the 2000 presidential election — the**

one that ended up with the entire rest of the nation watching, impatiently, as clumps of sleep-deprived South Florida election officials squinted at cardboard ballots, trying to figure out what the hell the voters were thinking when they apparently voted for two presidents, or no presidents, or part of a president, or, in some cases, simply drooled on the ballot.

–Dave Barry, "How to Vote in 1 Easy Step"

Both styles probably work, but they signal that the writers are about to make very different kinds of cases. Style alone tells you what to expect.

Manipulating style also enables writers to shape readers' responses to their ideas. Devices as simple as repetition and parallelism can give sentences remarkable power. Consider this selection from Andrew Sullivan, who argues for greater tolerance of homosexuals in American culture:

Homosexuals in contemporary America tend to die young; they sometimes die estranged from their families; they die among friends who have become their new families; they die surrounded by young death and by the arch symbols of cultural otherness. Growing up homosexual was to grow up normally but displaced; to experience romantic love, but with the wrong person; to entertain grand ambitions, but of the unacceptable sort; to seek a gradual self-awakening, but in secret, not in public.

–Andrew Sullivan, "What Are Homosexuals For?"

The style of this passage asks readers to pay attention and perhaps to sympathize. But the entire argument can't be presented in this key without exhausting readers—and it isn't. Style has to be modulated almost like music to keep readers tuned in.

Many writers prefer to edit for style after they've composed full drafts of their arguments. That makes sense, especially if you're a writer who likes to get lots of ideas on the page first. But the tone and spirit of an argument are also intimately related to subject matter, so style should not be a last-minute consideration. Often, how you express a thought can be as important as the thought itself. (For more about the style of arguments, see Chapters 14–17.)

MANAGING THE CONVENTIONS OF ARGUMENT

Persuasive writers know how to use sources well. They know how to present tables or graphs, how to document borrowed material, how to select and introduce quotations, how to tailor quotations to the grammar of surrounding sentences, how to shorten quoted passages, and so on. (For more about the conventions of argument, see Chapters 18–22.)

New conventions for argument are evolving in electronic environments. Just since the last edition of this book, Web logs, or *blogs*, have become one of the more potent forms of political discussion in the United States, proving what was only speculation a few years ago—that new environments and media will foster new tools of persuasion. That means that you will have to learn new ways to connect ideas and, in particular, to merge visual arguments with verbal ones. The prospects are quite exciting. (For more about visual and electronic arguments, see Chapters 15 and 16.)

COMPOSING A RHETORICAL ANALYSIS

As you now have seen, arguments have many twists, but how exactly do they work? Why does a Bose ad make you want to buy new speakers or an op-ed piece in the *Washington Post* suddenly change your thinking about school vouchers? A rhetorical analysis might help you understand. You perform a rhetorical analysis by analyzing how well the components of an argument work together to persuade or move an audience. You can study arguments of any kind—advertisements, for example, or editorials, political cartoons, perhaps even movies or photographs. (If everything really is an argument, then just about any communication can be opened up rhetorically.) And you can examine many different aspects of a piece to discover how it does its work.

Because arguments have so many components, you may need to be selective when you try your hand at a rhetorical analysis. You could begin by exploring issues such as the following raised in our first two chapters:

- Who is the audience for this argument? How does the argument connect with its audience?

- What is the purpose of this argument? What does it hope to achieve?

- What are the contexts—social, political, historical, cultural—for this argument? How does the argument fit into the world? Whose interests does it serve? Who gains or loses by it?

- What appeals does the argument use?

- What emotional arguments or techniques does it use?

- What values does it invoke or count on?

- What authorities does the argument rely on or appeal to? Who is making the argument, and are they trustworthy?

- What facts are used in the argument? What logic? What evidence? How is the evidence arranged and presented?

- What claims are advanced in the argument? What issues are raised and which are ignored or, perhaps, silenced?

- What shape does the argument take? How are arguments presented or arranged? What media do the argument use?

- How does the language or style of the argument work to persuade an audience?

Such questions should help you think about an argument. But a rhetorical analysis will be a persuasive piece itself: you'll need to make a claim about the item or article you are studying to explain how or how well it works. That's important because just summarizing what is "in" an argument usually isn't helpful and would be no more enlightening than describing Mona Lisa as a woman with a curious mouth or attributing the appeal of a BMW to its kidney-shaped grille. In performing a rhetorical analysis, you have to show how the key elements in an argument actually contribute to its success or mark it for failure, at least for some audiences. You need to show how the parts work together or, perhaps, work at odds with each other. If the argument startles audiences, or challenges them, or makes them angry or patriotic or lulls them into complacency, you need to explain, as best you can, how that happens.

You can usually do an adequate job by thinking first about the purpose and audience of a piece and then looking at the various appeals it uses. For example, to do a rhetorical analysis of the Texas Department of Transportation ad and poster on p. 34 of this chapter, you might begin by brainstorming its most compelling features and strategies.

- The poster has been created to reduce the incidence of drunk driving. The point it clearly supports is "Don't drink and drive," a claim stated in bold type at the bottom of the ad.

- The argument is probably aimed at a broad audience, but the fact that the drunk driving victim is only twenty-four years old probably will have an impact on younger drivers. The ad also aims to reach those who might dismiss the consequences of drunk driving.

- The poster is primarily a visual argument, dominated by two pictures of Jacqueline Saburido, a small one before her collision with a drunk driver and a much larger one taken four years later. The contrast between the two images will shock most readers, and the larger image may offend some. But they provide testimony that cannot be ignored or softened.

- The poster likely generates strong emotions: sympathy for Saburido and fear for the consequences of drunk driving. A person viewing the ad does not want to become either the victim of a drunk driver or the cause of such horrendous suffering.

- The few words in the ad, deliberately understated, reinforce the potent emotional appeal. A headline in bold type makes a point that might be reassuring if it weren't posed above Saburido's image: *Not everyone who gets hit by a drunk driver dies.* Two short sentences under the dominant image state the facts of Saburido's case simply and make an implicit argument: the consequences of drunk driving don't end with the accident it might cause.

- There are no words under the smaller image. None are needed.

- Many value arguments are implied in the poster. A young woman's life has been shattered by someone else's irresponsible choice. She can never recover the life she had. Yet she is showing enormous courage in allowing her image to be used on a poster to perhaps prevent others from enduring what she has suffered.

- The poster draws on the authority of the Texas Department of Transportation, which sponsors a "Save a Life" program and offers a Web site. Other public safety groups add their endorsement to the poster in small letters at the bottom. They also benefit from the argument that the ad makes. They seem less like meddlesome public agencies warring against social drinking when the consequences of alcohol abuse are made so powerfully clear.

Beginning with such a list, you would be prepared to show in considerable detail how the Texas Department of Transportation ad works by relying primarily upon dramatic visual elements to deliver an unforgettable emotional blow to anyone who might shrug off the consequences of drunk driving. (You probably know such drivers.)

Perhaps you might draw other conclusions from your study of the poster. Or find other elements in it omitted from our list. We have, for example, barely touched on the technical elements in the dominant photograph of Saburido: how she is posed, lighted, dressed. The more you look at the way arguments are composed, the more you will see. This principle holds for written arguments as well. Words, for example, have as much texture and color as pictures—though you might have to work harder to describe how they achieve their effects.

Then you could start writing, providing reasons and evidence to support whatever claims you decide to make about the argument you are analyzing. Following is an argument written by Derek Bok, followed by student Milena Ateyea's rhetorical analysis.

Protecting Freedom of Expression at Harvard

DEREK BOK

For several years, universities have been struggling with the problem of trying to reconcile the rights of free speech with the desire to avoid racial tension. In recent weeks, such a controversy has sprung up at Harvard. Two students hung Confederate flags in public view, upsetting students who equate the Confederacy with slavery. A third student tried to protest the flags by displaying a swastika.

These incidents have provoked much discussion and disagreement. Some students have urged that Harvard require the removal of symbols that offend many members of the community. Others reply that such symbols are a form of free speech and should be protected.

Different universities have resolved similar conflicts in different ways. Some have enacted codes to protect their communities from forms of speech that are deemed to be insensitive to the feelings of other groups. Some have refused to impose such restrictions.

It is important to distinguish between the appropriateness of such communications and their status under the First Amendment. The fact that speech is protected by the First Amendment does not necessarily mean that it is right, proper, or civil. I am sure that the vast majority of Harvard students believe that hanging a Confederate flag in public view—or displaying a swastika in response—is insensitive and unwise because any satisfaction it gives to the students who display these symbols is far outweighed by the discomfort it causes to many others.

I share this view and regret that the students involved saw fit to behave in this fashion. Whether or not they merely wished to manifest their pride in the South—or to demonstrate the insensitivity of hanging Confederate flags, by mounting another offensive symbol in return—they must have known that they would upset many fellow students and ignore the decent regard for the feelings of others so essential to building and preserving a strong and harmonious community.

To disapprove of a particular form of communication, however, is not enough to justify prohibiting it. We are faced with a clear example of the conflict between our commitment to free speech and our desire to foster a community founded on mutual respect. Our society has wrestled with this problem for many years. Interpreting the First Amendment, the Supreme Court has clearly struck the balance in favor of free speech.

While communities do have the right to regulate speech in order to uphold aesthetic standards (avoiding defacement of buildings) or to protect the public from disturbing noise, rules of this kind must be applied across the board and cannot be enforced selectively to prohibit certain kinds of messages but not others.

Under the Supreme Court's rulings, as I read them, the display of swastikas or Confederate flags clearly falls within the protection of the free-speech clause of the First Amendment and cannot be forbidden simply because it offends the feelings of many members of the community. These rulings apply to all agencies of government, including public universities.

Although it is unclear to what extent the First Amendment is enforceable against private institutions, I have difficulty understanding why a university such as Harvard should have less free speech than the surrounding society—or than a public university.

One reason why the power of censorship is so dangerous is that it is extremely difficult to decide when a particular communication is offensive enough to warrant prohibition or to weigh the degree of offensiveness against the potential value of the communication. If we begin to forbid flags, it is only a short step to prohibiting offensive speakers.

I suspect that no community will become humane and caring by restricting what its members can say. The worst offenders will simply find other ways to irritate and insult.

In addition, once we start to declare certain things "offensive," with all the excitement and attention that will follow, I fear that much ingenuity will be exerted trying to test the limits, much time will be expended trying to draw tenuous distinctions, and the resulting publicity will eventually attract more attention to the offensive material than would ever have occurred otherwise.

Rather than prohibit such communications, with all the resulting risks, it would be better to ignore them, since students would then have little reason to create such displays and would soon abandon them. If this response is not possible—and one can understand why—the wisest course is to speak with those who perform insensitive acts and try to help them understand the effects of their actions on others.

Appropriate officials and faculty members should take the lead, as the Harvard House Masters have already done in this case. In talking with students, they should seek to educate and persuade, rather than resort to ridicule or intimidation, recognizing that only persuasion is likely to produce a lasting, beneficial effect. Through such effects, I believe that we act in the manner most consistent with our ideals as an educational institution and most calculated to help us create a truly understanding, supportive community.

A Curse and a Blessing

MILENA ATEYA

In 1991, when Derek Bok's essay "Protecting Freedom of Expression at Harvard" was first published in the Boston Globe, I had just come to America to escape the oppressive Communist regime in Bulgaria. Perhaps my background explains why I support Bok's argument that we should not put arbitrary limits on freedom of expression. Bok wrote the essay in response to a public display of Confederate flags and a swastika at Harvard, a situation that created a heated controversy among the students. As Bok notes, universities have struggled to achieve a balance between maintaining students' right of free speech and avoiding racist attacks. When choices must be made, however, Bok argues for preserving freedom of expression.

Connects article to personal experience to create ethical appeal

Provides brief overview of Bok's argument

States Bok's central claim

In order to support his claim and bridge the controversy, Bok uses a variety of rhetorical strategies. The author first immerses the reader in the controversy by vividly describing the incident: two Harvard students had hung Confederate flags in public view, thereby "upsetting students who equate the Confederacy with slavery" (51). Another student, protesting the flags, decided to display an even more offen-

Transition sentence

Examines the emotional appeal the author establishes through description

sive symbol--the swastika. These actions provoked heated discussions among students. Some students believed that school officials should remove the offensive symbols, whereas others suggested that the symbols "are a form of free speech and should be protected" (51). Bok establishes common ground between the factions: he regrets the actions of the offenders but does not believe we should prohibit such actions just because we disagree with them.

The author earns the reader's respect because of his knowledge and through his logical presentation of the issue. In partial support of his position, Bok refers to U.S. Supreme Court rulings, which remind us that "the display of swastikas or Confederate flags clearly falls within the protection of the free-speech clause of the First Amendment" (52). The author also emphasizes the danger of the slippery slope of censorship when he warns the reader, "If we begin to forbid flags, it is only a short step to prohibiting offensive speakers" (52). Overall, however, Bok's work lacks the kinds of evidence that statistics, interviews with students, and other representative examples of controversial conduct could provide. Thus, his essay may not be strong enough to persuade all readers to make the leap from this specific situation to his general conclusion.

Throughout, Bok's personal feelings are implied but not stated directly. As a lawyer who was president of Harvard for twenty years, Bok knows how to present his opinions respectfully without offending the feelings of the students. However, qualifying phrases like "I suspect that," and "Under the Supreme Court's rulings, as I read them" could weaken the effectiveness of his position. Furthermore, Bok's attempt to be fair to all seems to dilute the strength of his proposed solution. He suggests that one should either ignore the insensitive deeds in the hope that students might change their behavior, or talk to the offending students to help them comprehend how their behavior is affecting other students.

Nevertheless, although Bok's proposed solution to the controversy does not appear at first reading to be very strong, it may ultimately be effective. There is enough flexibility in his approach to withstand various tests, and

Links author's credibility to use of logical appeals

Reference to First Amendment serves as warrant for Bok's claim

Comments critically on author's evidence

Examines how Bok establishes ethical appeal

Identifies qualifying phrases that may weaken claim

Analyzes author's solution

Raises points that suggest Bok's solution may work

Bok's solution is general enough that it can change with the times and adapt to community standards.

In writing this essay, Bok faced a challenging task: to write a short response to a specific situation that represents a very broad and controversial issue. Some people may find that freedom of expression is both a curse and a blessing because of the difficulties it creates. As one who has lived under a regime that permitted very limited, censored expression, I am all too aware that I could not have written this response in 1991 in Bulgaria. As a result, I feel, like Derek Bok, that freedom of expression is a blessing, in spite of any temporary problems associated with it.

Returns to personal experience in conclusion

WORK CITED

Bok, Derek. "Protecting Freedom of Expression on the Campus." Current Issues and Enduring Questions. Eds. Sylvan Barnet and Hugo Bedau. 6th ed. Boston: Bedford, 2002. 51-52. Rpt. of "Protecting Freedom of Expression at Harvard." Boston Globe 25 May 1991.

RESPOND●

1. Describe a persuasive moment you can recall from a speech, an article, an editorial, an advertisement, or your personal experience. Alternatively, research one of the following famous moments of persuasion and then describe the circumstances of the appeal: what the historical situation was, what issues were at stake, and what made the address memorable.

    Abraham Lincoln's "Gettysburg Address" (1863)

    Elizabeth Cady Stanton's draft of the "Declaration of Sentiments" for the Seneca Falls Convention (1848)

    Franklin Roosevelt's inaugural address (1933)

    Winston Churchill's addresses to the British people during the early stages of World War II (1940)

    Martin Luther King Jr.'s "Letter from Birmingham Jail" (1963)

    Ronald Reagan's tribute to the *Challenger* astronauts (1986)

    Toni Morrison's speech accepting the Nobel Prize (1993)

    George Bush's speech to Congress following the 9/11 terrorist attack (2001)

2. Working in a small group, make a list of some of the issues brought to your attention in a given week by people or groups engaged in political or social kinds of persuasion. What methods do they use to make you aware of their issues? How successful are they in engaging your attention? Do you worry about any of these issues or the groups advocating them? Why or why not?

3. Before class, find an editorial argument in a recent newspaper or periodical. Analyze this argument with regard to the six components summarized in this chapter: write a few sentences describing and evaluating the author's success at

    connecting to his or her readers

    arguing from the heart, values, character, and facts

    making a claim

    giving the argument shape

    giving the argument style

    managing the conventions of argument

    In class, exchange editorials with a partner and analyze the one you've just been given along the same lines. Compare your analysis with your partner's: Have you responded similarly to the editorials? If not, how do you account for the differences?

4. At one point, the chapter text poses this question: "What . . . could SUVs have to do with gender or class?" Take a stab at answering the question, based upon a day or two of examining SUVs, both the vehicles and the drivers. Summarize your observations in a fully developed paragraph that makes a claim about SUVs. Don't hesitate to add other categories to your analysis if they seem appropriate: age, race, sexual orientation, religion, physical size, academic major, and so on.

5. Browse a magazine, newspaper, or Web site to find an example of a powerful emotional argument made visually. Then, in a paragraph, defend a claim about how the argument works. For example, does an image itself make a claim, or does it draw you in to consider a verbal claim? What emotion does the argument generate? How does that emotion work to persuade you?

6. Review all the major examples in this chapter—from Bradsher, Crier, Brandt, Klock, Moore, Abbey, Coulter, Wilson, Cheney, Carlisle, Barry, and Sullivan—and try to draw some conclusions about style. Write a paragraph explaining how (if at all) style makes a writer powerful or appealing.

chapter three

Readers
and Contexts
Count

Note how artist and cartoonist Charles Schulz tackles the task of announcing his retirement—the end of the long-running hit comic "Peanuts." In this strip (see Figure 3.1), Schulz addresses his readers directly with "Dear Friends" and goes on to talk about the difficult decision to discontinue the comic that had been the "fulfillment of [his] childhood ambition." Schulz is careful to explain his reasoning to his readers and to acknowledge the contributions others have made to this strip, thereby addressing not only the readers of the comic strip but those who have worked on it as well. In fact, Schulz also appears to be writing partially to himself, as the last sentence ends unfinished: "Charlie Brown, Snoopy, Linus, Lucy . . . how can I ever forget them. . . ." Moreover, Schulz's letter suggests that he has been mulling over the

FIGURE 3.1 FINAL PEANUTS STRIP

way his readers will respond to and interpret his decision, and it raises the question of whether readers will ever forget these characters as well.

■ ■ ■

In the same way that this cartoon makes an argument (that Schultz's decision to retire was appropriate) and anticipates response, so all arguments call for *response*, for the voices of others. Even in thinking through a choice you have to make—for example, whether to major in psychology or in international affairs—you will want to give some response to yourself as you weigh the pros and cons of each choice. And because argument is (at least) a two-way street, thinking hard about the people your argument will engage is crucial to communicating clearly and effectively. This kind of thinking is complicated, however, because those in a position to respond to your arguments or to join you in the argument are always individually complex and varied. In fact, if you can count on any one thing about people, it may be that they are infinitely varied—so varied that it is dangerous to make quick assumptions about what they do or do not think, or to generalize about what will or will not appeal to them. Quick assumptions about your readers are especially troubling in our electronic age, when a click on "send" can convey your message literally around the world.

MAPPING THE TERRITORY OF READERS

Readers or audiences for argument exist across a range of possibilities—from the flesh-and-blood person sitting right across the table from you, to the "virtual" participants in an online conversation, to the imagined ideal readers a written text invites. The sketch in Figure 3.2 may help you think about this wide range of possible readers or audiences.

FIGURE **3.2** READERS AND WRITERS IN CONTEXT

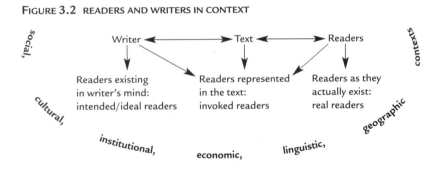

As you consider your argument and begin to write, you will almost always be addressing an intended reader, one who exists in your own mind. As we write this textbook, we are certainly thinking of those who will read it: you are our intended reader, and ideally you know something about and are interested in the subject of this book. Though we don't know you personally, a version of you exists very much in us as writers, for we are *intending* to write for you. In the same way, the writer bell hooks indicates in an essay that she carries intended readers within her:

> The most powerful resource any of us can have as we study and teach in university settings is full understanding and appreciation of the richness, beauty, and primacy of our familial and community backgrounds.
>
> –bell hooks, "Keeping Close to Home: Class and Education"

This sentence reflects hooks's intention of talking to a certain "us"—those who "study and teach in university settings."

But if texts—including visual texts—have intended readers (those the writer consciously intends to address), they also have invoked readers (those who can be seen represented in the text). Later in this chapter, "you" are invoked as one who recognizes the importance of respecting readers. For another example, look at the first paragraph of Chapter 1; it invokes readers who are interested in the goals of argument, whether those goals are overt or subtle. And bell hooks's text also invokes or inscribes a particular reader within its lines: an open, honest person who regards education as what hooks calls the "practice of freedom" and is willing to build bridges to others without losing the ability to think critically. As she says, "It is important that we know who we are speaking to, who we most want to hear us, who we most long to move, motivate, and touch with our words." To invoke the readers hooks wants, her text uses the pronouns us and we throughout.

But this device can be dangerous: those who read hooks's text (or any text) and do not fit the mold of the reader invoked there can feel excluded from the text—left out and thus disaffected. Such is the risk that Christopher Hitchens takes in a review of a book on animal rights:

> Without condescension but with a fine contempt [the author] introduces us to "canned hunting": the can't-miss virtual safaris that charge a fortune to fly bored and overweight Americans to Africa and "big game" destinations on other continents for an air-conditioned trophy trip and the chance to butcher a charismatic animal in conditions of guaranteed safety.
>
> –Christopher Hitchens, "Political Animals"

The words bored, overweight, and butcher, in particular, invoke readers who will agree with Hitchens's implicit condemnation of such people and the actions they take. Those who do not agree are not invited into this piece of writing; there is little space made for them there.

In addition to intended readers and the readers invoked by the text of the argument, any argument will have "real" readers—and these real people may not be the ones intended or even the ones that the text calls forth. You may pick up a letter written to someone else, for instance, and read it even though it is not intended for you. Even more likely, you will read email not sent to you but rather forwarded (sometimes unwittingly) from someone else. Or you may read a legal brief prepared for a lawyer and struggle to understand it, since you are neither the intended reader nor the knowledgeable legal expert invoked in the text. As these examples suggest, writers can't always (or even usually) control who the real readers of any argument will be. As a writer, then, you want to think carefully about these real readers and to summon up what you do know about them, even if that knowledge is limited.

When Julia Carlisle wrote an op-ed article for the *New York Times* about being "young, urban, professional, and unemployed," she intended to address readers who would sympathize with her plight; her piece invokes such readers through the use of the pronoun *we* and examples meant to suggest that she and those like her want very much to work at jobs that are not "absurd." But Carlisle ran into many readers who felt not only excluded from her text but highly offended by it. One reader, Florence Hoff, made clear in a letter to the editor that she did not sympathize with Carlisle at all. In fact, she saw Carlisle as self-indulgent and as asking for entitlement to one kind of job while rejecting others—the jobs that Hoff and others like her are only too glad to hold. In this instance, Carlisle needed to think not only of her intended readers or of the readers her text invited in, but also of all the various "real" readers who were likely to encounter her article in the *Times*.

CONSIDERING CONTEXTS

No consideration of readers can be complete without setting those readers in context. In fact, reading always takes place in what you might think of as a series of contexts—concentric circles that move outward from the most immediate context (the specific place and time in which the reading occurs) to broader and broader contexts, including local and community contexts, institutional contexts (such as school, church, or business), and cultural and linguistic contexts. Julia Carlisle's article, for instance, was written at a specific time and place (in New York City in 1991), under certain economic conditions (increasing unemployment of the kind currently seen across the United States in urban areas, particularly in the high-tech industry), and from the point of view of white, college-educated, and fairly privileged people. As we have seen, such broader contexts always affect both you as a writer of arguments and those who will read and respond to your arguments. As such, they deserve your careful investigation. As you compose arguments of your own, you need to think carefully about the contexts that surround your readers—and put your topic in context as well.

ESTABLISHING CREDIBILITY

Because readers are so variable and varied, and because the contexts in which arguments are made are so complex, it's almost impossible to guarantee that readers will always find you credible. Nevertheless, you can work toward establishing credibility by listening closely to those you want to reach, by demonstrating to readers that you are knowledgeable, by highlighting shared values, by referring to common experiences related to the subject at hand, by using language to build common ground, by respecting readers—and by showing that you are trying hard to understand them. (See also Chapter 6, "Arguments Based on Character.")

Demonstrate Knowledge

One good way to connect with readers is by demonstrating that you know what you are talking about—that you have the necessary knowledge to make your case. Notice how Lisa Takeuchi Cullen uses examples and statistics to demonstrate her claims to knowledge and to bolster her argument that white-collar workers are economically hard hit:

> It has come to this. White-collar workers are joining the jobless ranks in record numbers, tossed aside by the same companies that not long ago lavished them with signing bonuses and free lattes. Although the Labor department announced last week that overall unemployment fell slightly to 5.6% in September, the number of white-collar workers who are jobless has doubled from two years ago. Professionals, managers and technical and administrative workers now make up 43% of the unemployed, according to the government.
>
> —Lisa Takeuchi Cullen, "Will Manage for Food"

Highlight Shared Values

Even though all your readers will be somewhat different from you, they will not all be completely different. As a result, you can benefit from thinking about what values you hold and what values you may share with your readers. Jack Solomon is very clear about one value he hopes readers will share with him—the value of "straight talk":

> There are some signs in the advertising world that Americans are getting fed up with fantasy advertisements and want to hear some

straight talk. Weary of extravagant product claims and irrelevant associations, consumers trained by years of advertising to distrust what they hear seem to be developing an immunity to commercials.

–Jack Solomon, "Masters of Desire: The Culture of American Advertising"

Anthony Brandt faces a different kind of challenge in "Do Kids Need Religion?" for he assumes that his real readers will include those who would answer that question in very different ways. Because he wants to be attended to by readers on all sides of this issue, he highlights a widely shared value: the love for one's children and the wish for a good life for them. "I hope my children find a straighter road than I've found," he says near the end of the essay, concluding, "The longing for meaning is something we all share." To the extent that readers do share such a longing, they may be more receptive to Brandt's argument. (For more about arguments based on values, see Chapter 5.)

CULTURAL CONTEXTS FOR ARGUMENT

Listening well is an essential element of effective argument. When you are arguing a point with people from cultures other than your own, make a special effort to listen for meaning: What is it that they're *really* saying? Misunderstandings sometimes occur when people hear only the words and not the meaning.

- Ask people to explain or even repeat a point if you're not absolutely sure you understand what they're saying.
- Take care yourself to be explicit about what you mean.
- Invite response—ask if you're making yourself clear. This kind of back-and-forth is particularly easy (and necessary) in email.

A recent misunderstanding among a professor and two students helps to make these points. The issue was originality: the professor told the students to be more "original." One student (who was from the Philippines) thought this meant going back to the original and then relating her understanding of it in her own essay. The other student (who was from Massachusetts) thought it meant coming up with something on her own. The professor (who was French) had another definition altogether: he wanted students to read multiple sources and then come up with a point of their own about those sources. Once the students understood what he meant, they knew what they were supposed to do.

Refer to Common Experiences

In her article "The Signs of Shopping," Anne Norton draws on an experience common to many in her analysis of the ways symbolic messages are marketed to consumers: "A display window of Polo provides an embarrassment of semiotic riches. Everyone, from the architecture critic at the *New York Times* to kids in the hall of a Montana high school, knows what Ralph Lauren means."

In a very different kind of essay, Susan Griffin draws on a common experience among men to build credibility with readers: "Most men can remember a time in their lives when they were not so different from girls, and they also remember when that time ended." Such references assume that readers have enough in common with the writer to read on and to accept—at least temporarily—the writer's credibility.

Build Common Ground

We've already mentioned the ways in which the use of pronouns can include or exclude readers and define the intended audience. Writers who want to build credibility need to be careful with pronouns and, in particular, to make sure that *we* and *our* are used accurately and deliberately. In her essay entitled "In Search of Our Mothers' Gardens," Alice Walker's use of pronouns reveals her intended audience. She uses first-person singular and plural pronouns in sharing recollections of her mother and demonstrating the way her heritage led her to imagine generations of black women and the "creative spark" they pass down. When she refers to "our mothers and grandmothers," she is primarily addressing other black women. This intended audience is even more directly invoked when she shifts to the second person: "Did you have a genius of a great-great-grandmother who died under some ignorant and depraved white overseer's lash?" Through this rhetorical direct address, Walker seeks solidarity and identification with her audience and builds her own credibility with them.

Respect Readers

Another very effective means of building credibility and of reaching readers comes through a little seven-letter word made famous by Aretha Franklin: *respect*. Especially when you wish to speak to those who may disagree with you, or who may not have thought carefully about the issues you wish to raise, respect is crucial. In introducing an article on issues facing African American women in the workplace, editor-in-chief of *Essence* Diane Weathers considers the problems she faced with respecting all her readers:

> We spent more than a minute agonizing over the provocative cover line for our feature "White Women at Work." The countless stories we had heard from women across the country told us that this was a workplace issue we had to address. From my own experience at several major magazines, it was painfully obvious to me that Black and White women are not on the same track. Sure, we might all start out in the same place. But early in the game, most sisters I know become stuck—and the reasons have little to do with intelligence or drive. At some point we bump our heads against that ceiling. And while White women may complain of a glass ceiling, for us, the ceiling is concrete.
>
> So how do we tell this story without sounding whiny and paranoid, or turning off our White-female readers, staff members, advertisers and girlfriends? Our solution: Bring together real women (several of them highly successful senior corporate executives), put them in a room, promise them anonymity and let them speak their truth.
>
> —Diane Weathers, "Speaking Our Truth"

Of course, writers can also be deliberately disrespectful, particularly if they want to be funny or if they are very angry. Garrison Keillor, of the radio show "Prairie Home Companion," saddened by the untimely death of Minnesota senator Paul Wellstone and outraged at the election of Wellstone's opponent, Norman Coleman, wrote a fairly blistering attack on Coleman, addressed to readers who would be sure to include many of Coleman's supporters:

> Republicans don't like my criticism? Too bad. They have to answer for Norm Coleman's campaign, which exploited 9/11 in a way that was truly evil.
>
> The hoots and cackles of Republicans reacting to my screed against Norman Coleman, the ex-radical, former Democratic, now compassionate conservative senator-elect from Minnesota, was all to be expected, given the state of the Republican Party today. Its entire ideology, top to bottom, is We-are-not-Democrats, We-are-the-unClinton, and if it can elect an empty suit like Coleman, on a campaign as cheap and cynical and unpatriotic as what he waged right up to the moment Paul Wellstone's plane hit the ground, then Republicans are perfectly content. They are Republicans first and Americans second.
>
> —Garrison Keillor, "Minnesota's Shame"

Note that *hoots* and *cackles* carry negative connotations and that Keillor addresses Republican readers as *they* rather than *you*, thus further distancing himself from those he seeks to chastise. How do you think Keillor's message was received?

THINKING ABOUT READERS AND CONTEXTS

The following questions may help you craft an argument that will be compelling to your readers:

- How could (or do) you describe your intended readers? What characterizes the group of people you most want to reach? What assumptions do you make about your readers—about their values, goals, and aspirations?

- How does your draft represent or invoke readers? Who are the readers that it invites into the text, and who are those that it may exclude? What words and phrases convey this information?

- What range of "real" readers might you expect to read your text? What can you know about them? In what ways might such readers differ from you? From one another? What might they have in common with you? With one another?

- Whether readers are intended, invoked, or "real," what is their stance or attitude toward your subject? What are they likely to know about it? Who will be most interested in your subject, and why?

- What is your own stance or attitude toward your subject? Are you a critic, an advocate, an activist, a detached observer, a concerned consumer or citizen? Something else? In what ways may your stance be similar to or different from that of your readers?

- What is your stance or attitude toward your readers? That of an expert giving advice? A subordinate offering recommendations? A colleague asking for support? Something else?

- What kinds of responses from readers do you want to evoke?

- Within what contexts are you operating as you write this text? College course? Workplace? Community group? Local or state or national citizenry? Religious or spiritual group? Something else?

- What might be the contexts of your readers? How might those contexts affect their reading of your text?

- How do you attempt to establish your credibility with readers? Give specifics.

Considering and connecting with readers inevitably draws you into understanding what appeals—and what does not appeal—to them, whether they are imagined, invoked, or "real." Even though appeals are as varied as readers themselves, it is possible to categorize those that have been traditionally and most effectively used in Western discourse. These appeals are the subject of Part 2, "Lines of Argument."

RESPOND ●

1. Find an example of one of the following items. Explain the argument made by the piece and then describe, as fully as you can, the audience the text is designed to address or invoke.

    a request for a donation by a charitable group

    a poster for the latest hit film

    an editorial in a newspaper or magazine

    the cover of a political magazine or journal (such as *The Onion, New Republic, Nation,* or *Mother Jones*)

    a bumper sticker

2. What common experiences—if any—do the following objects, brand names, and symbols evoke, and for what audiences in particular?

    a USDA organic label

    the Nike swoosh

    the golden arches

    a dollar bill

    a can of Coca-Cola

    Sleeping Beauty's castle on the Disney logo

    Oprah Winfrey

    the Vietnam memorial

    the World Trade Towers

    the Sean Jean label, as seen on its Web site (see next page):

3. Carry out an informal demographic study of the readership of a local newspaper. Who reads the paper? What is its circulation? What levels of education and income does the average reader have? Are readers politically conservative, moderate, or liberal? How old is the average reader? You'll likely have to do some research—phone calls, letters, follow-ups—to get this information, and some of it might be unavailable.

   Then select an article written by one of the paper's own reporters (not a wire-service story), and analyze it in terms of audience. Who seem to be its intended readers? How does it invoke these readers? Does it seem addressed to the average reader you have identified?

4. Choose a chapter in this textbook and read it with a special eye for how it addresses its readers: Does the chapter follow the guidelines offered here—that is, does it demonstrate knowledge, highlight shared values, build common ground, and respect readers? How does the chapter use pronouns to establish a relationship between the writers of the text and its readers? What other strategies for connecting with readers can you identify?

PART 2

LINES OF argument

chapter four

Arguments from the Heart

What makes you glance at a magazine ad long enough to notice a product? These days, it's probably an image or design promising pleasure (a Caribbean beach), excitement (bikers at Moab), beauty (a model in low-rise jeans), security (a kindly physician), or good health (more models). In the blink of an eye, ads can appeal to your emotions, intrigue you, perhaps even seduce you. Look closer and you might find good reasons in the ads themselves for buying a product or service. But would you have even gotten there without an emotional tug to pull you into the page?

FIGURE 4.1 THIS IMAGE PARODIES ADS THAT EXPLOIT ONE OF THE MOST POWERFUL OF EMOTIONAL APPEALS.

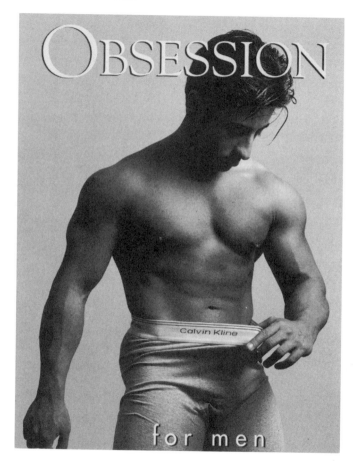

Emotional appeals (sometimes called appeals to *pathos*) are powerful tools for influencing what people think and believe. We all make decisions—even important ones—based on our feelings. We rent broken-down apartments or buy zonked-out cars because we fall in love with some small detail. On impulse, we collect whole racks of ties or blouses we're later too embarrassed to wear. We date, maybe even marry, people everyone else seemed to know are wrong for us—and sometimes it works out just fine.

That may be because we're not computers who use cost/benefit analyses to choose our friends or make our political decisions. Feelings belong in our lives. There's a powerful moment in Shakespeare's *Macbeth* when the soldier Macduff learns that his wife and children have been executed by the power-mad king. A well-meaning friend urges Macduff to "dispute it like a man." Macduff responds, gruffly, "But I must also feel it as a man" (*Macbeth*, 4.3.219–21). As a writer, you must learn like Macduff to appreciate legitimate emotions, particularly when you want to influence the public. When you hear that formal or academic arguments should rely solely on facts, remember that facts alone often won't carry the day, even for a worthy cause. The civil rights struggle of the 1960s is a particularly good example of a movement that persuaded people equally by means of the reasonableness and the passion of its claims.

But one doesn't have to look hard for less noble campaigns peppered by emotions such as hatred, envy, and greed. Democracies suffer when people use emotional arguments (and related fallacies such as personal attacks and name-calling) to drive wedges between groups, making them fearful and hateful. For that reason, writers can't use emotional appeals casually. (For more about emotional fallacies, see Chapter 19.)

UNDERSTANDING HOW EMOTIONAL ARGUMENTS WORK

You already know that words, images, and sounds can arouse emotions. In fact, the stirrings they generate are often physical. You've likely had the clichéd "chill down the spine" or felt something in the "pit of the stomach" when a speaker (or photograph or event) hits precisely the right note, as George W. Bush did when he unexpectedly took up a megaphone to assure rescue workers at the site of the 9/11 terrorist act (see Figure 4.2): "I can hear you. The rest of the world hears you. And the people who knocked down these buildings will hear all of us soon." Now, if writers and speakers can find the words and images to make people feel certain emotions, they might also move their audiences to sympathize with ideas they connect to those feelings, and even to act on them. Make people hate an enemy, and they'll rally against him; help people to imagine suffering, and they'll strive to relieve it; make people feel secure or happy, and they'll buy products that promise such good feelings.

FIGURE 4.2 PRESIDENT GEORGE W. BUSH STIRRED THE EMOTIONS OF MANY AMERICANS WITH HIS WORDS AT THE SITE OF THE WORLD TRADE CENTER ATTACK. HE WAS IN NEW YORK CITY ON SEPTEMBER 14, 2001.

Arguments from the heart probably count more when you are persuading than when you are arguing. When arguing, you might use reasons and evidence to convince readers something is true—for instance, that preserving wetlands is a worthy environmental cause. When persuading, however, you want people to take action, actually to join an environmental boycott, contribute money to an organization dedicated to wetlands protection, or write a well-researched op-ed piece for the local paper about a local marsh threatened by development.

Argument (discover a truth) ———➤ **conviction**

Persuasion (know a truth) ———➤ **action**

The practical differences between being convinced and acting on a conviction can be enormous. Your readers may agree that contributing to charity is a noble act, but that conviction may not be enough to persuade them to part with their spare change. You need a spur sharper than logic, and that's when emotion might kick in. You can embarrass readers into contributing to a good cause ("Change a child's life for the price of a pizza") or make them feel the impact of their gift ("Imagine the smile on that little child's face") or tell them a moving story ("In a tiny village in Central America . . ."). Doubtless, you've seen such techniques work.

USING EMOTIONS TO BUILD BRIDGES

You may sometimes want to use emotions to connect with readers, to assure them that you understand their experiences or, to use a famous political line, "feel their pain." Such a bridge is especially important when you are writing about matters that readers regard as sensitive. Before they will trust you, they'll want assurances that you understand the issues in depth. If you strike the right emotional note, you'll establish an important connection.

That's what presidential advisor Condoleezza Rice did while teaching a Sunday School class at the National Presbyterian Church, arguing that communities of faith should play a role in American politics. To reinforce her point, Rice lets us peer into her own experiences with religion, one of the most sensitive of all subjects:

> I think people who believe in a creator can never take themselves too seriously. I feel that faith allows me to have a kind of optimism about the future. You look around you and you see an awful lot of pain and suffering and things that are going wrong. It could be oppressive. But when I look at my own story or many others that I have seen, I think, "How could it possibly be that it has turned out this way?" Then my only answer is it's God's plan. And that makes me very optimistic that

this is all working out in a proper way if we all stay close to God and pray and follow in His footsteps.

I really do believe that God will never let you fall too far. There is an old gospel hymn, "He knows how much you can bear." I really do believe that.

–Condoleezza Rice, "Walking in Faith"

In no obvious way is Rice's recollection an actual argument. But it prepares her audience to accept the case she will make, because she seems to be teaching from an authentic experience with religion.

A more obvious way to build an emotional tie is simply to help readers identify with your experiences. If, like Georgina Kleege, you were blind and wanted to argue for more sensible attitudes toward blind people, you might ask readers in the very first paragraph of your argument to confront their prejudices. Here Kleege, a writer and college instructor, makes an emotional point by telling a story:

I tell the class, "I am legally blind." There is a pause, a collective intake of breath. I feel them look away uncertainly and then look back. After all, I just said I couldn't see. Or did I? I had managed to get there on my own—no cane, no dog, none of the usual trappings of blindness. Eyeing me askance now, they might detect that my gaze is not quite focused. . . . They watch me glance down, or towards the door where someone's coming in late. I'm just like anyone else.

–Georgina Kleege, "Call It Blindness"

Given the way she narrates the first day of class, readers are as likely to identify with the students as with Kleege, imagining themselves sitting in a classroom, facing a sightless instructor, confronting their own prejudices about the blind. Kleege wants to put them on edge emotionally.

Let's consider another rhetorical situation: How do you win over an audience when the logical claims you are making are likely to upset what many passionately believe? Once again, a slightly risky appeal to emotions on a personal level may work. That's the tack Dinesh D'Souza takes in trying to make the case that the evils of European colonialism may be exaggerated. He turns to his own experiences to meet the objections head on:

Much as it chagrins me to admit it—and much as it will outrage many third-world intellectuals for me to say it—my life would have been much worse had the British never ruled India.

How is that possible? Virtually everything that I am, what I do, and my deepest beliefs, all are the product of a worldview that was brought to India by colonialism. I am a writer, and I write in English. My ability to do this, and to reach a broad market, is entirely thanks to the British. My understanding of technology, which allows me, like so many Indians, to function successfully in the modern world, was largely the product of a Western education that came to India as a result of the British. So also my beliefs in freedom of expression, in self-government, in equality of rights under the law, and in the universal principle of human dignity—they are all the products of Western civilization.

–Dinesh D'Souza, "Two Cheers for Colonialism"

Although D'Souza's claims are, strictly speaking, logical, based on his own observations, he acknowledges that they will *outrage* most third-world intellectuals and many academics in the United States as well. But perhaps D'Souza is hoping his willingness to reveal personal background will build an emotional bridge among readers who respect someone willing to challenge intellectual orthodoxies. The strategy may have an unpredictable result (it can backfire), but it is also remarkably common.

USING EMOTIONS TO SUSTAIN AN ARGUMENT

You can also use emotional appeals to make logical claims stronger or more memorable. That is, in fact, the way photographs and other images add power to arguments. In a TV attack ad, the scowling black-and-white photograph of a political opponent may do as much damage as the claim that his bank laundered drug money. Or the attractive skier in a spot for lip balm may make us yearn for dry, chafing winter days. The technique is tricky, however. Lay on too much emotion—especially those like outrage, pity, or shame, which make people uncomfortable—and you may offend the very audiences you hoped to convince. But sometimes a strong emotion such as anger adds energy to a passage, as it does when Susan Faludi accuses writer Katie Roiphe of minimizing the significance of date rape:

Roiphe and others "prove" their case [that date rape is exaggerated] by recycling the same anecdotes of false accusations; they all quote the same "expert" who disparages reports of high rape rates. And they never interview any real rape victims. They advise us that a feeling of victimization is no longer a reasonable response to sexual violence; it's a hallucinatory state of mind induced by witchy feminists who cast a spell on impressionable co-eds. These date-rape revisionists claim to be liberating young women from the victim mind-set. But is women's sexual victimization just a mind trip—or a reality?

–Susan Faludi, "Whose Hype?"

Here, the threat in Faludi's sarcasm becomes part of the argument: if you make the kind of suggestion Roiphe has, expect this sort of powerful response.

In the same way, writers can generate emotions by presenting logical arguments in their starkest terms, stripped of qualifications or subtleties. Readers or listeners are confronted with core issues or important choices and asked to consider the consequences. It is hard to imagine an argument more serious than a debate about war and peace or one more likely to raise powerful feelings. Here is Andrew Sullivan on his Web log (commonly known as a *blog*) in late summer 2002, inviting opponents of a proposed American invasion of Iraq to put their cards on the table. That he favors military action is clear in the sharp and emotional way he outlines the consequences of the decision. We have italicized his more emotionally charged words and phrases:

> So far, very few have had the *cojones* to take such a stand [opposing action against Iraq], especially in Congress. (There are some honorable, principled exceptions among traditional pacifists, leftists and hard-core foreign policy 'realists.') But soon, even Howell Raines [editor of the *New York Times*] will have to take responsibility for backing a *passive policy of leaving America and our allies vulnerable to massive destruction.* Far from *ducking* this *vital* debate, those of us who believe *our national security is at stake* should *embrace* the discussion enthusiastically. And each side should be held accountable for the difficult and *unknowable* consequences of our respective stands. After all, what is at issue is the possible *future murder of thousands* of American citizens, *nuclear blackmail* from a *rogue state,* or *chemical warfare waged in American cities* by agents in close contact with the *Iran-Iraq-Syria-Saudi* axis. It's hard to think of a *graver moment in recent American history.*
> —Andrew Sullivan, <andrewsullivan.com>

You might imagine how an opponent of war might respond at this point: Would a more reasoned approach work, or would the reply have to be just as stirring as Sullivan's challenge, listing the potential consequences of ill-considered action? Or is this an opportunity to suggest alternatives to an either/or choice between war and peace?

It is possible, of course, for feelings to be an argument in themselves when they are powerfully portrayed. Here, for example, is the incomparable Camille Paglia hammering Harvard psychologist William Pollack for his view that American boys ought to be raised with greater, almost feminine, sensitivity. Again, the phrases with emotional kick are italicized.

> Specifically, I reject Pollack's position that mothers shouldn't *push growing boys away* and discourage displays of *weakness, fear and tears.*

Everywhere, I see the opposite problem: white, upper-middle-class mothers *clinging too much to their whiny sons* and turning them into companion daughters or substitute spouses. Boys are not girls: *the mocking epithets "sissy"* (i.e., "sister") and *"mollycoddle"* do describe something real—a stalling in the evolution of masculine identity, which requires boys to *leave the maternal nest* and make their way as independent adults.

Perhaps because of his background, Pollack overestimates the power of words in most men's lives. His program privileges female values and *simply cuts boys down to pliable ciphers* in a family matriarchy. It's actually a perfect recipe for *producing obedient office-workers, happy eunuchs in the corporate food chain.*

—Camille Paglia, "Guns and Penises"

As you can see, it is difficult to gauge how much emotion will work in a given argument. Some issues—such as date rape, abortion, gun control—provoke strong feelings and, as a result, are often argued on emotional terms. But even issues that seem deadly dull—such as funding for Medicare and Social Security—can be argued in emotional terms when proposed changes in these programs are set in human terms: Cut benefits and Grandma will have to eat cat food; don't cut benefits and the whole health care system will go broke, leaving nothing for aging baby boomers. Both alternatives might scare people into paying enough attention to take political action.

USING HUMOR

Humor has great power. Some days after terrorists attacked the World Trade Center and the Pentagon on September 11, 2001, comedian David Letterman, whose TV show originates in New York City, returned to the air. It was a memorable, emotionally riveting performance, with Letterman choking up during tributes to police and firefighters. But there were a few gibes and a few laughs, most of them at the expense of guest Regis Philbin. With remarkable grace that night, Letterman helped Americans to find themselves again.

Humor has always played an important role in argument, sometimes as the sugar that makes the medicine go down. You can certainly slip humor into an argument to put readers at ease, thereby making them more open to a proposal you have to offer. It is hard to say "no" when you're laughing. Humor also makes otherwise sober people suspend their judgment and even their prejudices, perhaps because the surprise and naughtiness of wit are combustive: they provoke laughter or smiles, not reflection. That may be why TV sitcoms like *All in the Family* or *Will and Grace* have been able to reach mainstream audiences, despite their some-times controversial subjects. Similarly, it is possible to make a point through humor that might not work at all in more sober writing. Consider the gross stereotypes about men that humorist Dave Barry presents here, tongue in cheek, explaining why people don't read the instructions that come with the products they buy:

> The third reason why consumers don't read manuals is that many consumers are men, and we men would no more read a manual than we would ask directions, because this would be an admission that the person who wrote the manual has a bigger . . . OK, a bigger grasp of technology than we do. We men would rather hook up our new DVD player in such a way that it ignites the DVDs and shoots them across the room—like small flaming UFOs—than admit that the manual-writer possesses a more manly technological manhood than we do.
> –Dave Barry, "Owners' manual Step No. 1: Bang head against the wall"

Our laughter testifies to a kernel of truth in Barry's observations and makes us more likely to agree with his conclusions.

A writer or speaker can use laughter to deal with especially sensitive issues. For example, sports commentator Bob Costas, given the honor of eulogizing the great baseball player Mickey Mantle, couldn't ignore well-known flaws in Mantle's character. So he argues for Mantle's greatness by admitting the man's weaknesses indirectly through humor:

> It brings to mind a story Mickey liked to tell on himself and maybe some of you have heard it. He pictured himself at the pearly gates, met by St. Peter who shook his head and said "Mick, we checked the record. We know some of what went on. Sorry, we can't let you in. But before you go, God wants to know if you'd sign these six dozen baseballs."
> –Bob Costas, "Eulogy for Mickey Mantle"

Similarly, politicians use humor to admit problems or mistakes they couldn't acknowledge in any other way. Here, for example, is President Bush at the annual Radio & TV Correspondents Dinner discussing his much-mocked intellect: "Those stories about my intellectual capacity do get under my skin. You know, for a while I even thought my staff believed it. There on my schedule first thing every morning it said, 'Intelligence briefing.'"

Not all humor is well intentioned. In fact, among the most powerful forms of emotional argument is ridicule—humor aimed at a particular target. Lord Shaftesbury, an eighteenth-century philosopher, regarded humor as a serious test for ideas, believing that sound ideas would survive prodding. In our own time, comedians poke fun at politicians and their ideas almost nightly, providing an odd barometer of public opinion. Even bumper stickers can be vehicles for succinct arguments:

Vote Republican: It's easier than thinking.
Vote Democrat: It's easier than working.

But ridicule is a two-edged sword that requires a deft hand to wield it. Humor that reflects bad taste discredits a writer completely, as does ridicule that misses its mark. Unless your target deserves assault and you can be very funny, it's usually better to steer clear of humor. (For more on humorous arguments, see Chapter 13.)

USING ARGUMENTS FROM THE HEART

You don't want to play puppetmaster with people's emotions when you write arguments, but it's a good idea to spend some time early in your writing or designing process thinking about how you want readers to feel as they consider your persuasive claims. Would readers of your editorial about campus traffic policies be more inclined to agree with you if you made them envy faculty privileges, or would arousing their sense of fairness work better? What emotional appeals might persuade meat eaters to consider a vegan diet—or vice versa? Would sketches of stage props on a Web site persuade people to buy a season ticket to the theater, or would you spark more interest by featuring pictures of costumed performers?

Consider, too, the impact that telling a story can have on readers. Writers and journalists routinely use what are called "human interest stories" to give presence to issues or arguments. You can do the same, using a particular incident to evoke sympathy, understanding, outrage, or amusement. Take care, though, to tell an honest story.

RESPOND ●

1. To what specific emotions do the following slogans, sales pitches, and maxims appeal?

"Just do it." (ad for Nike)

"Think different." (ad for Apple Computers)

"Reach out and touch someone." (ad for a long-distance phone company)

"In your heart, you know he's right." (1964 campaign slogan for U.S. presidential candidate Barry Goldwater, a conservative)

"It's the economy, stupid!" (1992 campaign theme for U.S. presidential candidate Bill Clinton)

"By any means necessary." (rallying cry from Malcolm X)

"When the going gets tough, the tough get going." (maxim used by many coaches)

"You can trust your car to the man who wears the star." (slogan for Texaco)

"We bring good things to life." (slogan for GE)

"Know what comes between me and my Calvins? Nothing!" (tag line for Calvin Klein jeans)

"Don't mess with Texas!" (antilitter campaign slogan)

2. Bring a magazine to class and analyze the emotional appeals in as many full-page ads as you can. Then classify those ads by types of emotional appeal and see whether you can connect the appeals to the subject or target audience of the magazine. Compare your results with those of your classmates and discuss your findings. For instance, do the ads in newsmagazines like *Time* and *Newsweek* appeal to different emotions and desires than ads in publications such as *Cosmo*, *Rolling Stone*, *Sports Illustrated*, *Automobile*, and *National Geographic*?

3. It's important to remember that argument—properly carried out—can be a form of inquiry: rather than a simple back-and-forth between established positions, good argument helps people discover their positions and modify them. Arguments from the heart can help in this process, as long as they are well tempered with reason.

   With this goal of inquiry in mind, as well as an awareness of the problems associated with emotional arguments, imagine how another Indian (or anyone who has lived in a former British colony) might respond to Dinesh D'Souza's argument that his life is probably better because the British once ruled his native land.

   You might also do this as a group exercise. Over several days, one group might read the entire D'Souza article, originally published in the *Chronicle of Higher Education* (May 10, 2002), while another examines the responses of his critics in the same journal (June 14, 2002). Then the groups could meet together to discuss the issues raised and the emotions evoked.

4. How do arguments from the heart work in different media? Are such arguments more or less effective in books, articles, television (both news and entertainment shows), films, brochures, magazines, email, Web sites, the theater, street protests, and so on? You might focus on a single medium, exploring how it handles emotional appeals, or compare different media. For example, why do Internet news groups seem to encourage angry outbursts? Are newspapers an emotionally colder source of information than television news programs? If so, why?

chapter five

Arguments Based on Values

   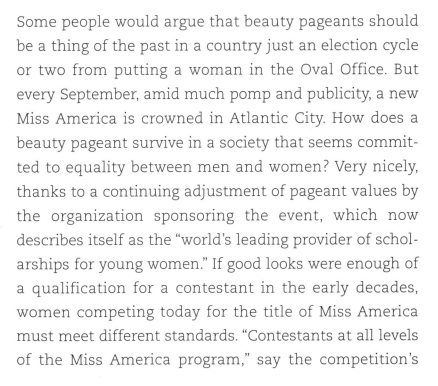

Some people would argue that beauty pageants should be a thing of the past in a country just an election cycle or two from putting a woman in the Oval Office. But every September, amid much pomp and publicity, a new Miss America is crowned in Atlantic City. How does a beauty pageant survive in a society that seems committed to equality between men and women? Very nicely, thanks to a continuing adjustment of pageant values by the organization sponsoring the event, which now describes itself as the "world's leading provider of scholarships for young women." If good looks were enough of a qualification for a contestant in the early decades, women competing today for the title of Miss America must meet different standards. "Contestants at all levels of the Miss America program," say the competition's

FIGURE **5.1** IN 1921, MARGARET GORMAN BECAME THE FIRST MISS AMERICA.

rules, "are required to clearly define a social issue to which they are sincerely committed and for which each will be an activist during her year of service." So crowning a Miss America is really an argument about contemporary values, the person selected supposedly representing a contemporary ideal of womanhood. Of course, critics of the pageant complain that the competition is still out of step with the times. And they, too, are making an argument based on values.

Arguments like these usually occur within or between groups—in this case the 280 million people who describe themselves as Americans. Most groups are much smaller. But they stay together because, consciously or not, their members share core beliefs about issues such as politics, religion, ethics, art, work, or family. You shouldn't be surprised if arguments based on values often involve other sorts of claims. For instance, writing about love of country as a value might stir emotional memories or lead to passionate claims about character—*she is a real patriot; he's a traitor*. But appeals based on value are powerful in their own right because they ask people to look inside themselves. Thus it is only common sense to try to find out all you can about the beliefs of people you want to persuade. That also means you need to be aware of how your own core values shape your view of the world.

UNDERSTANDING HOW VALUES ARGUMENTS WORK

Sometimes the values shared by members of a group are clearly spelled out in a statement of principles, a platform, a creed, or a document such as the Declaration of Independence. Here's how the Knighthood of BUH, a college group dedicated to creative humor, rather seriously defines its counterculture values:

> Among its members . . . the Knighthood is about more than just comedy. It is about being an individual, and thinking for yourself. A lot of the time, it is easier to feel the way a movie wants us to . . . than it is to generate our own emotions. It seems the world is a place for being the guy next to you. The Knighthood is about being you, about thinking for yourself, and about believing what you have decided is believable, not simply what your parents or your pastor told you. It is about creativity, but not creativity as your third grade teacher meant it, which is to say bright colors and lots of glitter, but creativity in the true and not-so-easy-to-have sense of the word—divergent thinking.
>
> —The Knighthood of BUH

At other times, the beliefs evolve as part of the history and traditions of a club or movement or political party; for example, what it means to be a traditional Navajo, a committed feminist, or an environmentalist may

never be entirely clear, but it is always somehow understood. Moreover, many groups prefer to keep their principles a little blurred around the edges so they can attract new members or change with the times. Arguments about principles may be, in fact, what help many groups evolve. Sharon Clahchischilliage, a Navajo woman from New Mexico, faced such a conflict of values when she decided to run for Secretary of State, as a news report from the *Washington Times* explains:

> By placing her face on billboards around the state and publicizing her justcallmesharon.com Web site, she is bucking tribal customs. Navajos as a rule do not stare people in the eyes, nor ask for money or boast about their capabilities.

FIGURE 5.2
SHARON CLAHCHISCHILLIAGE

"I'm going against the norms of my culture," she admits, "just by being a candidate."

–Julia Duin, "Navajo Woman Vies for Political Distinction"

Because principles do change, appeals to values typically involve a comparison between *what is* and *what ought to be*:

- A person or group does not live up to current values.
- Past values were better or nobler than current ones.
- Future values can be better or worse than current ones.

USING VALUES TO DEFINE

You will likely find appeals to values whenever members of a group disagree about who belongs in the group or what its core principles are. *What does it mean to be an American? A faithful Muslim? A good Christian? A true Texan? A patriot? A concerned liberal?* Everyone who belongs to such a group likely has an answer—as do people who stand outside—and their opinions might generate plenty of talk.

How, for instance, would you define an American? Here is Hector St. Jean de Crèvecoeur, a Frenchman, trying in 1782 to do exactly that, speaking in the imagined voice of an American:

> We are a people of cultivators, scattered over an immense territory, communicating with each other by means of good roads and navigable rivers, united by the silken bands of mild government, all respecting the laws without dreading their power, because they are equitable. We are all animated with the spirit of industry which is unfettered and unrestrained, because each person works for himself.
>
> –Hector St. Jean de Crèvecoeur, "What Is an American?"

Crèvecoeur lived in a different era (few Americans are farmers now), but the core values he describes might still stir a mainstream crowd on the Fourth of July: limited government, fair laws, hard work, self-reliance. Appeals to such shared (and flattering) principles are so common that even advertisers exploit them. In Texas, for example, one truck manufacturer used to advertise its products as "Texas tough," making the assumption that Texans like to think of themselves as rugged.

But let's consider an entirely different way of imagining American values, one far less idealistic (and perhaps parodic). This time the writer is Dana Cloud, an associate professor of Communication Studies writing to a student newspaper to applaud a California federal court's decision (later suspended) forbidding public schools from using the phrase "one nation, under God" as part of the Pledge of Allegiance. Cloud's version of America is less comforting than Crèvecoeur's and much different from that in the familiar Pledge of Allegiance, which she parodies:

> My daughter, who is 11, and I were delighted at the California court decision omitting the words "under God" from the Pledge of Allegiance. She and I have always been uncomfortable saying the pledge, not only because of the religious imposition, but because it seems very strange to pledge loyalty to a scrap of cloth representing a corrupt nation that imposes its will, both economic and military, around the world by force. So she inspired me to rewrite the Pledge.
>
> Imagine schoolchildren every day reciting the following:
>
> *I pledge allegiance to all the ordinary people around the world,*
> *to the laid off Enron workers and the WorldCom workers*
> *the maquiladora workers*
> *and the sweatshop workers from New York to Indonesia,*
> *who labor not under God but under the heel of multinational corporations; I*
>   *pledge allegiance*
> *to the people of Iraq,*
> *Palestine and Afghanistan,*
> *and to their struggles to survive and resist*
> *slavery to corporate greed,*
> *brutal wars against their families,*
> *and the economic and environmental ruin wrought by global capitalism; I*
>   *pledge allegiance*
> *to building a better world*
> *where human needs are met*
> *and with real liberty, equality and justice for all.*
>
> The original pledge does not include or represent us godless radicals. The backlash against the California decision shows just how thin our democracy is.
>
> —Dana Cloud, *The Daily Texan*

You can imagine the local backlash to Cloud's letter to the editor, but her words were also soon sprinting across the Internet, where they were the subject of both denunciation and praise on various Web logs. Are Crèvecoeur's "silken bands of mild government" in any way compatible with Cloud's "heel of multinational corporations"? Can both of these views represent an authentic version of American values? As a writer, you may find that any real America exists in the turbulence between such conflicting views — in the arguments about values that you, like Crèvecoeur and Cloud, may help to shape.

EMBRACING OR REJECTING VALUES

You can often make a strong argument by connecting your own beliefs and values to core principles that are better established and more widely respected. This strategy is particularly effective when your position seems to threaten traditional values. For example, when Terry Tempest Williams is arrested for protesting nuclear weapons testing, she claims her action represents an American value as old and honorable as the Boston Tea Party:

> **I crossed the line at the Nevada Test Site and was arrested with nine other Utahns for trespassing on military lands. They are still conducting nuclear tests in the desert. Ours was an act of *civil disobedience*. (emphasis added)**
> **– Terry Tempest Williams, "The Clan of One-Breasted Women"**

By linking her own arrest to the respected tradition of civil disobedience, she makes an argument in defense of her entire cause. Similarly, advocates of abortion rights and school vouchers — people usually on different ends of the political spectrum — both claim to favor "choice," a value fundamental to any democracy.

But appeals to core values of a culture can cut in different ways. What happens when principles of equality lead to new kinds of discrimination? For instance, some argue that Title IX of a 1972 federal education act barring gender discrimination compels colleges and universities to shut down men's sports teams when the number of men playing sports exceeds their proportion of the school's population. Does an ideal of equity conflict, then, with a related value of fairness? Welch Suggs, a writer for the *Chronicle of Higher Education*, explores exactly that question:

> **Why should courts and administrators presume that men's interests in competing in college sports are being met simply by providing them with opportunities proportional to their enrollment at a university? Curt A. Levey, a lawyer for the Center for Individual Rights . . . says that athletics is the only area in education where quotas are permitted.**
>
> **Should a university's nursing school, he wonders, be forced to enroll men in numbers proportional to their overall enrollment at the university?**

As you might guess, there's another side to the argument that also appeals to principles of fairness. Suggs continues his report on the controversy:

> Sports programs are different, responds Mary Frances O'Shea, who oversees Title IX compliance in athletics for the U.S. Department of Education's Office for Civil Rights.
>
> "Athletic programs are the only programs wherein schools can establish [teams] set aside for men and women," Ms. O'Shea says. "You can't have Algebra I-A for boys and Algebra I-B for girls, but in athletics, because of the nature of the program, you can." As such, rules must be in place to ensure that men and women are treated equitably in athletic programs, Ms. O'Shea says.
>
> —Welch Suggs, "Colleges Consider Fairness of Cutting Men's Teams to Comply with Title IX"

Conflicts about core values keep courts and newspaper editorialists very busy.

COMPARING VALUES

Many arguments based on values involve comparisons. Something is faulted for not living up to an ideal, or the ideal is faulted for not reaching far enough, or one value is presented as preferable to another or in need of redefinition. It would be hard to find an argument based on values more clearly stated than the following example from a book by Stephen Carter that explores what he sees as a trend toward intolerance of religion among America's legal and political elites:

> The First Amendment guarantees the "free exercise" of religion but also prohibits its "establishment" by the government. There may have been times in our history when we as a nation have tilted too far in one direction, allowing too much religious sway over politics. But in late-twentieth-century America, despite some loud fears about the weak and divided Christian right, we are upsetting the balance afresh by tilting too far in the other direction—and the courts are assisting in the effort.
>
> —Stephen Carter, *The Culture of Disbelief*

In this case, Carter makes his argument by appealing to the balance between "free exercise" and "establishment" of religion guaranteed by the First Amendment to the U.S. Constitution. If readers share his interpretation of the First Amendment, they also likely agree with him that disrupting this equilibrium would be bad. Carter's argument is relatively easy to make because most Americans do have a high—almost religious—regard for the First Amendment. He doesn't have to defend it. But consider how much tougher it would be to get the same consensus for the Second Amendment's protection of the right to bear arms. It provides a shakier premise for arguments, one that requires more backing. (See Chapter 8 for more on using evidence.)

Adrienne Rich, a poet and writer, provides a clear example of a second type of value comparison, one in which a current value—in this case, power—is redefined for a different group so that it can be embraced in a new way. Notice especially how she unpacks the meaning of power:

> The word *power* is highly charged for women. It has been long associated for us with the use of force, with rape, with the stockpiling of weapons, with the ruthless accrual of wealth and the hoarding of resources, with the power that acts only in its own interest, despising and exploiting the powerless—including women and children. . . . But for a long time now, feminists have been talking about redefining power, about that meaning of power which returns to the root—*posse, potere, pouvoir*: to be able, to have the potential, to possess and use one's energy of creation—transforming power.
>
> –Adrienne Rich, "What Does a Woman Need to Know?"

As you can see, arguments based on values are challenging and sophisticated. That's because they often take you right into the heart of issues.

USING ARGUMENTS BASED ON VALUES

Knowing your audience is a key to arguing successfully. The more you know about the values your readers hold dear, the better you will be at selecting the options available to you for making an argument. Corporations and political organizations do massive demographic studies to figure out who their consumers and constituencies are and what they want. Companies that track what you buy or even what you browse on their Web sites are doing a similar kind of audience study. But you don't have to be quite so intrusive. Although you want to influence readers, you need not do that by violating your own principles. Instead, you should study the values of others to appreciate the ways they differ from you and, when possible, to find common ground. Precisely because people are so complicated and because their values can change, you are in a position as a writer to explore values in ways that can make a difference.

1. Listed here are groups whose members likely share some specific interests and values. Choose a group you recognize (or find another special interest group on your own), research it on the Web or in the library, and, in a paragraph, explain its core values for someone less familiar with the group.

   parrotheads

   Harley Davidson owners

   Trekkies

   Log Cabin Republicans

   PETA members

   hip-hop fans

   survivalists

2. A number of selections in this chapter deal with specifically American values. Can you list 30 values—core values—associated with the people of the United States? 100? 200? List as many as you can, and then ask yourself when the list stops being representative of core values. Why does this problem arise? (If you are not from the United States, you might instead list the core values of your home country or another country you know well.)

   Now make a list of core values for a small group—the members of your college's English department, for instance, or a church philanthropy committee, or an athletic team. Any small group will do. How many core values can you list? How does the list compare to the list you generated for the people of the United States?

3. Using the list of core values you've developed for the smaller group, write a paragraph arguing that a public figure—such as Jesse Jackson, Jennifer Lopez, or Serena Williams—meets the standards of that group.

4. Several years ago, a group of animal rights activists raided a mink "ranch" and released several thousand animals from their cages. Many of the minks died during and after their release. Soon thereafter, other animal rights groups criticized this action, arguing that it did not represent the values of true animal rights activists.

   What might these values be? And how would those responsible for the release characterize their own values? Write a statement from one of the other groups, using arguments based on values to express your disapproval of the release. Then write a statement from the releasing group, explaining why its actions were consonant with the values of true animal lovers. In each of these letters, you'll have to decide whether you're writing to a public audience or directly to the opposing group; the values you refer to might change, depending on the audience.

5. A contestant in the Miss America competition is now expected to demonstrate "a commitment to a social issue." Study the pageant's Web site at <missamerica.org> to get a sense of the organization's values. Then make a list of social issues the most contestants would likely avoid. Be prepared to explain why these issues might be controversial or even contrary to the values of the pageant.

chapter six

Arguments Based on Character

In the introduction to his book about men, Dave Barry tries to explain the difference between *men* and *guys*. Naturally, in making such a distinction, he makes readers wonder how he will define each term. Here is what he has to say about the second:

> And what, exactly, do I mean by "guys"? I don't know. I haven't thought much about it. One of the major characteristics about guyhood is that guys don't spend a lot of time pondering our deep innermost feelings.
>
> —Dave Barry, "Guys vs. Men"

If you know that Barry is a famous humorist (there was even a TV sitcom based on his life), you understand just how to take his self-deprecating remarks. He's not writing a serious piece, a fact he stresses in the very first line of his introduction:

> This is a book about guys. It's not a book about men. There are already way too many books about men and most of them are way too serious.

But imagine for a moment that you've never heard of Dave Barry and have somehow missed all the comedy in his introduction. What might you think of a writer who confessed, "I don't know. I haven't thought much about it," it being the subject of his book? Chances are you'd close the volume and choose another by someone smarter.

That's because in argument, as in politics, character matters. Readers usually won't consider an argument unless they trust the person or group offering it. You earn a reader's trust by seeming to know what you are talking about and demonstrating your authority.

You must also seem honest—and sometimes, likable—if you are to persuade an audience. Opponents of Richard Nixon, the controversial thirty-sixth president of the United States, once raised doubts about his integrity by asking a single ruinous question: *Would you buy a used car from this man?* Put that question under the photograph of any controversial politician, and you've composed a powerful visual argument about their *ethos*, or character. Being smart doesn't matter if you aren't perceived as honest.

In composing an argument, you have to convey both authority and honesty through an appeal based on character—what the ancient Greeks called *ethos*. You can do so in various ways, both direct and subtle.

FIGURE 6.1 PUBLIC FIGURES TRY TO CONTROL THEIR IMAGES FOR OBVIOUS REASONS. WOULD YOU BUY A USED CAR FROM ANY OF THESE DISTINGUISHED MEN AND WOMEN?

UNDERSTANDING HOW ARGUMENTS BASED ON CHARACTER WORK

Because life is complicated, we often need shortcuts to help us make choices; we can't weigh every claim to its last milligram or trace every fragment of evidence to its original source. And we have to make such decisions daily: *Which college or university should I attend? For whom should I vote in the next election? Which reviewers of* The Matrix Reloaded *will I believe? What pain reliever will get me through the 10K race?*

To answer the more serious questions, people typically rely on professionals for wise, well-informed, and honest advice: a doctor, lawyer, teacher, pastor. But people look to equally trustworthy individuals to guide them in less momentous matters as well: a coach, a friend, maybe even a waitperson (*Is the fish really fresh?*). Depending on the subject, an *expert* can be anyone with knowledge and experience, from a professor of nuclear physics at a local college to a short-order cook at the local diner.

Readers give people (or companies) they know a hearing they might not automatically grant to a stranger or to someone who hasn't earned their respect or affection. That indicates the power of arguments based on character and accounts for why people will trust the opinion of the "car guy" in their neighborhood more than the reviews in *Consumer Reports*. And they'll take *Consumer Reports* more seriously than the SUV ads in *People*.

CLAIMING AUTHORITY

When you read an argument, especially one that makes an aggressive claim, you have every right to wonder about the writer's authority: *What does he know about the subject? What experiences does she have that make her especially knowledgeable? Why should I pay attention to this writer?*

When you offer an argument yourself, you have to anticipate pointed questions exactly like these and be able to answer them, directly or indirectly. Sometimes the claim of authority will be bold and uncompromising, as it is when writer and activist Terry Tempest Williams attacks those who poisoned the Utah deserts with nuclear radiation. What gives her the right to speak on this subject? Not scientific expertise, but gut-wrenching personal experience:

> **I belong to the Clan of One-Breasted Women. My mother, my grandmothers, and six aunts have all had mastectomies. Seven are dead.**

The two who survive have just completed rounds of chemotherapy and radiation.
I've had my own problems: two biopsies for breast cancer and a small tumor between my ribs diagnosed as a "borderline malignancy."
—Terry Tempest Williams, "The Clan of One-Breasted Women"

We are willing to listen to her claims because she has lived with the nuclear peril she will deal with in the remainder of her essay.

But just as often, writers make claims of authority in other and more subtle ways. We may not have lords and dukes in the United States, but it seems everyone has a job title that confers some clout. When writers attach such titles to their names, they are saying "This is how I've earned the right to be heard"—they are medical doctors or have law degrees or have been board certified to work as psychotherapists. Similarly, writers can assert authority by mentioning who employs them—their institutional affiliations—and how long they have worked in a given field. Bureaucrats often identify themselves with government agencies, and professors always mention what schools they represent. As a reader, you'll likely pay more attention to an argument about global warming if it's offered by a professor of atmospheric and oceanic science at the University of Wisconsin, Madison, than by your Uncle Sid who sells tools at Sears. But you'll prefer your uncle to the professor when you need advice about a reliable rotary saw.

When your readers are apt to be skeptical of both you and your claim—as is usually the case when your subject is controversial—you may have to be even more specific about your credentials. That's exactly the strategy Richard Bernstein uses to establish his right to speak on the delicate subject of teaching multiculturalism in American colleges and universities. At one point in a lengthy argument, he challenges those who make simplistic pronouncements about non-Western cultures, specifically "Asian culture." But what gives a New York writer named *Bernstein* the authority to write about Asian peoples? Bernstein tells us in a sparkling example of an argument based on character:

The Asian culture, as it happens, is something I know a bit about, having spent five years at Harvard striving for a Ph.D. in a joint program called History and East Asian Languages and, after that, living either as a student (for one year) or a journalist (six years) in China and Southeast Asia. At least I know enough to know there is no such thing as the "Asian culture."
—Richard Bernstein, *Dictatorship of Virtue*

Clearly, Bernstein understates the case when he says he knows "a bit" about Asian culture and then mentions a Ph.D. program at Harvard and years of living in Asia. But the false modesty may be part of his argumentative strategy, too.

Bjørn Lomborg, an associate professor of statistics and author of *The Skeptical Environmentalist*, faces a problem much like Bernstein's. Lomborg claims that many environmental threats to the natural world have been exaggerated, sometimes wildly. But what, one might ask, does a statistician know about topics such as global warming, deforestation, or water pollution? Lomborg anticipates that question in the introduction to his book, where he explains what a statistician can add to the discussion (emphasis added):

> **I teach statistics at the University of Aarhus and basically my skills consist in knowing how to handle international statistics. Normally you associate statistics with a boring run-through of endless rows of numbers—a problem I must every semester convince new students is not necessarily true. Actually, statistics can be thoroughly exciting because it *confronts our myths with data and allows us to see the world more clearly*.**

You need not agree with Lomborg's conclusions, but it makes sense for him to defend his credentials this way. His expertise may make it possible to understand the facts better.

When you write for readers who trust you and your work, you may not have to make such an open claim to authority. But you should know that making this type of appeal is always an option. A second lesson is that it certainly helps to know your subject when you are making a claim.

Even if an author does not make an explicit effort to assert authority, authority can be conveyed through tiny signals that readers may pick up almost subconsciously. Sometimes it comes just from a style of writing that presents ideas with robust confidence. For example, years ago when Allan Bloom wrote a controversial book about problems in American education, he used tough, self-assured prose to argue for what needed to be done. We've italicized the words that convey his confident ethos:

> *Of course*, the only *serious* solution [to the problems of higher education] is the one that is almost universally rejected: the *good old* Great Books approach. . . . I am *perfectly aware of*, and actually agree with, the objections to the Great Books Cult. . . . But *one thing is certain:*

wherever the Great Books make up a central part of the curriculum, the students are excited and satisfied.

–Allan Bloom, *The Closing of the American Mind*

Bloom's "of course" seems arrogant; his concession—"I am perfectly aware"—is poised; his announcement of truth is unyielding—"one thing is certain." Writing like this can sweep readers along; the ideas feel carved in stone. Bloom was a professor at the University of Chicago, respected and knowledgeable and often able to get away with such a style even when his ideas provoked strong opposition. Indeed, there is much to be said for framing arguments directly and confidently, as if you really mean them. (And it helps if you do.)

CULTURAL CONTEXTS FOR ARGUMENT

In the United States, students writing arguments are often asked to establish authority by drawing on certain kinds of personal experience, by reporting on research they or others have conducted, and by taking a position for which they can offer strong evidence and support. But this expectation about student authority is by no means universal. Indeed, some cultures regard student writers as novices who can most effectively make arguments by reflecting back on what they have learned from their teachers and elders—those who hold the most important knowledge, wisdom, and, hence, authority. Whenever you are arguing a point with people from cultures other than your own, therefore, you need to think about what kind of authority you are expected to have:

- Whom are you addressing, and what is your relationship with him or her?
- What knowledge are you expected to have? Is it appropriate or expected for you to demonstrate that knowledge—and if so, how?
- What tone is appropriate? If in doubt, always show respect: politeness is rarely if ever inappropriate.

ESTABLISHING CREDIBILITY

Writers with authority seem smart; those with credibility seem trustworthy. As a writer you usually want to convey both impressions, but sometimes, to seem credible, you have to admit limitations: *This is what I know; I won't pretend to fathom more.* Readers pay attention to writers who are willing to be honest and who appear modest about their claims.

Imagine, for instance, that you are the commencement speaker at a prestigious women's college. You want the graduates to question all the material advantages they have enjoyed. But you yourself have enjoyed many of the same privileges. How do you protect your argument from charges of hypocrisy? The poet Adrienne Rich defuses this very conflict simply by admitting her status:

> And so I want to talk today about privilege and tokenism and about power. Everything I can say to you on this subject comes hard-won from the lips of a woman privileged by class and skin color, a father's favorite daughter, educated at Radcliffe.
> –Adrienne Rich, "What Does a Woman Need to Know?"

Candor is a strategy that can earn writers immediate credibility. It's a tactic used by people as respected in their fields as was the late biologist Lewis Thomas, who in this example ponders whether scientists have overstepped their bounds in exploring the limits of DNA research:

> Should we stop short of learning some things, for fear of what we, or someone, will do with the knowledge? My own answer is a flat no, but I must confess that this is an intuitive response and I am neither inclined nor trained to reason my way through it.
> –Lewis Thomas, "The Hazards of Science"

When making an argument, many people would be reluctant to write "I suppose" or "I must confess," but those are the very concessions that might increase a reader's confidence in Lewis Thomas. Note, too, how Thomas's honesty differs from the giddy celebration of ignorance in Dave Barry's comic piece on guys that opened this chapter.

You can invite readers to see you as honest in other ways, too. Nancy Mairs, in an essay entitled "On Being a Cripple," wins the attention and maybe the respect of her readers by facing her disability with a riveting directness:

> First, the matter of semantics. I am a cripple. I choose this word to name me. I choose from among several possibilities, the most common of which are "handicapped" and "disabled." I made the choice a number of years ago, without thinking, unaware of my motives for doing so. Even now, I am not sure what those motives are, but I recognize that they are complex and not entirely flattering. People— crippled or not—wince at the word "cripple," as they do not at "handi-

capped" or "disabled." Perhaps I want them to wince. I want them to see me as a tough customer, one to whom the fates/gods/viruses have not been kind, but who can face the brutal truth of her existence squarely. As a cripple, I swagger.

–Nancy Mairs, "On Being a Cripple"

The paragraph takes some risks because the writer is expressing feelings that may make readers unsure how to react because Mairs herself doesn't completely understand her own feelings and motives. Yet the very uncertainty helps her to build a bridge to readers.

Thus a reasonable way to approach an argument—especially an academic or personal one—is to be honest with your readers about who you are and what you do and do not know. If it is appropriate to create a kind of dialogue with readers, as many writers do, then you want to give readers a chance to identify with you, to see the world from your perspective, and to appreciate why you are making specific claims.

In fact, a very powerful technique for building credibility is to acknowledge outright any exceptions, qualifications, or even weaknesses in your argument. Making such concessions to objections that readers might raise, called *conditions of rebuttal*, sends a strong signal to the audience that you've scrutinized your own position with a sharp critical eye and can therefore be trusted when you turn to arguing its merits. W. Charisse Goodman, arguing that the media promote prejudice against people who aren't thin, points out that some exceptions do exist:

Television shows . . . occasionally make an effort. Ricki Lake, who has since lost weight, was featured in the defunct series *China Beach*; Delta Burke once co-starred in *Designing Women* and had her own series; and Roseanne's show has long resided among the Top 10 in the Nielsen ratings. Although these women are encouraging examples of talent overcoming prejudice, they are too few and far between. At best, TV shows typically treat large female characters as special cases whose weight is always a matter of comment, rather than integrating women of all sizes and shapes into their programs as a matter of course.

–W. Charisse Goodman, "One Picture Is Worth a Thousand Diets"

Notice how pointing out these exceptions helps build Goodman's credibility as a critic. Conceding some effort on the part of television shows allows her to make her final judgment more compellingly.

You can also use language in other ways to create a relationship of trust with readers. Speaking to readers directly, using *I* or *you*, for instance, enables you to come closer to them when that strategy is appropriate.

Using contractions will have the same effect because they make prose sound more colloquial. Consider how linguist Robert D. King uses such techniques (as well as an admission that he might be wrong) to add a personal note to the conclusion of a serious essay arguing against the notion that language diversity is endangering the United States (emphasis added):

> If *I'm wrong*, then the great American experiment will fail—not because of language but because it no longer means anything to be an American; because we have forfeited that "willingness of the heart" that F. Scott Fitzgerald wrote was America; because we are no longer joined by Lincoln's "mystic chords of memory."
>
> We are not even close to the danger point. *I suggest* that we relax and luxuriate in our linguistic richness and our traditional tolerance of language differences. Language does not threaten American unity. Benign neglect is a good policy for any country when it comes to language, and it's *a good policy* for America.
>
> —Robert D. King, "Should English Be the Law?"

On the other hand, you may find that a more formal tone gives your claims greater authority. Choices like these are yours to make as you search for the ethos that best represents you in a given argument.

Another fairly simple way of conveying both authority and credibility is to back up your claims with evidence and documentation—or, in an electronic environment, to link your claims to sites with reliable information. Citing trustworthy sources and acknowledging them properly shows that you have done your homework.

Indeed, any signals you give readers to show that you have taken care to present ideas clearly and fairly will help your credibility. A helpful graph, table, chart, or illustration may carry weight, as does the physical presentation of your work (or your Web site, for that matter). Even proper spelling counts.

USING ARGUMENTS FROM CHARACTER

A number of studies over the years have shown that tall, thin, good-looking people have an advantage in getting a job or getting a raise. Apparently, employers respond to their attractive appearance and make assumptions about their competence that have no basis in fact. You probably act the same way in some circumstances, even if you resent the practice. So you might recall these studies when you make an argument, knowing that like it or not, readers and audiences are going to respond to how you present yourself as a person. Fortunately, you need not add inches to your height or character to your cheekbones to be persuasive in writing. What you do need is to sound confident, knowledgeable, and honest. Sounding friendly may help too, though many persuasive writers manage without that trait.

Be sure that your writing also conveys competence visually. Choose a medium that shows you at your best. Some writers love the written text, garnished with quotations, footnotes, charts, graphs, and bibliography. Others can make a better case online or in some purely visual form. Design arguments that tell readers they can trust you.

RESPOND ●

1. Consider the ethos of each of the following figures. Then describe one or two public arguments, campaigns, or products that might benefit from their endorsements as well as several that would not.

   Eminem—rap artist

   Ricki Lake—TV talk-show host

   Jesse Ventura—former governor of Minnesota and professional wrestler

   Katie Holmes—actress featured on *Dawson's Creek*

   Donald Rumsfeld—secretary of defense in the Bush administration

   Jesse Jackson—civil rights leader

   Queen Latifah—actress and rap artist

   Dave Barry—humorist and columnist

   Jeff Gordon—NASCAR champion

   Madeleine Albright—secretary of state in the Clinton administration

   Bill O'Reilly—TV news show host

   Marge Simpson—sensible wife and mother on *The Simpsons*

   Ozzy Osbourne—rock personality

2. Voice is a choice. That is, writers modify the tone and style of their language depending on who they want to seem to be. In the excerpts from this chapter, Allan Bloom wants to appear poised and confident;

his language aims to convince us of his expertise. Terry Tempest Williams wants to appear serious, knowledgeable, and personally invested in the problems of radiation poisoning; the descriptions of her family's illness try to convince us. In different situations, even when writing about the same topics, Bloom and Williams would adopt different voices. (Imagine Williams explaining "The Clan of One-Breasted Women" to a young girl in her family—she might use different words, a changed tone, and simpler examples.)

Rewrite the Williams passage on p. 90, taking on the voice—the character—of someone speaking to a congressional committee studying nuclear experiments in Utah. Then rewrite the selection in the voice of someone speaking to a fourth-grade class in New Hampshire. You'll need to change the way you claim authority, establish credibility, and demonstrate competence as you try to convince different audiences of your character.

3. Create your own version of the famous "Would you buy a used car from this man?" argument aimed against Richard Nixon when he was a candidate for political office. Begin by choosing an intriguing or controversial person or group and finding an image online. Download the image into a word-processing file. Create a caption for the photo modeled after the question asked about Nixon—*Would you give this woman your email password? Would you share a campsite with this couple? Would you eat lasagna this guy prepared?* Finally, write a serious 300-word argument that explores the character flaws (or strengths) of your subject(s).

FIGURE 6.2 WOULD YOU BUY LONG-DISTANCE SERVICE FROM CARROT TOP?

4. A well-known television advertisement from the 1980s featured a soap-opera actor promoting a pain relief medication. "I'm not a doctor," he said, "but I play one on TV." Likewise, Michael Jordan trades on his good name to star in Nike advertisements. Actress Susan Sarandon uses the entertainment media to argue for political causes. One way or another, each of these cases relies on arguments based on character.

Develop a one-page print advertisement for a product or service you use often—anything from soap to auto repair to cell phone service. There's one catch: Your advertisement should rely on arguments based on character, and you should choose as a spokesperson someone who would seem the least likely to use or endorse your product or service. The challenge is to turn an apparent disadvantage into an advantage by exploiting character.

chapter seven

Arguments Based on Facts and Reason

"Logic and practical information do not seem to apply here."

"You admit that?"

"To deny the facts would be illogical, Doctor."

–Spock and McCoy, "A Piece of the Action"

When the choice is between logic and emotion, a great many of us are going to side with *Star Trek*'s Dr. McCoy rather than the stern Spock. Most of us respect logical appeals—arguments based on facts, evidence, reason, and logic—but, like the good doctor, we are inclined to test the facts against our feelings and against the character and values of those making the appeal. As McCoy observes in another *Star Trek* episode, "You can't evaluate a man by logic alone."

The fact is that human beings aren't computers and most human issues don't present themselves like problems in geometry. When writers need to persuade, they usually try their best to give readers or listeners good reasons to believe them or to enter into a conversation with them. Not infrequently, they will tell a story to make their point, dramatizing their case by showing how an issue affects the lives of individuals or a community. Sometimes these well-reasoned cases get listened to sympathetically; at other times, even the most reasonable efforts to persuade fail. Then people try harder—perhaps by strengthening their good reasons with stronger appeals to the heart or to their personal credibility. (For more on these types of appeals, see Chapters 4 and 6.)

Still, when you argue logically, you've got plenty of resources to draw upon—far too many to list in a text this brief. Here we can only summarize some ways of arguing logically. Aristotle, one of the first philosophers to write about persuasion, gives us a place to begin. He divided logical proofs into two kinds: those based on what we'd call *hard evidence* (what Aristotle called *inartistic appeals*—facts, clues, statistics, testimonies, witnesses) and those based upon *reason and common sense* (what Aristotle called *artistic appeals*). Though these categories overlap and leak (what, after all, is *common sense?*), they are useful even today. For instance, when lawyers in a trial question witnesses, judges usually restrict them to questions about evidence and fact. But when the same lawyers make their closing arguments to juries, they can draw on those facts and testimony to raise broader questions of guilt or innocence. They can speak more openly about motives, mitigating circumstances, and reasonable doubt. In other words, they can *interpret* the hard evidence they have assembled (as at the O.J. Simpson trial when Simpson was asked to try on a bloody glove)

FIGURE 7.1   DURING HIS TRIAL FOR THE MURDER OF HIS EX-WIFE, O. J. SIMPSON WAS ASKED TO TRY ON A PAIR OF BLOODY GLOVES SAID TO BE HIS. THEY DIDN'T FIT.

to urge conviction or exoneration (in Johnnie Cochran's words, *If it does not fit, you must acquit*). We'll examine both types of logical appeals in this chapter.

HARD EVIDENCE

It wasn't so in Aristotle's time, but people today probably prefer arguments based on facts and testimony to those grounded in reason. In a courtroom as well as in the popular media, for example, lawyers or reporters look for the "smoking gun"—that piece of hard evidence that ties a defendant or politician to a crime. It might be an audiotape, a fingerprint, a stained dress, or, increasingly, a videotape or DNA evidence. Popular crime shows such as *CSI: Crime Scene Investigation* focus intensely on gathering this sort of "scientific" support for a prosecution. Less dramatically, the factual evidence in an argument might be columns of data carefully collected over time to prove a point about climate change or racial profiling or the effects of Title IX on collegiate sports. After decades of exposure to science and the wonders of technology, audiences today have more faith in claims that can be counted, measured, photographed, or analyzed than in those that are merely defended with words. If you've ever been ticketed after a camera caught you running a red light, you know what hard evidence means.

Factual evidence, however, comes in many forms. Which ones you use will depend on the kind of argument you are writing. In fact, providing accurate evidence ought to become a habit whenever you write an argument. The evidence makes your case plausible; it may also supply the details that make writing interesting. Just recall Aristotle's claim that all arguments can be reduced to two components:

Statement + Proof

Here's another way of naming those parts:

Claim + Supporting Evidence

When you remember to furnish evidence for every important claim you make, you go a long way toward understanding how to argue responsibly. The process can be remarkably straightforward. In a scholarly article, you can actually see this process occurring in the text and in the notes. As an example, we reprint a single page from a much-cited review of Michael Bellesiles's *Arming America: The Making of America's Gun Culture* by James Lindgren published in the *Yale Law Review*. Bellesiles had used evidence gathered from eighteenth-century documents to argue that gun ownership in frontier America was much rarer than advocates of the right to bear arms believed. Upon publication, *Arming America* was hailed by gun critics for weakening the claim of gun advocates today that the ownership of weapons has always been a part of American culture. But Lindgren, as well as many other critics and historians, found so many evidentiary flaws in Bellesiles's arguments that questions were soon raised about his scholastic integrity. Lindgren's review of *Arming America* runs for more than 50 meticulous pages (including an appendix of errors

FIGURE 7.2 THIS SELECTION FROM JAMES LINDGREN'S REVIEW OF MICHAEL BELLE-SILES'S *ARMING AMERICA* FIRST APPEARED IN THE *YALE LAW REVIEW*, VOL. 111 (2002).

LINDGRENFINAL.DOC   APRIL 26, 2002 4/26/02 12:34 PM

2002]   *Arming America*   2203

B. *How Common Was Gun Ownership?*

The most contested portions of *Arming America* involve the book's most surprising claim, that guns were infrequently owned before the mid-1800s. As I show below, the claim that colonial America did not have a gun culture is questionable on the evidence of gun ownership alone. Compared to the seventeenth and eighteenth centuries, it appears that guns are not as commonly owned today. Whereas individual gun ownership in every published (and unpublished) study of early probate records that I have located (except Bellesiles's) ranges from 40% to 79%; only 32.5% of households today own a gun.[44] This appears to be a much smaller percentage than in early America—in part because the mean household size in the late eighteenth century was six people,[45] while today it is just under two people.[46] The prevailing estimate of 40% to 79% ownership differs markedly from Bellesiles's claim that only about 15% owned guns.[47] In the remainder of this Section, I explain why.

1. *The Gun Censuses*

Bellesiles bases his claims of low gun ownership primarily on probate records and counts of guns at militia musters.[48] He also discusses censuses of all guns in private and public hands, but on closer examination, none of these turns out to be a general census of all guns.

The trend is set in Bellesiles's first count of guns in an American community—the 1630 count of all the guns in the Massachusetts Bay Colony of about 1000 people. Bellesiles's account is quite specific: " In 1630 the Massachusetts Bay Company reported in their possession: '80 bastard musketts, . . . [10] Fowling peeces, . . . 10 Full musketts . . . .'" There were thus exactly one hundred firearms for use among seven towns

44. This results from my analysis of the March 2001 release of the National Opinion Research Center's *General Social Survey. 2000* [hereinafter 2000 NORC GSS]. The data are also available at Nat'l Opinion Research Ctr., General Social Survey, *at* http://www.icpsr.umich.edu/GSS/ (last visited Apr. 8, 2002). According to the survey, 32.5% of households owned any gun, 19.7% owned a rifle, 18.6% owned a shotgun, and 19.7% owned a pistol or revolver. 2000 NORC GSS, *supra.* Only 1.2% of respondents refused to respond to the question. *Id.*
45. Inter-Univ. Consortium for Political & Soc. Research (ICPSR), Census Data for the Year 1790, http://fisher.lib.virginia.edu/cgi-local/censusbin/census/cen.pl?year=790 (last visited Aug. 10, 2001).
46. 2000 NORC GSS, *supra* note 44.
47. BELLESILES, *supra* note 3, at 445 tbl.1.

in Bellesiles's work) and contains 212 footnotes. You can see a factual argument in action just by looking at how Lindgren handles evidence on a single page. You may never write an argument as detailed as Lindgren's review, but you should have the same respect for evidence.

Facts

"Facts," said John Adams, "are stubborn things," and so they make strong arguments, especially when readers believe they come from honest sources. Gathering such information and transmitting it faithfully practically defines what we mean by journalism in one realm and scholarship in another. We'll even listen to people we don't agree with when they overwhelm us with evidence. Here, for example, a reviewer for the conservative journal *National Review* praises the work of William Julius Wilson, a liberal sociologist, because of how well he presents his case (emphasis added):

> **In his eagerly awaited new book, Wilson argues that ghetto blacks are worse off than ever, victimized by a near-total loss of low-skill jobs in and around inner-city neighborhoods. In support of this thesis, he** *musters mountains of data, plus excerpts from some of the thousands of surveys and face-to-face interviews that he and his research team conducted among inner-city Chicagoans.* **It is a book that deserves a wide audience among thinking conservatives.**
> —John J. Dilulio Jr., **"When Decency Disappears"**

Here, the facts are trusted even above differences in political thinking.

When your facts are compelling, they may stand on their own in a low-stakes argument, supported by little more than a tag that gives the source of your information. Consider the power of phrases such as "reported by the *New York Times*," "according to CNN," or "in a book published by Oxford University Press." Such sources gain credibility if they have, in readers' experience, reported facts accurately and reliably over time. In fact, one reason you document the sources you use in an argument is to let the credibility of those sources reflect positively on you—one important reason to find the best, most reliable authorities and evidence to support your claims.

But arguing with facts also sometimes involves challenging claims made by reputable sources. You don't have to look hard to find critics of the *Times* or CNN. Web loggers (commonly known as *bloggers*) particularly enjoy pointing out the biases or factual mistakes of major media outlets. Here, for example, is blogger Andrew Sullivan charging that a headline of a story in the *New York Times*, his favorite target, distorts the facts reported in a poll:

THE TIMES AND POLLS: It's gotten to the point now that I always check the actual poll when reading the *New York Times*' version. This particular story is from the AP, so I'm not sure where the bias lies. But the *Times* headline is a complete distortion of the poll numbers. The *Times*' story reads: "Poll: Support For Iraq Action Drops." The poll itself shows that on the generic question of supporting military action against Iraq, those supporting it numbered 59 percent in June and 64 percent today. Those opposing it dropped from 34 percent to 21 percent. Lies, damned lies, and the *New York Times*!

–Andrew Sullivan, <andrewsullivan.com>

In an ideal world, good information would always drive out bad. But you'll soon learn that such is not always the case. That's why as a reader and researcher, you should look beyond headlines, scrutinizing any facts you collect before using them yourself, testing their reliability and reporting them with all the needed qualifiers. As a writer, you have to give your readers not only the facts but where they came from and what they may mean.

Statistics

Let's deal with a cliché right up front: *figures lie and liars figure*. Like most clichés, it contains a grain of truth. It is possible to lie with numbers, even those that are accurate. Anyone either using or reading statistics has good reason to ask how the numbers were gathered and how they have been interpreted. Both factors bear on the credibility of statistical arguments.

However, the fact remains that contemporary culture puts great stock in tables, graphs, reports, and comparisons of numbers. People use such numbers to understand the past, evaluate the present, and speculate about the future. These numbers almost always need writers to interpret them. And writers almost always have agendas that influence their interpretations.

For example, you might want to herald the good news that unemployment in the United States stands just a little over 5 percent. That means 95 percent of Americans have jobs, a figure much higher than that of most other industrial nations. But let's spin the figure another way. In a country as populous as the United States, unemployment at 5 percent means that millions of Americans are without a daily wage. Indeed, *one out of every twenty adults* who wants work can't find it. That's a remarkably high number. As you can see, the same statistics can be cited as a cause for celebration or shame.

We don't mean to suggest that numbers are meaningless or untrustworthy or that you have license to use them in any way that serves your

FIGURE 7.3 *USA TODAY* IS FAMOUS FOR THE TABLES, PIE CHARTS, AND BAR GRAPHS IT CREATES TO PRESENT STATISTICS AND POLL RESULTS. WHAT CLAIMS MIGHT THE EVIDENCE IN THIS CHART SUPPORT? HOW DOES THE DESIGN OF THE ITEM INFLUENCE YOUR READING OF IT?

purposes. Quite the contrary. But you do have to understand the role you play in giving numbers a voice and a presence.

Consider the matter we mentioned earlier about using cameras at highway intersections to catch drivers who run red lights. The cameras may intrude a little into our privacy, but they are an effective way to deal with a serious traffic hazard, aren't they? Well, no, not according to former House Majority Leader Dick Armey. In an article on his Web site entitled "The Truth about Red Light Cameras," Armey uses numbers and statistics to raise doubts about the motives that cities and police forces have for installing cameras at traffic lights. We've highlighted his use of figures:

> Safety was never the primary consideration [for installing traffic light cameras in San Diego]. In fact, none of the devices were placed at any of San Diego's *top-ten most dangerous intersections.* Instead, the documents tell us how the camera operators consciously sought out mistimed intersections as locations for new red light cameras.
>
> Yellow signal time at intersections turns out to be directly related to "red light running." Simply put, when the yellow light is short, more people enter on red. Inadequate yellow time causes a condition where individuals approaching an intersection are unable either to come to a safe stop or [to] proceed safely before the light turns red.

Though dangerous, this condition also turns out to be very profitable. Each time someone ends up in an intersection on red in San Diego, *the city collects $271*. And $70 of that fine is paid as bounty to the city's private contractor. Combine hefty fines with mistimed signals and you've found the formula for big money. A single camera brought the city *$6.8 million in just 18 months.* . . .

Consider the intersection of Mission Bay Drive and Grand Avenue in San Diego. With *a yellow time of 3 seconds*, the intersection produced about *2,300 violations every month*.

Documents show that the *yellow time was increased to 4.7 seconds* at that particular intersection on July 28, 2000. Immediately after the change, *red light entries dropped 90 percent* — and they stayed down.

The simple and inexpensive step of adding a little over a second to the yellow time produced a significant safety benefit. Did the city tell the world of its success? Did the city refocus its efforts to correct signal timing at other intersections? No. That's because this "success" *cost the City of San Diego $3 million* in yearly revenue it would have otherwise collected from the mistimed signal.

Red light entries similarly dropped about 70 percent in Mesa, Arizona, after the city increased yellow times at its intersections in response to motorist complaints. The problem subsided so dramatically that their camera program turned into a big money loser. The incredible truth about Mesa, however, is that the city had to break its contract with the camera operators to achieve this safety benefit.

Inadequate yellows are more dangerous, but they are also more profitable. It's hard to conceive another explanation for a contract that prevents engineering safety measures that could dilute profits.

–Dick Armey, "The Truth About Red Light Cameras"

This is hardly the last word on traffic light cameras. Proponents (including insurance companies) might cite different numbers and studies that report reductions in collisions after cameras were installed or savings on insurance claims. Perhaps a compromise is possible — longer yellow signals *and* traffic light cameras?

Surveys, Polls, and Studies

Surveys and polls produce statistics. These measures play so large a role in people's political and social lives that writers, whether interpreting them or fashioning surveys themselves, need to give them special attention.

Surveys and polls provide persuasive appeals when they verify the popularity of an idea or proposal because, in a democracy, majority opinion offers a compelling warrant: *a government should do what most people want.* Polls come as close to expressing the will of the people as anything short of an election—the most decisive poll of all. (For more on warrants, see Chapter 8, p. 129.)

However, surveys, polls, and studies can do much more than help politicians make decisions. They can also provide persuasive reasons for action or intervention. When studies show, for example, that most American sixth-graders can't locate France or Wyoming on the map, that's an appeal for better instruction in geography. When polls suggest that consumer confidence is declining, businesses may have reason to worry about their bulging inventories. By this point, you should appreciate the responsibility to question any study or report. It always makes sense to ask who is reporting the results and numbers and what stake the source has—financial, political, ethical—in the outcome.

Are we being too suspicious? No. In fact, this sort of scrutiny is exactly what you should anticipate from your readers whenever you use such material to frame an argument. Especially with polls and surveys, you should be confident that you or your source surveyed enough people to be accurate, that the people you chose for the study were representative of the selected population as a whole, and that you chose them randomly— not selecting those most likely to say what you hoped to hear.

Surveys and polls can be affected, too, by the way questions are asked or results are reported. Professional pollsters generally understand that their reputations depend on asking questions in as neutral a way as possible. But some researchers aren't above skewing their results by asking leading questions. There's even a term for using polls to sway the people being polled rather than to survey public opinion: *push polling.* Consider how differently people might respond to the following queries on roughly the same subject:

> **Do you support cuts in Medicare to help balance the federal budget?**
>
> **Do you support adjustments in Medicare to keep the system solvent?**
>
> **Do you support decisive action to prevent the bankruptcy of Medicare?**

You must also read beyond the headlines to be sure you understand the claims made in a poll. A recent headline on a Gallup poll was potentially confusing: "Fewer Americans Favor Private Investment of Social Security Taxes." Fewer than what? Does the headline mean that a majority of Americans oppose privatizing Social Security or that support for the idea has declined? Fortunately a subheading clarified the matter: "Proposal still gets majority approval." A less honest pollster might have omitted that important line. The simple lesson here is to use polls, surveys, and other studies responsibly.

Testimonies, Narratives, and Interviews

We don't want to give the impression that numbers and statistics make the only good evidence. Indeed, writers support arguments with all kinds of human experiences, particularly those they or others have lived or reported. The testimony of reliable witnesses counts in almost any situation in which a writer seeks to make a case for action, change, or sympathetic understanding.

In a court, for example, decisions are often based upon detailed descriptions of what happened. Following is a reporter's account of a court case in which a panel of judges decided, based on the testimony presented, that a man had been sexually harassed by another man. The narrative, in this case, supplies the evidence:

> The Seventh Circuit, in a 1997 case known as Doe v. City of Belleville, drew a sweeping conclusion allowing for same-sex harassment cases of many kinds. Title VII was sex-neutral, the court ruled; it didn't specifically prohibit discrimination against men or women. Moreover, the judges argued, there was such a thing as gender stereotyping, and if someone was harassed on that basis, it was unlawful. This case, for example, centered on teenage twin brothers working a summer job cutting grass in the city cemetery of Belleville, Ill. One boy wore an earring, which caused him no end of grief that particular summer — including a lot of menacing talk among his co-workers about sexually assaulting him in the woods and sending him "back to San Francisco." One of his harassers, identified in court documents as a large former marine, culminated a verbal campaign by backing the earring-wearer against a wall and grabbing him by the testicles to see "if he was a girl or a guy." The teenager had been "singled out for this abuse," the court ruled, "because the way in which he projected the sexual aspect of his personality" — meaning his gender — "did not conform to his co-workers' view of appropriate masculine behavior."
>
> –Margaret Talbot, "Men Behaving Badly"

Personal experience carefully reported can also support a claim convincingly, especially if a writer has earned the trust of readers. In the following excerpt, Christian Zawodniak describes his experiences as a student in a first-year college writing course. Not impressed by his instructor's performance, Zawodniak provides specific evidence of the instructor's failings:

My most vivid memory of Jeff's rigidness was the day he responded to our criticisms of the class. Students were given a chance anonymously to write our biggest criticisms one Monday, and the following Wednesday Jeff responded, staunchly answering all criticisms of his teaching: "Some of you complained that I didn't come to class prepared. It took me five years to learn all this." Then he pointed to the blackboard on which he had written all the concepts we had discussed that quarter. His responses didn't seem genuine or aimed at improving his teaching or helping students to understand him. He thought he was always right. Jeff's position gave him responsibilities that he officially met. But he didn't take responsibility in all the ways he had led us to expect.

–Christian Zawodniak, "Teacher Power, Student Pedagogy"

Zawodniak's portrait of a defensive instructor gives readers details by which to assess the argument. If readers believe Zawodniak, they learn something about teaching. (For more on establishing credibility with readers, see Chapter 6.)

Shifting from personal experience to more distanced observations of people and institutions, writers move into the arena of ethnographic observation, learning what they can from the close study of human behavior and culture. Ethnography is a specific discipline with clearly defined methods of studying phenomena and reporting data, but the instinct to explore and argue from observation is widespread. Notice that instinct in play as English professor Shelby Steele assembles evidence to explain why race relationships on college campuses may be deteriorating:

To look at this mystery, I left my own campus with its burden of familiarity and talked with black and white students at California schools where racial incidents had occurred: Stanford, UCLA, and Berkeley. I spoke with black and white students—not with Asians and Hispanics—because, as always, blacks and whites represent the deepest lines of division, and because I hesitate to wander into the complex territory of other minority groups. A phrase by William H. Gass—"the hidden internality of things"—describes, with maybe a little too much grandeur, what I hoped to find. But it is what I wanted to find, for this is the kind of problem that makes a black person nervous, which is not to say that it doesn't unnerve whites as well. Once every six months or so someone yells "nigger" at me from a passing car. I don't like to think that these solo artists might soon make up a chorus, or worse, that this chorus might one day soon sing to me from the paths of my own campus.

–Shelby Steele, "The Recoloring of Campus Life"

Steele's method of observation also includes a rationale for his study, giving it both credibility and immediacy. Chances are, readers will pay attention to what he discovers. It may be worth noting that personal narratives and ethnographic reports can sometimes reach into the "hidden internality of things" where more scientific approaches cannot inquire so easily or reveal so much.

As you can see, with appropriate caution and suitable qualifications you can offer personal experiences and careful observations as valid forms of argument.

REASON AND COMMON SENSE

"Facts are stupid things," Ronald Reagan once misspoke, delighting his critics with what they thought was evidence of his lack of sophistication. But Reagan was right in at least one sense. In and of themselves, facts can be mute. They need to be interpreted. Or, in the absence of reliable facts, claims must be supported with other kinds of reasoning.

The *Washington Times* made precisely such a distinction between facts and reasoning in reporting on an argument raging in Washington, D.C., in September 2002 over whether Osama bin Laden was dead or alive, describing the dilemma in terms Aristotle might have admired (emphasis added): "An increasing number of government analysts believe Osama bin Laden is dead, but *the assessment is based on rational deduction, not hard evidence*." Because bin Laden's body had not been found and no reliable witnesses had confirmed his death, the paper offered a list of good reasons (rather than cold facts) for believing that the leader of Al Qaeda — not seen in public for months — might, in fact, be deceased:

- *Bin Laden has an enormous ego*, and with it, a need to appear in public. . . . "He has too big an ego to stay quiet this long," said a senior military officer. . . .

- *It is easier to hide bin Laden's death than his life.* . . . If bin Laden were alive, he must be talking to Al Qaeda members at some point, who in turn talk to other followers. Those conversations would surface in communications "chatter" and be picked up by U.S. intelligence. . . .

- *Al Qaeda supporters have put out videotapes of anti-Western speeches by bin Laden, claiming that they are new.* U.S. analysts say all tapes since December [2001] are old. Some surmise that Al Qaeda is putting out phony tapes to cover up bin Laden's death.

Lacking a smoking gun (or, in this case, a cold corpse), government officials were falling back on probabilities and likelihoods, drawing their inferences from the scant knowledge about bin Laden they did have. Yet the process is one we all use when we can't speak with certainty about an issue—and that's the case most of the time. When we argue about matters that are unsettled or unknown, we use reason to give voice to the facts we do possess. In short, evidence and reason work hand in hand.

Logic is the formal study of principles of reasoning, but few people—except perhaps mathematicians and philosophers—present their arguments using formal logic; the extent of what most people know about it is the most famous of all syllogisms (a vehicle of formal deductive logic):

> **All human beings are mortal.**
>
> **Socrates is a human being.**
>
> **Therefore, Socrates is mortal.**

Fortunately, even as gifted a logician as Aristotle recognized that most people could argue very well using informal logic (some might say common sense). Consciously or not, people are constantly stating propositions, drawing inferences, assessing premises and assumptions, and deriving conclusions whenever they read or write. Mostly, we rely on the cultural assumptions and habits of mind we share with readers or listeners.

In the next chapter, we describe a system of informal logic you may find useful in shaping credible arguments—Toulmin argument. Here, we want to examine the way informal logic works in people's daily lives.

Once again, we begin with Aristotle, who used the term *enthymeme* to describe a very ordinary kind of sentence, one that includes both a claim and a reason.

> **Enthymeme = Claim + Reason**

Enthymemes are logical statements that everyone makes almost effortlessly. The following sentences are all enthymemes:

> **We'd better cancel the picnic because it's going to rain.**
>
> **Flat taxes are fair because they treat everyone in the same way.**
>
> **I'll buy a Honda Civic because it's cheap and reliable.**
>
> **Barry Bonds will be in the baseball Hall of Fame because he's already accomplished more than most players already there.**

Enthymemes are persuasive statements when most readers agree with the assumptions within them. Sometimes the statements seem so commonsensical that readers aren't aware of the inferences they are drawing in accepting them. Consider the first example:

We'd better cancel the picnic because it's going to rain.

When a person casually makes such a claim, it's usually based on more specific information, so let's expand the enthymeme a bit to say what the speaker really means:

We'd better cancel the picnic this afternoon because the weather bureau is predicting a 70 percent chance of rain for the remainder of the day.

Embedded in this argument are all sorts of assumptions and bits of cultural information that help make it persuasive, among them:

Picnics are ordinarily held outdoors.

When the weather is bad, it's best to cancel picnics.

Rain is bad weather for picnics.

A 70 percent chance of rain means that rain is more likely to occur than not.

When rain is more likely to occur than not, it makes sense to cancel picnics.

The weather bureau's predictions are reliable enough to warrant action.

You'd sound ridiculous if you drew out all these inferences just to suggest that a picnic should be canceled because of rain. For most people, the original statement carries all this information on its own; it is a compressed argument, based on what audiences know and will accept.

But what if a claim isn't so self-evident? Compare these examples:

You'd better stop driving. The oil level in your engine is very low.

You'd better stop driving. The oil level in your engine is very high.

Most drivers know that not having enough oil in the crankcase of an engine can damage a vehicle, so the first enthymeme doesn't need much explanation or defense. But what happens when a crankcase has too much oil? Is that condition harmful enough to require a driver to do something immediately? Most people don't know whether too much oil can also damage an engine (it can, though not as quickly as too little oil), so you'd have to do some technical backfilling to support the second enthymeme. Otherwise, readers might not understand the assumption on which it is based. But even when readers get the assumption, you may still have to prove that a particular claim is true—for example, that the weather bureau has actually predicted bad weather for the day of the picnic or that the dipstick does in fact show that the oil level is low. In other words, to be persuasive, you have to make reasonable claims based upon assumptions your readers accept and then provide whatever evidence your readers need.

Cultural Assumptions

Some of the assumptions in an argument will be based on culture and history. In the United States, for example, few arguments work better than those based on principles of fairness and equity. Most Americans believe that all people should be treated in the same way, no matter who they are or where they come from. That principle is announced in the Declaration of Independence: all men are created equal.

Because fairness is culturally accepted, in American society enthymemes based on equity ordinarily need less support than those that challenge it. That's why, for example, both sides in debates over affirmative action programs seek the high ground of fairness: Proponents claim that affirmative action is needed to correct enduring inequities from the past; opponents suggest that the preferential policies should be overturned because they cause inequity today. Here's Linda Chavez drawing deeply on the equity principle:

> Ultimately, entitlements based on their status as "victims" rob Hispanics of real power. The history of American ethnic groups is one of overcoming disadvantage, of competing with those who were already here and proving themselves as competent as any who came before. Their fight was always to be treated the same as other Americans, never to be treated as special, certainly not to turn the temporary disadvantages they suffered into permanent entitlement. Anyone who thinks this fight was easier in the earlier part of this century when it was waged by other ethnic groups does not know history.
> –Linda Chavez, "Towards a New Politics of Hispanic Assimilation"

Chavez expects Hispanics to accept her claims because she believes they do not wish to be treated differently than other ethnic groups in the society.

Naturally, societies in other times and places have operated from very different premises—they may have privileged a particular race, gender, religion, or even aristocratic birth. Within particular organizations, you may see such powerful assumptions operating. Understanding such core cultural assumptions is a key to making successful arguments.

STRUCTURES FOR ARGUMENTS

Some types of argument seem less tightly bound to particular cultural assumptions. They work on their own to make a plausible case that readers can readily comprehend—even when they don't necessarily agree with it. In the second part of this book we examine in detail some structures of arguments we use almost daily: *arguments of definition, evaluative arguments, causal arguments*, and *proposal arguments*. Although we present them individually, you'll cross boundaries between types of arguments all the time when you make a case on your own. Arguments should be consistent, but they need not follow a single pattern.

In fact, there are many types of logical arguments to draw on— structures that your readers will recognize without the need for much explanation. Arguments about *greater or lesser* are of this type. In the novel *The Fountainhead*, novelist Ayn Rand asks the question: "If physical slavery is repulsive, how much more repulsive is the concept of servility of the spirit?" Most readers understand immediately the point she intends to make about mental slavery because they already appreciate the cruelty of physical slavery. Rand may still have to offer evidence that "servility of the spirit" is, in fact, worse than bodily servitude, but she has begun with a structure readers can understand. This type of argument can be made in many forms and in many circumstances:

- If I can get a ten-year warranty on a humble Hyundai, shouldn't I get the same or better treatment from Mercedes or BMW?
- The widespread benefits to be derived from using human stem cells in research will outweigh the largely theoretical ethical qualms of harvesting the cells from fetuses.
- Better a conventional war now than a nuclear confrontation later.

Analogies offer another structure of argument that people understand intuitively. They usually involve explaining something that is not well known by comparing it to something much more familiar. We reject or accept such analogies, depending on the quality of the comparison. Here, for example, is a controversial analogy that Maryland governor Kathleen Kennedy Townsend used during her campaign, comparing affirmative action to other race-based activities. The question, of course, is whether her analogy makes affirmative action seem like the desirable policy she believes it is.

> He [her Republican opponent, Robert Erhlich] opposes affirmative action based on race. Slavery was based on race. Lynching was based on race. Discrimination was based on race. Jim Crow was based on race. Affirmative action should be based on race.
>
> –Kathleen Kennedy Townsend

Townsend demonstrates that analogies can be slippery types of arguments, but they do have power when readers believe that a comparison works. And analogies aren't the only type of argument of similarity. Consider a claim like the following:

> If motorists in most other states can pump their own gas safely, surely the state of New Jersey can trust its own drivers to be as capable. It's time for New Jersey to permit self-service gas stations.

You can probably think of dozens of arguments that follow a similar pattern.

Arguments from precedent are related to arguments of analogy and similarity in that they both involve comparisons. But precedents deal with issues of time: *We did it before; we can do it again.* Cases in court are routinely argued this way. What previous courts have decided often determines how courts will rule on a similar issue. Even parents will use precedents in dealing with their children: *We never let your older sister date while she was in high school, so we're not about to let you go to the prom either.* It is easy to see the appeal in overturning precedents, particularly in a society as fond of rebellious stances as American culture. But there is no denying that you can support a claim effectively by showing that it is consistent with previous policies, actions, or beliefs.

You'll encounter additional kinds of logical structures as you create your own arguments. You'll find some of them in the following chapter on Toulmin argument and still more in Chapter 19, "Fallacies of Argument."

USING LOGICAL ARGUMENTS

Nothing might seem more obvious than to enter an argument by listing all the reasons you can think of both for and against your claim. In some cases you'll be gathering statistics, testimonies, and studies right from the start. And you'll certainly want to put into words —preferably complete sentences—the good reasons people might have for believing you as well as the respectable reasons people might have for dissenting from your view.

When you've done that, you can begin arranging your evidence and thoughts strategically, looking for relationships and sequences. Inevitably, some arguments will seem more persuasive than others. When some of those strong arguments are on the other side of your claim, deal with them honestly. Quite often, you'll want to modify or moderate your own opinions to reflect what you've learned when you open your mind to different points of view. All the while, keep your audience in mind as you shape an argument.

RESPOND ●

1. Discuss whether the following statements are examples of hard evidence or rational appeals. Not all cases are clear-cut.

   "The bigger they are, the harder they fall."

   Drunk drivers are involved in more than 50 percent of traffic deaths.

   DNA tests of skin found under the victim's fingernails suggest that the defendant was responsible for the assault.

   Polls suggest that a large majority of Americans favor a constitutional amendment to ban flag burning.

   A psychologist testified that teenage violence could not be blamed on computer games.

   Honey attracts more flies than vinegar.

   Historical precedents demonstrate that cutting tax rates usually increases tax revenues because people work harder when they can keep more of what they earn.

   "We have nothing to fear but fear itself."

   Air bags ought to be removed from vehicles because they can kill young children and small-framed adults.

2. We suggest in this chapter that statistical evidence becomes useful only when responsible authors interpret the data fairly and reasonably. As an exercise, go to the USA Today Web site or to the newspaper itself and look for the daily graph, chart, or table called the "USA Today snapshot." (On the Web site, you'll have a series of these items to choose from.) Pick a snapshot and use the information in it to support at least three different claims. See if you can get at least two of the

claims to make opposing or very different points. Share your claims with classmates.

We don't mean to suggest that you learn to use data dishonestly, but it is important that you see firsthand how the same statistics can serve a variety of arguments.

3. Testimony can be just as suspect as statistics. For example, movie reviews are often excerpted by advertising copywriters for inclusion in newspaper ads. A reviewer's stinging indictment of a shoot-'em-up film—"This summer's blockbuster will be a great success at the box office; as a piece of filmmaking, though, it is a complete disaster"— could be reduced to "A great success."

Bring to class a full review of a recent film that you enjoyed. (If you haven't enjoyed any films lately, select a review of one you hated.) Using testimony from that review, write a brief argument to your classmates explaining why they should see that movie (or why they should avoid it). Be sure to use the evidence from the review fairly and reasonably, as support for a claim that you are making.

Then exchange arguments with a classmate and decide whether the evidence in your peer's argument helps convince you about the movie. What is convincing about the evidence? If it does not convince you, why not?

4. Choose an issue of some consequence, locally or nationally, and then create a series of questions designed to poll public opinion on the issue. But design the questions to evoke a range of responses. See if you can design a reasonable question that would make people strongly inclined to favor or approve an issue, a second question that would lead them to oppose the same proposition just as intensely, a third that tries to be more neutral, and additional questions that provoke different degrees of approval or disapproval. If possible, try out your questions on your classmates.

PART 3

WRITING
arguments

chapter eight

Structuring Arguments

Even if you aren't a political junkie, you've probably tuned in to cable TV talk shows to watch hosts like Bill O'Reilly and Greta Van Susteren on FOX or James Carville and Tucker Carlson on CNN turn discussions of political and social issues into WWE Smackdowns. In the heart of prime time, they duke it out with their guests on matters from war in the Middle East to the cultural sway of Eminem. In these shows argument becomes entertainment, just a bit more civilized than hair-pulling and head-butting. Yet these people do know how to think on their feet. Quick as NBA guards, they offer claims, counterclaims, rebuttals, and apologies in about the time it takes viewers to pop open a can of Coke.

But these highly paid pundits can hardly claim to have invented political debate in the United States. From the earliest days of the American revolution, spirited citizens have been engaged in serious argument about the welfare of the state. You probably remember Tom Paine, the ardent revolutionary who wrote pamphlets to keep the American Revolution alive, his most famous words today probably being those that open *The American Crisis* (1776):

> THESE are the times that try men's souls. The summer soldier and the sunshine patriot will, in this crisis, shrink from the service of their country; but he that stands it now, deserves the love and thanks of man and woman. Tyranny, like hell, is not easily conquered; yet we have this consolation with us, that the harder the conflict, the more glorious the triumph. What we obtain too cheap, we esteem too lightly.

Then, just a decade later, Alexander Hamilton shares the nom de plume "Publius" with James Madison and John Jay to produce *The Federalist Papers* (1787–88), a series of influential political pamphlets written to rally support for the proposed new United States Constitution. The pace of Hamilton's eighteenth-century prose in this excerpt may not be to your taste, but read carefully and you'll hear the voice of a skilled writer and politician moving you to think favorably about the new Constitution.

> Yes, my countrymen, I own to you that, after having given it an attentive consideration, I am clearly of opinion it is your interest to adopt it.

FIGURE 8.1   BILL O'REILLY

I am convinced that this is the safest course for your liberty, your dignity, and your happiness. I affect not reserves which I do not feel. I will not amuse you with an appearance of deliberation when I have decided. I frankly acknowledge to you my convictions, and I will freely lay before you the reasons on which they are founded. The consciousness of good intentions disdains ambiguity. I shall not, however, multiply professions on this head. My motives must remain in the depository of my own breast. My arguments will be open to all, and may be judged of by all. They shall at least be offered in a spirit which will not disgrace the cause of truth.

–Alexander Hamilton, *Federalist No. 1*

As you might guess, Publius had to face crossfire from opponents, who produced pamphlets now collectively know as the *Anti-Federalist Papers*.

Following ratification of that Constitution (1789), the country would spend half a century arguing the monumental issue of slavery, culminating (verbally at least) in the famous Lincoln-Douglas Debates in Illinois (1858). Here is Abraham Lincoln from the first debate with Stephen A. Douglas on August 21, 1858:

This declared indifference, but, as I must think, covert real zeal for the spread of slavery, I cannot but hate. I hate it because of the monstrous injustice of slavery itself. I hate it because it deprives our republican example of its just influence in the world—enables the enemies of free institutions, with plausibility, to taunt us as hypocrites—causes the real friends of freedom to doubt our sincerity, and especially because it forces so many really good men amongst ourselves into an open war with the very fundamental principles of civil liberty—criticizing the Declaration of Independence, and insisting that there is no right principle of action but self-interest.

All of these examples of argument appear in environments stirring with controversy and political ideas. The participants are engaged with important issues and capable of generating complex and richly developed arguments: *The Federalist Papers* ended up as a series of 85 pamphlets; Lincoln and Douglas talked for hours before large crowds in seven different cities during their famous competition for the Illinois Senate seat. (Douglas won.) Yet contemporary issues are no less complex or important.

We won't pretend that learning how to make (or analyze) an argument is easy. Nor will we offer you any foolproof guidelines for being persuasive because arguments are as complicated and different as the people who make them. Five-step plans for changing minds or scoring big on *The O'Reilly Factor* won't work. But making effective arguments isn't a mystery either. As you'll see shortly, you understand, almost intuitively, most of the basic moves in effective logical arguments. But it helps to give them names and to appreciate how they work. When you can recognize a reasonable claim, you can make one of your own. When you know that claims need to be supported with both sound reasons and reliable evidence, you'll expect to see both in what you read and what you write yourself. You'll also see that all arguments rest on assumptions, some far more controversial than others. And when you do, you'll be prepared to air your differences with some degree of confidence.

TOULMIN ARGUMENT

To look at argument, we'll borrow some of the key terms and strategies introduced by British philosopher Stephen Toulmin in *The Uses of Argument* (1958). Toulmin was looking for a method that accurately described the way people make convincing and reasonable arguments. Because Toulmin argument takes into account the complications in life—all those situations when we have to qualify our thoughts with words such as *sometimes, often, presumably, unless,* and *almost*—his method isn't as airtight as formal logic, that is, the kind that uses syllogisms (see Chapter 7). But for exactly that reason, Toulmin logic has become a powerful and, for the most part, practical tool for shaping argument in the real world.

You'll find Toulmin argument especially helpful as a way to come up with ideas and test them. Moreover, it will help you understand what goes where in many kinds of arguments. The method won't predict the shape of every possible line of reasoning, and it may not help you out in a late-night dorm-room squabble. But then again, it just might—because you'll acquire good critical thinking habits when you think in Toulmin's terms.

Making Claims

In the Toulmin model, arguments begin with claims, which are statements or assertions you hope to prove. With a claim, you stake out a position others will likely find controversial and debatable. Notice that in this model the arguments depend on conditions set by others—your audience or readers. *It's raining* might be an innocent statement of fact in one situation; in another, it might provoke a debate: *No, it's not. That's sleet.* And so an argument begins, involving a question of definition.

FIGURE 8.2 CLAIM

Claim

Claims worth arguing tend to be controversial; there's no point worrying about points on which most people agree. For example, there are assertions in the statements *Twelve inches make a foot* and *Earth is the third planet from the sun.* But except in unusual circumstances, such claims aren't worth much time.

Claims should also be debatable; they can be demonstrated using logic or evidence, the raw material for building arguments. Sometimes the line between what's debatable and what isn't can be thin. You push back your chair from the table in a restaurant and declare, *That was delicious!* A debatable point? Not really. If you thought the meal was appetizing, who can challenge your taste, particularly when your verdict affects no one but yourself?

But now imagine you're a restaurant critic working for the local newspaper, leaning back from the same table and making the same observation. Because of your job, your claim about the restaurant's cannelloni would have different status and wider implications. People's jobs might be at stake. *That was delicious!* suddenly becomes a claim you have to support, bite by bite.

Many writers stumble when it comes to making claims because facing issues squarely takes thought and guts. A claim is your answer to the sometimes-hostile question: *So what's your point?* Some writers would rather ignore the question and avoid taking a stand altogether. But when you make a claim worth writing about, you step slightly apart from the crowd and ask that it notice you.

Is there a danger that you might oversimplify an issue by making too bold a claim? Of course. But making that sweeping claim is a logical first step toward eventually saying something more reasonable and subtle. Here are some fairly simple, undeveloped claims:

The Electoral College has outlived its usefulness.

It's time to lower the drinking age.

NASA should launch a human expedition to Mars.

Vegetarianism is the best choice of diet.

New York City is the true capital of the United States.

Note that these claims are statements, not questions. There's nothing wrong with questions per se; in fact, they're what you ask to reach a claim:

Questions   What should NASA's next goal be? Should the space agency establish a permanent moon base? Should NASA launch more robotic interstellar probes? Should NASA send people to Mars or Venus?

Statement   NASA should launch a human expedition to Mars.

Don't mistake one for the other.

Good claims—those that lead toward arguments people want to hear—often spring from personal experience. Almost all of us know enough about something to merit the label *expert*—though we don't always realize it. If you are a typical first-year college student, for example, you're probably an expert about high school. You could make trustworthy claims (or complaints) about a range of consequential issues, from competency testing to the administration of athletic programs. And if you aren't a typical college student, what makes you different—perhaps your experiences at work, in the military, or with a family—should make claims sprout like crabgrass. Whether you are a typical or nontypical college stu-

CULTURAL CONTEXTS FOR ARGUMENT

In the United States, many people (especially those in the academic and business worlds) expect a writer to "get to the point" as directly as possible and to articulate that point efficiently and unambiguously. Student writers are typically expected to make their claims explicit, leaving little unspoken. Such claims usually appear early on in an argument, often in the first paragraph. But not all cultures take such an approach. Some prefer that the claim or thesis be introduced subtly and indirectly, expecting that readers "read between the lines" to understand what is being said. Some even save the thesis until the very end of a written argument. Here are a couple of tips that might help you think about how explicitly you should (or should not) make your points:

- What general knowledge does your audience have about your topic? What information do they expect or need you to provide?

- Does your audience tend to be very direct, saying explicitly what they mean? Or are they more subtle, less likely to call a spade a spade? Look for cues to determine how much responsibility you have as the writer and how you can most successfully argue your points.

dent, you might also know a lot about music or urban living or retail merchandising, or inequities in government services and so on — all of them fertile ground for authoritative, debatable, and personally relevant claims.

Offering Data and Good Reasons

A claim is a lonely and unpersuasive statement until it is accompanied by some data and good reasons. You can begin developing a claim simply by drawing up a list of reasons to support it or finding evidence that backs up the point. In doing so, you'll likely generate still more claims in need of more support; that's the way arguments work.

FIGURE 8.3 CLAIM, DATA, REASON

One student writer, for instance, wanted to gather good reasons in support of an assertion that his college campus needed more space for motorcycle parking. He had been doing some research — gathering statistics about parking space allocation, numbers of people using particular parking lots, and numbers of motorcycles registered on campus. Before he went any further with this argument, however, he decided to list the primary reasons he had identified for more motorcycle parking:

- *Personal experience*: At least three times a week for two terms, he had been unable to find a parking space for his bike.

- *Anecdotes*: Several of his best friends told similar stories; one had even sold her bike as a result.

- *Facts*: He had found out that the ratio of car to bike parking spaces was 200 to 1, whereas the ratio of cars to bikes registered on campus was 25 to 1.

- *Authorities*: The campus police chief had indicated in an interview with the college newspaper that she believed a problem existed for students trying to park motorcycles.

On the basis of his preliminary listing of possible reasons in support of the claim, this student decided that his subject was worth still more research. He was on the way to amassing a set of good reasons sufficient to support his claim.

In some arguments you read, claims might be widely separated from the reasons offered to support them. In shaping your own arguments, try putting claims and reasons together early in the writing process to create what Aristotle called *enthymemes*, or arguments in brief. Think of these enthymemes as test cases or even as topic sentences:

> **The Electoral College has outlived its usefulness because it gives undue power to small and mid-sized states in presidential elections.**

> **It's time to lower the drinking age because I've been drinking since I was fourteen and it hasn't hurt me.**

> **NASA should launch a human expedition to Mars because Americans need a unifying national goal.**

> **Vegetarianism is the best choice of diet, the only one that doesn't require the suffering of animals.**

As you can see, attaching a reason to a claim often spells out the major terms of an argument. In rare cases, the full statement is all the argument you'll need:

> **Don't eat that mushroom—it's poisonous.**

> **We'd better stop for gas because the gauge has been reading empty for more than thirty miles.**

More often, your work is just beginning when you've put a claim together with its supporting reasons and data. If your readers are capable—and you should always assume they are—they will then begin to question your statement. They might ask whether the reasons and data you are offering really are connected to the claim: *Should the drinking age be changed simply because you've managed to drink since you were fourteen? Should the whole state base its laws on what's worked for you?* They might ask pointed questions about your data: *Exactly how do small states benefit from the Electoral College?* Eventually, you've got to address both issues: quality of assumptions and quality of evidence. The connection between claim and reason(s) is a concern at the next level in Toulmin argument. (For more on enthymemes, see Chapter 7, p. 112.)

Determining Warrants

Crucial to Toulmin argument is appreciating that there must be a logical and persuasive connection between a claim and the reasons and data supporting it. Toulmin calls this connection the *warrant*; it answers the question *How exactly do I get from the claim to the data?* Like the warrant in legal situations (a search warrant, for example), a sound warrant in an argument gives you authority to proceed with your case.

FIGURE 8.4 CLAIM, REASON, WARRANT

It tells readers what your assumptions are—for example, that no states should have undue influence on presidential elections or that what works for you ought to work for them as well. If readers accept your warrant (as they might in the first case), you can then present specific evidence to develop your claim.

FIGURE 8.5 EXAMPLE OF CLAIM, REASON, WARRANT

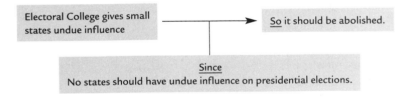

But if readers dispute your warrant (as they might in the second instance), you'll have to defend it before you can move on to the claim itself.

FIGURE 8.6 EXAMPLE OF CLAIM, REASON, WARRANT

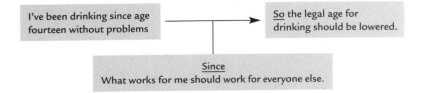

When you state a warrant accurately, you sometimes expose a fatal flaw in an argument.

However, stating warrants can be tricky because they can be phrased in various ways. What you are looking for is the general principle that enables you to justify the move from a reason to a specific claim, the bridge connecting them. The warrant is the assumption that makes the claim seem plausible. It is often a value or principle you share with your readers. Let's demonstrate this logical movement with an easy example.

Don't eat that mushroom—it's poisonous.

The warrant supporting this enthymeme can be stated in several ways, always moving from the reason ("it's poisonous") to the claim ("Don't eat that mushroom"):

That which is poisonous shouldn't be eaten.

If something is poisonous, it's dangerous to eat.

Here is the relationship, diagrammed:

FIGURE 8.7 EXAMPLE OF CLAIM, REASON, WARRANT

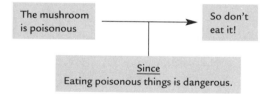

Perfectly obvious, you say? Exactly—and that's why the statement is so convincing. If the mushroom in question is indeed a death angel or toadstool (and you might still need expert testimony to prove that's what it is), the warrant does the rest of the work, making the claim it supports seem logical and persuasive.

Let's look at a similar example, beginning with the argument in its basic form:

We'd better stop for gas because the gauge has been reading empty for more than thirty miles.

In this case, you have data so clear (a gas gauge reading empty) that the reason for getting gas doesn't even have to be stated: the tank is almost empty. The warrant connecting the data to the claim is also compelling and pretty obvious:

If the fuel gauge of a car has been reading empty for more than thirty miles, that car is about to run out of gas.

Since most readers would accept this warrant as reasonable, they would also likely accept the statement the warrant supports.

Naturally, factual information might undermine the whole argument—the fuel gauge might be broken, or the driver might know from previous experience that the car will go another fifty miles even though the fuel gauge reads empty. But in most cases, readers would accept the warrant.

Let's look at a third easy case, one in which stating the warrant confirms the weakness of an enthymeme that doesn't seem convincing on its own merits:

Grades in college should be abolished because I don't like them!

Moving from stated reason to claim, we see that the warrant is a silly and selfish principle:

What I don't like should be abolished.

Most readers won't accept this assumption as a principle worth applying generally. It would produce a chaotic or arbitrary world, like that of the Queen of Hearts in *Alice in Wonderland*. ("Off with the heads of anyone I don't like!")

So far, so good. But how does understanding warrants make you better at writing arguments? The answer is simple: warrants tell you what arguments you have to make and at what level you have to make them. If your warrant isn't controversial, you can immediately begin to defend your claim. But if your warrant is controversial, you must first defend the warrant—or modify it or look for better assumptions on which to support it. Building an argument on a weak warrant is like building a house on a questionable foundation. Sooner or later, the structure will crack.

Let's consider how stating and then examining a warrant can help you determine the grounds on which you want to make a case. Here's a political enthymeme of a familiar sort:

Flat taxes are fairer than progressive taxes because they treat all tax-payers in the same way.

Warrants that follow from this enthymeme have power because they appeal to a core American value—equal treatment under the law:

Treating people equitably is the American way.

All people should be treated in the same way.

You certainly could make an argument on these grounds. But stating the warrant should also raise a flag if you know anything about tax policy. If the principle is so obvious and universal, why are federal income taxes progressive, requiring people at higher levels of income to pay at higher tax rates than people at lower income levels? Could it be that the warrant isn't as universally popular as it might seem at first glance? To explore the argument further, try stating the contrary argument and warrant:

Progressive taxes are fairer than flat taxes because they tax people according to their ability to pay.

Taxing people according to their ability to pay is the American way.

Now you see how different the assumptions behind opposing positions really are. In a small way, we've stated one basic difference between political right and political left, between Republicans and Democrats. If you decided to argue in favor of flat taxes, you'd be smart to recognize that some members of your audience might have fundamental reservations about your position. Or you might even decide to shift your entire argument. After all, you aren't obligated to argue any particular proposition. So you might explore an alternative rationale for flat taxes:

Flat taxes are preferable to progressive taxes because they simplify the tax code and reduce the likelihood of fraud.

Here you have two stated reasons, supported by two new warrants:

Taxes that simplify the tax code are desirable.

Taxes that reduce the likelihood of fraud are preferable.

As always, you have to choose your warrant knowing your audience, the context of your argument, and your own feelings. Moreover, understanding how to state a warrant and how to assess its potential makes subsequent choices better informed.

Offering Evidence: Backing and Grounds

As you might guess, claims and warrants provide only the skeleton of an argument. The bulk of a writer's work—the richest, most interesting part— still remains to be done after the argument has been outlined. Claims and warrants clearly stated do suggest the scope of the evidence you have yet to assemble.

An example will illustrate the point. Here's an argument in brief—suitably debatable and controversial, if somewhat abstract:

> NASA **should launch a human expedition to Mars because Americans need a unifying national goal.**

Here's the warrant that supports the enthymeme, at least one version of it:

> **What unifies the nation ought to be a national priority.**

To run with this claim and warrant, a writer needs, first, to place both in context because most points worth arguing have a rich history. Entering an argument can be like walking into a conversation already in progress. In the case of the politics of space exploration, the conversation has been a lively one, debated with varying intensity since the launch in 1957 of the Soviet Union's *Sputnik* satellite (the first man-made object to orbit the earth) and sparked again recently after the *Columbia* disaster. A writer stumbling into this dialogue without a sense of history won't get far. Acquiring background knowledge (through reading, conversation, inquiry of all kinds) is the price you have to pay to write on the subject. Without a minimum amount of information on this—or any comparable subject—all the moves of Toulmin argument won't do you much good. You've got to do the legwork before you're ready to make a case. (See Chapter 6 for more on gaining authority.)

If you want examples of premature argument, just listen to talk radio or C-SPAN phone-ins for a day or two. You'll soon learn that the better callers can hold a conversation with the host or guests, fleshing out their basic claims with facts, personal experience, and evidence. The weaker callers usually offer a claim supported by a morsel of data. Then such callers begin to repeat themselves, as if saying over and over again that "Republicans are starving our children" or "Democrats are scaring our senior citizens" will make the statement true.

If you are going to make a claim about the politics of space exploration, you need to defend both your warrant and your claim with authority, knowledge, and some passion (see Chapters 4–7), beginning with the warrant. Why? Because there is no point defending any claim until you've satisfied readers that any questionable warrants the claim is based on are, in fact, defensible. Evidence you offer to support a warrant is called *backing*.

Warrant

What unifies the nation ought to be a national priority.

Backing

On a personal level, Americans want to be part of something bigger than themselves. (Emotional claim)

A country as regionally, racially, and culturally diverse as the United States of America needs common purposes and values to hold its democratic system together. (Ethical claim)

In the past, enterprises such as westward expansion, World War II, and the Apollo moon program enabled many—though not all—Americans to work toward common goals. (Logical claim)

Once you are confident that most readers will agree with your warrant, you can move on to demonstrate the truth of your claim. Evidence you offer in support of your claim is sometimes called the *grounds*—the specific data that supports your point. Toulmin himself doesn't make this distinction between backing and grounds in *The Uses of Argument*, but you might find it helpful simply as a reminder that you'll need evidence for every questionable claim you make.

Argument in brief (Enthymeme)

NASA should launch a human expedition to Mars because Americans need a unifying national goal.

Grounds

The American people are politically divided along lines of race, ethnicity, religion, gender, and class. (Factual claim)

A common challenge or problem often unites people to accomplish great things. (Emotional claim)

Successfully managing a Mars mission would require the cooperation of the entire nation—financially, logistically, and scientifically. (Logical claim)

A human expedition to Mars would be a valuable scientific project for the nation to pursue. (Logical claim)

Notice that you would likely have to do research to flesh out the backing or grounds, finding out more about the space program than you know now. After all, uninformed opinion doesn't have much status in argument.

Note, too, that you can draw from the full range of argumentative appeals to provide support for your arguments. Appeals to values and emotions might be just as appropriate as appeals to logic and facts, and all such claims will be stronger if a writer presents a convincing ethos. Although one can study such appeals separately, they work together in arguments, reinforcing each other. (See Chapter 6 for more on ethos.)

Finally, understand that arguments can quickly shift downward from an original set of claims and warrants to deeper, more basic claims and reasons. In a philosophy course, for example, you might dig many layers deep to reach what seem to be first principles. In general, however, you need to pursue an argument only as far as your audience demands, always presenting readers with adequate warrants and convincing evidence. There comes a point, as Toulmin himself acknowledges, at which readers have to agree to some basic principles or else the argument becomes pointless.

Using Qualifiers

What makes Toulmin's system work so well in the real world is that it acknowledges that *qualifiers*—words and phrases that place limits on claims such as *usually, sometimes, in many cases*—play an essential role in arguments. By contrast, formal logic requires universal premises: *All men are mortal*, for example. Unfortunately, politics and life don't lend themselves well to many such sturdy truths. If we could argue only about these types of sweeping claims, we'd be silent most of the time.

Toulmin logic, in fact, encourages you to limit your responsibilities in an argument through the effective use of qualifiers. You can save time if you qualify a claim early in the writing process. But you might not figure out how to limit a claim effectively until after you have explored your subject or discussed it with others.

FIGURE 8.8 CLAIM, REASON, WARRANT, QUALIFIER

FIGURE 8.9 EXAMPLE OF CLAIM, REASON, WARRANT, QUALIFIER

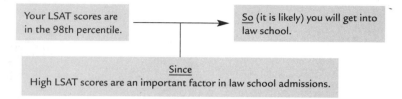

One way to qualify an argument is by spelling out the terms of the claim as precisely as possible. Never assume that readers understand the limits you have in mind. You'll have less work to do as a result, and your argument will seem more reasonable. In the following examples, the first claim in each pair would be much harder to argue convincingly and responsibly—and tougher to research—than the second claim.

> **People who don't go to college earn less than those who do. (Unqualified claim)**
>
> *In most cases,* **people who don't go to college earn less than those who do. (Qualified claim)**
>
> **Welfare programs should be cut. (Unqualified claim)**
>
> *Ineffective federal* **welfare programs should be** *identified, modified,* **and,** *if necessary, eliminated.* **(Qualified claim)**

Experienced writers cherish qualifying expressions because they make writing more precise and honest.

QUALIFIERS

few	it is possible
rarely	it seems
some	it may be
sometimes	more or less
in some cases	many
in the main	routinely
most	one might argue
often	perhaps
under these conditions	possibly
for the most part	if it were so

Notice that the second qualified claim above does not use terms from this list but instead specifies and limits the action proposed.

Understanding Conditions of Rebuttal

There's a fine old book on writing by Robert Graves and Alan Hodges entitled *The Reader over Your Shoulder* (1943), in which the authors advise writers always to imagine a crowd of "prospective readers" hovering over their shoulders, asking questions. At every stage in Toulmin argument—making a claim, offering a reason, or studying a warrant—you might converse with those nosy readers, imagining them as skeptical, demanding, even a bit testy. They may well get on your nerves. But they'll likely help you foresee the objections and reservations real readers will have regarding your arguments.

In the Toulmin system, potential objections to an argument are called *conditions of rebuttal*. Understanding and reacting to these conditions are essential not only to buttress your own claims where they are weak, but also to understand the reasonable objections of people who see the world differently. For example, you may be a big fan of the Public Broadcasting Service (PBS) and the National Endowment for the Arts (NEA) and prefer that federal tax dollars be spent on these programs. So you offer the following claim:

Claim   **The federal government should support the arts.**

Of course, you need reasons to support this thesis, so you decide to present the issue as a matter of values:

Argument   **The federal government should support the arts because it**
in Brief   **also supports the military.**

Now you've got an enthymeme and can test the warrant, or the premises of your claim:

Warrant   **If the federal government can support the military, it can also support other programs.**

But the warrant seems frail—something is missing to make a convincing case. Over your shoulder you hear your skeptical friends wondering what wouldn't be fundable according to your very broad principle. They restate your warrant in their own mocking fashion: *Because we pay for a military, we should pay for everything!* You could deal with their objection in the body of your paper, but revising your claim might be a better way to parry the objections. You give it a try:

Revised   **If the federal government can spend huge amounts of money**
Argument   **on the military, it can afford to spend moderate amounts on arts programs.**

Now you've got a new warrant, too:

> **Revised**   **A country that can fund expensive programs can also afford**
> **Warrant**   **less expensive programs.**

This is a premise you feel more able to defend, believing strongly that the arts are just as essential to the well-being of the country as a strong military. (In fact, you believe the arts are more important; but remembering those readers over your shoulder, you decide not to complicate your case by overstating it.) To provide backing for this new and more defensible warrant, you plan to illustrate the huge size of the federal budget and the proportion of it that goes to various programs.

Although the warrant seems solid, you still have to offer strong grounds to support your specific and controversial claim. Once again you cite statistics from reputable sources, this time comparing the federal budgets for the military and the arts; you break them down in ways readers can visualize, demonstrating that much less than a penny of every tax dollar goes to support the arts.

But once more you hear those voices over your shoulder, pointing out that the "common defense" is a federal mandate; the government is constitutionally obligated to support a military. Support for public television or local dance troupes is hardly in the same league. And the nation still has a huge federal debt.

Hmmm. You'd better spend a paragraph explaining all the benefits the arts provide for the very few dollars spent, and maybe you should also suggest that such funding falls under the constitutional mandate to "promote the general welfare." Though not all readers will accept these grounds, they will at least see that you haven't ignored their point of view. You gain credibility and authority by anticipating a reasonable objection.

As you can see, dealing with conditions of rebuttal is a natural part of argument. But it is important to understand rebuttal as more than mere opposition. Anticipating objections broadens your horizons and likely makes you more open to change. One of the best exercises for you or for any writer is to learn to state the views of others in your own favorable words. If you can do that, you're more apt to grasp the warrants at issue and the commonalities you may share with others, despite differences.

Fortunately, today's wired world is making it harder to argue in isolation. Newsgroups and Web logs on the Internet provide quick and potent responses to positions offered by participants in discussions. Email and instant messaging make cross-country connections feel almost like face-to-face conversations. Even the links on Web sites encourage people to think of communication as a network, infinitely variable, open to many voices and different perspectives. Within the Toulmin system, conditions of rebuttal—the voices over the shoulder—remind us that we're part of this bigger world. (For more on arguments in electronic environments, see Chapter 16.)

A TOULMIN ANALYSIS

You might wonder how Toulmin's method works when applied to a full-length argument, not just to a few sentences. Do real arguments work the way Toulmin predicts? Such an exercise can be both revealing and a bit embarrassing. Knowledgeable readers often won't agree even on what the core claim in a piece is, let alone its warrants, stated or implied. Yet such an analysis can be rewarding because it can't help but raise basic questions about purpose, structure, quality of evidence, and rhetorical strategy. The following short argument by Alan Dershowitz, a professor of law, provides an interesting opportunity for applying Toulmin's terms and method to a challenging piece. Here, Dershowitz is responding to a proposal by Harvard Law School in late 2002 to impose a speech code on its students.

Testing Speech Codes
....

ALAN M. DERSHOWITZ

We need not resort to hypothetical cases in testing the limits of a proposed speech code or harassment policy of the kind that some students and faculty members of Harvard Law School are proposing. We are currently experiencing two perfect test cases.

The first involves Harvard's invitation to Tom Paulin to deliver a distinguished lecture for which it is paying him an honorarium. Paulin believes that poetry cannot be separated from politics, and his politics is hateful and bigoted.

He has urged that American Jews who make aliya to the Jewish homeland and move into the ancient Jewish quarters of Jerusalem or Hebron "should be shot dead." He has called these Jews "Nazis" and has expressed "hatred" toward "them." "Them" is many of our students and graduates who currently live on land captured by Israel during the defensive war in 1967 or who plan to move there after graduation.

The Jewish quarters of Jerusalem and Hebron have been populated by Jews since well before the birth of Jesus. The only period in which they were Judenrein was between 1948 and 1967, when it was under Jordanian control, and the Jordanian government destroyed all the synagogues and ethnically cleansed the entire Jewish populations.

Though I (along with a majority of Israelis) oppose the building of Jewish settlements in Arab areas of the West Bank and Gaza, the existence of these settlements—which Israel has offered to end as part of an overall peace—does not justify the murder of those who believe they have a religious right to live in traditional Jewish towns such as Hebron.

Paulin's advocacy of murder of innocent civilians, even if it falls short of incitement, is a paradigm of hate speech. It would certainly make me uncomfortable to sit in a classroom or lecture hall listening to him spew his murderous hatred. Yet I would not want to empower Harvard to censor his speech or include it within a speech code or harassment policy.

Or consider the case of the anti-Semitic poet Amiri Baraka, who claims that "neo-fascist" Israel had advance knowledge of the terrorist attack on the World Trade Center and warned Israelis to stay away. This lie received a standing ovation, according to *The Boston Globe*, from "black students" at Wellesley last week. Baraka had been invited to deliver his hate speech by Nubian, a black student organization, and [was] paid an honorarium with funds provided by several black organizations. Would those who are advocating restrictions on speech include these hateful and offensive lies in their prohibitions? If not, would they seek to distinguish them from other words that should be prohibited?

These are fair questions that need to be answered before anyone goes further down the dangerous road to selective censorship based on perceived offensiveness. Clever people can always come up with distinctions that put their cases on the permitted side of the line and other people's cases on the prohibited side of the line.

For example, Paulin's and Baraka's speeches were political, whereas the use of the "N-word" is simply racist. But much of what generated controversy at Harvard Law School last spring can also be deemed political. After all, racism is a political issue, and the attitudes of bigots toward a particular race is a political issue. Paulin's and Baraka's poetry purports to be "art," but the "N-word" and other equally offensive expressions can also be dressed up as art.

The real problem is that offensiveness is often in the eyes and experiences of the beholder. To many African Americans, there is nothing more offensive than the "N-word." To many Jews, there is nothing more offensive than comparing Jews to Nazis. (Ever notice that bigots never compare Sharon to Pinochet, Mussolini, or even Stalin, only to Hitler!)

It would be wrong for a great university to get into the business of comparing historic grievances or experiences. If speech that is deeply offensive to many African Americans is prohibited, then speech that is deeply offensive to many Jews, gays, women, Asians, Muslims, Christians, atheists, etc. must also be prohibited. Result-oriented distinctions will not suffice in an area so dominated by passion and historical experience.

Unless Paulin's and Baraka's statements were to be banned at Harvard — which they should not be — we should stay out of the business of trying to pick and choose among types and degrees of offensive, harassing, or discriminatory speech. Nor can we remain silent in the face of such hate speech. Every decent person should go out of his or her way to condemn what Tom Paulin and Amiri Baraka have said, just as we should condemn racist statements made last spring at Harvard Law School.

The proper response to offensive speech is to criticize and answer it, not to censor it.

Analysis

Dershowitz uses an inverted structure for his argument, beginning with his evidence — two extended examples — and then extracting lessons from it. Indeed, his basic claim occurs, arguably, in the final sentence of the piece, and it is supported by three major reasons — although the third reason might be seen as an extension of the second:

> **The proper response to offensive speech is to criticize and answer it, not to censor it [because]**
>
> - **Clever people can always come up with distinctions that put their cases on the permitted side of the line and other people's cases on the prohibited side of the line.**
> - **It would be wrong for a great university to get into the business of comparing historic grievances or experiences.**
> - **[W]e should stay out of the business of trying to pick and choose among types and degrees of offensive, harassing, or discriminatory speech.**

Dershowitz opens the essay by focusing on two lengthy examples that provide evidence or data for the arguments he offers near the end of the essay. As Dershowitz presents them, the cases of Tom Paulin and Amiri Baraka suggest that smart people can always find reasons for defending the legitimacy of their offensive speech.

The closest Dershowitz gets to stating a warrant for his argument may be in the following sentence:

> **The real problem is that offensiveness is often in the eyes and experiences of the beholder.**

He doesn't want individuals dictating the limits of free speech because if they did, freedom would likely be restrained by the "eyes and experiences" of specific people and groups, not protected by an absolute and unwavering principle. Dershowitz doesn't actually offer such a warrant, perhaps because he assumes that most readers will understand that protecting free speech is a primary value in American society.

Dershowitz establishes his ethos by making it clear that although he is powerfully offended by the speech of both Paulin and Baraka, he would not censor them—even though Paulin especially says things offensive to him. An implicit claim is that if Dershowitz is willing to allow such hate speech to be experienced on his own campus, surely the university itself should be able to show such tolerance toward its students.

BEYOND TOULMIN

Can all arguments be analyzed according to Toulmin's principles? The honest answer is no, if you expect most writers to express themselves in perfectly sequenced claims or warrants. You might not think of Toulmin's terms yourself as you build arguments. Once you are into your subject, you'll be too eager to make a point to worry about whether you're qualifying a claim or finessing a warrant.

That's not a problem if you appreciate Toulmin argument for what it teaches:

- *Claims should be stated clearly and qualified carefully.* If you expect to find a single claim neatly stated in most arguments in magazines or newspapers, you'll be disappointed. Skilled writers often develop a single point, but to make that point they may run through a complex series of claims. They may open with an anecdote, use the story to raise the issue that concerns them, examine alternative perspectives on the subject, and then make a half-dozen related claims only as they move toward a conclusion. Even so, you can enter an argument through any of its separate claims, examining what they say exactly and studying the connections between them, working backward through the essay if necessary. You have the same freedom to develop your own arguments, as long as you know how to make clear and reasonable claims.

- *Claims should be supported with data and good reasons.* Remember that a Toulmin analysis provides just the framework of an argument. Real arguments are thick with ideas and with many different kinds of evidence. You may not think of photographs or graphs as evidence, but they can serve that purpose. So can stories, even those that go on for many paragraphs or pages. A tale may not look like "data," but if it supports an author's claim, it is. Once you acquire the habit of looking for reasons and data, you will be able to separate real supportive evidence from filler, even in arguments offered by professional writers. When you write arguments, you'll discover that it is far easier to make claims than to back them up.

- *Claims and reasons should be based on assumptions readers will likely accept.* Toulmin's focus on warrants confuses a lot of people, but that's because it forces readers and writers to think about their assumptions — something they would often just as soon skip. It is tough for a writer, particularly in a lengthy argument, to be consistent about warrants. At one point a writer might offer arguments based on warrants that make "free speech" a first principle. But later he might rail against those who contribute too much money to political campaigns, making democracy a higher value than free speech. Because most people read at the surface, they may not detect the discrepancy. Toulmin pushes you to probe into the values that support any argument and to think of those values as belonging to particular audiences. You can't go wrong if you are both thoughtful and aware of your readers when you craft an argument.

- *All parts of an argument need the support of solid evidence.* Arguments come in all shapes and sizes, including massive studies produced by federal departments and full-length articles in scholarly journals. But it's hard to deny that much political and social argument in the most influential media rarely runs more than a few pages, screens, or columns. Thus any writer wanting to make a convincing argument had better know how to find and present the best possible evidence succinctly and powerfully — and often visually.

- *Effective arguments anticipate objections readers might offer.* Argument seems more partisan than ever today. In fact, the term *spin* describes a kind of political advocacy that makes any fact or event, however unfavorable, serve a politician's purpose. Yet there's still plenty of respect for people who can make a powerful, even passionate case for what they believe without dismissing the objections of others as absurd or idiotic. They are also willing to admit the limits of their own knowledge. Toulmin argument appreciates that any claim can crumble under certain conditions, so it encourages a complex view of argument, one that doesn't demand absolute or unqualified positions. It is a principle that works for many kinds of successful and responsible arguments.

It takes considerable experience to write arguments that meet all these conditions. Using Toulmin's framework brings them into play automatically; if you learn it well enough, constructing good arguments can become a habit.

CULTURAL CONTEXTS FOR ARGUMENT

As you think about how to organize your writing, remember that cultural factors are at work: the patterns that you find satisfying and persuasive are probably ones that are deeply embedded in your culture. The organizational patterns favored by U.S. engineers in their writing, for example, hold many similarities to the system recommended by Cicero some two thousand years ago. It is a highly explicit pattern, leaving little or nothing unexplained: introduction and thesis, background, overview of the parts that follow, evidence, other viewpoints, and conclusion. If a piece of writing follows this pattern, Anglo-American readers ordinarily find it "well organized."

In contrast, writers who are accustomed to different organizational patterns may not. Those accustomed to writing that is more elaborate or that sometimes digresses from the main point may find the U.S. engineers' writing overly simple, even childish. Those from cultures that value subtlety and indirectness tend to favor patterns of organization that display these values instead.

When arguing across cultures, think about how you can organize material to convey your message effectively. Here are a couple of points to consider:

- Determine when to state your thesis—at the beginning? At the end? Somewhere else? Not at all?
- Consider whether digressions are a good idea, a requirement, or an element that is best avoided.

RESPOND●

1. Following is a claim followed by five possible supporting reasons. State the warrant that would support each of the arguments in brief. Which of the warrants would need to be defended? Which would a college audience likely accept without significant backing?

    We should amend the Constitution to abolish the Electoral College

    —because a true democracy is based on the popular vote, not the votes of the usually unknown electors.

    —because under the Electoral College system the votes of people who have minority opinions in some states end up not counting.

    —because then Al Gore would have won the 2000 election.

    —because the Electoral College is an outdated relic of an age when the political leaders didn't trust the people.

    —because the Electoral College skews power toward small and mid-size states for no good reason.

2. Claims aren't always easy to find—sometimes they are buried deep within an argument, and sometimes they are not present at all. An important skill in reading and writing arguments is the ability to identify claims, even when they are not obvious.

    Collect a sample of eight to ten letters to the editor of a daily newspaper (or a similar number of argumentative postings from a political Web log). Read each item and try to reduce it to a single sentence, beginning with "I believe that . . ."—this should represent the simplest version of the writer's claim. When you have compiled your list of claims, look carefully at the words the writer or writers use when stating their positions. Is there a common vocabulary? Can you find words or phrases that signal an impending claim? Which of these seem most effective? Which seem least effective? Why?

3. At their simplest, warrants can be stated as *X is good* or *X is bad*. Consider the example from page 130, *Don't eat that mushroom—it's poisonous*. In this case, the warrant could be reduced to *Poison is bad*. Of course, this is an oversimplification, but it may help you to see how warrants are based in shared judgments of value. If the audience members agree that poison is bad (as they are likely to do), they will accept the connection the writer makes between the claim and the reason.

    As you might expect, warrants are often hard to find, relying as they do on unstated assumptions about value. Return to the letters to the editor or Web log postings that you analyzed in exercise 2, this time looking for the warrant behind each claim. As a way to start, ask yourself these questions: *If I find myself agreeing with the letter writer, what assumptions about the subject matter do I share with the letter writer?*

If I disagree, what assumptions are at the heart of that disagreement? The list of warrants you generate will likely come from these assumptions.

4. Toulmin logic is a useful tool for understanding existing arguments, but it can also help you through the process of inventing your own arguments. As you decide what claim you would like to make, you'll need to consider the warrants, different levels of evidence, conditions of rebuttal, and qualifiers. The argument about federal support for the arts provides a good illustration of the Toulmin system's inventional power. By coming to terms with the conditions of rebuttal, you revised your claim and reconsidered the evidence you'd use.

Using a paper you are writing for this class — it doesn't matter how far along you are in the process — do a Toulmin analysis of the argument. At first, you may struggle to identify the key elements, and you might not find all the categories easy to fill. When you're done, see which elements of the Toulmin scheme are represented. Are you short of evidence to support the warrant? Have you considered the conditions of rebuttal?

Next, write a brief revision plan: How will you buttress the argument in the places where your writing is weakest? What additional evidence will you offer for the warrant? How can you qualify your claim to meet the conditions of rebuttal? Having a clearer sense of the logical structure of your argument will help you revise more efficiently.

It might be instructive to show your paper to a classmate and have him or her do a Toulmin analysis, too. A new reader will probably see your argument in a very different way than you do and suggest revisions that may not have occurred to you.

5. You can find transcripts of TV talk/news programs at CNN.com, MSNBC.com, and FOXNews.com. Locate one such transcript (you may have to look under the site for a particular program), and then find a segment where several guests discuss one particular issue — perhaps between commercials. Do a Toulmin analysis of the section, trying to identify as many specific claims, reasons or data, warrants, evidence, and qualifiers as possible. Note in particular how often — or more likely, how rarely — you find a fully developed argument in one of these segments. What might the transcript suggest about the differences between oral and written arguments?

chapter nine

Arguments of Definition

A traffic committee must define what a small car is in order to enforce parking restrictions in a campus lot where certain spaces are marked "Small Car Only!" Owners of compact luxury vehicles, light trucks, and motorcycles have complained that their vehicles are being unfairly ticketed.

A panel of judges must decide whether computer-enhanced images will be eligible in a contest for landscape photography. At what point is an electronically manipulated image no longer a photograph?

A scholarship committee must decide whether the daughter of two European American diplomats, born while her parents were assigned to the U.S. embassy in Nigeria, will be eligible to apply for grants designated specifically for "African American students." The student claims that excluding her from consideration would constitute discrimination.

A priest chastises some members of his congregation for being "cafeteria Catholics" who pick and choose which parts of Catholic doctrine they will accept and follow. A member of that congregation responds to the priest in a letter explaining her view of what a "true Catholic" is.

A young man hears a classmate describe hunting as a "blood sport." He disagrees and argues that hunting for sport has little in common with "genuine blood sports" such as cock fighting.

A committee of the student union is accused of bias by a conservative student group, which claims that the committee has brought a disproportionate share of left-wing speakers to campus. The committee defends its program by challenging the definition of "left wing" used to classify its speakers.

■ ■ ■

UNDERSTANDING ARGUMENTS OF DEFINITION

Vandalism happens all the time. It's no big deal when someone spray paints a slogan on a billboard. Or is it? On November 29, 2002, <Instapundit .com>, a Web log (or blog) run by University of Tennessee professor of law Glenn Reynolds, posted an image of a defaced billboard in St. Paul congratulating Minnesota senator-elect Norm Coleman. Coleman's contest with former vice president Walter Mondale (following the death of the incumbent, Senator Paul Wellstone) had attracted enormous press coverage and significant national attention because much was at stake in the election: Coleman's victory tilted the U.S. Senate from Democratic to Republican control.

On the billboard, someone had painted swastikas on Coleman's forehead and lapel and scrawled "Newest Member of the SS" under the words "Congratulations Senator Norm Coleman." In his Web entry, Reynolds labels this vandalism a *hate crime*. What would move the graffiti into this serious category?

Is it enough that the vandal is implying that Coleman is a Nazi, a diatribe the political Left hurls against conservatives about as often as Republicans brand liberals Socialists? Or is it the more specific charge that Coleman is a member of the SS—Hitler's elite henchmen? If that's a

FIGURE **9.1** A VANDALIZED BILLBOARD IN MINNESOTA BECOMES AN ARGUMENT OF
DEFINITION NATIONWIDE WHEN IT ATTRACTS A BLOGGER'S ATTENTION.

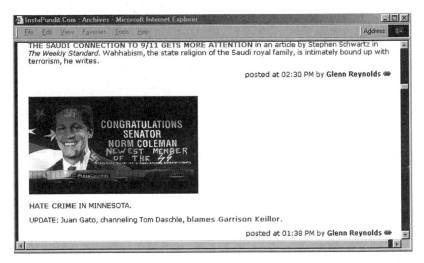

political comment, it clearly crosses the line, but hate crimes usually
involve an attack on a person as a member of an ethnic or cultural group.
This is where the argument for a hate crime turns: Norman Coleman is a
Jew. Blind political rage or malicious vandalism changes to something different when the motive for an attack shifts from the political to the personal. In effect, the act has moved from one category to another and
taken on a different name. What you call something matters. That's what
arguments of definition are about.

Even in the biblical book of Genesis when Adam names the animals, he
gains authority over them because to name things is, partly, to control
them. That's why arguments of definition are so important and so very
contentious. They can be about the power to say what someone or something is or can be. As such, they can also be arguments that include or
exclude: A creature is an endangered species or it isn't; an act is harassment or it isn't; a person is a homicide bomber or, perhaps, a freedom
fighter.

Another way of approaching definitional arguments, however, is to
think of what comes between *is* and *is not*. In fact, the most productive
definitional arguments probably occur in this murky realm. Consider the
controversy over how to define human intelligence. Some might argue
that human intelligence is a capacity measured by tests of verbal and

mathematical reasoning. In other words, it's defined by IQ and SAT scores. Others might define intelligence as the ability to perform specific practical tasks. Still others might interpret intelligence in emotional terms, as a competence in relating to other people. Any of these positions could be defended reasonably, but perhaps the wisest approach would be to construct a definition of intelligence rich enough to incorporate all three perspectives—and maybe more.

In fact, it's important to realize that many political, social, and scientific definitions are constantly "under construction," reargued and reshaped whenever they need to be updated for the times. Writing for a campus newsletter, Katherine Anundson, for instance, revisits the definition of *eco-terrorism* in light of other world events and enumerates its characteristics: "Eco-terrorism is terrorism, plainly put. It is the moral equivalent to the September 11th attacks: Innocent people are hurt, expenses are incurred, and property is destroyed." Similarly, just a few weeks after the attacks of 9/11, Peter Ferrara, a law professor at George Mason University, thought it was appropriate to refine the meaning of the word *American* in response to a call in Pakistan to kill all people of that nationality. Here are the opening and conclusion of what proved to be an "extended definition" of the term— a lengthy exploration of the many dimensions of the word, some of which people might have not considered earlier:

> You probably missed it in the rush of news last week, but there was actually a report that someone in Pakistan had published in a newspaper there an offer of a reward to anyone who killed an American, any American.
>
> So I just thought I would write to let them know what an American is, so they would know when they found one.
>
> An American is English . . . or French, or Italian, Irish, German, Spanish, Polish, Russian or Greek. An American may also be African, Indian, Chinese, Japanese, Australian, Iranian, Asian, or Arab, or Pakistani, or Afghan.
>
> An American is Christian, or he could be Jewish, or Buddhist, or Muslim. In fact, there are more Muslims in America than in Afghanistan. The only difference is that in America they are free to worship as each of them choose.
>
> An American is also free to believe in no religion. For that he will answer only to God, not to the government, or to armed thugs claiming to speak for the government and for God. . . .
>
> So you can try to kill an American if you must. Hitler did. So did General Tojo and Stalin and Mao Tse-Tung, and every bloodthirsty tyrant in the history of the world. But in doing so you would just be

killing yourself. Because Americans are not a particular people from a particular place. They are the embodiment of the human spirit of freedom. Everyone who holds to that spirit, everywhere, is an American.
                                    –Peter Ferrara, "What Is an American?"

Clearly, Ferrara's definition is in fact an argument in favor of American values and principles. The definition makes an unabashed political point.

In case you are wondering, you usually *can't* resolve important arguments of definition by consulting dictionaries. (Ferrara certainly wouldn't have found any of his definitions of an American in *Webster's*.) Dictionaries themselves just reflect the way particular groups of people used words at a specified time and place. And, like any form of writing, these reference books mirror the prejudices of their makers — as shown, perhaps most famously, in the entries of lexicographer Samuel Johnson (1709–1784), who gave the English language its first great dictionary. Johnson, no friend of the Scots, defined *oats* as "a grain which in England is generally given to horses, but in Scotland supports the people." (To be fair, he also defined *lexicographer* as "a writer of dictionaries, a harmless drudge.") Thus it is quite possible to disagree with dictionary definitions or to regard them merely as starting points for arguments.

KINDS OF DEFINITION

Because there are different kinds of definitions, there are also different ways to make a definition argument. Fortunately, identifying a particular type of definition is less important than appreciating when an issue of definition is at stake. Let's explore some common definitional issues.

Formal Definitions

Formal definitions are what you find in dictionaries. Such definitions involve placing a term in its proper genus and species — that is, first determining the larger class to which it belongs and then identifying the features that distinguish it from other members of that class. That sounds complicated, but a definition will help you see the principle. A minivan might first be identified by placing it among its peers — light trucks. Then the formal definition would go on to identify the features necessary to distinguish minivans from other light trucks — sliding side doors, enclosed luggage area, six- to nine-passenger capacity, family-friendly interior.

People can make arguments from either part of a formal definition, from the genus or the species, so to speak. Does the object or idea really belong to the larger class to which it is traditionally assigned? *Are all minivans really light trucks, or are some of them just gussied-up station wagons?* That's the genus argument. Maybe the object doesn't have all the features required to meet the definition. *Is a Pacifica roomy enough to be a respectable minivan?* That's the species argument.

QUESTIONS RELATED TO GENUS

- What is a minivan?
- Is tobacco a drug or a crop?
- Should hate speech be a criminal offense?
- Is *On the Record with Greta Van Susteren* a news program? A tabloid? Both?

QUESTIONS RELATED TO SPECIES

- Is a Pacifica or an FX45 really a minivan?
- Is tobacco a harmless drug? A dangerously addictive one? Something in between?
- Is using a racial epithet always an instance of hate speech?
- Do tabloids report the news or sensationalize it?

Operational Definitions

Operational definitions identify an object not by what it is so much as by what it does or by the conditions that create it: *A line is the shortest distance between two points; Sexual harassment is an unwanted and unsolicited imposition.* You'll get arguments that arise from operational definitions when people debate the conditions that define something and whether these conditions have been met. (See also the discussion of "stasis theory" in Chapter 1, p. 15.)

QUESTIONS RELATED TO CONDITIONS

- Must sexual imposition be both unwanted and unsolicited to be considered harassment?
- Can institutional racism occur in the absence of individual acts of racism?
- Is a volunteer who is paid still a volunteer?
- Does someone who ties the record for home runs in one season deserve the title *Hall of Famer*?

QUESTIONS RELATED TO FULFILLMENT OF CONDITIONS

- Was the act really sexual harassment if the accused believed the interest was mutual?
- Has the institution supported traditions or policies that might lead to racial inequities?
- Was the compensation given to volunteers really "pay" or just "reimbursement" for expenses?
- Has a person actually tied a home-run record if the player has hit the same number of homers in a long season that someone else has hit in a shorter season?

Definitions by Example

Resembling operational definitions are definitions by example, which define a class by listing its individual members. For example, one might define planets by listing all nine major bodies in orbit around the sun, or true American sports cars by naming the Corvette and the Viper.

Arguments of this sort focus on who or what may be included in a list that defines a category: great movies, great presidents, groundbreaking painters. Such arguments often involve comparisons and contrasts with the items most readers would agree from the start belong in this list. One might, for example, wonder why planet status is denied to asteroids, when both planets and asteroids are bodies in orbit around the sun. A comparison between planets and asteroids might suggest that size is one essential feature of the nine recognized planets that asteroids don't meet.

Similarly, you might define great English novelists simply by listing Jane Austen, Emily Brontë, Charlotte Brontë, and Virginia Woolf. Does Iris Murdoch belong in this company? You could argue that she does if she shares the qualities that place the other writers indisputably in this select group.

QUESTIONS RELATED TO MEMBERSHIP IN A NAMED CLASS

- Is any rock artist today in a class with Chuck Berry, Elvis, the Beatles, Madonna, or Aretha Franklin?
- Is the Mustang a Viper-class sports car?
- Who are the Madame Curies or Albert Einsteins of the current generation?
- Does Washington, D.C., deserve the status of a state?

Other Issues of Definition

Many issues of definition cross the line between the types described here and some other forms of argument. For example, if you decided to explore whether banning pornography on the Internet violates First Amendment guarantees of free speech, you'd first have to establish a definition of free speech—either a legal one already settled on by, let's say, the Supreme Court, or another definition closer to your own beliefs. Then you'd have to argue that types of pornography on the Internet are (or are not) in the same class or share (or do not share) the same characteristics as free speech. In doing so, you'd certainly find yourself slipping into an evaluative mode because matters of definition are often also questions of value. (See Chapter 10.)

When exploring or developing an idea, you shouldn't worry about such slippage—it's a natural part of the process of writing. But do try to focus an argument on a central issue or question, and appreciate the fact that any definition you care to defend must be examined honestly and rigorously. Be prepared to explore every issue of definition with an open mind and with an acute sense of what will be persuasive to your readers.

DEVELOPING A DEFINITIONAL ARGUMENT

Definitional arguments don't just appear out of the blue; they evolve out of the occasions and conversations of daily life, both public and private. You might get into an argument over the definition of "ordinary wear and tear" when you return a rental car with some battered upholstery. Or you might be asked to write a job description for a new position to be created in your office: you have to define the position in a way that doesn't step on anyone else's turf on the job. Or maybe someone in your family has to deal with a government agency trying to define farm property they own as "wetlands." Or someone derides one of your best friends as "just a typical fratboy." In a dozen ways every day, you encounter situations that turn out to be issues of definition. They are so frequent and indispensable that you barely notice them for what they are.

Formulating Claims

In addressing matters of definition, you'll likely formulate tentative claims—declarative statements that represent your first response to such situations. Note that these initial claims usually don't follow a single definitional formula.

CLAIMS OF DEFINITION

• A person paid to do public service is not a volunteer.

• Institutional racism can exist—maybe even thrive—in the absence of overt civil rights violations.

• A wetland is just a swamp with powerful friends.

• A municipal fee is often the same darn thing as a tax.

• The District of Columbia has nothing in common with states and ought not to be one.

• It is more accurate to call a suicide bomber a homicide bomber.

None of the claims listed here could stand on its own. Such claims often reflect first impressions and gut reactions. That's because stating a claim of definition is typically a starting point, a moment of bravura that doesn't last much beyond the first serious rebuttal or challenge. Statements of this sort aren't arguments until they're attached to reasons, data, warrants, and evidence. (See Chapter 8.)

Finding good reasons to support a claim of definition usually requires formulating a general definition by which to explore the subject. To be persuasive, the definition must be broad and not tailored to the specific controversy:

• A volunteer is . . .

• Institutional racism is . . .

• A wetland is . . .

• A tax is . . .

• A state is . . .

• A terrorist is . . .

Now consider how the following claims might be expanded with a general definition in order to become full-fledged definitional arguments:

ARGUMENTS OF DEFINITION

• Someone paid to do public service is not a volunteer because volunteers are people who . . .

• Institutional racism can exist even in the absence of overt violations of civil rights because, by definition, institutional racism is . . .

• A swampy parcel of land becomes a federally protected wetland when . . .

• A municipal fee is the same darn thing as a tax. Both fees and taxes are . . .

- Washington, D.C., ought not to be considered eligible for statehood because states all . . .—and the District of Columbia doesn't!
- Someone who straps on a bomb with the intention to kill other people differs from the suicide victim who intends to kill no one but herself.

Notice, too, that some of the issues here involve comparisons between things: swamp/wetland; fees/taxes.

Crafting Definitions

Imagine that you decide to tackle the concept of "paid volunteer" in the following way:

> **Participants in the federal AmeriCorps program are not really volunteers because they are paid for their public service. Volunteers are people who work for a cause without compensation.**

In Toulmin terms, the argument looks like this:

Claim   Participants in AmeriCorps aren't volunteers . . .

Reason   . . . because they are paid for their service.

Warrant   People who are compensated for their services are, ordinarily, employees.

As you can see, the definition of *volunteers* will be crucial to the shape of the argument. In fact, you might think you've settled the matter with this tight little formulation. But now it's time to listen to the readers over your shoulder (see Chapter 8) pushing you further. Do the terms of your definition account for all pertinent cases of volunteerism—in particular, any related to the types of public service AmeriCorps volunteers might be involved in?

Consider, too, the word *cause* in your original statement of the definition:

> **Volunteers are people who work for a cause without compensation.**

Cause has political connotations that you may or may not intend. You'd better clarify what you mean by *cause* when you discuss its definition in your paper. Might a phrase such as "the public good" be a more comprehensive or appropriate substitute for "a cause"?

And then there's the matter of compensation in the second half of your definition:

> **Volunteers are people who work for a cause without compensation.**

Aren't people who volunteer to serve on boards, committees, and commissions sometimes paid, especially for their expenses? What about members of the so-called all-volunteer military? They are financially compensated for their years of service, and they enjoy substantial benefits after they complete their tour of duty.

As you can see, you can't just offer up a definition as part of your argument and assume that readers will understand or accept it. Every part of the definition has to be weighed, critiqued, and defended. That means you'll want to investigate your subject in the library, on the Internet, or in conversation with others. You might then be able to present your definition in a single paragraph, or you may have to spend several pages coming to terms with the complexity of the core issue.

Were you to get involved in an environmental case involving the meaning of *wetlands*, for instance, you might have to examine a range of definitions from any number of sources before arriving at the definition you believe will be acceptable to your readers. Here are just three definitions of wetlands we found on the Internet, suggesting the complexity of the issue:

> In general terms, wetlands are lands where saturation with water is the dominant factor determining the nature of soil development and the types of plant and animal communities living in the soil and on its surface.
> —U.S. Fish and Wildlife Service

> WETLANDS are lands transitional between terrestrial and aquatic systems where the water table is usually at or near the surface or the land is covered by shallow water.
> —U.S. Fish and Wildlife Service

> [Wetlands are] land where the water table is at, near, or above the land surface long enough to promote the formation of hydric soils or to support the growth of hydrophytes, and shall also include types of wetlands where vegetation is lacking and soil is poorly developed or absent as a result of frequent drastic fluctuations of surface water levels, wave action, water flow, turbidity or high concentration of salts or other substances in the substrate. Such wetlands can be recognized by the presence of surface water or saturated substrate at some [time] during each year and their location within, or adjacent to vegetated wetland or deepwater habitats.
> —California Department of Fish and Game

The definitions, taken together, would help you to distinguish the conditions that are *essential* and *sufficient* for defining whether a given plot of land is wetlands. *Essential conditions* are elements that must be part of a definition but that—in themselves—aren't enough to define the term.

Clearly, a wetland needs water and land in proximity, but it isn't a suffi-cient condition since a riverbank or beach might meet that condition without being a wetland.

A *sufficient condition* is any element or conjunction of elements that is enough to define a term. The sufficient condition for wetlands seems to be a combination of land and water sufficient to form a regular (if some-times temporary) ecological system.

One might add *accidental conditions* to a definition as well—elements that are often associated with a term but are not present in every case or sufficient to identify it. An important accidental feature of wetlands, for example, might be specific forms of plant life or species of birds.

After conducting research of this kind, you might be in a position to write an extended definition well enough informed to explain to your readers what you believe makes a wetland a wetland, a volunteer a vol-unteer, a tax a tax, and so on. At the end of this chapter, writer Lynn Peril provides just such a definition of the mind-set she claims is imposed on women in this country, what she calls "Pink Think."

Matching Claims to Definitions

Once you've formulated a definition readers will accept—a demanding task in itself—you might need to look at your particular subject to see if it fits that general definition, providing evidence to show that

- it is a clear example of the class defined,
- it falls outside the defined class,
- it falls between two closely related classes,

  or

- it defies existing classes and categories and requires an entirely new definition.

It's possible that you might have to change your original claim at this point if the evidence you've gathered suggests that qualifications are nec-essary. It is amazing how often seemingly cut-and-dry issues of definition become blurry—and open to compromise and accommodation—when you learn more about them. That has proved to be the case as various campuses across the country have tried to define hate speech or sexual harassment—very tricky matters. And even the Supreme Court has never quite been able to say what "pornography" is. Just when matters seem set-tled, new legal twists develop. Should virtual child pornography created with software be as illegal as the real thing? Is a virtual image—even a lewd one — an artistic expression protected like other works of art by the First Amendment? That's an issue of definition the Court may have to decide someday soon. (See Chapter 8.)

KEY FEATURES OF DEFINITIONAL ARGUMENTS

In writing an argument of definition of your own, consider that it is likely to include the following parts:

- a claim involving a question of definition
- a general definition of some key concept
- a careful look at your subject in terms of that general definition
- evidence for every part of the argument
- a consideration of alternative views and counterarguments
- a conclusion, drawing out the implications of the argument

It is impossible, however, to predict what emphasis each of those parts might receive or what the ultimate shape of an argument of definition will be.

Whatever form an argument takes, the draft should be shared with others who can examine its claims, evidence, and connections. It is remarkably easy for a writer in isolation to think narrowly — and not to imagine that others might define *volunteer* or *institutional racism* in a completely different way than they do. Thus it is important to keep a mind open to criticism and suggestions. Look very carefully at the terms of any definitions you offer. Do they really help readers distinguish one concept from another? Are the conditions offered sufficient or essential? Have you mistaken accidental features of a concept or object for more important features?

Don't hesitate to look to other sources for comparisons with your definitions. You can't depend on dictionaries to offer the last word about any disputed term, but you can at least begin there. Check the meaning of terms in encyclopedias and other reference works. And search the Web intelligently to find how your key terms are presented there. (In searching for the definition of *wetland*, for example, you could type *wetland definition* into a search engine like Google and get a limited number of useful hits.)

Finally, be prepared for surprises in writing arguments of definition. That's part of the delight in expanding the way you see the world. "You're not a terrier; you're a police dog," exclaims fictional detective Nick Charles after his fox terrier, Asta, helps him solve a case. Such is the power of definition.

GUIDE to writing an argument of definition

Finding a Topic

You are likely entering an argument of definition when you

- formulate a controversial definition: *Discrimination is the act of judging someone on the basis of unchangeable characteristics.*
- challenge a definition: *Judging someone on the basis of unchangeable characteristics is not discrimination.*
- try to determine whether something fits an existing definition: *Affirmative action is/is not discrimination.*

Look for issues of definition in your everyday affairs—for instance, in the way jobs are classified at work; in the way key terms are described in your academic major; in the way politicians characterize the social issues that concern you; in the way you define yourself or others try to define you. Be especially alert to definitional arguments that may arise whenever you or others deploy adjectives such as *true*, *real*, *actual*, or *genuine*: *a true Texan*, *real environmental degradation*, *actual budget projections*, *genuine rap music*.

Researching Your Topic

You can research issues of definition by using the following sources:

- college dictionaries and encyclopedias
- unabridged dictionaries
- specialized reference works and handbooks, such as legal and medical dictionaries
- your textbooks (check their glossaries)
- newsgroups and listservs that focus on particular topics

Be sure to browse in your library reference room. Also, use the search tools of electronic indexes and databases to determine whether or how often controversial phrases or expressions are occurring in influential materials: major online newspapers, journals, and Web sites.

Formulating a Claim

After exploring your subject, begin to formulate a full and specific claim, a thesis that lets readers know where you stand and what issues are at stake. In moving toward this thesis, begin with the following types of questions of definition:

160

- questions related to genus: *Is assisting in suicide a crime?*
- questions related to species: *Is tobacco a relatively harmless drug or a dangerously addictive one?*
- questions related to conditions: *Must the imposition of sexual attention be both unwanted and unsolicited to be considered sexual harassment?*
- questions related to fulfillment of conditions: *Has our college kept in place traditions or policies that might constitute racial discrimination?*
- questions related to membership in a named class: *Is any rock artist today in a class with Elvis, Dylan, the Beatles, or the Rolling Stones?*

Your thesis should be an actual statement. In one sentence, you need to make a claim of definition and state the reasons that support your claim. In your paper or project itself, you may later decide to separate the claim from the reasons supporting it. But your working thesis should be a fully expressed thought. That means spelling out the details and the qualifications: *Who? What? Where? When? How many? How regularly? How completely?* Don't expect readers to fill in the blanks for you.

Examples of Definitional Claims

- Assisting a gravely ill person to commit suicide should not be considered murder when the motive behind the act is to ease a person's suffering, not to do harm or to benefit from the death.
- Although tobacco is admittedly addictive and ultimately harmful to health, it should not be classified as a dangerous drug because its immediate effects are far less damaging to the individual and society than those of heroin, marijuana, and cocaine.
- Flirting with the waitstaff in a restaurant should be considered sexual harassment when the activity is repeated, obviously offensive, unsolicited, and unappreciated.
- Giving college admission preference to children of alumni is an example of class discrimination because most such policies privilege families that are rich and already advantaged.

Preparing a Proposal

If your instructor asks you to prepare a proposal for your project, here's a format you might use.

State your thesis completely. If you are having trouble doing so, try outlining it in Toulmin terms:

> Claim:
>
> Reason(s):
>
> Warrant(s):

Explain why this argument of definition deserves attention. What is at stake? Why is it important for your readers to consider?

Explain whom you hope to reach through your argument and why this group of readers would be interested in it.

Briefly discuss the key challenges you anticipate in preparing your argument: Defining a key term? Establishing the essential and sufficient elements of your definition? Demonstrating that your subject will meet those conditions?

Determine what strategies you will use in researching your definitional argument. What sources do you expect to consult: Dictionaries? Encyclopedias? Periodicals? The Internet?

Consider what format you expect to use for your project: A conventional research essay? A letter to the editor? A Web page?

Thinking about Organization

Your argument of definition may take various forms, but it is likely to include elements such as the following:

- a claim involving a matter of definition: *Pluto ought not to be considered a genuine planet.*

- an attempt to establish a definition of a key term: *A genuine planet must be a body in orbit around the sun, spherical (not a rock fragment), large enough to sustain an atmosphere, and . . .*

- an explanation or defense of the terms of the definition: *A planet has to be large enough to support an atmosphere in order to be distinguished from lesser objects within the solar system . . .*

- an examination of the claim in terms of the definition and all its criteria: *Although Pluto does orbit the sun, it may not in fact be spherical or have sufficient gravity to merit planetary status . . .*

- evidence for every part of the argument: *Evidence from radio telescopes and other detailed observations of Pluto's surface suggest . . . , and so . . .*
- a consideration of alternative views and counterarguments: *It is true, perhaps, that Pluto is large enough to have a gravitational effect on . . .*

Getting and Giving Response

All arguments benefit from the scrutiny of others. Your instructor may assign you to a peer group for the purpose of reading and responding to each other's drafts; if not, make the effort yourself to get some careful response. You can use the following questions to evaluate a draft. If you are evaluating someone else's draft, be sure to illustrate your points with examples. Specific comments are always more helpful than general observations.

The Claim

- Is the claim clearly an issue of definition?
- Is the claim significant enough to interest readers?
- Are clear and specific criteria established for the concept being defined? Do the criteria define the term adequately? Using this definition, could most readers identify what is being defined and distinguish it from other related concepts?

Evidence for the Claim

- Is enough evidence furnished to explain or support the definition? If not, what kind of additional evidence is needed?
- Is the evidence in support of the claim simply announced, or are its significance and appropriateness analyzed? Is a more detailed discussion needed?
- Are all the conditions of the definition met in the concept being examined?
- Are any objections readers might have to the claim, criteria, or evidence, or to the way the definition is formulated, adequately addressed?
- What kinds of sources are cited? How credible and persuasive will they be to readers? What other kinds of sources might be more credible and persuasive?
- Are all quotations introduced with appropriate signal phrases (such as "As Himmelfarb argues,") and blended smoothly into the writer's sentences?

Organization and Style

- How are the parts of the argument organized? Is this organization effective, or would some other structure work better?

- Will readers understand the relationships among the claim, supporting reasons, warrants, and evidence? If not, what could be done to make those connections clearer? Are more transitional words and phrases needed? Would headings or graphic devices help?

- Are the transitions or links from point to point, paragraph to paragraph, and sentence to sentence clear and effective? If not, how could they be improved?

- Is the style suited to the subject? Is it too formal? Too casual? Too technical? Too bland?

- Which sentences seem particularly effective? Which ones seem weakest, and how could they be improved? Should some short sentences be combined, or should any long ones be separated into two or more sentences?

- How effective are the paragraphs? Do any seem too skimpy or too long?

- Which words or phrases seem particularly effective, vivid, and memorable? Do any seem dull, vague, unclear, or inappropriate for the audience or the writer's purpose? Are definitions provided for technical or other terms that readers might not know?

Spelling, Punctuation, Mechanics, Documentation, Format

- Are there any errors in spelling, punctuation, capitalization, and the like?

- Is an appropriate and consistent style of documentation used for parenthetical citations and the list of works cited or references? (See Chapter 22.)

- Does the paper or project follow an appropriate format? Is it appropriately designed and attractively presented? If it is a Web site, do all the links work?

RESPOND •

1. Briefly discuss the criteria you might use to define the italicized terms in the following controversial claims of definition. Compare your definitions of the terms with those of your classmates.

   Burning a nation's flag is a *hate crime*.

   The Bushes have become America's *royal family*.

   Matt Drudge and Larry Flynt are legitimate *journalists*.

   College sports programs have become *big businesses*.

   Plagiarism can be an act of *civil disobedience*.

   Satanism is a *religion* properly protected by the First Amendment.

   Wine (or beer) is a *health food*.

   Campaign contributions are acts of *free speech*.

   The District of Columbia should have all the privileges of an American *state*.

   Committed gay and lesbian couples should have the legal privileges of *marriage*.

2. This chapter opens with sketches of six rhetorical situations that center on definitional issues. Select one of these situations, and write definitional criteria using the strategy of formal definition. For example, identify the features of a photograph that make it part of a larger class (art, communication method, journalistic technique). Next, identify the features of a photograph that make it distinct from other members of that larger class.

   Then use the strategy of operational definition to establish criteria for the same object: What does it do? Remember to ask questions related to conditions (*Is a computer-scanned photograph still a photograph?*) and questions related to fulfillment of conditions (*Does a good photocopy of a photograph achieve the same effect as the photograph itself?*).

3. In an essay at the end of this chapter entitled "Pink Think," Lynn Peril makes a variety of claims about a concept she identifies as *pink think*, which she defines in part as "a set of ideas and attitudes about what constitutes proper female behavior." After reading this selection carefully, consider whether Peril has actually defined a concept that operates today. If you think "pink think" still exists, prove it by showing how some activities, behaviors, products, or institutions meet the definition of the concept. Write, too, about the power this concept has to define behavior.

Alternatively, define a concept of your own that applies to a similar kind of stereotypical behavior—for example, *jock think* or *frat think* or *theater think* or *geek think*. Then argue that your newly defined concept does, in fact, influence people today. Be sure to provide clear and compelling examples of the concept in action as it shapes the way people act, think, and behave.

TWO SAMPLE ARGUMENTS OF DEFINITION

Creating a Criminal

....

MICHAEL KINGSTON

In reaction to the Vietnamese American practice of raising canines for food, Section 598b of the California Penal Code was recently amended to read as follows:

> (a) Every person is guilty of a misdemeanor who possesses, imports into this state, sells, buys, gives away, or accepts any carcass or part of any carcass of any animal traditionally or commonly kept as a pet or companion with the sole intent of using or having another person use any part of that carcass for food.

The California Penal Code defines what actions constitute a misdemeanor.

> (b) Every person is guilty of a misdemeanor who possesses, imports into this state, sells, buys, gives away, or accepts any animal traditionally or commonly kept as a pet or companion with the sole intent of killing or having another person kill that animal for the purpose of using or having another person use any part of the animal for food.

This is a fascinating new law, one that brings up a complex set of moral, political, and social questions. For example: What constitutes a "pet"? Do pets have special "rights" that other animals aren't entitled to? How should these "rights" be balanced with the real political rights of the human populace? How do we define the civil rights of an ethnic minority whose actions reflect cultural values that are at odds with those of the majority? Section 598b does not mention these issues. Rather, it seems to simply walk around them, leaving us to figure out for ourselves whose interests (if any) are being served by this strange new law.

All the questions Kingston raises here arise from an issue of definition: What is a pet?

Michael Kingston wrote "Creating a Criminal" while he was a student at the University of California, Riverside. Kingston argues that a law banning the consumption of animals regarded as pets targets specific immigrant groups. Key to the argument are definitions of *pet* and *racial discrimination*.

The first thing one might wonder is whether the purpose of Section 598b is to improve the lot of pets throughout California. What we do know is that it seeks to prevent
people from eating animals traditionally regarded as pets
(dogs and cats). But for the most part, the only people who
eat dogs or cats are Vietnamese Americans. Furthermore,
they don't consider these animals "pets" at all. So, pets
aren't really being protected. Maybe Section 598b means
to say (in a roundabout manner) that *all* dogs and cats are
special and therefore deserve protection. Yet, it doesn't
protect them from being "put to sleep" in government
facilities by owners who are no longer willing to have
them. Nor does it protect them from being subjected to
Kingston compares painful, lethal experiments designed to make cosmetics
the ostensible safe for human use. Nor does it protect them from
purpose of the new unscrupulous veterinarians who sometimes keep one or
statutes with what two on hand to supply blood for anemic pets of paying
he regards as their customers. No, the new law simply prevents Vietnamese
real purpose. Americans from using them as food.

Is the consumption of dogs or cats so horrible that it
merits its own law? One possible answer is that these practices pose a special threat to the trust that the pet-trading
network relies upon. Or in other words: that strange man
who buys one or more of your puppies might just be one
of those dog-eaters. But this scenario just doesn't square
with reality. A Vietnamese American, canine-eating family
is no more a threat to the pet-trading industry than is a
family of European heritage that chooses to raise rabbits
(another popular pet) for its food. Predictably, there is a
The case for loophole in Section 598b that allows for the continued eat-
prejudice can be ing of pet rabbits. Its circular logic exempts from the new
built on a loophole law any animal that is part of an *established* agricultural
in the law's industry.
definition of pet —
one that favors the It seems as though Vietnamese Americans are the only
culinary habits ones who can't eat what they want, and so it is hard not to
of the European think of the issue in terms of racial discrimination. And why
American majority. shouldn't we? After all, the Vietnamese community in California has long been subjected to bigotry. Isn't it conceivable
that latent xenophobia and racism have found their way
into the issue of dog-eating? One needs only to look at the

law itself for the answer. This law protects animals "traditionally . . . kept as a pet." Whose traditions? Certainly not the Vietnamese's.

The meaning of traditions now becomes a key issue.

Of course, the typical defense for racially discriminatory laws such as this one is that they actually protect minorities by forcing assimilation. The reasoning here is that everything will run much smoother if we can all just manage to fall in step with the dominant culture. This argument has big problems. First, it is morally bankrupt. How does robbing a culture of its uniqueness constitute a protection? Second, it doesn't defuse racial tensions at all. Racists will always find reasons for hating the Vietnamese. Finally, any policy that seeks to label minorities as the cause of the violence leveled against them is inherently racist itself.

A counterargument is considered and refuted.

Whatever the motives behind Section 598b, the consequences of the new law are all too clear. The government, not content with policing personal sexual behavior, has taken a large step toward dictating what a person can or cannot eat. This is no small infringement. I may never have the desire to eat a dog, but I'm rankled that the choice is no longer mine, and that the choice was made in a climate of racial intolerance. Whatever happened to the right to life, liberty, and the pursuit of happiness?

In this paragraph, Kingston draws on emotional and ethical appeals.

Unfortunately, we may suffer more than just a reduction in personal choice. Crimes such as dog-eating require a certain amount of vigilance to detect. More than likely, the police will rely upon such dubious measures as sifting through garbage left at curbside, or soliciting anonymous tips. Laws that regulate private behavior, after all, carry with them a reduction in privacy.

The threat the new law poses to privacy rights adds an emotional kick to the conclusion.

We sure are giving up a lot for this new law. It's sad that we receive only more criminals in return.

Pink Think

LYNN PERIL

From the moment she's wrapped in a pink blanket, long past the traumatic birthday when she realizes her age is greater than her bust measurement, the human female is bombarded with advice on how to wield those feminine wiles. This advice ranges from rather vague proscriptions along the lines of "nice girls don't chew gum/swear/wear pants/fill-in-the-blank," to obsessively elaborate instructions for daily living. How many women's lives, for example, were enriched by former Miss America Jacque Mercer's positively baroque description of the proper way to put on a bathing suit, as it appeared in her guide *How to Win a Beauty Contest* (1960)?

> [F]irst, roll it as you would a girdle. Pull the suit over the hips to the waist, then, holding the top away from your body, bend over from the waist. Ease the suit up to the bustline and with one hand, life one breast up and in and ease the suit bra over it. Repeat on the other side. Stand up and fasten the straps.

Instructions like these made me bristle. I formed an early aversion to all things pink and girly. It didn't take me long to figure out that many things young girls were supposed to enjoy, not to mention ways they were supposed to behave, left me feeling funny—as if I was expected to pound my square peg self into the round hold of designated girliness. I didn't know it at the time, but the butterflies in my tummy meant I had crested the first of many hills on the roller coaster ride of femininity—or, as I soon referred to it, the other f-word. Before I knew what was happening, I was hurtling down its track, seemingly out of control, and screaming at the top of my lungs.

After all, look what I was up against. The following factoids of femininity date from the year of my birth (hey, it wasn't *that* long ago):

- In May of 1961, Betsy Martin McKinney told readers of *Ladies' Home Journal* that, for women, sexual activity commenced with intercourse and was completed with pregnancy and childbirth. Therefore, a woman who used contraceptives denied "her own creativity, her own sexual role, her very femininity." Furthermore, McKinney asserted that "one of the most stimulating predisposers to orgasm in a woman may be childbirth followed by

---

Lynn Peril is the publisher of the 'zine *Mystery Date*. This essay is excerpted from the introduction to *Pink Think*, a book that examines the influence of the feminine ideal.

several months of lactation." (Mmm, yes, must be the combination of epi-siotomy and sleep deprivation that does it.) Politely avoiding personal examples, she neglected to mention how many little McKinneys there were.

- During the competition for the title of Miss America 1961, five finalists were given two questions to answer. First they were asked what they would do if "you were walking down the runway in the swimsuit competi-tion, and a heel came off one of your shoes?" The second question, how-ever, was a bit more esoteric: "Are American women usurping males in the world, and are they too dominant?" Eighteen-year-old Nancy Fleming, of Montague, Michigan, agreed that "there are too many women working in the world. A woman's place is in the home with her husband and chil-dren." This, along with her pragmatic answer to the first question ("I would kick off both shoes and walk barefooted") and her twenty-three-inch waist (tied for the smallest in pageant history), helped Nancy win the crown.

- In 1961, toymaker Transogram introduced a new game for girls called Miss Popularity ("The True American Teen"), in which players competed to see who could accrue the most votes from four pageant judges—three of whom were male. Points were awarded for such attributes as nice legs, and if the judges liked a contestant's figure, voice, and "type." The prize? A special "loving" cup, of course! Who, after all, could love an unpopular girl?

These are all prime examples of "pink think." Pink think is a set of ideas and attitudes about what constitutes proper female behavior; a groupthink that was consciously or not adhered to by advice writers, manufacturers of toys and other consumer products, experts in many walks of life, and the public at large, particularly during the years spanning the mid-twentieth century—but enduring even into the twenty-first century. Pink think assumes there is a standard of behavior to which all women, no matter their age, race, or body type, must aspire. "Femininity" is sometimes used as a code word for this mythical standard, which suggests that women and girls are always gentle, soft, delicate, nurturing beings made of "sugar and spice and everything nice." But pink think is more than a stereotyped vision of girls and women as poor drivers who are afraid of mice and snakes, adore babies and small dogs, talk incessantly on the phone, and are incapable of keeping secrets. Integral to pink think is the belief that one's success as a woman is grounded in one's allegiance to such behavior. For example, a woman who fears mice isn't necessarily following the dictates of pink think. On the other hand, a woman who isn't afraid of mice but pretends to be because she thinks such helplessness adds to her appearance of femininity is toeing the pink think party line. When you hear the words "charm" or "personality" in the context of successful womanhood, you can almost always be sure you're in the presence of pink think.

While various self-styled "experts" have been advising women on their "proper" conduct since the invention of the printing press, the phenomenon defined here as pink think was particularly pervasive from the 1940s to the 1970s. These were fertile years for pink think, a cultural mindset and consumer behavior rooted in New Deal prosperity yet culminating with the birth of women's liberation. During this time, pink think permeated popular books and magazines aimed at adult women, while little girls absorbed rules of feminine behavior while playing games like the aforementioned Miss Popularity. Meanwhile, prescriptions for ladylike dress, deportment, and mindset seeped into child-rearing manuals, high school home economics textbooks, and guides for bride, homemaker, and career girl alike.

It was almost as if the men and women who wrote such books viewed proper feminine behavior as a panacea for the ills of a rapidly changing modern world. For example, myriad articles in the popular press devoted to the joys of housewifery helped coerce Rosie the Riveter back into the kitchen when her hubby came home from the war and expected his factory job back. During the early cold war years, some home economics texts seemed to suggest that knowing how to make hospital corners and a good tuna casserole were the only things between Our Way of Life and communist incursion. It was patriotic to be an exemplary housewife. And pink-thinking experts of the sixties and seventies, trying to maintain this ideal, churned out reams of pages that countered the onrushing tide of both the sexual revolution and the women's movement. If only all women behaved like our Ideal Woman, the experts seemed to say through the years, then everything would be fine.

You might even say that the "problem with no name" that Betty Friedan wrote about in *The Feminine Mystique* (1963) was a virulent strain of pink-thinkitis. After all, according to Friedan, "the problem" was in part engendered by the experts' insistence that women "could desire no greater destiny than to glory in their own femininity"—a pink think credo.

The pink think of the 1940s to 1970s held that femininity was necessary for catching and marrying a man, which was in turn a prerequisite for childbearing—the ultimate feminine fulfillment. This resulted in little girls playing games like Mystery Date long before they were ever interested in boys. It made home economics a high school course and college major, and suggested a teen girl's focus should be on dating and getting a boyfriend. It made beauty, charm, and submissive behavior of mandatory importance to women of all ages in order to win a man's attention and hold his interest after marriage. It promoted motherhood and housewifery as women's only meaningful career, and made sure that women who worked outside the home brought "feminine charm" to their workplaces lest a career make them too masculine.

Not that pink think resides exclusively alongside antimacassars and 14.4 modems in the graveyard of outdated popular culture: Shoes, clothing, and movie stars may go in and out of style with astounding rapidity, but attitudes have an unnerving way of hanging around long after they've outlived their usefulness—even if they never had any use to begin with.

chapter ten

Evaluations

"We don't want to go *there* for Tex-Mex. Their tortillas aren't fresh, their quesadillas are mush, and they get their salsa from New York City!"

After a twenty-two-year stint, the president of a small liberal arts college decides to retire. After the announcement a committee is formed to choose a new leader, with representatives from the faculty, administration, alumni, and student body. The first task the group faces is to describe the character of an effective college president in the twenty-first century.

A senior is frustrated by the "C" he received on an essay written for a history class, so he makes an appointment to talk with the teaching assistant who graded the paper. "Be sure to review the assignment sheet first," she warns.

174

The student notices that the sheet, on its back side, includes a checklist of requirements for the paper; he hadn't turned it over before.

"We have a lousy home page," a sales representative observes at a district meeting. "What's wrong with it?" the marketing manager asks. "Everything," she replies, then quickly changes the subject when she notices the manager's furrowed brow. But the manager decides to investigate the issue. Who knows what an effective Web site looks like these days.

You've just seen *Citizen Kane* for the first time and want to share the experience with your roommate. Orson Welles's masterpiece is playing at the Student Union for only one more night, but *Die Hard X: The Battery* is featured across the street in THX sound. Guess which movie Bubba wants to see? You intend to set him straight.

■ ■ ■

UNDERSTANDING EVALUATIONS

Kristin Cole has a problem. The holiday break is approaching, she is headed out of town, and she still has not found a pet-sitter for Baldrick, her lovable cockatiel. When her first email appeal to colleagues in a large academic department fails to turn up a volunteer, she tries a second, this one more aggressively singing the praises of her companion:

> **Apologies for all duplications, folks! Since nobody's stepped forward to birdsit for me from 15–30 or 31 December, I must repeat my plea.**
> **Please take my bird for this time. I'll pay. If you have other pets, all I ask is that your little darlings can't get at my little darling.**
> **And let me repeat that Baldrick could be the poster child for birds: he's quiet, loves people, and couldn't be happier than to sit on your shoulder while you go about your day. He'll whistle and make kissy noises in your ear, since he's a huge flirt. I must admit that he loves to chew paper and pens, but that's controllable. And he loves feet—that can be positive, negative, or neutral, depending on you.**
> **He is much easier than a cat or dog—no litter boxes, walks, or poop in the yard. And his food smells like candy. He's pretty much allergy-free, and the mess he makes is easily vacuumable with the dustbuster I will lend you. He just needs contact with people and a fair amount of supervised out-of-cage time per day.**

Please do let me know if you can help me out. He's a great pet—he converted me, who had always thought a proper pet needed fur and four legs!

−Kristin

In just a few lines, Kristin offers about a half-dozen reasons for birdsitting Baldrick, many of them based on the evaluative claim "he's a great pet." The petition deploys several different lines of argument, including appeals to the heart ("he's a huge flirt"), the head ("I'll pay"), and even values ("he converted me, who had always thought a proper pet needed fur and four legs"). About the only potential device Kristin misses is a visual argument—for example, a photo of Baldrick, which she might have attached to the email easily enough.

Kristin makes Baldrick seem lovable and charming for a reason: to persuade someone to board the cockatiel over the holidays. In this respect her strategy is typical of many arguments of evaluation. They are written to clarify or support other decisions in our lives: what to read, whom to hire, what to buy, which movies to see, for whom to vote. (In case you are wondering, Kristin's email worked.)

Evaluations are everyday arguments. By the time you leave home in the morning, you've likely made a dozen informal evaluations. You've selected dressy clothes because you have a job interview in the afternoon with a law firm; you've chosen low-fat yogurt and shredded wheat over artery-clogging eggs and bacon; you've clicked the remote past cheery

FIGURE 10.1 BALDRICK—THE POSTER CHILD FOR BIRDS

Katie Couric for what you consider more adult programming on C-SPAN. In each case, you've applied criteria to a particular problem and then made a decision.

Some professional evaluations require much more elaborate standards, evidence, and paperwork (imagine what an aircraft manufacturer has to do to certify a new jet for passenger service), but such work doesn't differ structurally from the simpler choices that people make routinely. And, of course, people do love to voice their opinions, and always have: a whole mode of ancient rhetoric — called the ceremonial, or epideictic — was devoted entirely to speeches of praise and blame. (See Chapter 1.)

Today, rituals of praise and blame are part of American life. Adults who'd choke at the very notion of debating causal or definitional claims will happily spend hours appraising the Miami Hurricanes or the Fighting Irish. Other evaluative spectacles in our culture include awards shows, beauty pageants, most-valuable-player presentations, lists of best-dressed or worst-dressed celebrities, "sexiest people" magazine covers, literary prizes, political opinion polls, consumer product magazines, and — the ultimate formal public gesture of evaluation — elections. Indeed, making evaluations is a form of entertainment in America — one that generates big audiences (think of *American Idol*) and revenues.

FIGURE 10.2 *PEOPLE* DEDICATES AN ISSUE EVERY YEAR TO CHOOSING THE SEXIEST MAN. CRITERION? THE WINNERS ARE ALMOST ALWAYS ACTORS.

CRITERIA OF EVALUATION

Whether arguments of evaluation produce simple rankings and winners or lead to more profound decisions about our lives, they involve standards. The particular standards we establish for judging anything—whether an idea, a work of art, a person, or a product—are called *criteria of evaluation*. Sometimes criteria are pretty self-evident. You probably know that a truck that gets ten miles per gallon is a gas hog or that a steak that's charred and rubbery should be returned. But criteria are often more complex when a potential subject is more abstract. *What makes a politician or a teacher effective? What features make a film a classic? How do we measure a successful foreign policy or college education?* Struggling to identify such difficult criteria of evaluation can lead to important insights into your values, motives, and preferences.

Why make such a big deal about criteria when many acts of evaluation seem almost effortless? Because we should be most suspicious of our judgments precisely when we start making them carelessly. It's a cop-out simply to think that everyone is entitled to an opinion, however stupid and uninformed it might be. Evaluations always require reflection. And when we look deeply into our judgments, we sometimes discover important "why" questions that typically go unasked:

- You may find yourself willing to challenge the grade you received in a course, but not the practice of grading itself.

- You argue that Miss Alabama would have been a better Miss America than the contestant from New York, but perhaps you don't wonder loudly enough whether such competitions make sense at all.

- You argue passionately that a Republican Congress is better for America than a Democratic alternative, but you fail to ask why voters get only two choices.

- You can't believe people take Britney Spears seriously as a singer, but you never consider what her impact on young girls might be.

Push an argument of evaluation hard enough, and even simple judgments become challenging and intriguing.

In fact, for many writers, grappling with criteria is the toughest step in producing an evaluation. They've got an opinion about a movie or book or city policy, but they also think that their point is self-evident and widely shared by others. So they don't do the work they need to do to specify the criteria for their judgments. If you know a subject well enough to evaluate it, your readers should learn something from you when you offer an opinion. Do you think, for instance, that you know what makes a grilled hamburger good? The following criteria offered on the *Cooks Illustrated* Web site will probably make you more thoughtful the next time you maul a Big Mac:

> I'll admit it: I have, at times, considered becoming a vegetarian. I could give up steaks and pork chops and leg of lamb, but when I bite into a juicy grilled hamburger with all the trimmings, I'm back with the carnivores.
>
> I'm not talking about one of those pasty, gray "billions served" or "have it your way" specimens. And I'm not talking about the typical backyard barbecue burger, either. You know the one I mean, because we've all made them. This burger is tough, chewy, and dry, and, after one flip with a spatula, more of its crust—if it formed one at all—sticks to the grill than to the patty. And of course there's the shape—domed, puffy, and round enough to let all the condiments slide right off. The ideal grilled burger, however, is altogether different: moist and juicy, with a texture that's tender and cohesive, not dense and heavy. Just as important, it's got a flavorful, deeply caramelized, reddish brown crust that sticks to the meat, and a flat shape to hold the goodies.
>
> —Adam Ried and Julia Collin, "Grilling Great Hamburgers"

We've all eaten burgers, but have we thought about them this much? If we intend to evaluate them convincingly, we'd better. It's not enough to claim merely that a good burger is juicy or tasty. It's also not very interesting.

Criteria of evaluation aren't static either. They will differ according to time and audience. Much market research, for example, is designed to find out what particular consumers want now and in the future—what their criteria for buying a product are. Consider what the researchers at Honda discovered when they asked Y-generation men—a targeted demographic of consumers who generally don't consider Honda products— what they wanted in a new car. The answer, reported in the *New York Times*, was surprising:

> The Honda group found that young adults wanted a basic, no-nonsense vehicle with lots of space—and they didn't seem to care much about the exterior style. "We found that vehicles, in this generation, were not the top priority," Mr. Benner said. "They're the means, not the end. The car is a tool." . . .
>
> What distinguishes younger buyers, all car companies seem to agree, is that they don't seem to care as much about cars as young people used to—putting more stock in the style of their cellphones or P.D.A.'s than in the style of what they drive.
>
> —Phil Patton, "Young Man, Would You Like That in a Box?"

FIGURE 10.3 YOUNG PEOPLE THINK A CAR SHOULD BE A TOOL. DOES THIS HONDA ELEMENT MEET THAT CRITERION?

Such an evaluation of criteria actually led Honda to build the Element, a boxy—some would say homely—truck with swing-out side doors and an easily reconfigurable interior designed to be a "place" more than a vehicle. Its success would depend on how well the designers understood the values of their target audience and how well their vehicle met those criteria.

CHARACTERIZING EVALUATION

One way of understanding evaluative arguments is to consider the types of evidence they use. A distinction we explored in Chapter 7 between hard evidence and arguments based on reason is helpful here. You may recall that we defined hard evidence as facts, statistics, testimony, and other kinds of arguments that can be measured, recorded, or even found—the so-called "smoking gun" in a criminal investigation. Arguments based on reason are those shaped by language, using various kinds of logic.

We can study arguments of evaluation the same way, looking at some as *quantitative* and others as *qualitative*. Quantitative arguments of evaluation rely on criteria that can be measured, counted, or demonstrated in some mechanical fashion—something is taller, faster, smoother, quieter, more powerful than something else. In contrast, qualitative arguments rely on criteria that must be explained through words, relying on such matters as values, traditions, and even emotions: something is more ethical, more beneficial, more handsome, more noble. Needless to say, a claim of evaluation might be supported by arguments of both sorts. We separate them below merely to present them more clearly.

Quantitative Evaluations

At first glance, quantitative evaluations would seem to hold all the cards, especially in a society as enamored of science and technology as our own. Once you have defined a quantitative standard, making judgments should be as easy as measuring and counting—and in a few cases, that's the way things work out. *Who is the tallest or heaviest or loudest person in your class?* If your colleagues allow themselves to be measured, you could find out easily enough, using the right equipment and internationally sanctioned standards of measurement: the meter, the kilo, or the decibel.

But what if you were to ask, *Who is the smartest person in class?* You could answer this more complex question quantitatively too, using IQ tests or college entrance examinations that report results numerically. In fact, almost all college-bound students in the United States submit to this kind of evaluation, taking either the SAT or ACT to demonstrate their verbal and mathematical prowess. Such measures are widely accepted by educators and institutions, but they are also vigorously challenged. What do they actually measure? They predict likely success in college, which is not the same thing as intelligence.

Like any standards of evaluation, quantitative criteria must be scrutinized carefully to make sure that what they measure relates to what is being evaluated. For example, in evaluating a car, you might use 0–60 mph times as a measure of acceleration, 60–0 mph distances as a measure of braking capability, skidpad numbers (0.85) as a measure of handling ability, and coefficient of drag (0.29) as a test of aerodynamic efficiency. But all these numbers are subject to error. And even when the numbers are gathered accurately and then compared, one vehicle with another, they may not tell the whole story, because some cars generate great test numbers and yet still feel less competent than vehicles with lower scores. The same disparity between numbers and feel occurs with other items—compact disc recordings, for example. CDs can produce awesome sonic accuracy numbers, but some listeners feel the music they produce may lack aural qualities important to listening pleasure. Educators, too, acknowledge that some students test better than others, which doesn't necessarily indicate greater intelligence.

We don't mean to belittle quantitative measures of quality, only to offer a caveat: even the most objective measures have limits. They have been devised by fallible people looking at the world from their own inevitably limited perspectives. Just a few decades ago, teachers hoped that they might figure out how to measure quality of writing by applying quantitative measures relating to "syntactical maturity." The endeavor now seems almost comical because the more complex the human activity, the more it resists quantification. And writing is very complicated.

Yet experts in measurement assert with confidence that quantitative measures are almost always more reliable than qualitative criteria — no matter what is being evaluated. It is a sobering claim, and one not easily dismissed.

Qualitative Evaluations

Many issues of evaluation closest to people's hearts simply aren't subject to quantification. *What makes a movie great?* If you suggested a quantitative measure like length, your friends would probably hoot. Get serious! But what about box office receipts, especially if they could be adjusted to reflect inflation? Would films that made the most money — an easily quantifiable measure — really be the "best pictures"? In that select group would be movies such as *Star Wars*, *The Sound of Music*, *Gone with the Wind*, *Titanic*, and *Harry Potter and the Sorcerer's Stone*. An interesting group of films, but the best? To argue for box office revenue as a criterion of film greatness, you'd have to defend the criteria vigorously because many people in the audience would express doubts about it — major ones.

More likely, then, in defining the criteria for "great movie," you would look for standards to account for the merit of films widely respected among serious critics. For example, the American Film Institute, which ranks the top hundred American films of the past century (see <AFI.com/tv/movies.asp>), lists the following as its top ten:

1. *Citizen Kane* (1941)
2. *Casablanca* (1942)
3. *The Godfather* (1972)
4. *Gone with the Wind* (1939)
5. *Lawrence of Arabia* (1962)

6. *The Wizard of Oz* (1939)

7. *The Graduate* (1967)

8. *On the Waterfront* (1954)

9. *Schindler's List* (1993)

10. *Singin' in the Rain* (1952)

You might consider the qualities common to such respected movies, exploring such elements as their societal impact, cinematic technique, dramatic structures, casting, and so on. Most of these markers of quality could be defined with some precision, but not measured or counted. Lacking hard numbers, you would have to convince the audience to accept your standards and make your case rhetorically. As you might guess, a writer using qualitative measures could spend as much time defending criteria of evaluation as providing evidence that these standards are present in the film under scrutiny.

But establishing subtle criteria is what can make arguments of evaluation so interesting. They require you, time and again, to challenge conventional wisdom. Look at the way Nick Gillespie in *reasononline* celebrates MTV on the occasion of its twentieth anniversary not so much for the music it has presented but for the new openness it has fostered in American culture. As you'll see, most of Gillespie's selection is about his criterion of evaluation—which may be as controversial as MTV itself.

> Most rock-and-roll purists have never liked MTV, arguing that the channel is relentlessly, blandly commercial and that the music-video form inevitably swings the spotlight away from uncompromising artistes and shines it on good-looking posers whose only musical bona fides are perfect hair and teeth. On MTV, goes this line of thinking, strategically coifed divas like Christina Aguilera rule and raw punk priestesses like Ani DiFranco need not apply.
>
> Such critics make some valid points. MTV has certainly never been avant garde and much of its programming is mediocre and unmemorable (anyone remember *Austin Stories?*). But these critics miss the larger contribution that the cable channel has made, both to pop music and to pop culture: MTV has been an exceptionally vital force in the growth of the wide variety of new and ever-shifting identities that characterize our times. It has been perhaps the premier showcase—in the nation's living rooms no less—for what anthropologist Grant McCracken calls "plenitude," or the "quickening speciation of social groups, gender types, and lifestyles that characterizes our times."

From the start, MTV has been an unending and gloriously attractive parade of freaks, gender-benders, and weirdos who push the boundaries of good taste and break down whatever vestiges of mainstream sensibilities remain. Can anyone forget just how awesomely odd bands like Devo, Eurythmics, and Culture Club seemed to us once upon a time? Or how totally normal they now look?

In the years since video killed the radio star, America has become a much looser place. We're less uptight with difference and we're more interested in customized experiences, whether we're talking about 50 types of coffee, special-blend whiskeys—or highly individualized ways of dress, sexuality, and being in the world.

That trend may bother some, but for most of us, it has been both liberating and exciting.

To the extent that MTV has contributed to it, may its next 20 years be as rich as its first two decades.

—Nick Gillespie, "Happy Birthday, MTV"

As Gillespie acknowledges, not everyone will agree that America is a better place because it now accepts a "parade of freaks, gender-benders, and weirdos." But we do understand why he values MTV. His evaluation makes sense, given the criterion he has offered and defended.

DEVELOPING AN EVALUATIVE ARGUMENT

Developing an argument of evaluation can seem like a simple process, especially if you already know what your claim is likely to be:

Citizen Kane is the finest film ever made by an American director.

Having established a claim, you would then explore the implications of your belief, drawing out the reasons, warrants, and evidence that might support it.

Claim	*Citizen Kane* is the finest film ever made by an American director . . .
Reason	. . . because it revolutionizes the way we see the world.
Warrant	Great films change viewers in fundamental ways.
Evidence	Shot after shot, *Citizen Kane* presents the life of its protagonist through cinematic images that viewers can never forget.

The warrant here is, in effect, a statement of criteria—in this case, the quality that defines "great film" for the writer.

In developing an evaluative argument, you'll want to pay special attention to criteria, claims, and evidence.

Formulating Criteria

Most often neglected in evaluations is the discussion of criteria. Although even thoughtless evaluations ("The band stinks!") might be traced to reasonable criteria, most people don't bother defending their positions until they are challenged ("Oh yeah?"). Yet when writers address audiences whom they understand well or with whom they share core values, they don't defend most of their criteria in detail. One wouldn't expect a film critic like Roger Ebert to restate all his principles every time he writes a movie review. Ebert assumes his readers will—over time—come to appreciate his standards.

Still, the criteria can make or break the piece. In an essay from *Salon.com*'s series of evaluative arguments called "Masterpieces," writer Stephanie Zacharek can barely contain her enthusiasm for the Chrysler Building in downtown Manhattan:

> **Architects, who have both intuition and training on their side, have some very good reasons for loving the Chrysler Building. The rest of us love it beyond reason, for its streamlined majesty and its inherent sense of optimism and promise for the future, but mostly for its shimmery, welcoming beauty—a beauty that speaks of humor and elegance in equal measures, like a Noel Coward play.**
>
> **How can a mere building make so many people so happy—particularly so many ornery New Yorkers, who often pretend, as part of their act, not to like anything? There may be New Yorkers who dislike the Chrysler Building, but they rarely step forward in public. To do so would only invite derision and disbelief.**

Certainly it may seem odd to suggest that one measure of a great building is that it makes people happy. And so the writer has a lot to prove. She's got to provide evidence that a building can, in fact, be delightful. And she seems to do precisely that later in the same essay when she gives life even to the windows in the skyscraper:

> **Looking at the Chrysler Building now, though, it's hard to argue against its stylish ebullience, or its special brand of sophisticated cheerfulness. . . . Particularly at night, the crown's triangular windows— lit up, fanned out and stacked high into the sky—suggest a sense of movement that has more in common with dance than with architecture: Those rows of windows are as joyous and seductive as a chorus line of Jazz Age cuties, a bit of sexy night life rising up boldly from an otherwise businesslike skyline.**

FIGURE 10.4 WHY DOES THIS BUILDING MAKE PEOPLE HAPPY?

The criteria Zacharek uses lead to an inventive and memorable evaluation, one that may teach readers to look at buildings a whole new way.

Don't take criteria of evaluation for granted. If you offer vague, dull, or unsupportable principles, expect to be challenged. You are most likely to be vague about your beliefs when you haven't thought enough about your subject. So push yourself at least as far as you imagine the readers will. Imagine the readers looking over your shoulder, asking difficult questions.

Say, for example, that you intend to argue that serious drivers will obviously prefer a 5-Series BMW to an E-Class Mercedes. What standards would serious drivers apply to these sedans? Razor-sharp handling? But what does that mean? Perhaps it's the ability to hold the road in tight curves with minimal steering correction. That's a criterion you could defend. Serious drivers would likely expect precise braking, too. Might that mean that the brake pedal should be firm, responding linearly to driver input? Are such standards getting too technical? Or do you need to assert such sophisticated criteria to establish your authority to write about the subject? These are appropriate questions to ask.

Making Claims

Claims can be stated directly or, in rare instances, strongly implied. For most writers the direct evaluative claim probably works better, with the statement carefully qualified. Consider the differences between the following claims and how much less the burden of proof would be for the second and third ones:

> John Paul II was the most important leader of the twentieth century.

> John Paul II may have been one of the three or four most influential leaders of the twentieth century.

> John Paul II may come to be regarded as one of the three or four most influential spiritual leaders of the twentieth century.

The point of qualifying a statement is not to make evaluative claims bland, but to make them responsible and manageable. Consider how sensitively Christopher Caldwell frames his claim in the eulogy he writes for former Beatle George Harrison. (A eulogy is a very important kind of evaluative argument.)

> Leaving aside the screaming Beatlemaniacs in thrall to the idiosyncrasies of sex appeal, there were never any George People or Ringo People. But George Harrison's death from cancer Thursday at the age of 58 reminds us that there ought to have been. If any of the four could be called "typical" of the group, the most Beatley Beatle, the heart of the Fab Four, the means of bridging Paul's appeal and John's, and thus the glue that held the band together, it was George.
> –Christopher Caldwell, "All Things Must Pass"

Caldwell will have to prove this claim, offering evidence that George contributed in important ways to a musical group dominated by John Lennon and Paul McCartney. But he doesn't have to show that George was the most important Beatle, just the group's binding element. And that's a much more manageable task.

Of course, claims themselves might be more responsible if they were always written after a sober study of facts and evidence. But most people don't operate that way. They start with an opinion and then look for reasons and evidence to support it. If people are honest, though, they'll at least modify their claims in the face of contrary evidence.

In fact, bringing strongly held claims to the table can work well in situations where different opinions collide. That's what makes discussions on listservs so potentially exciting: people with different values make contradictory claims and then negotiate their differences, sometimes over days and weeks. Committees and study groups can work in this way, too. For example, imagine Congress contemplating alternatives to the current federal income tax system. A committee assigned to explore better systems of taxation would likely work best if it included people willing to champion the merits of different plans, everything from a flat tax to the current progressive income tax. Each of these positions, well argued, would broaden the scope of what the committee knew and might help the group move toward consensus. Or it might not.

Presenting Evidence

The more evidence the better in an evaluation, provided that the evidence is relevant. For example, in evaluating the performance of two computers, the speed of their processors would certainly be important, but the quality of their keyboards or the availability of service might be less crucial, perhaps irrelevant.

Just as important as relevance in selecting evidence is presentation. Not all pieces of evidence are equally convincing, nor should they be treated as such. Select evidence most likely to impress your readers, and arrange the paper to build toward your best material. In most cases, that best material will be evidence that is specific, detailed, and derived from credible sources. Look at the details in these paragraphs by David Plotz evaluating rapper, producer, and entertainer Sean "Puffy" Combs:

> Combs is a Renaissance man, but only by the standards of a P.T. Barnum world. Rarely has someone become so famous by being so mediocre at so many things—a boy wonder without any wonder. Puffy is a famous rapper who can't rap, and he's becoming a movie actor who can't act. He's a restaurateur who serves ho-hum food; a magazine publisher whose magazine was immediately forgettable (Notorious—see, you've forgotten already); a music producer whose only talents are stealing old songs and recycling the work of his dead friend the Notorious B.I.G.
>
> Combs can be seen as the inverse of the past century's great Renaissance man, Paul Robeson, a truly wonderful singer, actor, athlete, and political activist. Puffy has none of that talent, but unlike the Communist Robeson, he has a profound understanding of capitalism. Puffy has thrived because he has achieved his mediocrity with immense panache, with bling-bling hoopla and PR genius. Puffy is the Sam Glick of hip-hop—a man without wit, talent, charm, or convictions, but so full of drive that he made $230 million anyway.
> —David Plotz, "Sean Combs: Why Is Puffy Deflating?"

The details are rich enough to make the case that Sean Combs lacks the talent of a real artist or genius. But notice that Plotz admits what's obvious to anyone aware of the man's fame: he's a success by contemporary standards. Combs's income can't be ignored in this argument.

However, don't be afraid to concede such a point when evidence goes contrary to the overall claim you wish to make. If you are really skillful, you can even turn a problem into an argumentative asset, as Bob Costas does in acknowledging the flaws of baseball great Mickey Mantle in the process of praising him:

> **None of us, Mickey included, would want to be held to account for every moment of our lives. But how many of us could say that our best moments were as magnificent as his?**
> —Bob Costas, "Eulogy for Mickey Mantle"

KEY FEATURES OF EVALUATIONS

In drafting an evaluation, you should consider three basic elements:

- an evaluative claim that makes a judgment about a person, idea, or object

- the criterion or criteria by which you'll measure your subject

- evidence that the particular subject meets or falls short of the stated criteria

All these elements will be present in one way or another in arguments of evaluation, but they won't follow a specific order. In addition, you'll often need an opening paragraph to explain what you are evaluating and why. Tell readers why they should care about your subject and take your opinion seriously.

Nothing adds more depth to an opinion than letting others challenge it. When you can, use the resources of the Internet or more local online networks to get responses to your opinions. It can be eye-opening to realize how strongly people react to ideas or points of view that you regard as perfectly normal. When you are ready, share your draft with colleagues, asking them to identify places where you need additional support for your ideas, either in the discussion of criteria or in the presentation of evidence.

Finding a Topic

You are entering an argument of evaluation when you

- make a judgment about quality: Citizen Kane *is probably the finest film ever made by an American director.*

- challenge such a judgment: Citizen Kane *is vastly overrated by most film critics.*

- construct a ranking or comparison: Citizen Kane *is a more intellectually challenging movie than* Casablanca.

Issues of evaluation arise daily—in the judgments you make about public figures or policies; in the choices you make about instructors and courses; in the recommendations you make about books, films, or television programs; in the preferences you exercise in choosing products, activities, or charities. Be alert to evaluative arguments whenever you read or use terms that indicate value or rank: *good/bad, effective/ineffective, best/worst, competent/incompetent, successful/ unsuccessful.* Finally, be aware of your own areas of expertise. Write about subjects or topics about which others regularly ask your opinion or advice.

Researching Your Topic

You can research issues of evaluation using the following sources:

- journals, reviews, and magazines (for current political and social issues)
- books (for assessing judgments about history, policy, etc.)
- biographies (for assessing people)
- research reports and scientific studies
- books, magazines, and Web sites for consumers
- periodicals and Web sites that cover entertainment and sports
- Web logs for exploring current affairs

Surveys and polls can be useful in uncovering public attitudes: *What books are people reading? Who are the most admired people in the country? What activities or businesses are thriving or waning?* You'll discover that Web sites, newsgroups, and Web logs thrive on evaluation. Browse these public forums for ideas and, when possible, explore your own topic ideas there.

Formulating a Claim

After exploring your subject, begin to shape a full and specific claim, a thesis that lets readers know where you stand and on what criteria you will base your judgments. Look for a thesis that is challenging enough to attract readers' attention, not one that merely repeats views already widely held. In moving toward this thesis, you might begin with questions of this kind:

- What exactly is my opinion? Where do I stand?
- Can I make my judgment more specific?
- Do I need to qualify my claim?
- According to what standards am I making my judgment?
- Will readers accept my criteria, or will I have to defend them, too?
- What major reasons can I offer in support of my evaluation?

Your thesis should be a complete statement. In one sentence, you need to make a claim of evaluation and state the reasons that support your claim. Be sure your claim is specific enough. Anticipate the questions readers might have: *Who? What? Where? Under what conditions? With what exceptions? In all cases?* Don't expect readers to guess where you stand.

Examples of Evaluative Claims

- Though they may never receive Oscars for their work, Sandra Bullock and Keanu Reeves deserve credit as actors who have succeeded in a wider range of film roles than most of their contemporaries.
- Many computer users are discovering that Mac OS X is a more intuitive, stable, robust, and elegant operating system than anything currently available on PC platforms.
- Jimmy Carter has been highly priaised as an ex-president of the United States, but history may show that even his much-derided term in office laid the groundwork for the foreign policy and economic successes now attributed to later administrations.
- On a hot day, nothing tastes better than a scoop of ice cream rich in butter fat, expertly blended, creatively concocted, and free of off-putting preservatives, emulsifiers, and artificial flavors.
- Because knowledge changes so quickly and people switch careers so often, an effective education today is one that trains people *how to learn* more than it teaches them *what to know*.

Preparing a Proposal

If your instructor asks you to prepare a proposal for your project, here's a format you might use.

State your thesis completely. If you are having trouble doing so, try outlining it in Toulmin terms:

Claim:

Reason(s):

Warrant(s):

Explain why this issue deserves attention. What is at stake?

Specify whom you hope to reach through your argument and why this group of readers would be interested in it.

Briefly discuss the key challenges you anticipate. Defining criteria? Defending them? Finding quantitative evidence to support your claim? Developing qualitative arguments to bolster your judgment?

Determine what research strategies you will use. What sources do you expect to consult?

Consider what format you expect to use for your project. A conventional research essay? A letter to the editor? A Web page?

Thinking about Organization

Your evaluation may take various forms, but it is likely to include elements such as the following:

- a specific claim: *Most trucks are unsuitable for the kind of driving most Americans do.*

- an explanation or defense of the criteria (if necessary): *The overcrowding and pollution of American cities and suburbs might be relieved if more Americans drove small, fuel-efficient cars. Cars do less damage in accidents than heavy trucks and are also less likely to roll over.*

- an examination of the claim in terms of the stated criteria: *Most trucks are unsuitable for the kind of driving Americans do because they are not designed for contemporary urban driving conditions.*

- evidence for every part of the argument: *Trucks get very poor gas mileage; they are statistically more likely than cars to roll over in accidents . . .*

- consideration of alternative views and counterarguments: *It is true, perhaps, that trucks make drivers feel safer on the roads and give them a better view of traffic conditions . . .*

Getting and Giving Response

All arguments benefit from the scrutiny of others. Your instructor may assign you to a peer group for the purpose of reading and responding to each other's drafts; if not, make the effort yourself to get some careful response. You can use the following questions to evaluate a draft. If you are evaluating someone else's draft, be sure to illustrate your points with examples. Specific comments are always more helpful than general observations.

The Claim

- Is the claim clearly an argument of evaluation? Does it make a judgment about something?

- Does the claim establish clearly what is being evaluated?

- Is the claim too sweeping? Does it need to be qualified?

- Will the criteria used in the evaluation be clear to readers? Do the criteria need to be defined more explicitly or precisely?

- Are the criteria appropriate ones to use for this evaluation? Are they controversial? Does evidence of their validity need to be added?

Evidence for the Claim

- Is enough evidence provided to ensure that what is being evaluated meets the criteria established for the evaluation? If not, what kind of additional evidence is needed?

- Is the evidence in support of the claim simply announced, or are its significance and appropriateness analyzed? Is a more detailed discussion needed?

- Are any objections readers might have to the claim, criteria, or evidence adequately addressed?

- What kinds of sources are cited? How credible and persuasive will they be to readers? What other kinds of sources might be more credible and persuasive?

- Are all quotations introduced with appropriate signal phrases (for instance, "As Will argues,") and blended smoothly into the writer's sentences?

Organization and Style

- How are the parts of the argument organized? Is this organization effective, or would some other structure work better?

- Will readers understand the relationships among the claims, supporting reasons, warrants, and evidence? If not, what could be done to make those connections clearer? Are more transitional words and phrases needed? Would headings or graphic devices help?

- Are the transitions or links from point to point, paragraph to paragraph, and sentence to sentence clear and effective? If not, how could they be improved?

- Is the style suited to the subject? Is it too formal? Too casual? Too technical? Too bland?

- Which sentences seem particularly effective? Which ones seem weakest, and how could they be improved? Should some short sentences be combined, or should any long ones be separated into two or more sentences?

- How effective are the paragraphs? Do any seem too skimpy or too long?

- Which words or phrases seem particularly effective, vivid, and memorable? Do any seem dull, vague, unclear, or inappropriate for the audience or the writer's purpose? Are definitions provided for technical or other terms that readers might not know?

Spelling, Punctuation, Mechanics, Documentation, Format

- Are there any errors in spelling, punctuation, capitalization, and the like?

- Is an appropriate and consistent style of documentation used for parenthetical citations and the list of works cited or references? (See Chapter 22.)

- Does the paper or project follow an appropriate format? Is it appropriately designed and attractively presented? If it is a Web site, do all the links work?

RESPOND •

1. Choose one item from the following list that you understand well enough to evaluate. Develop several criteria of evaluation you could defend to distinguish excellence from mediocrity in the area. Then choose another item from the list, this time one you do not know much about at all, and explain the research you might do to discover reasonable criteria of evaluation for it.

   fashion designers

   Navajo rugs

   action films

   hip-hop music

   American presidents

   NFL quarterbacks

   contemporary painting

   professional journalists

   TV sitcoms

   fast food

   rock musicians

2. Review Kristin Cole's appeal for a pet-sitter for Baldrick (see p. 175), and then write an email of your own in which you try to persuade friends to care for someone or something while you are away. Be sure that the argument includes strong elements of evaluation. Why should friends be eager to pamper your pit bull Killer, care for your fragile collection of tropical orchids, or baby-sit your ten-year-old twin siblings Bonnie and Clyde?

3. In the last ten years, there has been a proliferation in awards programs for movies, musicians, sports figures, and other categories. For example, before the Oscars are handed out, a half-dozen other organizations have given prizes to the annual crop of films. Write a short opinion piece assessing the merits of a particular awards show or a feature such as *People*'s annual "sexiest man" issue. What should a proper event of this kind accomplish? Does the event you are reviewing do so?

4. Local news-and-entertainment magazines often publish "best of" issues or articles that list readers' and editors' favorites in such categories as "best place to go on a first date," "best softball field," and "best dentist." Sometimes the categories are very specific: "best places to say, 'I was retro before retro was cool,'" or "best movie theater

seats." Imagine that you are the editor of your own local magazine and that you want to put out a "best of" issue tailored to your hometown. Develop ten categories for evaluation. For each category, list the evaluative criteria you would use to make your judgment.

Next, consider that because your criteria are warrants, they are especially tied to audience. (The criteria for "best dentist," for example, might be tailored to people whose major concern is avoiding pain, to those whose children will be regular visitors, or to those who want the cheapest possible dental care.) For several of your evaluative categories, imagine that you have to justify your judgments to a completely different audience. Write a new set of criteria for that audience.

5. Develop an argument using (or challenging) one of the criteria of evaluation presented in this chapter. Among the criteria you might explore are the following:

   A car should be a tool.

   Buildings should make people happy.

   Great films change viewers in fundamental ways.

   Good pets need not have fur and four legs.

   Great burgers need just the right shape and texture.

6. For examples of powerful evaluation arguments, search the Web or library for obituaries of famous, recently deceased individuals. Try to locate at least one such item and analyze the types of claims it makes about the deceased. What criteria of evaluation are employed? What kinds of evidence does it present?

TWO SAMPLE EVALUATIONS

Why I Hate Britney

NISEY WILLIAMS

I'm afraid of having children. Not because of labor pains, but because of the odds that I may actually have a girl. Today, efficiently raising a daughter is almost impossible because of pop culture's persistent emphasis on sex. It's rare to watch MTV or BET and not be bombarded with images of women's bare midriffs, protruding cleavage and round rumps. Bellies, breasts and booties. I can't imagine how much more difficult it will be to protect my daughter from this in 15 years when she'd be approaching puberty.

And for my fear of motherhood, I blame Britney Spears. *The thesis is stated clearly and emphatically.*

Well, in all fairness, Britney's not the only one to influence our youth. There is a growing group of sexualized, so-called entertainers who seem to be multiplying like roaches: Britney Spears, Destiny's Child, Christina Aguilera, 3LW, Mariah Carey, Shakira, Jessica Simpson, Pink, J.Lo, etc.—hereafter known as Britney et al. Daily, these destructive divas serve young girls with an earful and eyeful of sex, tempting children to mimic their musical heroes. So much so that the media has coined such phrases as "Baby Britneys," "Teeny Christinees," and "Junior J.Los." Still, while there are other female artists who also discourage the healthy development of our youth—most

When she wrote this paper Nisey Williams was a senior at the University of Texas, Austin, an African American Studies and Cultural Anthropology major who plans on teaching honors English to high school students. Although she enjoys all realms of creative writing, her passion is poetry. She hopes to publish poetry and short stories.

"Why I Hate Britney" is her response to an assignment that asked for an argument with a personal voice suitable for publication in a newspaper or magazine. Sources were to be documented in the paper itself, not through formal documentation.

recently J.Lo with her serial marrying/divorcing practices—Britney remains the most culpable.

A *Dallas Morning News* reporter claims it's "always convenient to blame the sinister influence of Britney," but it's much more than "convenient"—it's practical. *Forbes* magazine voted Britney as the most powerful celebrity of 2002, beating such influential personalities as Steven Spielberg and Oprah Winfrey. With such recognition comes responsibilities. It's undeniable that Britney is at the forefront of this sex-crazed phenomenon and I, like many others, hold her accountable. On a website called *Pax Vobiscum*, one concerned father of two teenage daughters refers to Britney as "the chief apostlette for the sexualization of our little girls" with her "revealing clothing and 'come-hither' image." This couldn't be more accurate.

Evidence suggests that Spears is responsible for influencing young women.

While she says she hopes to save her virginity for marriage, she also wears see-through outfits and dances like a stripper on the MTV Video Music Awards. Actions speak louder than words; her chastity claim falls short beside her sleazy image. Britney's marketing management is pimping her and she's without the dignity or strength to step off the street corner and hail a cab from Lolita Lane to Respectable Road.

Several other female artists don't sell their bodies in order to sell their music. Among them is Avril Lavigne, one of Arista's latest signers, who openly criticizes Britney for her confusing and contradictory image. In a recent interview with *Chart Attack*, Avril explains that: "The clothes I wear onstage are the clothes I would wear to school or to go shopping. Britney Spears goes up onstage and dresses like a showgirl. She's not being herself. I mean, the way she dresses . . . would you walk around the street in a bra? It's definitely not what I'm going to do." And so far, Avril hasn't had to compromise herself to be a success. Her first album, *Let Go*, debuted at No. 8 on the Billboard charts and has since gone double platinum. She was also awarded Best New Artist at the 2002 MTV Video Music Awards. Avril is known as the "Anti-Britney" because, as AskMen.com explained, she "stands out in the current sea of female teen vocalists as a distinctly unmanufactured artist whose

An alternative to Spears's approach to success is offered.

success can be directly linked to her musical talent." Can't say the same for Miss Spears.

It's amazing how Britney ignores her influence on children. In *Rolling Stone*, her response to critics judging her clothing style was a reference to her younger days of playing dress-up in her mother's closet—within the confines of her home. She explained: "We put on our mom's clothes and we dressed up. It was our time to daydream and fantasize." Does she seriously think wearing Mom's clothes is the same as having your own and flaunting them at the mall or in the classroom?

Then in an *In Style* interview, she says she has no patience for those who criticize her skin-baring. In her words: "I mean, I'm a girl! Why not?" Great message for the kiddies, Brit: if you got it, flaunt it. And what about those girls who don't "got it"? Britney basically tells girls that body image is of primary importance—a difficult problem for many young females. Some girls who feel this constant pressure to attain unrealistic goals end up with destructive behaviors such as eating disorders and low self-esteem. Many girls who strive to be Britney look-alikes do not realize they lack her resources, such as makeup artists, silicone enhancements, and millions of dollars.

Spears does not live up to criteria for responsible behavior —given her role as a model for young girls.

The main argument against those like me who bash Britney is that it's up to parents—not celebrities—to teach their children morals and appropriate behavior. While I agree with elements of that claim, there is only so much a parent can do. Sexual material is so intertwined in pop culture that even cautious parents have a hard time keeping their children away from it. In the *Milwaukee Journal Sentinel*, one psychiatrist explains that parents "often don't even think about it [keeping children away from pop culture] because it's an overwhelming task," while another equated "trying to insulate a child from sexual material" with "fighting a tornado."

An alternative perspective is explored and rejected.

During the crucial years of adolescence, popular opinion sometimes overrides that of parents. In the same Milwaukee article, one mother reports that her daughter threw a fit in the department store when she refused to buy her thongs. The mother was completely baffled by her

Numerous
examples enforce
the claim that
children are being
sexualized too early
by "Britney et al."

child's reaction until the 12-year-old admitted that the other girls in the locker room teased her for wearing bikini underwear instead of thongs. Many kids will do anything to fit in because peer approval is so necessary to a child learning her place in school.

Experts are torn on the long-term effects our sex-heavy pop culture may have on children, but many agree that there are likely negative consequences. According to Diane Levin, an education professor who has studied the effects of media on children's development for over 20 years, our sex-saturated culture will rub off on children in the most undesired ways. On *ABCNews.com*, Levin explains that "the kind of increased sexual images that children are seeing parallel with when they get a little older. They start becoming sexually active earlier." Currently, the Alan Guttmacher Institute reports that two out of ten girls and three out of ten boys have had sexual intercourse by age 15, while there are also several widespread reports of increased sexual activity—including oral sex—among middle-school students. How much worse will these statistics be by the time my daughter reaches the age of 15?

Although there is no documented evidence of how pop culture's over-sexualization affects children, an August 14th taping of *Good Morning, America,* entitled "From Oshkosh to Oh My Gosh," revealed some startling reactions. The show divided the children by sex and then interviewed the two groups separately about issues surrounding pop culture. The result was a roomful of shocked parents who had no idea the word *sexy* was such a frequent and familiar part of their children's vocabulary. When the girls' group watched a Jennifer Lopez video, the relationship between the mature concept of sexiness and popular music became obvious. After one young girl predicted the video's ending was J.Lo removing her shirt, another girl explained that J.Lo did this "to look sexy."

Being sexy is the latest fad for girls of all ages and with the current fashions available, their dreams can become a reality. Clothing designers work side by side with the entertainment industry. There is at least a $90 billion market targeting "tweens"—children between the ages of 8 and 12 who are in the in between stages of adolescence and teenagehood. It is this up-and-coming group who fuel pop culture. They listen to the music, worship the singers and crave their clothing. From Wal-Mart to the Limited Too, stores are fully aware of what their young consumers want and promote their merchandise accordingly.

Modest girls' clothing is hard to find among the racks of grown-up fashions like low-riding hip huggers, tight midriff-revealing shirts, high-heeled platforms and miniskirts. One of my co-workers said she had such a difficult time school shopping for her 13-year-old daughter that she ended up taking her to Academy for wind suits, free-flowing T-shirts and soccer shorts. Sporting stores will soon be the last option for frustrated parents, as more retailers prey on the tween market.

As a consequence of Spears's influence, parents are finding it more difficult to raise children, underscoring the initial claim in the argument.

However, my beef is not with these merchants. The clothing is harmless by itself. It would sit untouched and undesired if it weren't for Britney et al. flaunting revealing fashions in music videos, posters, magazine covers and award shows. As *FashionFollower.com* revealed: "Queen Britney single-handedly made the bare midriff a staple of 15-year-old wardrobes across the globe. Now that's something every mother should be proud of."

Pop culture seems to be in downward spiral, continually going from bad to worse. It's bad enough to have to endure countless images of exposed female bodies on every music channel, but it's so much worse to see those same "barely there" outfits on children. Hopefully, there will come a day when it's no longer trendy to be so overtly sexual and pop culture will replace Britney et al. with more respectable female icons.

My America

ANDREW SULLIVAN

Thursday, November 28, 2002

A THANKSGIVING POST: My old colleague, the legendary British journalist and drunk Henry Fairlie, had a favourite story about his long, lascivious love affair with America. He was walking down a suburban street one afternoon in a suit and tie, passing familiar rows of detached middle-American dwellings and lush, green Washington lawns. In the distance a small boy— aged perhaps six or seven—was riding his bicycle towards him.

And in a few minutes, as their paths crossed on the pavement, the small boy looked up at Henry and said, with no hesitation or particular affectation: "Hi." As Henry told it, he was so taken aback by this unexpected outburst of familiarity that he found it hard to say anything particularly coherent in return. And by the time he did, the boy was already trundling past him into the distance.

In that exchange, Henry used to reminisce, so much of America was summed up. That distinctive form of American manners, for one thing: a strong blend of careful politeness and easy informality. But beneath that, something far more impressive. It never occurred to that little American boy that he should be silent, or know his place, or defer to his elder. In America, a six-year-old cyclist and a 55-year-old journalist were equals. The democratic essence of America was present there on a quiet street on a lazy summer afternoon.

Henry couldn't have imagined that exchange happening in England—or Europe, for that matter. Perhaps now, as European—and especially British— society has shed some of its more rigid hierarchies, it could. But what thrilled him about that exchange is still a critical part of what makes America an enduringly liberating place. And why so many of us who have come to live here find, perhaps more than most native Americans, a reason to give thanks this Thanksgiving.

Andrew Sullivan, an émigré from England, is the former editor of The New Republic and the author of Almost Normal (1995) and Love Undetectable (1998). He has written for the New York Times Magazine and many other publications such as Time and Salon.com. Sullivan maintains one of the most read and often-cited Web logs at <andrewsullivan.com>.

"My America" was first published November 24, 1996, in the Sunday Times of London.

When I tuck into the turkey on Thursday, I'll have three things in particular in mind. First, the country's pathological obsession with the present. America is still a country where the past is anathema. Even when Americans are nostalgic, they are nostalgic for a myth of the future. What matters for Americans, in small ways and large, is never where you have come from—but where you are going, what you are doing now, or what you are about to become. In all the years I have lived in America—almost a decade and a half now—it never ceases to amaze me that almost nobody has ever demanded to know by what right I belong here. Almost nobody has asked what school I went to, what my family is like, or what my past contains. (In Britain I was asked those questions on a daily, almost hourly, basis.) Even when I took it on myself to be part of the American debate, nobody ever questioned my credentials for doing so. I don't think that could ever happen in a European context (when there's a gay American editor of *The Spectator*, let me know). If Europeans ever need to know why Ronald Reagan captured such a deep part of the American imagination, this is surely part of the answer. It was his reckless futurism (remember Star Wars and supply-side economics?) and his instinctive, personal generosity.

Second, I'm thankful for the American talent for contradiction. The country that sustained slavery for longer than any other civilised country is also the country that has perhaps struggled more honestly for the notion of racial equality than any other. The country that has a genuine public ethic of classlessness also has the most extreme economic inequality in the developed world. The country that is most obsessed with pressing the edge of modernity also has the oldest intact constitution in the world. The country that still contains a powerful religious right has also pushed the equality of homosexuals further than ever before in history. A country that cannot officially celebrate Christmas (it would erase the boundary between church and state) is also one of the most deeply religious nations on the planet. Americans have learnt how to reconcile the necessary contradictions not simply because their country is physically big enough to contain them, but because it is spiritually big enough to contain them. Americans have learnt how to reconcile the necessary contradictions of modern life with a verve and a serenity few others can muster. It is a deeply reassuring achievement.

Third, I'm thankful because America is, above all, a country of primary colours. Sometimes the pictures Americans paint are therefore not as subtle, or as elegant, or even as brilliant as masterpieces elsewhere. But they have a vigour and a simplicity that is often more viscerally alive. Other nations may have become bored with the Enlightenment, or comfortable in post-modern ennui. Americans find such postures irrelevant. Here the advertisements are cruel, the battles are stark and the sermons are terrifying. And here, more than anywhere else, the most vital of arguments still go on. Does God exist? Are the races equal? Can the genders get along? Americans believe that these debates can never get tired, and that their resolution still matters, because what happens in America still matters in the broader world. At its worst, this can bespeak a kind of arrogance and crudeness. But at its best, it reflects a resilient belief that the great questions can always be reinvented and that the answers are always relevant. In the end, I have come to appreciate this kind of naivety as a deeper form of sophistication. Even the subtlest of hues, after all, are merely primary colours mixed.

At the end of November each year this restless, contradictory and simple country finds a way to celebrate itself. The British, as befits a people at ease with themselves, do not have a national day. When the French do, their insecurity shows. Even America, on the Fourth of July, displays a slightly neurotic excess of patriotism. But on Thanksgiving, the Americans resolve the nationalist dilemma. They don't celebrate themselves, they celebrate their good fortune. And every November, as I reflect on a country that can make even an opinionated Englishman feel at home, I know exactly how they feel.

chapter eleven

Causal Arguments

Laid-off workers at a formerly prosperous technology firm have a hunch that the layoffs are related to mismanagement by their CEO. They quietly begin to track down possible causes of the layoffs, hoping to prove their hunch correct.

A local school board member notes that students at one high school consistently outscore all others in the district on standardized math tests. She decides to try to identify the cause(s) of these students' success.

Researchers in Marin County, California, discover that the occurrence of breast cancer cases is significantly higher than in any other urban area in California. They immediately begin work to investigate possible causes.

A large clothing manufacturer wants to increase its worldwide market share among teenage buyers of blue jeans. Its executives know that another company has been the overwhelming market leader for years — and they set out to learn exactly why.

Convinced that there is a strong and compelling causal link between secondhand smoke and lung cancer, the mayor of New York moves to institute a total ban of smoking, even in bars.

A state legislator notes that gasoline prices are consistently between twenty-five and fifty cents higher in one large city in the state than else-where. After some preliminary investigation, the legislator decides to bring a class action lawsuit on behalf of the people of this city, arguing that price fixing and insider deals are responsible for the price difference.

■ ■ ■

UNDERSTANDING CAUSAL ARGUMENTS

Arguments about causes and effects inform many everyday decisions and choices: You decide to swear off desserts since they inevitably lead to weight gain; because you failed last week's midterm you decide to form a study group, convinced that the new technique will bring up your test scores. Suppose you are explaining, in a petition for a grade change, why you were unable to submit the final assignment on time. You'd probably try to trace the causes of your failure to submit the assignment — the death of your grandmother followed by an attack of the flu followed by the theft of your car — in hopes that the committee reading the petition would see these causes as valid and change your grade. In identifying the causes of the situation, you are implicitly arguing that the effect — your failure to turn in the assignment on time — should be considered in a new light.

Like all arguments, those about causes can also be used to amuse or to poke fun. The drawing on page 207 takes a tongue-in-cheek look at the causal relationship between the cost and the quality of health care.

FIGURE 11.1   CAUSAL RELATIONSHIP EXPLAINED IN A CARTOON

"And, in our continuing effort to minimize surgical costs, I'll be hitting you over the head and tearing you open with my bare hands."

As this cartoon suggests, causal arguments exist in many forms and frequently appear as parts of other arguments (such as evaluations or proposals). It may help focus your work on causal arguments to separate them into three major categories:

- arguments that state a cause and then examine its effect(s)
- arguments that state an effect and then trace the effect back to its cause(s)
- arguments that move through a series of links: A causes B, which leads to C and perhaps to D

Arguments that state a cause and then examine one or more of its effects

This type of argument might begin, for example, with a cause—say, putting women into combat—and then demonstrate the effects that such a cause would have. In such an argument, you will be successful if you can show compellingly that the cause would indeed lead to the described effects. Take a look at the opening of an article exploring the causes of a slump in the sale of CDs; in this case, the cause does not lead to the expected effect.

> There is a lot of propaganda about MP3s being detrimental to the sales of music CDs. . . .
>
> As the popularity of MP3s continues to exponentially grow, it's been expected that sales of CDs will decline. Surprisingly, 1999 U.S. sales reports show an increase in music CD sales by 100 million units. To what or who does the RIAA [Recording Industry Association of America] credit such great success for 1999 sales?
>
> —StellaYu, "IWantMyMP3"

Arguments that begin with an effect and then trace the effect back to one or more causes

This type of argument might begin with a certain effect—for example, the fact that America's seventh-largest company, Enron, utterly collapsed in 2002—and then trace the effect or set of effects to the most likely causes—in this case, corporate greed, "cooking" the books, spectacular mismanagement, and the freefall in the value of Enron shares. Again, the special challenge of such arguments is to make the causal connection compelling to the audience. In 1962, scientist Rachel Carson seized the attention of millions with a causal argument about the effects of the overuse of chemical poisons in agricultural control programs. Here is an excerpt from the beginning of her book-length study of this subject; note how she begins with the *effects* before saying she will go on to explore the causes:

> [A] strange blight crept over the area and everything began to change. Some evil spell had settled on the community: mysterious maladies swept the flocks of chickens; the cattle and sheep sickened and died. Everywhere was a shadow of death. The farmers spoke of much illness among their families. . . . There had been several sudden and unexplained deaths, not only among adults but even among children, who would be stricken suddenly while at play and die within a few hours. . . .
>
> The roadsides, once so attractive, were now lined with browned and withered vegetation as though swept by fire. These, too, were silent, deserted by all living things. Even the streams were now lifeless. Anglers no longer visited them, for all the fish had died.
>
> In the gutters under the eaves and between the shingles of the roofs, a white granular powder still showed a few patches; some

weeks before it had fallen like snow upon the roofs and the lawns, the fields and streams.

No witchcraft, no enemy action had silenced the rebirth of new life in this stricken world. The people had done it themselves. . . .

What has already silenced the voices of spring in countless towns in America? This book is an attempt to explain.

–Rachel Carson, *Silent Spring*

Arguments that move through a series of links: Cause A leads to B, which leads to C and possibly to D

In an environmental science class, for example, you might decide to argue that a national law regulating smokestack emissions from utility plants is needed

1. because emissions from utility plants in the Midwest cause acid rain,

2. because acid rain causes the death of trees and other vegetation in eastern forests,

3. because powerful lobbyists have prevented midwestern states from passing strict laws to control emissions from these plants, and

4. as a result, acid rain will destroy most eastern forests by 2020.

In this case, the first link is that emissions cause acid rain; the second, that acid rain causes destruction in eastern forests; and the third, that states have not acted to break the cause-effect relationship established by the first two points. These links set the scene for the fourth link, which ties the previous points together to argue from effect: unless X, then Y.

At their most schematic, causal arguments may be diagrammed in relatively straightforward ways, as shown in Figure 11.2.

FIGURE 11.2 CAUSAL ARGUMENTS

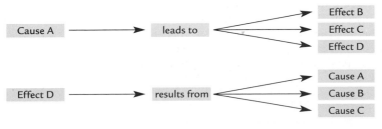

CHARACTERIZING CAUSAL ARGUMENTS

Causal arguments tend to share several characteristics.

They are often part of other arguments.

Causal arguments often work to further other arguments, especially pro-posals, so you should remember that they can be useful in establishing the good reasons for arguments in general. For example, a proposal to limit the amount of time children spend playing video games would very likely draw on causal "good reasons" for support, ones that would attempt to establish that playing video games causes negative results — such as increased violent behavior, decreased attention spans, and so on.

They are almost always complex.

The complexity of most causal arguments makes establishing causes and effects extremely difficult. For example, scientists and politicians con-tinue to disagree over the extent to which acid rain is actually responsible for the so-called dieback of many eastern forests. If you can show that X *definitely* causes Y, though, you will have a powerful argument at your dis-posal. That is why, for example, so much effort has gone into establishing a definite link between certain dietary habits and heart disease: providing the causal link amid the complex of factors that might be associated with heart disease would argue most forcefully for changing eating behavior in very significant ways.

They are often definition-based.

One reason causal arguments are so complex is that they often depend on extremely careful definitions. Recent figures from the U.S. Department of Education, for example, show that the number of high school dropouts is rising and that this rise has caused an increase in youth unemployment. But exactly how does the study define *dropout*? A closer look may suggest that some students (perhaps a lot) who drop out actually "drop back in" later and go on to complete high school. Further, how does the study define *employ-ment*? Until you can provide explicit definitions that answer such questions, you should proceed cautiously with a causal argument like this one.

They usually yield probable rather than absolute conclusions.

Because causal relationships are almost always extremely complex, they seldom yield more than a high degree of probability. Scientists in particular are wary of making causal claims—that environmental factors cause infertility, for example, because it is highly unlikely that a condition as variable as infertility could be linked to any one cause. Even *after* an event, proving what caused it can be hard. No one would disagree that the Japanese bombing of Pearl Harbor took place on December 7, 1941, or that the United States entered World War II shortly thereafter. But what is the causal connection? Did the bombing "cause" the U.S. entry into the war? Even if you are convinced that the bombing was the most immediate cause, what of other related causes: the unstable and often hostile relationship between the U.S. and Japanese governments in the years leading up to the bombing; U.S. policies toward Japanese immigration; common U.S. stereotypes of "Oriental" peoples; U.S. reactions to the Japanese invasion of China; and so on? As another example, during the campus riots of the late 1960s, a special commission was charged with determining the "causes" of riots on a particular campus. After two years of work—and almost a thousand pages of evidence and reports—the commission was unable to pinpoint anything but a broad network of contributing causes and related conditions. Thus causal claims must be approached with care and supported with the strongest evidence available in order to demonstrate the highest probability that A caused B.

DEVELOPING CAUSAL ARGUMENTS

Formulating a Claim

Of course, you might decide to write a wildly exaggerated or parodic causal argument for humorous purposes. Dave Barry does precisely this in an article supposedly explaining the causes of El Niño and other weather effects: "So we see that the true cause of bad weather, contrary to what they have been claiming all these years, is TV weather forecasters, who have also single-handedly destroyed the ozone layer via overuse of hair spray."

Most of the causal reasoning you do, however, will probably take a more serious approach to subjects you, your family, and friends care about. To begin creating a strong causal claim, try listing some of the effects—events or phenomena—you would like to know the causes of. *Why do you tend to panic before meeting new people? What's responsible for the latest tuition hike? What has led to postings of "contamination" along your favorite creek?* Or try moving in the opposite direction, listing some events or causes you are interested in and then hypothesizing what kinds of effects they may produce. *What will happen if your academic major begins requiring a five-year program for a B.S.? What will be the effects of a total crackdown on peer-to-peer file sharing?*

When you find several possible causal relationships that interest you, try them out on friends and colleagues. Can they suggest ways to refocus or clarify what you want to do? Can they offer leads to finding information about your subject? If you have hypothesized various causes or effects, can they offer counterexamples or refutations?

Finally, map out a rough statement about the causal relationship you want to explore:

A causes (or is caused by) B for the following reasons:

1. _____
2. _____
3. _____

Developing the Argument

Once you have drafted a claim, you can explore the cause-effect relationship(s), drawing out the reasons, warrants, and evidence that can support the claim most effectively.

Claim	Losing seasons caused the football coach to lose his job.
Reason	The team lost more than half its games for three seasons in a row.
Warrant	Winning is the key to success for major-team college coaches.
Evidence	For the last ten years, coaches with more than two losing seasons in a row have lost their jobs.
Claim	Certain career patterns cause women to be paid less than men.
Reason	Women's career patterns differ from men's, and in spite of changes in the relative pay of other groups, women's pay still lags behind that of men.
Warrant	Successful careers are made during the period between ages twenty-five and thirty-five.
Evidence	Women often drop out of or reduce work during the decade between ages twenty-five and thirty-five in order to raise families.

In further developing a causal argument, you can draw on many of the strategies we have already touched on in this book. In the article from which the following passage is excerpted, for instance, Stephen King uses dozens of examples — from *The Texas Chainsaw Massacre*, *The Gory Ones*, and *Invasion of the Body Snatchers* to *Night of the Living Dead*, *Psycho*, *The Amityville Horror*, and *The Thing* — in explaining why people love horror movies:

> The mythic horror movie, like the sick joke, has a dirty job to do. It deliberately appeals to all that is worst in us. It is morbidity unchained, our most base instincts let free, our nastiest fantasies realized . . . and it all happens, fittingly enough, in the dark. For those reasons, good liberals often shy away from horror films. For myself, I like to see the most aggressive of them — *Dawn of the Dead*, for instance — as lifting a trap door in the civilized forebrain and throwing a basket of raw meat to the hungry alligators swimming around in that subterranean river beneath.
>
> Why bother? Because it keeps them from getting out, man. It keeps them down there and me up here. It was Lennon and McCartney who said that all you need is love, and I would agree with that.
>
> As long as you keep the gators fed.
> —Stephen King, "Why We Crave Horror Movies"

Another way to support a causal argument is through the use of analogies. In such an argument, the strength will lie in how closely you can relate the two phenomena being compared. In exploring why women consistently earn less pay than men even when they are performing the same jobs, Sarah Banda Purvis draws an analogy between working women and sports:

> An analogy I use when describing my experiences as a female manager in corporate America is that I was allowed to sit on the bench but never given a chance to get on the field and play in the game.
> —Sarah Banda Purvis, "What Do Working Women Want in the 21st Century?"

She goes on to trace the effects that constantly being relegated to the "bench" has on earning power.

Establishing causes for physical effects — like diseases — often calls for another means of support: testing hypotheses, or theories about possible causes. This kind of reasoning helped to determine the causes of recent school poisonings in Georgia, and some years ago it helped to solve a mystery disease that had struck some fifty people in Quebec City. Puzzled by cases all involving the same effects (nausea, shortness of breath, cough, stomach pain, weight loss, and a marked blue-gray coloration), doctors at first investigated the hypothesis that the cause was severe vitamin deficiency. But too many cases in too short a time made this hypothesis unlikely, because vitamin deficiency does not ordinarily appear as a sudden epidemic. In addition, postmortem examinations of the twenty people who died revealed severe damage to the heart muscle and the liver, features that were inconsistent with the vitamin-deficiency hypothesis. The doctors therefore sought a clue to the mysterious disease in something the fifty victims were found to have shared: all fifty had been lovers of beer and had, in fact, drunk a particular brand of beer.

It seemed possible that the illness was somehow connected to the beer, brewed in Quebec City and Montreal. But Montreal had no incidence of the disease. The hypothesis, then, was further refined: perhaps the significant difference existed in the process of brewing. Eventually, this hypothesis was borne out. The Quebec brewery had added a cobalt compound to its product in order to enhance the beer's foaminess; the Montreal brewery had not. Furthermore, the compound had been added only a month before the first victims became ill.

In spite of the strength of this causal hypothesis, doctors in this case were still cautious, because the cobalt had not been present in sufficient quantities to kill a normal person. Yet twenty had died. After persistent study, the doctors decided that this fact must be related to the victims' drinking habits, which in some way reduced their resistance to the chemical. For those twenty people, a normally nonlethal dose of cobalt had been fatal.

The difficulties of such causal analysis were in the news a lot after the September 11, 2001, attacks on the Pentagon and World Trade Center. In the ensuing months, many sought to determine the causes of the crash of "the fourth plane," United flight #93, that went down in Pennsylvania. As the investigation unfolded, citizens saw investigators reject several hypotheses about the cause of the crash—it was not, for example, shot down by the U.S. military. When the flight recorder tape was finally played for family members some seven months after the crash, they came away convinced that the investigation had finally targeted the correct cause: the plane crashed into the Pennsylvania countryside as passengers fought to seize control of the plane from the hijackers. Even this information, however, cannot clarify completely the technical causes that led to the crash.

Causal arguments can also be supported by experimental evidence that is based less on strictly scientific investigation than on ethnographic observation—the study of the daily routines of ordinary people in a particular community. In an argument that attempts to explain why, when people meet head-on, some step aside and some do not, investigators Frank Willis, Joseph Gier, and David Smith observed "1,038 displacements involving 3,141 persons" at a Kansas City shopping mall. In results that surprised the investigators, "gallantry" seemed to play a significant role in causing people to step aside for one another—more so than other causes the investigators had anticipated (such as deferring to someone who is physically stronger or higher in status).

Yet another method of supporting a causal argument is through the use of one or more correlations. In such an argument you try to show that if A occurs, B is also likely to occur. You may be most familiar with correlations from statistical procedures that enable you to predict, within a degree of certainty, how likely it is that two elements or events will occur together. Recent advances in the human genome project, for example, have identified "clusters" of genes that, when found in correlation with one another, strongly suggest the occurrence of certain cancers. But correlation works in more informal ways as well. Kate Shindle, who was crowned Miss America 1998, objects strenuously to the correlation between beauty and brainlessness:

> I thought my work on the front lines of a life-and-death issue made it clear that there is more to the Miss America program than swimsuits and evening gowns. I quickly realized that wasn't the case. Though I was a dean's list student at Northwestern, suddenly people assumed I didn't have a brain. Administrators at one highly ranked university canceled an appearance, claiming that Miss America couldn't possibly have anything in common with their students. Another time, a representative of the group I had flown in to speak to picked me up at the airport, grabbed the heaviest of my three suitcases, and said, "Is this the one that holds all the makeup?" I didn't bother to explain that it held my files on AIDS research.
>
> –Kate Shindle, "Miss America: More Than a Beauty Queen?"

FIGURE **11.3** MISS AMERICA, KATE SHINDLE

Finally, you may want to consider using personal experience in support of a causal argument. Indeed, people's experiences generally lead them to seek out or to avoid various causes and effects. If you are consistently praised for your writing ability, chances are that you will look for opportunities to produce that pleasant effect. If three times in a row you get sick after eating shrimp, you will almost certainly identify the shellfish as the cause of your difficulties and stop eating it. Personal experience can also help build your credibility as a writer, gain the empathy of your listeners, and thus support your cause. Although one person's experiences cannot ordinarily be universalized, they can still argue eloquently for causal relationships. Leslie Marmon Silko uses personal experience to explain her shift from studying to become a lawyer to becoming a writer/photographer/activist, arguing that the best way to seek justice is not through the law but through the power of stories:

> When I was a sophomore in high school I decided law school was the place to seek justice. . . . I should have paid more attention to the lesson of the Laguna Pueblo land claims lawsuit from my childhood: The lawsuit was not settled until I was in law school. The U.S. Court of Indian Claims found in favor of the Pueblo of Laguna, but the Indian Claims Court never gives back land wrongfully taken; the court only pays tribes for the land. . . . The Laguna people wanted the land they cherished; instead, they got twenty-five cents for each of the six million acres stolen by the state. The lawsuit had lasted twenty years, so the lawyers' fees amounted to nearly $2 million.
>
> I completed three semesters in the American Indian Law School Fellowship Program before I realized that injustice is built into the Anglo-American legal system. . . . But I continued in law school until our criminal law class read an appeal to the U.S. Supreme Court to stop the execution of a retarded black man convicted of strangling a white librarian in Washington, D.C., in 1949. The majority on the Court refused to stop the execution, though it was clear that the man was so retarded that he had no comprehension of his crime. That case was the breaking point for me. I wanted nothing to do with such a barbaric legal system.
>
> My time in law school was not wasted: I had gained invaluable insights into the power structure of mainstream society, and I continue to follow developments in the law to calculate prevailing political winds. It seems to me there is no better way to uncover the deepest values of a culture than to observe the operation of that culture's system of justice.
>
> [But] I decided the only way to seek justice was through the power of stories.
> —Leslie Marmon Silko, *Yellow Woman and a Beauty of Spirit: Essays on Native American Life Today*

All these strategies—the use of examples, analogies, testing hypotheses, experimental evidence, correlations, and personal experience—can help you build good reasons in support of a causal argument. However, the success of the argument may ultimately depend on your ability to convince your readers that the reasons you offer are indeed good ones. In terms of causal arguments, that will mean distinguishing among immediate, necessary, and sufficient reasons. In the case of the mysterious illness in Quebec City, the immediate reasons for illness were the symptoms themselves: nausea, shortness of breath, and so on. But they were not the base or root causes of the disease. Drinking the particular beer in question served as a necessary reason: without the tainted beer, the illness would not have occurred. However, the researchers had to search much harder for the sufficient reason—the reason that will cause the effect (the illness) if it is present. In the case of the Quebec City beer, that reason turned out to be the addition of cobalt.

This example deals with the scientific investigation of a disease, but everyday causal analysis can draw on this distinction among reasons as well. What caused you, for instance, to pursue a college education? Immediate reasons might be that you needed to prepare for a career of some kind or that you had planned to do so for years. But what are the necessary reasons, the ones without which your pursuit of higher education could not occur? Adequate funds? Good test scores and academic record? The expectations of your family? You might even explore possible sufficient reasons, those that—if present—will guarantee the effect of your pursuing higher education. In such a case, you may be the only person with enough information to determine what the sufficient reasons might be.

KEY FEATURES OF CAUSAL ARGUMENTS

In drafting your own causal argument, keep in mind the following five elements:

- examination of each possible cause and effect
- description and explanation of the relationship among any links, especially in an argument based on a series of links in a causal chain
- evidence that your description and explanation are accurate and thorough

- evidence to show that the causes and effects you have identified are highly probable and that they are backed by good reasons, usually presented in order of their strength and importance
- consideration of alternative causes and effects, and evidence that you have considered them carefully before rejecting them

Fully developing a causal argument will probably call for addressing each of these elements, though you can order them in several ways. You may want to open your essay with a dramatic description of the effect, for example, and then "flash back" to multiple causes. Or you might decide to open with a well-known phenomenon, identify it as a cause, and then trace its effects. In the same way, you might decide to lead off the body of the argument with your strongest, most compelling piece of evidence, or to hold that evidence for the culmination of your argument. In any case, you should make a careful organizational plan and get a response to that plan from your instructor, friends, and colleagues before proceeding to a full draft. When the draft is complete, you should again seek a response, testing out the strength of your causal argument on at least several readers.

Finding a Topic

Chances are that a little time spent brainstorming—either with friends or other students, or on paper—will turn up some good possibilities for causal arguments of several kinds, including those that grow out of your personal experience. *Just exactly what did lead to your much higher GPA last term?* Beyond your own personal concerns, you may find a good number of public issues that lend themselves to causal analysis and argument: *What factors have led to the near bankruptcy of the nation's major airlines? What will happen if the United States continues to refuse to sign the Kyoto Protocol aimed at reducing greenhouse emissions? What effects have been caused by the move to pay professional basketball players astronomical sums of money?* Finally, as you are brainstorming possibilities for a causal argument of your own, don't ignore important current campus issues: *What have been the effects of recent increases in tuition (or what factors caused the increases)? What are the likely outcomes of shifting the academic calendar from a quarter to a semester system? If, as some argue, there has been a significant increase of racism and homophobia on campus, what has caused that increase? What are its consequences?*

Researching Your Topic

Causal arguments will lead you to a number of different resources:

- current news media—especially magazines and newspapers (online or in print)
- online database
- scholarly journals
- books written on your subject (here you can do a keyword search, either in your library or online)
- Web sites, listservs, or newsgroups devoted to your subject

In addition, why not carry out some field research of your own? You could conduct interviews with appropriate authorities on your subject, for instance, or create a questionnaire aimed at getting a range of opinion on a particular aspect of your subject. The information you get from interviews or from analyzing responses to a questionnaire can provide strong evidence to back up the claim you are making.

Formulating a Claim

You may begin to formulate your claim by identifying the particular kind of causal argument you want to make—one moving from cause(s) to effect(s);

one moving from effect(s) to cause(s); or one involving a series of links, with Cause A leading to B, which then leads to C. (See pp. 207–209 for a review of these kinds of arguments.)

Your next move may be to explore your own relationship to your subject. What do you know about the subject and its causes and effects? On what basis do you agree with the claim? What significant reasons can you offer in support of it?

In short, you should end this process of exploration by formulating a brief claim or thesis about a particular causal relationship. It should include *a statement that says, in effect, A causes (or does not cause, or is caused by) B, and a summary of the reasons supporting this causal relationship.* Remember to make sure that your thesis is as specific as possible and that it is sufficiently controversial or interesting to hold your readers' interest.

Examples of Causal Claims

- Lax current gun laws are responsible, in large part, for an increase in gun-related violent crimes.

- Rising support for third-party political candidates in three key states and increasing disillusionment with the major parties are paving the way for moving beyond the two-party system.

- The proliferation of images in film, television, and computer-generated texts is bringing profound changes to literacy.

- The many extensions to the copyright terms have led to a serious imbalance between the necessary incentive to creators and the right of the public to information, closing off the public commons, doing away, in effect, with the fair use doctrine, and adding billions of dollars to the coffers of Disney and other huge entertainment conglomerates.

Preparing a Proposal

If your instructor asks you to prepare a proposal for your project, here's a simple format that may help.

State the thesis of your argument fully, perhaps using the Toulmin schema:

> Claim:
>
> Reason(s):
>
> Warrant(s):

Explain why this argument deserves attention. Why is it important for your readers to consider?

Specify those whom you hope to reach with this argument, and explain why this group of readers is an appropriate audience. What interest or investment do they have in the issue? Why will they (or should they) be concerned?

Briefly identify and explore the major challenges you expect to face in supporting your argument. Will demonstrating a clear causal link between A and B be particularly difficult? Will the data you need to support the claim be hard to obtain?

List the strategies you expect to use in researching your argument—will you be interviewing? Surveying opinion? Conducting library and online searches? Other?

List the major sources you will need to consult—and note whether they are readily available to you.

Briefly identify and explore the major counterarguments you might expect in response to your argument.

Consider what format and genre will work best for your argument: Will you be preparing a Web site? A press release? An editorial for the local newspaper? A report for an organization you belong to?

Thinking about Organization

Whatever genre or format you decide to use, your causal argument should address the following elements:

- a specific causal claim: *Devastating flash floods associated with El Niño were responsible for the dramatic loss of homes in central California in early 2003.*

- an explanation of the claim's significance or importance: *Claims for damage from flooding put some big insurance companies out of business; as a result, homeowners couldn't get coverage and many who lost their homes had to declare bankruptcy.*

- supporting evidence sufficient to support each cause or effect—or, in an argument based on a series of causal links, evidence to support the relationships among the links: *The amount of rain that fell in central California in early 2003 was 50 percent above normal, leading inexorably to rapidly rising rivers and creeks.*

- consideration of alternative causes and effects, and evidence that you understand these alternatives and have thought carefully about them before rejecting them: *Although some say that excessive and sloppy logging and poor building codes were responsible for the loss of homes, the evidence supporting these alternative causes is not convincing.*

Getting and Giving Response

All arguments can benefit from the scrutiny of others. Your instructor may assign you to a peer group for the purpose of reading and responding to each other's drafts; if not, make the effort yourself to get some careful response. You can use the following questions to evaluate a draft. If you are evaluating someone else's draft, be sure to supply examples to illustrate your points. Specific comments are always more helpful than general observations.

The Claim

- What is most effective about the claim? What are its strengths?
- Is the claim sufficiently qualified?
- Is the claim specific enough to be clear? How could it be narrowed and focused more clearly?
- How strong is the relationship between the claim and the reasons given to support it? How could that relationship be made more explicit?
- Is it immediately evident why the claim is important? How could it be rephrased in a way that more forcefully and clearly suggests its significance?
- Does the claim reveal a causal connection? How could it be revised to make the causal links clearer?

Evidence for the Claim

- What is the strongest evidence offered for the claim? What, if any, evidence needs to be strengthened?
- Is enough evidence offered that these particular causes are responsible for the effect that has been identified, that these particular effects result from the identified cause, or that a series of causes and effects are linked? If not, what kind of additional evidence is needed? What kinds of sources might provide this evidence?
- How credible and persuasive will the sources likely be to potential readers? What other kinds of sources might be more credible and persuasive?

- Is the evidence in support of the claim simply announced, or is it analyzed in terms of its appropriateness and significance? Is a more detailed discussion necessary?
- Have all the major alternative causes and effects as well as objections to the claim been considered? What support is offered for rejecting these alternatives? Where is additional support needed?

Organization and Style

- How are the parts of the argument organized? Is this organization effective, or would some other structure work better?
- Will readers understand the relationships among the claims, supporting reasons, warrants, and evidence? If not, what could be done to make those connections clearer? Are more transitional words and phrases needed? Would headings or graphic devices help?
- Are the transitions or links from point to point, paragraph to paragraph, and sentence to sentence clear and effective? If not, how could they be improved?
- Is the style suited to the subject? Is it too formal? Too casual? Too technical? Too bland? How can it be improved?
- Which sentences seem particularly effective? Which ones seem weakest, and how could they be improved? Should some short sentences be combined, or should any long ones be separated into two or more sentences?
- How effective are the paragraphs? Do any seem too skimpy or too long, and how can they be improved?
- Which words or phrases seem particularly effective, vivid, and memorable? Do any seem dull, unclear, or inappropriate for the audience or the writer's purpose? Are definitions provided for terms that readers might not know?

Spelling, Punctuation, Mechanics, Documentation, Format

- What errors in spelling, punctuation, capitalization, and the like can you identify?
- Is an appropriate and consistent style of documentation used for parenthetical citations and the list of works cited or references? (See Chapter 22.)
- Does the paper or project follow an appropriate format? Is it appropriately designed and attractively presented? How can it be improved? If it is a Web site, do all the links work?

RESPOND●

1. The causes of some of the following events and phenomena are quite well known and frequently discussed. But do you understand them well enough yourself to spell out the causes to someone else? Working in a group, see how well (and in how much detail) you can explain each of the following events or phenomena. Which explanations are relatively clear-cut, and which seem more open to debate?

   rain

   the Burning Man festival

   the collapse of communism in 1989

   earthquakes

   the common cold

   the popularity of the Harry Potter films

   the itching caused by a mosquito bite

   the economic slump of 2002–2003

   a skid in your car on a slippery road

   the destruction of the space shuttle *Columbia*

   the rise in cases of autism

2. One of the fallacies of argument discussed in Chapter 19 is the *post hoc, ergo propter hoc* fallacy: "after this, therefore because of this." Causal arguments are particularly prone to this kind of fallacious reasoning, in which a writer asserts a causal relationship between two entirely unconnected events. After Elvis Presley's death, for instance, oil prices in the United States rose precipitously—but it would be a real stretch to argue that the King's passing caused gas prices to skyrocket.

   Because causal arguments can easily fall prey to this fallacy, you might find it useful to take absurd causal positions and see where they go—if only to learn how to avoid making such mistakes. As a class, have some fun creating an argument that goes from cause to effect—or from effect to cause—in a series of completely ridiculous steps (A leads to B leads to C leads to D). Start with one person stating a cause (such as someone sleeping late or missing a test) and move on one by one through the class, building effects on effects. (For example: *Because Jamie stepped on a crack in the sidewalk, he failed his physics exam.* Next person: *Because he failed his physics exam, he couldn't face any of his friends.* Next person: *Because he couldn't face any of his friends. . . .* In an exercise like this, the more absurd or silly the causal links, the better!)

3. In an article at the end of this chapter, Damien Cave conducts an interview with economist Stan Liebowitz, who has spent a great deal of time and effort trying to identify the causes of slumping CD sales and, more specifically, to answer the question, *Does MP3 file trading hurt the music industry?* Cave's article traces the changes in Liebowitz's answer to this question as he analyzes thirty years of record sales figures. Read this article carefully and then, working with another person in your class, decide how strong the causal evidence is for the conclusion Liebowitz puts forth.

TWO SAMPLE CAUSAL ARGUMENTS

What Makes a Serial Killer?

....

LA DONNA BEATY

Jeffrey Dahmer, John Wayne Gacy, Mark Allen Smith, Richard Chase, Ted Bundy—the list goes on and on. These five men alone have been responsible for at least ninety deaths, and many suspect that their victims may total twice that number. They are serial killers, the most feared and hated of criminals. What deep, hidden secret makes them lust for blood? What can possibly motivate a person to kill over and over again with no guilt, no remorse, no hint of human compassion? What makes a serial killer?

Serial killings are not a new phenomenon. In 1798, for example, Micajah and Wiley Harpe traveled the backwoods of Kentucky and Tennessee in a violent, year-long killing spree that left at least twenty—and possibly as many as thirty-eight—men, women, and children dead. Their crimes were especially chilling as they seemed particularly to enjoy grabbing small children by the ankles and smashing their heads against trees (Holmes and DeBurger 28). In modern society, however, serial killings have grown to near epidemic proportions. Ann Rule, a respected author and expert on serial murders, stated in a seminar at the University of Louisville on serial murder that between 3,500 and 5,000 people become victims of serial murder each year in the United States alone (qtd. in Holmes and DeBurger 21). Many others estimate that there are close to 350 serial killers currently at large in our society (Holmes and DeBurger 22).

The cause-effect relationship is raised in a question: What (the causes) makes a serial killer (the effect)?

An important term (serial killer) is defined through examples.

Authority is cited to emphasize the importance of the causal question.

La Donna Beaty wrote this essay while she was a student at Sinclair Community College in Dayton, Ohio. In the essay, she explores the complex web of possible causes—cultural, psychological, genetic, and others—that may help to produce a serial killer. The essay follows MLA style.

Fascination with murder and murderers is not new, but researchers in recent years have made great strides in determining the characteristics of criminals. Looking back, we can see how naive early experts were in their evaluations: in 1911, for example, Italian criminologist Cesare Lombrosco concluded that "murderers as a group [are] biologically degenerate [with] bloodshot eyes, aquiline noses, curly black hair, strong jaws, big ears, thin lips, and menacing grins" (qtd. in Lunde 84). Today, however, we don't expect killers to have fangs that drip human blood, and many realize that the boy-next-door may be doing more than woodworking in his basement. While there are no specific physical characteristics shared by all serial killers, they are almost always male and 92 percent are white. Most are between the ages of twenty-five and thirty-five and often physically attractive. While they may hold a job, many switch employment frequently as they become easily frustrated when advancement does not come as quickly as expected. They tend to believe that they are entitled to whatever they desire but feel that they should have to exert no effort to attain their goals (Samenow 88, 96). What could possibly turn attractive, ambitious human beings into cold-blooded monsters?

Evidence about general characteristics of serial killers is presented.

One popular theory suggests that many murderers are the product of our violent society. Our culture tends to approve of violence and find it acceptable, even preferable, in many circumstances (Holmes and DeBurger 27). According to research done in 1970, one out of every four men and one out of every six women believed that it was appropriate for a husband to hit his wife under certain conditions (Holmes and DeBurger 33). This emphasis on violence is especially prevalent in television programs. Violence occurs in 80 percent of all prime-time shows, while cartoons, presumably made for children, average eighteen violent acts per hour. It is estimated that by the age of eighteen, the average child will have viewed more than 16,000 television murders (Holmes and DeBurger 34). Some experts feel that children demonstrate increasingly aggressive behavior with each violent act they view (Lunde 15) and become so accustomed to violence that these acts

One possible cause is explored: violence in society.

Evidence, including statistics and authority, is offered to support the first cause.

seem normal (35). In fact, most serial killers do begin to show patterns of aggressive behavior at a young age. It is, therefore, possible that after viewing increasing amounts of violence, such children determine that this is acceptable behavior; when they are then punished for similar actions, they may become confused and angry and eventually lash out by committing horrible, violent acts.

A second possible cause is introduced: family context.

Another theory concentrates on the family atmosphere into which the serial killer is born. Most killers state that they experienced psychological abuse as children and never established good relationships with the male figures in their lives (Ressler, Burgess, and Douglas 19). As children, they were often rejected by their parents and received little nurturing (Lunde 94; Holmes and DeBurger 64–70). It has also been established that the families of serial killers often move repeatedly, never allowing the child to feel a sense of stability; in many cases, they are also forced to live outside the family home before reaching the age of eighteen (Ressler, Burgess, and Douglas 19–20). Our culture's tolerance for violence may overlap with such family dynamics: with 79 percent of the population believing that slapping a twelve-year-old is either necessary, normal, or good, it is no wonder that serial killers relate tales of physical abuse (Holmes and DeBurger 30; Ressler, Burgess, and Douglas 19–20) and view themselves as the "black sheep" of the family. They may even, perhaps unconsciously, assume this same role in society.

Evidence is offered in support of the second cause.

An alternative analysis of the evidence in support of the second cause is explored.

While the foregoing analysis portrays the serial killer as a lost, lonely, abused, little child, another theory, based on the same information, gives an entirely different view. In this analysis, the killer is indeed rejected by his family but only after being repeatedly defiant, sneaky, and threatening. As verbal lies and destructiveness increase, the parents give the child the distance he seems to want in order to maintain a small amount of domestic peace (Samenow 13). This interpretation suggests that the killer shapes his parents much more than his parents shape him. It also denies that the media can influence a child's mind and turn him into something that he doesn't already long to be. Since most children view similar amounts of violence, the argument goes, a responsible child filters what he sees and will not resort to criminal activity no matter how acceptable it seems to be (Samenow 15–18). In 1930, the noted psychologist Alfred Adler seemed to find this true of any criminal. As he put it, "With criminals it is different: they have a private logic, a private intelligence. They are suffering from a wrong outlook upon the world, a wrong estimate of their own importance and the importance of other people" (qtd. in Samenow 20).

Most people agree that Jeffrey Dahmer or Ted Bundy had to be "crazy" to commit horrendous multiple murders, and scientists have long maintained that serial killers are indeed mentally disturbed (Lunde 48). While the percent- *A third possible* age of murders committed by mental hospital patients is *cause is introduced:* much lower than that among the general population (35), *mental instability.* it cannot be ignored that the rise in serial killings hap- pened at almost the same time as the deinstitutionaliza- tion movement in the mental health care system during the 1960s (Markman and Bosco 266). While reform was *Evidence in support* greatly needed in the mental health care system, it has *of the third cause,* now become nearly impossible to hospitalize those with *including a series of* severe problems. In the United States, people have a con- *examples, is offered.* stitutional right to remain mentally ill. Involuntary com- mitment can only be accomplished if the person is deemed dangerous to self, dangerous to others, or gravely disabled. However, in the words of Ronald Markman, "According to the way that the law is interpreted, if you can go to the mailbox to pick up your Social Security check, you're not gravely disabled even if you think you're living on Mars"; even if a patient is thought to be danger- ous, he or she cannot be held longer than ninety days unless it can be proved that the patient actually commit- ted dangerous acts while in the hospital (Markman and Bosco 267). Many of the most heinous criminals have had long histories of mental illness but could not be hospital- ized due to these stringent requirements. Richard Chase, the notorious Vampire of Sacramento, believed that he needed blood in order to survive, and while in the care of a psychiatric hospital, he often killed birds and other small animals in order to quench this desire. When he was released, he went on to kill eight people, one of them an eighteen-month-old baby (Biondi and Hecox 206). Edmund Kemper was equally insane. At the age of fifteen, he killed both of his grandparents and spent five years in a psychiatric facility. Doctors determined that he was "cured" and released him into an unsuspecting society. He killed eight women, including his own mother (Lunde 53–56). In another case, the world was soon to be disturbed by a cataclysmic earthquake, and Herbert Mullin knew that he had been appointed by God to prevent the catastrophe. The fervor of his religious delusion resulted in a death toll of thirteen (Lunde 63–81). All of these men had been treated for their mental disorders, and all were released by doctors who did not have enough proof to hold them against their will.

A fourth possible cause is introduced: genetic makeup.

Recently, studies have given increasing consideration to the genetic makeup of serial killers. The connection between biology and behavior is strengthened by research in which scientists have been able to develop a violently aggressive strain of mice simply through selective inbreeding (Taylor 23). These studies have caused scientists to become increasingly interested in the limbic system of the brain, which houses the amygdala, an almond-shaped structure located in the front of the temporal lobe. It has long been known that surgically altering that portion of the brain, in an operation known as a lobotomy, is one way of controlling behavior. This surgery was used frequently in the 1960s but has since been discontinued as it also erases most of a person's personality. More recent developments, however, have shown that temporal lobe epilepsy causes electrical impulses to be discharged directly into the amygdala. When this electronic stimulation is re-created in the laboratory, it causes violent behavior in lab animals. Additionally, other forms of epilepsy do not cause abnormalities in behavior, except during seizure activity. Temporal lobe epilepsy is linked with a wide range of antisocial behavior, including anger, paranoia, and aggression. It is also interesting to note that this form of epilepsy produces extremely unusual brain waves. These waves have been found in only 10 to 15 percent of the general population, but over 79 percent of known serial killers test positive for these waves (Taylor 28–33).

Statistical evidence in support of the fourth cause is offered.

The look at biological factors that control human behavior is by no means limited to brain waves or other brain abnormalities. Much work is also being done with neurotransmitters, levels of testosterone, and patterns of trace minerals. While none of these studies is conclusive, they all show a high correlation between antisocial behavior and chemical interactions within the body (Taylor 63–69).

One of the most common traits that all researchers have noted among serial killers is heavy use of alcohol. Whether this correlation is brought about by external factors or whether alcohol is an actual stimulus that causes certain behavior is still unclear, but the idea deserves consideration. Lunde found that the majority of those who commit murder had been drinking beforehand and commonly had a urine alcohol level of between .20 and .29, nearly twice the legal level of intoxication (31–32). Additionally, 70 percent of the families that reared serial killers had verifiable records of alcohol abuse (Ressler, Burgess, and Douglas 17). Jeffrey Dahmer had been arrested in 1981 on charges of drunkenness and, before his release from prison on sexual assault charges, his father had written a heartbreaking letter which pleaded that Jeffrey be forced to undergo treatment for alcoholism, a plea that, if heeded, might have changed the course of future events (Davis 70, 103). Whether alcoholism is a learned behavior or an inherited predisposition is still hotly debated, but a 1979 report issued by Harvard Medical School stated that "[a]lcoholism in the biological parent appears to be a more reliable predictor of alcoholism in the children than any other environmental factor examined" (qtd. in Taylor 117). While alcohol was once thought to alleviate anxiety and depression, we now know that it can aggravate and intensify such moods (Taylor 110), which may lead to irrational feelings of powerlessness that are brought under control only when the killer proves he has the ultimate power to control life and death.

A fifth possible cause — heavy use of alcohol — is introduced and immediately qualified.

The complexity of causal relationships is emphasized: one cannot say with certainty what produces a particular serial killer.

The conclusion looks toward the future: the web of causes examined here suggests that much more work needs to be done to understand, predict, and ultimately control the behavior of potential serial killers.

"Man's inhumanity to man" began when Cain killed Abel, but this legacy has grown to frightening proportions, as evidenced by the vast number of books that line the shelves of modern bookstores—row after row of titles dealing with death, anger, and blood. We may never know what causes a serial killer to exact his revenge on an unsuspecting society. But we need to continue to probe the interior of the human brain to discover the delicate balance of chemicals that controls behavior. We need to be able to fix what goes wrong. We must also work harder to protect our children. Their cries must not go unheard. Their pain must not become so intense that it demands bloody revenge. As today becomes tomorrow, we must remember the words of Ted Bundy, one of the most ruthless serial killers of our time: "Most serial killers are people who kill for the pure pleasure of killing and cannot be rehabilitated. Some of the killers themselves would even say so" (qtd. in Holmes and DeBurger 150).

Works Cited

Biondi, Ray, and Walt Hecox. *The Dracula Killer*. New York: Simon, 1992.

Davis, Ron. *The Milwaukee Murders*. New York: St. Martin's, 1991.

Holmes, Ronald M., and James DeBurger. *Serial Murder*. Newbury Park, CA: Sage, 1988.

Lunde, Donald T. *Murder and Madness*. San Francisco: San Francisco Book, 1976.

Markman, Ronald, and Dominick Bosco. *Alone with the Devil*. New York: Doubleday, 1989.

Ressler, Robert K., Ann W. Burgess, and John E. Douglas. *Sexual Homicide—Patterns and Motives*. Lexington, MA: Heath, 1988.

Samenow, Stanton E. *Inside the Criminal Mind*. New York: Times, 1984.

Taylor, Lawrence. *Born to Crime*. Westport, CT: Greenwood, 1984.

File Sharing: Guilty as Charged?

DAMIEN CAVE

DOES MP3 FILE TRADING HURT THE MUSIC INDUSTRY?

It's a question that has caused heated debate ever since Napster exploded on the scene in 1999. And as sales of recorded music have declined over the past two years, it's a question that has taken on ever-greater importance — for the music business, Congress and music fans.

Up until recently, there has been little hard data to support anyone's claims that file trading is hurting — or helping — music sales. But at least one researcher, University of Texas (at Dallas) economist Stan Liebowitz, author of an upcoming book titled *Rethinking the Network Economy*, is digging hard for quantitative answers.

In May, Liebowitz published a paper suggesting that the record industry would soon be seriously harmed by MP3s. But in June, by the time Salon caught up with him, he was questioning his own conclusions after having examined the numbers and finding little solid proof that file sharing was hurting CD sales.

Two months later, he's changed his mind again. Sort of. In an insightful, yet-to-be published paper that analyzes 30 years of record sales figures, Liebowitz argues that MP3s are in fact having a significant negative effect on the CD market. He acknowledges that new data could once again lead to new conclusions, but for now, Liebowitz says, "I've moved somewhat closer to the record company position."

Salon called Liebowitz at his home in Dallas to discuss his findings.

When we last spoke, you said you had yet to find proof of harm from MP3s. What's changed?
The one big piece of evidence that I didn't have when we talked before was a half-year 2002 number [that appears to indicate a 9.8 percent decrease in album sales]. There has to be a caveat in here, which is that I don't know if this number is correct. It's a half-year number that I saw in *USA Today*, from SoundScan.

Damien Cave, a senior writer for Salon.com, has written numerous articles on technology. The selection reprinted here, from August 23, 2002, contains an interview with Stan Liebowitz, an economist at the University of Texas.

If it were the case that there was a 9.8 percent drop on albums, when you look at the historical record of the ups and downs of the CD industry, [that's] a bigger decline than we've seen in 30 years. It starts to look unusual.

How much bigger is the decline? Is it a significant drop or a slight depression?

I haven't figured out the percentage but it's definitely bigger than the other ones. Now, let me add another point. When we last spoke, we were talking about a 5 percent decline in sales and I said, "Look, if this is a recession then a 5 percent decline isn't so unusual." At that time, I had assumed that record sales moved with income; during a recession, you could expect fewer records to be sold. When I actually ran the numbers, with income as a variable, it had a very small impact. It was what is known as statistically significant but it was so small that you could ignore it. So in fact, you couldn't conclude that because we're having a recession, you might expect a 5 percent reduction in record sales. That's the other prop I was leaning on. . . . There's evidence that something different is going on.

But assuming SoundScan's figures are correct, your paper seems to hang on a matter of degree. If 2002 sales are down 9.8 percent, you argue, and if this continues, the decline will be the biggest in 30 years. But aren't there other possible reasons for the decline?

I mention that there are these supposed instances of doldrums in musical creativity and you read about them from time to time. But it's a hard thing, at the moment, to measure that.

But isn't it possible that the intersection of several other unprecedented factors wholly independent of MP3s could be causing the decline in sales?

That's right. It is certainly not conclusive, by any means, that there's real damage going on from MP3s. It could be that we're having a bit of doldrums in terms of taste; it could be that we're all using CDs now and nothing else, so since they're a little more durable than other formats that could be part of it. But it is at least beginning to look like there is damage being caused. But remember, the original story was that there's so much MP3 downloading going on so we should see a really big impact fairly easy. And now we're seeing a medium impact, which still could be explained by other things—but we can't discount the MP3 possibility.

If the record industry is somehow not able to stop the downloading, I think we'll know by 2003. We'll get the end of the 2002 year numbers when December's over. We'll see what actually happened. And I expect that by 2003, whatever's going to happen will have happened. This is a great experiment for people who are curious about issues like this. We'll eventually find out. So while it's premature to say this is the smoking gun that shows that harm is there, it is certainly more indicative of harm than what had been there with just the 2001 numbers.

In your paper you argue that MP3s will create a 20 percent decline in sales. How did you get this figure?
I may be going out on a limb in trying to do that but what I'm saying is, let's throw out the fact that cassettes are dying, because that seems to be happening on its own. If we remove that, and assume that half the computer owners have CD burners—a number that I've seen—you just double the decline that's already occurred. It should be less than that because the people who would be doing the most burning would be the ones who already have the burners. So that's where I come up with that number. That's not the death of the industry, but it's a severe decline.

Is this decline significant enough to justify new laws, like the Berman bill, which would give copyright owners the power to hack into people's computers to stop copying and trading?
In my own mind, I don't think a 20 percent decline warrants letting them override the other laws we have out there saying that you're not supposed to tamper with people's computers. That's my own view.

If [file-trading] was going to kill the record industry, you could understand why the record industry would be willing to go to any lengths to get [the Berman bill] passed. They also might be willing to do that for 20 percent if they're not paying the costs. But is society willing to impose a law like this on the public to protect the industry from a 20 percent decline?

If the industry wants to prosecute 18-year-old kids, they can make that decision. But I suspect I wouldn't be in favor of that if the government is going to be prosecuting 18-year-old kids. You don't want to, in my mind, create a situation in which we're saying that a large proportion of our population are criminals unless you think that there's some really strong reason to do that.

People can debate whether, say, criminalizing marijuana and making so many people violate the law is good or bad, but at least you have to understand what the costs and benefits are. And at least the people who are in favor of criminalizing it think it's a terrible, terrible thing. If you're going to do that [with file trading], you have to ask if in fact there's a terrible thing going on. Is a 20 percent decline enough of a problem to say that we should go after these kids? If the record industry wants to foot the bill, because they think the benefits are greater than the costs, fine. But I don't want my district attorney spending my money going after 18-year-old kids who are downloading if it's only going to cause a 20 percent decline in sales for the industry.

When we last spoke, you said that a key historical sign would come from whether the introduction of audiocassettes had a negative effect on music sales. Your analysis here argues that tapes had no effect on sales, and if anything, sales went up when cassettes were introduced. What makes you think MP3s will be different?
The net effect of tapes was positive. But it doesn't mean that it wouldn't have been more positive if people weren't making more copies. [What is clear is that] there's no evidence in the data that the tapes caused a decline.

MP3s wouldn't do the same thing. The reason cassettes led to growth was that before cassettes existed, you didn't have portable music. You couldn't play recorded music in your car, and you couldn't play it walking around, in a Walkman. It was the little cassette that basically allowed you to do that. To be technically correct, there were 8-track players prior to cassettes. But they didn't have quite the same penetration. My theory as to what went on is that [the rise in cassettes] coincides almost perfectly with the penetration rate of the portable, Walkman type of thing. So it opened up this whole new market, which overwhelmed any copying that went on.

You mention that price doesn't matter because album prices have tracked with inflation for the last 30 years: A 10-song recording today costs as much as it did in the '70s. This runs counter to the public perception that CDs are wildly overpriced, and I'm wondering if people think CDs are expensive because other musical components such as CD players have decreased in price, while CDs have not . . .
It's possible, but the technology in creating stereos is not necessarily related to the technology used to create CDs. If you take a look at the book *Entertainment Industry Economics*, the author goes through the cost of a CD, and in his older editions, he goes through the cost of an LP or a cassette. And the majority of the cost is not the production of the actual physical item. That may go down, but the majority of the costs are the other costs:

publicizing albums, finding talent. There's no reason to think that those are going down because they're not technology-based. The small part, technology, is 15 percent of the item and that may be going down, but it doesn't have much of an impact. It's really amazing how prices have tracked so closely with inflation. It's almost as if the industry just bumps up prices with the inflation rate.

You also point out in your paper that there's been no differentiation in price when it comes to music, which is radically different from most markets for other products, such as TVs, for example, which come in a variety of sizes and prices. Do you think the industry needs to abandon this business model? Could this be a solution to the problem of MP3s?
I don't know if that's necessary but one of the things that the entertainment industry has always been really good at is differentiating products. With movies, you have the theater, the tapes, the pay-per-view, the HBO, then the TV. To me, the interesting thing is that historically, the record industry hasn't done much differentiation. What you might have expected was, say, a CD that was half the price of current high-quality CDs that just has a lower sampling rate. With MP3s, for example, when you rip a CD, you have a choice about whether you want to have CD-quality or near-CD quality or FM-radio quality. When you're playing music on low-quality stereos, you wouldn't really hear the difference. So one of the things the industry could do with their downloads is have different prices. People with high-quality stereos aren't going to want to put the low-quality material on, and the people who have lower-quality stereos, with speakers that are incapable of producing the frequencies that let you hear the difference, then they'll buy the cheap ones. That would be a way to broaden the market and increase their revenues. In a way it's surprising that the industry hasn't done that. And as they are trying to figure out their models for online sales, that would be one way of doing it.

How willing do you think the industry is to make such changes?
That depends on the individuals involved. But the fact of the matter is that if they're too rigid, they'll get replaced by some start-up that's not. That much is certain. You can't be terribly inefficient, terribly rigid and hang on.

chapter twelve

Proposals

A student looking forward to a much-needed vacation emails three friends proposing that they pool their resources and rent a cottage at a nearby surfing beach.

A cartoonist works to develop a cartoon arguing that for-profit health care may well kill the (national) patient.

The members of a club for business majors begin to talk about their common need to create informative, appealing—and easily scannable—résumés. After much talk, three members suggest that the club develop a Web site that will guide members in building such résumés and provide links to other resources.

A project team at a large consulting engineering firm works for three months developing a proposal in response to an RFP (request for proposal) to convert a military facility to a community camp.

Members of a youth activist organization propose to start an afterschool program for neighborhood kids, using the organization's meeting place and volunteering their time as tutors and mentors.

The undergraduate student organization at a large state university asks the administration for information about how long it takes to complete a degree in each academic major. After analyzing this information, the group recommends a reduction in the number of hours needed to graduate.

■ ■ ■

UNDERSTANDING AND CATEGORIZING PROPOSALS

How many proposals do you make or respond to every day? Chances are, more than a few: Your roommate suggests you both skip breakfast in order to get in an extra hour of exercise; you and a colleague decide to go out to dinner rather than work late once again; you call your best friend to propose checking out a new movie; you decide to approach your boss about implementing an idea you've just had. In each case, the proposal implies that some action should take place and implicitly suggests that there are good reasons why it should.

In their simplest form, proposal arguments look something like this:

A should do B because of C.

⌐A⌐ ⌐———————————— B ————————————⌐
We should see Eminem's *Eight Mile* tonight
⌐——————————————————— C ———————————————————⌐
because both the *New York Times* and *Rolling Stone* (reluctantly) gave it good reviews.

Because proposals come at us in so many ways, it's no surprise that they cover a dizzyingly wide range of possibilities, from very local and concrete practices (*A student should switch dorms immediately; A company should switch from one supplier of paper to another*) to very broad matters of policy (*The United States Congress should repeal the Homeland Security Act*). So it may help to think of proposal arguments as divided roughly into two kinds—those that focus on practices, and those that focus on policies. Here are several examples:

PROPOSALS ABOUT PRACTICES

- The city should use brighter lightbulbs in employee parking garages.
- The college should allow students to pay tuition on a month-by-month basis.
- College Bowl games should all be held during a two-day period.

PROPOSALS ABOUT POLICIES

- Congress should institute a national youth service plan.
- The college should adopt a policy guaranteeing a "living wage" to all campus workers.
- The state should repeal all English Only legislation.

CHARACTERIZING PROPOSALS

Proposals have three main characteristics:

- They call for action.
- They focus on the future.
- They center on the audience.

Proposals always call for some kind of action; they aim at getting something done. So while proposals may rely on analysis and careful reflection about ideas and information, these strategies all aim to urge the audience to decide what to do. This feature of proposals will almost always present a challenge, one put very well in the old saying, "You can lead a horse to water, but you can't make it drink." You can present a proposal as cogently and compellingly as possible—but most of the time you can't *make* the audience take the action you propose. Thus proposal arguments must stress the ethos of the writer: if your word and experience and judgment are all credible, the audience is more likely to carry out the action you propose.

In addition, proposal arguments focus on the future, which the actions proposed will affect. Aristotle referred to such arguments as *deliberative* and associated them with the work of government, which is most often concerned with what a society should do over the upcoming years or decades. This future orientation also presents special challenges, since few of us have crystal balls that predict the future. Proposal arguments must therefore concentrate on marshaling all available evidence to demonstrate that the proposed action is very likely to produce the effects it sets out to achieve.

Finally, proposal arguments are highly focused on audience and audience response, since the success of the argument often (if not always) depends on the degree to which the audience agrees to carry out the proposed action.

Let's say that as president of your church youth organization, you decide to propose that the group take on a community tutoring project. Your proposal aims at action: you want members to do volunteer tutoring in an after-school program at the local community center. Your proposal is also future-oriented: you believe that such a project would help teach your group's members about conditions in the inner city as well as help inner-city children in ways that could make them more successful in future schooling. And certainly your proposal is heavily audience-dependent, because only if you can convince members that such service is needed, that it is feasible and likely to achieve the desired effects, and that it will be beneficial to members and to the organization, is your proposal likely to be acted on positively.

In a humorous proposal argument called "Gloom, Gloom, Go Away," Walter Kirn focuses on action—he wants the United States to institute an "emergency extension of daylight saving time, whose ending a couple of weeks ago plunged a lot of folks I know into a funk they still haven't recovered from." Arguing that "desperate times call for desperate measures," Kirn points out that one such measure has traditionally been "to goose our biorhythms by monkeying with the clock." This tongue-in-cheek proposal is certainly action- and future-oriented. But it also appeals directly to its audience, assuming that "winter brings darkness that we don't need right now" and describing the uplifting benefits of "sunlit winter evenings."

In the advertisement on the following page, Americans for the Arts argues "there's not enough art in our schools." The argument targets its audience—parents—in several explicit ways.

FIGURE 12.1 THIS ADVERTISEMENT BY AMERICANS FOR THE ARTS MAKES A CLEAR
PROPOSAL.

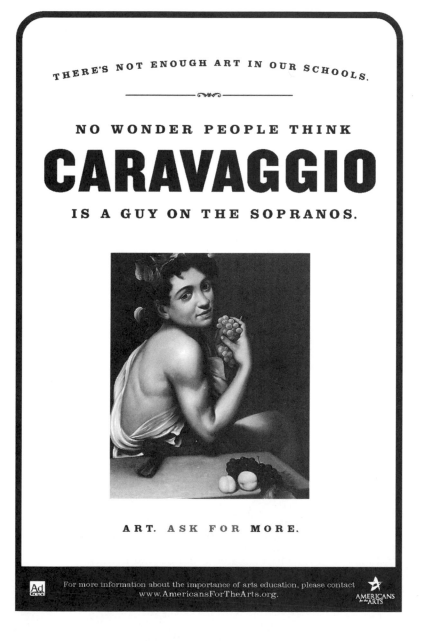

DEVELOPING PROPOSALS

How do you develop an effective proposal? Start by making a strong and clear claim; then go on to show that the proposal meets a need or solves a problem; present good reasons why adopting the proposal will effectively address the need or problem; and show that the proposal is feasible and should therefore be adopted.

Making a Strong and Clear Claim

Begin with a *claim* (what X or Y should do) followed by the *reason(s)* why X or Y should act and the *effects* of adopting the proposal:

Claim	Communities should encourage the development of charter schools
Reason	because they are not burdened by the bureaucracy associated with most public schooling, and
Effects	because instituting such schools will bring more effective educational progress to the community and offer a positive incentive to the public schools to improve their programs as well.

Having established a claim, you can explore its implications by drawing out the reasons, warrants, and evidence that can support it most effectively:

Claim	Congress should pass a bill legalizing the use of marijuana for medical purposes.
Reason	Medical marijuana is an effective pain reliever for millions suffering from cancer and AIDS.
Warrant	The relief of intractable chronic pain is desirable.
Evidence	Nine states have already approved the use of cannabis for medical purposes, and referendums are planned in many other states. Evidence gathered in large double-blind studies demonstrates that marijuana relieves pain associated with cancer and AIDS.

In this proposal argument the reason sets up the need for the proposal, whereas the warrant and evidence demonstrate that the proposal is just and could meet its objective.

Relating the Claim to a Need or Problem

To be effective, claims must be clearly related to a significant need or problem. Thus establishing that the need or problem exists is one of the most important tasks the writer of a proposal argument faces. For this reason, you should explore this part of any proposal you want to make very early on; if you can't establish a clear need for the proposal or show that it solves an important problem, you should probably work toward a revision or a new claim.

You'll often establish the need or problem at the beginning of your introduction—as a way of leading up to your claim. But in some cases you could put the need or problem right *after* your introduction as the major reason for adopting the proposal. In the preceding examples about charter schools and the use of medical marijuana, a writer might choose either strategy.

Regardless of the practical choices about organization, the task of establishing a need or problem calls on you to

- paint a picture of the need or problem in concrete and memorable ways
- show how the need or problem affects the audience for the argument as well as the larger society
- explain why the need or problem is significant

In an argument proposing that a state board of higher education institute courses that involve students in community service in all state colleges, for example, you might begin by painting a fairly negative picture of a "me first and only" society that is self-absorbed and concentrated only on instant gratification. After evoking such a scene, you might explore how this particular problem affects society in general and the state's colleges in particular: It results in hyper-competition that creates a kind of pressure-cooker atmosphere on campuses; it leaves many of society's most vulnerable members without resources or helping hands; it puts the responsibility of helping people solely in the hands of government, thereby adding to the size and cost of government and raising taxes for all; it deprives many of the satisfaction that helping others can bring, a satisfaction that should be a part of every student's education. Finally, you might demonstrate this problem's importance by relating it to the needs of those who would benefit from various kinds of volunteer service: child care, elder care, health care, community learning, arts and cultural projects—the list of areas affected could go on and on.

Look at how Craig R. Dean, a lawyer and executive director of the Equal Marriage Rights Fund, relates his claim—that the United States should legalize same-sex marriage—to a significant problem (and how he evokes, or renders, the problem):

> In November 1990, my lover, Patrick Gill, and I were denied a marriage license because we are gay. In a memorandum explaining the District's decision, the clerk of the court wrote that "the sections of the District of Columbia code governing marriage do not authorize marriage between persons of the same sex." By refusing to give us the same legal recognition that is given to heterosexual couples, the District has degraded our relationship as well as that of every other gay and lesbian couple.
>
> At one time, interracial couples were not allowed to marry. Gays and lesbians are still denied this basic civil right in the U.S.—and around the world. Can you imagine the outcry if any other minority group was denied the right to legally marry today?
>
> Marriage is more than a piece of paper. It gives societal recognition and legal protection to a relationship. It confers numerous benefits to spouses; in the District alone, there are more than 100 automatic marriage-based rights. In every state in the nation, married couples have the right to be on each other's health, disability, life insurance and pension plans. Married couples receive special tax exemptions, deductions and refunds. Spouses may automatically inherit property and have rights of survivorship that avoid inheritance tax. Though unmarried couples—both gay and heterosexual—are entitled to some of these rights, they are by no means guaranteed.
>
> For married couples, the spouse is legally the next of kin in case of death, medical emergency or mental incapacity. In stark contrast, the family is generally the next of kin for same-sex couples. In the shadow of AIDS, the denial of marriage rights can be even more ominous. . . .
>
> Some argue that gay marriage is too radical for society. We disagree. According to a 1989 study by the American Bar Association, eight to 10 million children are currently being reared in three million gay households. Therefore, approximately 6 percent of the U.S. population is made up of gay and lesbian families with children. Why should these families be denied the protection granted to other families?
>
> Allowing gay marriage would strengthen society by increasing tolerance. It is paradoxical that mainstream America perceives gays and lesbians as unable to maintain long-term relationships while at the same time denying them the very institutions that stabilize such relationships.
>
> −Craig R. Dean, "Legalize Gay Marriage"

Showing That the Proposal Addresses the Need or Problem

An important but tricky part of making a successful proposal lies in relating the claim to the need or problem it addresses. Everyone you know may agree that rising tuition costs at your college constitute a major problem. But will your spur-of-the-moment letter to the college newspaper proposing to reduce the size of the faculty and eliminate all campus bus services really address the problem effectively? Chances are, you would have a very hard time making this connection. On the other hand, proposing that the college establish a joint commission of students, administrators and faculty, and legislative leaders charged with studying the problem and proposing a series of alternatives for solving it would be much more likely to present a clear connection between the problem and the claim.

If you were working on the argument about charter schools, you'd need to show that establishing such schools could successfully tackle at least one of the problems associated with current public education. And in the passage from "Legalize Gay Marriage," the writer must show explicitly how carrying out the recommended action would directly affect the problems he has identified.

Showing That the Proposal Is Workable

To be effective, proposals must be workable: that is, the action proposed can be carried out in a reasonable way. Demonstrating "workability" calls on you to present more evidence—from similar cases, from personal experience, from observational data, from interview or survey data, from Internet research, or from any other sources that help show that what you propose can indeed be done. In addition, it will help your case if you can show that the proposal can be carried out with the resources available. If instead the proposal calls for personnel or funds far beyond reach or reason, your audience is unlikely to accept it. As you think about revising your proposal argument, you can test it against these criteria. In addition, you can try to think of proposals that others might say are better, more effective, or more workable than yours—and you can ask friends to help you think of such counterproposals. If your own proposal can stand up to counterproposals, it's likely a strong one.

Using Personal Experience

If your own experience demonstrates the need or problem your proposal aims to address, or backs up your claim, consider using it to develop your proposal (as Craig R. Dean does in the opening of his proposal to legalize gay marriage). Consider the following questions in deciding when to include your own experiences in making a proposal:

- Is your experience directly related to the need or problem you seek to address, or to your proposal about it?

- Will your experience be appropriate and speak convincingly to the audience? Will the audience immediately understand its significance, or will it require explanation?

- Does your personal experience fit logically with the other reasons you are using to support your claim?

KEY FEATURES OF PROPOSALS

In drafting a proposal, make sure you include:

- a claim that proposes a practice or policy to address a problem or need and that is oriented toward action, directed at the future, and appropriate to your audience

- statements that clearly relate the claim to the problem or need

- evidence that the proposal will effectively address the need or solve the problem, and that it is workable

Fully developing your proposal will call for addressing all these elements, though you may choose to order them in several different ways. As you organize your proposal, you may decide to open with an introductory paragraph that paints a dramatic picture of the problem you are addressing, and you may decide to conclude with a kind of flashback to this dramatic scene. Or you may choose to start right off with your claim and offer strong support for it before showing the ways in which your proposal addresses a need or solves a problem. In any case, organize your proposal carefully and get response to your organizational plan from your instructor and classmates.

Considering Design

Because proposals often address very specific audiences, they can take any number of forms: a letter or memo, a Web page, a feasibility report, a brochure, a prospectus. Each form has different design requirements; indeed, the design may add powerfully to—or detract significantly from—the effectiveness of the proposal. Even in a college essay written on a computer, the use of white space and margins, headings and subheadings, and variations in type (such as boldface or italics) can guide readers through the proposal and enhance its persuasiveness. So before you produce a final copy of any proposal, make a careful plan for its design. Then get response to the proposal in terms of its content and its design, asking friends, classmates, or instructors to read the proposal and give you their responses. Finally, revise to address all the concerns they raise.

Finding a Topic

Your everyday experience calls on you to make proposals all the time; for example, to spend the weekend snowboarding or doing some other much-loved sport, to change your academic major for some very important reasons, or to add to the family income by starting a small, home-based business. In addition, your community group work or your job may require you to make proposals—to a boss, a board of directors, the local school board, someone you want to impress—the list could go on and on. Of course, you also have many opportunities to make proposals to online groups—with email one click away, the whole world could be the audience for your proposal. In all these cases, you will be aiming to call for action: so why not make an informal list of proposals you'd like to explore in a number of different areas? Or do some freewriting on a subject of great interest to you and see if it leads to a proposal? Either method of exploration is likely to turn up several possibilities for a good proposal argument.

Researching Your Topic

Proposals often call for some research. Even a simple one like "Let's all paint the house this weekend" would raise questions that require some investigation: *Who has the time for the job? What sort of paint will be the best? How much will the job cost?* A proposal that your school board adopt block scheduling would call for careful research into evidence supporting the use of such a system. *Where has it been effective, and why?* And for proposals about social issues (for example, that information on the Internet be freely accessible to everyone, even youngsters), extensive research would be necessary to provide sufficient support. For many proposals, you can begin your research by consulting the following types of sources:

- newspapers, magazines, reviews, and journals (online and print)
- online databases
- government documents and reports
- Web sites and listservs or newsgroups
- books
- experts in the field, some of whom might be right on your campus

In addition, you might decide to carry out some field research: a survey of student opinion on Internet accessibility, for example, or interviews with people who are well informed about your subject.

Formulating a Claim

As you think about and explore your topic, begin formulating a claim about it. To do so, come up with a clear and complete thesis that makes a proposal and states the reasons why this proposal should be followed. To get started on formulating a claim, explore and respond to the following questions:

- What do I know about the proposal I am making?
- What reasons can I offer to support my proposal?
- What evidence do I have that implementing my proposal will lead to the results I want?

Examples of Proposal Claims

- Because Senator Dianne Feinstein is highly principled, is a proven leader, and has a powerful political story to tell, Democrats should consider nominating her as the first woman Presidential candidate.
- Hospitals, state and local security agencies, and even citizens should stockpile surgical masks that could help prevent the rapid spread of plague pneumonia.
- Congress should repeal the Copyright Extension Act, since it disrupts the balance between incentives for creators and the right of the public to information set forth in the U.S. Constitution.
- The Environmental Protection Agency must move immediately to regulate power-plant emissions of carbon dioxide, a leading cause of global warming.

Preparing a Proposal

If your instructor asks you to prepare a proposal for your project, here's a format that may help.

State the thesis of your proposal completely. If you are having trouble doing so, try outlining it in terms of the Toulmin system:

Claim:

Reason(s):

Warrant(s):

Explain why your proposal is important. What is at stake in taking, or not taking, the action you propose?

Identify and describe those readers you most hope to reach with your proposal. Why is this group of readers most appropriate for your proposal? What are their interests in the subject?

Briefly discuss the major difficulties you foresee in preparing your argument. Demonstrating that the action you propose is necessary? Demonstrating that it is workable? Moving the audience beyond agreement to action? Something else?

List the research you need to do. What kinds of sources do you expect to consult?

Note down the format or genre you expect to use: An academic essay? A formal report? A Web site?

Thinking about Organization

Proposals, which can take many different forms, generally include the following elements:

- a clear and strong proposal, including the reasons for taking the action proposed and the effects that taking this action will have: *Our neighborhood should establish a "Block Watch" program that will help reduce break-ins and vandalism, and involve our kids in building neighborhood pride.*

- a clear connection between the proposal and a significant need or problem: *Break-ins and vandalism have been on the rise in our neighborhood for the last three years.*

- a demonstration of ways in which the proposal addresses the need: *A Block Watch program establishes a rotating monitor system for the streets in a neighborhood and a voluntary plan to watch out for others' homes.*

- evidence that the proposal will achieve the desired outcome: *Block Watch programs in three other local areas have significantly reduced break-ins and vandalism.*

- consideration of alternative ways to achieve the desired outcome, and a discussion of why these are not preferable: *We could ask for additional police presence, but funding would be hard to get.*

- a demonstration that the proposal is workable and practical: *Because Block Watch is voluntary, our own determination and commitment are all we need to make it work.*

Getting and Giving Response

All arguments can benefit from the scrutiny of others. Your instructor may assign you to a peer group for the purpose of reading and responding to each other's drafts; if not, make the effort yourself to get some careful response. You can use the following questions to evaluate a draft. If you are evaluating someone else's draft, be sure to illustrate your points with examples. Specific comments are always more helpful than general observations.

The Claim

- Does the claim clearly call for action? Is the proposal as clear and specific as possible?
- Is the proposal too sweeping? Does it need to be qualified? If so, how?
- Does the proposal clearly address the problem it intends to solve? If not, how could the connection be strengthened?
- Is the claim likely to get the audience to act rather than just to agree? If not, how could it be revised to do so?

Evidence for the Claim

- Is enough evidence provided to get the audience to support the proposal? If not, what kind of additional evidence is needed? Does any of the evidence provided seem inappropriate or otherwise ineffective? Why?
- Is the evidence in support of the claim simply announced, or are its significance and appropriateness analyzed? Is a more detailed discussion needed?
- Are any objections readers might have to the claim or evidence adequately addressed?
- What kinds of sources are cited? How credible and persuasive will they be to readers? What other kinds of sources might be more credible and persuasive?
- Are all quotations introduced with appropriate signal phrases ("As Ehrenreich argues") and blended smoothly into the writer's sentences?
- Are all visuals titled and labeled appropriately? Have you introduced them and commented on their significance?

Organization and Style

- How are the parts of the argument organized? Is this organization effective, or would some other structure work better?
- Will readers understand the relationships among the claims, supporting reasons, warrants, and evidence? If not, what could be done to make those connections clearer? Are more transitional words and phrases needed? Would headings or graphic devices help?

- How have you used visual design elements to make your proposal more effective?

- Are the transitions or links from point to point, paragraph to paragraph, and sentence to sentence clear and effective? If not, how could they be improved?

- Is the style suited to the subject? Is it too formal? Too casual? Too technical? Too bland? How can it be improved?

- Which sentences seem particularly effective? Which ones seem weakest, and how could they be improved? Should some short sentences be combined, or should any long ones be separated into two or more sentences?

- How effective are the paragraphs? Do any seem too skimpy or too long? How can they be improved?

- Which words or phrases seem particularly effective, vivid, and memorable? Do any seem dull, vague, unclear, or inappropriate for the audience or the writer's purpose? Are definitions provided for technical or other terms that readers might not know?

Spelling, Punctuation, Mechanics, Documentation, Format

- What errors in spelling, punctuation, capitalization, and the like can you identify?

- Is an appropriate and consistent style of documentation used for parenthetical citations and the list of works cited or references? (See Chapter 22.)

- Does the paper or project follow an appropriate format? Is it appropriately designed and attractively presented? How could it be improved? If it is a Web site, do all the links work?

RESPOND•

1. For each problem and solution, make a list of readers' likely objections to the off-the-wall solution offered. Then propose a more defensible solution of your own and explain why you think it is more workable.

   Problem   Future bankruptcy of the Social Security system in the United States.

   Solution   Raise the age of retirement to eighty.

   Problem   Traffic gridlock in major cities.

   Solution   Allow only men to drive on Mondays, Wednesdays, and Fridays and only women on Tuesdays, Thursdays, and Saturdays. Everyone can drive on Sunday.

   Problem   Increasing rates of obesity in the general population.

   Solution   Ban the sale of all high-fat items in fast-food restaurants, including hamburgers, fries, and shakes.

   Problem   Increasing school violence.

   Solution   Authorize teachers and students to carry handguns.

   Problem   Excessive drinking on campus.

   Solution   Establish an 8:00 P.M. curfew on weekends.

2. We write proposal arguments to solve problems, to change the way things are. But problems are not always obvious; what troubles some people might be no big deal to others.

   To get an idea of the range of problems people face on your campus—some of which you may not even have thought of as problems—divide into groups and brainstorm about things that annoy you on and around campus, including everything from bad food in the cafeterias to 8:00 A.M. classes to long lines at the registrar's office. Ask each group to aim for at least twenty gripes. Then choose one problem and, as a group, discuss how you'd go about writing a proposal to deal with it. Remember that you will need to (a) make a strong and clear claim, (b) show that the proposal meets a clear need or solves a significant problem, (c) present good reasons why adopting the proposal will effectively address the need or problem, and (d) show that the proposal is workable and should be adopted.

3. In the essay "The Fat Tax" (see pages 259–61), Jonathan Rauch playfully proposes a tax on overweight folks as a way to decrease obesity and increase health. Using the Toulmin model discussed in Chapter 8, analyze the proposal's structure. What claim(s) does Rauch make, and what reasons does he give to support the claim? What are the warrants that connect the reasons to the claim? What evidence does he provide? Alternatively, make up a rough outline of Rauch's proposal and track the good reasons he presents in support of his claim.

TWO SAMPLE PROPOSALS

Devastating Beauty

···

TEAL PFEIFER

Collarbones, hipbones, cheekbones — so many bones. She looks at the camera with sunken eyes, smiling, acting beautiful. Her dress is Versace, or Gucci, or Dior, and it is revealing, revealing every bone and joint in her thin, thin body. She looks fragile and beautiful, as if I could snap her in two. I look at her and feel the soft cushion of flesh that surrounds my own joints, my own shoulders and hips that are broad, my own ribs surrounded by skin and muscle and fat. I am not nearly as fragile or graceful or thin. I look away and wonder what kind of self-discipline it takes to become beautiful like the model in my magazine.

By age seventeen a young woman has seen an average of 250,000 ads featuring a severely underweight woman whose body type is, for the most part, unattainable by any means, including extreme ones such as anorexia, bulimia, and drug use, according to Allison LaVoie. The media promote clothing, cigarettes, fragrances, and even food with images like these. In a culture that has become increasingly visual, the images put out for public consumption feature women that are a smaller size than ever before. In 1950, the White Rock Mineral Water girl was 5'4" tall and weighed 140 pounds; now she is 5'10" tall and weighs only 110 pounds, signifying the growing deviation between the weight of models and that of the normal female population (Pipher 184).

Teal Pfeifer wrote this essay during her sophomore year at Stanford University, where she has just declared an English major. Teal plans to complete her undergraduate education in a speedy three years and hopes to travel and write about diverse cultures, including the Native American ones she knows best.

This media phenomenon has had a major effect on the female population as a whole, both young and old. Five to ten million women in America today suffer from an eating disorder related to poor self-image, and yet advertisements continue to prey on insecurities fueled by a woman's desire to be thin. Current estimates reveal that eighty percent of women are dissatisfied with their appearance and forty-five percent of those are on a diet on any given day ("Statistics," *National Eating Disorders Association*). Yet even the most stringent dieting will generally fail to create the paper-thin body so valued in the media, and continuing efforts to do so can lead to serious psychological problems such as depression.

Causal relationship between ads and women's body image is considered.

While many young women express dissatisfaction with their bodies, they are not the only victims of the emaciated images so frequently presented to them. Young girls are equally affected by these images, if not more so. Eighty percent of girls under age ten have already been on a diet and expressed the desire to be thinner and more beautiful (*Slim Hopes*). Thus from a young age, beauty is equated to a specific size. The message girls get is an insidious one: In order to be your best self, you should wear size 0 or 1, yet these clothing sizes are not even available in the children's section of clothing stores. The pressure only grows more intense as girls grow up. According to Liz Dittrich, when eleven- to seventeen-year-old girls were asked to name their number one wish, they overwhelmingly said they wanted to be thinner; twenty-seven percent reported that the images of models exerted direct pressure on them to lose weight. Yet only twenty-nine percent of the girls who wanted to lose weight were medically overweight; the rest were a size that is healthy and should be considered desirable.

Evidence that the problem extends across age groups is provided.

Logical appeals are emphasized.

It is tragic to see so much of the American population obsessed with weight and reaching an ideal that is, for the most part, ultimately unattainable. Equally troubling is the role magazines play in feeding this obsession. When a researcher asked female students from Stanford University to flip through several magazines

The role magazines play in perpetuating the problem is established.

FIGURE 1. YOUNG WOMAN READING MAGAZINE (PERSONAL
PHOTOGRAPH). THIS MAGAZINE'S COVER IMAGE EXEMPLIFIES THE
SEXY, THIN STEREOTYPE.

containing images of glamorized, super-thin models,
sixty-eight percent of the women felt significantly worse
about themselves after viewing the magazine models
(Dittrich). This same study showed that looking at models on a long-term basis leads to stress, depression,
guilt, and lowered self-worth. As Naomi Wolfe points
out in *The Beauty Myth*, thinking obsessively about fat
and dieting has actually been shown to change thought
patterns and brain chemistry.

How do we reject images that are so harmful to the
women and young girls who view them (such as those
appearing in magazines like the one in Figure 1)? Legislation regarding what can be printed and distributed is not
an option because of First Amendment rights. Equally
untenable is the idea of appealing to the industries that

*Alternative propos-
als to address the
problem are consid-
ered and rejected.*

employ emaciated models. As long as the beauty and clothing industry are making a profit from the physically insecure women who view their ads, nothing will change.

What, however, might happen if those women stopped viewing such destructive images and buying the magazines that print them? A boycott is the most effective way to rid the print medium of emaciated models and eliminate the harmful effects they cause. If women stopped buying magazines that target them with such harmful advertising, magazines would be forced to change the selection of ads they print. Such a boycott would send a clear message that women reject the victimization that takes place every time a woman or young girl looks at a skeletally thin model and feels worse about herself. Consumers can ultimately control what is put on the market: If we don't buy, funding for such ads will dry up fast.

The proposal claim: a boycott would effectively solve the problem.

In the past, boycotts have proved effective in effecting change quickly. Rosa Parks, often identified as the mother of the modern-day civil rights movement, played a pivotal role in the Montgomery Bus Boycott in December 1955. In protest of the mistreatment of African Americans on the public transit system, people chose to walk instead of employ the buses. This act was successful not because of the status or influence of the people involved; rather, when seventy-five percent of the people who rode the bus chose to walk instead, the buses lost too much money and were forced to change their treatment of African Americans. The boycott put the people in charge of the public transit system in a new way.

Precedent/example in support of the claim is presented.

Between 1965 and 1973, Cesar Chavez also used boycotts successfully to change wage policies and working conditions for millions of Mexicans and Mexican Americans who were being exploited by growers of grapes and lettuce. In his boycott efforts, Chavez moved on two fronts, asking the workers to withhold their labor and, at the same time, asking consumers to refrain from purchasing table grapes (and later, lettuce) in order to show their support for the workers. In these instances, not only did the boycott force an industry to improve existing

Second precedent/ example in support of the claim is presented.

conditions, but it also created a profound awareness of pressing labor issues, often forming a bond between the workers and the community their labor was benefiting.

As a society, we have much to learn from boycotts of the past, and their lessons can help us confront contemporary social ills. As I have shown, body image and eating disorders are rising at an alarming rate among young girls and women in American society every year. This growing desire for an unrealistically thin body affects our minds and our spirits, especially when we are pummeled dozens of times a day with glamorized images of emaciated and unhealthy women. The resulting anorexia and bulimia that women suffer from are not only diseases that can be cured; they are also ones that can be prevented—if women will take a solid stand against such advertisements and the magazines that publish them. While we are not the publishers or advertisers who choose the pictures of starving women represented in magazines, we are the ones who decide whether or not their images will be consumed. This is where power lies—in the hands of those who hand over the dollars that support the glorification of unhealthy and unrealistic bodies. It is our choice to exert this power and to reject magazines that promote such images.

Severity of the problem is reiterated.

Appeals to emotion underscore the importance of the proposal.

Proposal is reiterated.

WORKS CITED

Dittrich, Liz. "About-Face Facts on the Media." *About Face.* 10 March 2003 <http://www.about-face.org/r/facts/ses.html>.

LaVoie, Allison. "Media Influence on Teens." *The Green Ladies.* 11 March 2003 <http://kidsnrg.simplenet.com/grit.dev/london/g2_jan12/green_ladies/media/>.

Pipher, Mary. *Reviving Ophelia.* New York: Ballantyne, 1994.

Slim Hopes. Dir. Sut Jhally. Prod. Jean Kilbourne. Videocassette. Media Education Foundation, 1995.

"Statistics." *National Eating Disorders Association.* 2002. 14 March 2003 <http://www.nationaleatingdisorders.org>.

Wolfe, Naomi. *The Beauty Myth.* New York: Harper, 2002.

Young woman reading magazine. Personal photograph by author. 14 March 2003.

The Fat Tax:
A Modest Proposal

JONATHAN RAUCH

In September, McDonald's announced plans to cook its fries in healthier oil. And not a moment too soon. Just a few days later the Centers for Disease Control and Prevention announced that in 2000 (the latest year for which final figures are available) the death rate in America, adjusted for the fact that the population is aging, reached an all-time low. Not only that, but life expectancy reached an all-time high, of about seventy-seven years. Obviously, those numbers can mean only one thing: America is in the grip of a gigantic public-health crisis. To wit—an obesity epidemic!

That America is marching fatward seems not to be in doubt. Obesity has risen substantially in recent years, to 31 percent of adults, according to the most recent data from the National Center for Health Statistics. Soft-drink cups are bigger, restaurant portions are larger, and health campaigns condemning fatty foods have persuaded people, wrongly, that they can eat twice as much bread as before, provided that they cut down on the butter. Also not in doubt is that other things being equal, being blubbery, is not good. Still, one cannot help scratching one's head. If Americans are living longer, and if they are dying less (so to speak), and if, as the CDC reports, the proportion rating their own health as excellent or very good has remained at a solid 69 percent for the past five years, what exactly is the problem?

Call me oversensitive, but I think I detect a hint of snobbery in the national anti-fat drive. More than occasionally I read things like a recent article from the online *Bully Magazine*, which was headlined "AMERICA: LAND OF THE FAT, DRUNKEN SLOBS." The author, one Ken Wohlrob, writes, "We're quickly becoming a society of sloths who spend their free hours driving around in SUVs and staring at televisions or computer monitors. . . . [As] if we need more fat, bloated people in America." Do I sniff a trace of condescension here? In the September issue of *The Atlantic* a letter writer named Ken Weiss pointedly (and wrongly) mentioned that

Jonathan Rauch, a senior writer for *National Journal*, wrote this article for *The Atlantic*. Inspired by Jonathan Swift's "A Modest Proposal," another satirical proposal to amend society's ills, "The Fat Tax" presents evidence of an obesity epidemic and offers a solution.

"more than 50 percent of our population is obese" amid a list of ways in which America is inferior to Europe, beginning with our shorter vacations, continuing through our lack of a national health plan, and ending, inevitably, with our "polluting SUVs." It's not just that Americans are fat, apparently. It's that Americans are the kind of people who *would* be fat, in the kind of country that would encourage their piggishness.

What is to be done? The letters pages of magazines are often good places to preview the great bad ideas of tomorrow, and recently three letters in *The New Republic* offered a peek. The first, co-signed by the executive director of the Center for Science in the Public Interest and an academic nutritionist, said that the government should "slap small taxes on junk foods like soft drinks" to generate money for public-health campaigns. The next letter, from someone with the Center for the Advancement of Public Health, in Washington, D.C., said, "No one is suggesting the creation of a refrigerator police, but so long as the government is spending $360 billion per year at the federal level on health through Medicare, Medicaid, and the Children's Health Insurance Program, the government's interest in trying to prevent needless illness and death from obesity is kind of simple." The third letter came from a professor of public-interest law who wrote that he had helped to sue McDonald's for "failing to disclose the fat content of its French fries." He warned that more such suits could be on the way. "As with smoking," he wrote, "health advocates may increasingly be forced" — forced? — "to turn to the courts if legislatures continue to do little or nothing about the problem."

If obesity really is such a big crisis, I want to suggest a different approach, because the ones above seem deficient. For one thing, snack taxes that pay for public-health campaigns, and lawsuits against food companies, seem pretty likely to fatten the wallets of the people advocating them — public-health activists and lawyers — without necessarily making anyone any thinner. Besides, most people snack sensibly, so why should they pay to harangue lazy gluttons? And I know of no conclusive evidence that people are fat because food companies fail to disclose that fries and bacon cheeseburgers are fattening.

It seems to me that the only honest and effective way to confront this issue is to tax not fattening foods or fattening companies but fat people. It is they, after all, who drive up the government's health-care costs, so it is they who should pay. What I propose, then, is to tax people by the pound.

This needn't be very complicated. Fat-tax rates would be set by a National Avoirdupois Governing System (NAGS). To hit the worst offenders the hardest, the tax could be graduated. People would pay one per-pound rate above the "overweight" threshold, and a stiffer rate above the "obese" threshold. Fat people might not like this tax, but of course they could avoid it by becoming thinner.

In fact, I might go further. Carrots often work even better than sticks, so I propose a skinny subsidy to complement the fat tax. People who maintain trim, firm physiques should be rewarded for their public-spiritedness with large tax credits—funded, of course, by the fat tax.

My plan would address the nation's fat epidemic equitably and efficiently. It would make Americans put their money where their mouths are. And did I mention that I weigh 135 pounds?

chapter thirteen

Humorous Arguments

When the local city council passes an ordinance requiring bicyclists to wear helmets to protect against head injuries, a cyclist responds by writing a letter to the editor of the local newspaper suggesting other requirements the council might impose to protect citizens—including wearing earplugs in dance clubs, water wings in city pools, and blinders in City Hall.

A distinguished professor at a prestigious school dashes off a column for the campus paper on a controversial issue, perhaps spending a little less time than she should backing up her claims. The op-ed gets picked up by a Web logger who circulates it nationally and responses flood in—including one from a student who grades the paper like a freshman essay. The professor doesn't get an "A."

An undergraduate who thinks his school's new sexual harassment policy amounts to puritanism parodies it for the school humor magazine by describing in a short fictional drama what would happen if Romeo and Juliet strayed onto campus.

Tired of looking at the advertisements that cover every square inch of the campus sports arena walls, a student sends the college newspaper a satirical "news" article entitled "Sports Arena for Sale—to Advertisers!"

■ ■ ■

UNDERSTANDING HUMOR AS ARGUMENT

Breathes there a college student who doesn't read *The Onion* in its print or online versions? Sure, its humor can be sophomoric, yet that's just fine with many undergraduates. But it's not just four-letter words and bathroom jokes that make young people fans of *The Onion* today or that made their parents avid readers of *The National Lampoon* or even *Mad Magazine*. Nor has *Saturday Night Live* survived almost thirty years on TV because viewers (again, mainly young) want to hear Madonna sing "Fever" or watch the Rolling Stones creak through "Brown Sugar" one more time. No, we suspect that these productions—print and video—have attracted and held audiences for years because they use humor to argue passionately against all that is pompous, absurd, irritating, irrational, venal, hypocritical, and even evil in the adult world. *The Onion* (see Figure 13.1) describes itself as *satire*, and satires are, down deep, powerful assaults on the way things are by people who'd like to see some changes.

In particular, no one who read it is likely to forget the impact of *The Onion*'s post-9/11 issue, famously known as the "Holy F—king Sh-t" issue. Offensive? Sure—potentially. Yet the phrase rang true. It described what many Americans were feeling that dismal autumn but didn't dare admit, even to themselves. The headlines and stories in that issue of *The Onion* helped them put the cataclysmic events in an oddly human perspective: "God Angrily Clarifies 'Don't Kill' Rule"; "Hijackers Surprised to Find Themselves in Hell"; "Not Knowing What Else to Do, Woman Bakes American-Flag Cake"; and, perceptively, "A Shattered Nation Longs to Care About Stupid Bullsh-t Again." Clearly, humor has a point and a place even—perhaps especially—in the toughest of times. It's a powerful form of argument.

FIGURE 13.1 JUST ONE OF MANY SATIRICAL STORIES IN THE OCTOBER 3, 2001 ISSUE OF
THE ONION

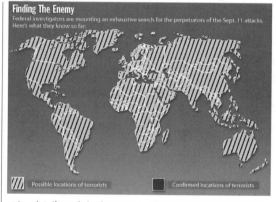

VOLUME 37 ISSUE 34   AMERICA'S FINEST NEWS SOURCE™   27 SEPTEMBER–3 OCTOBER 2001

U.S. Vows To Defeat Whoever It Is We're At War With

WASHINGTON, DC—In a televised address to the American people Tuesday, a determined President Bush vowed that the U.S. would defeat "whoever exactly it is we're at war with here."

"America's enemy, be it Osama bin Laden, Saddam Hussein, the Taliban, a multinational coalition of terrorist organizations, any of a rogue's gallery of violent Islamic fringe groups, or an entirely different, non-Islamic aggressor we've never even heard of... be warned," Bush said during an 11-minute speech from the Oval Office. "The United States is preparing to strike, directly and decisively, against you, whoever you are, just as soon as we have a rough idea of your identity and a reasonably decent estimate as to where your base is located."

Added Bush: "That is, assuming you have a base."

Bush is acting with the full support of Congress, which on Sept. 14 authorized him to use any necessary force against the undetermined attackers. According to House Speaker Dennis Hastert (R-IL), the congressional move enables the president to declare war, "to the extent that war can

Finding The Enemy
Federal investigators are mounting an exhaustive search for the perpetrators of the Sept. 11 attacks. Here's what they know so far:

Possible locations of terrorists   Confirmed locations of terrorists

again, what if we declared war on Afghanistan and they didn't send anyone to fight us? It's plausible that we could

"Christ," McCain continued, "what if the terrorists' base of operation turns out to be Detroit? Would we declare war on the state

---

By its very nature, humor is risky. Playing fast and loose with good taste and sound reason, humorists turn what is comfortable and familiar inside out and hope readers get the joke. If they play it too safe, they lose their audiences; if they step over an unseen line, people groan or hiss or act offended. Humor, especially satire, is a knife's edge that had better cut deep or not at all.

To manage humor, you must understand people and the foibles of human nature. That's because humor often works best when it deals with ordinary life and current events. (You'd be surprised how many Americans get their daily news from the comic monologues of late-night comedians.) Timeliness is what makes comedians seem hip and smart: their sharp minds decide what many people will be chuckling and *thinking* about the next day. But for the same reason, a lot of humor doesn't have the shelf life of lettuce. And some humor doesn't easily cross canyons that divide ethnic groups, classes, or generations. Catholics laugh hardest at jokes about Catholic schools, and Jews doubtless understand Jewish mothers and princesses better than the goyim do.

Obviously, then, humor cannot be learned quickly or easily. But it is too powerful a tool to leave to comedians. For writers and speakers, humor can sharpen any rhetorical strategy, giving heightened presence to appeals to reason, emotion, character, or value.

Humor can simply make people pay attention or feel good—or make them want to buy stuff or do what others ask. That's the rationale behind many "soft sell" commercials, from classic VW pitches of a generation ago ("Think small") to more recent ads for products as different as insurance ("AFLAC!") and computers ("Dude, you're getting a Dell!"). Advertisers use humor to capture your interest and make you feel good about their products. Who focused on AFLAC insurance prior to the duck, Geico before the gecko, or Energizer pre-bunny?

Humor has a darker side, too; it can make people feel superior to its targets of ridicule. And most of us don't want to associate with people who seem ridiculous. Bullies and cliques in secondary school often use humor to torment their innocent victims, behavior that is really nasty. In the political arena, however, politicians may be fairer game, given their resources and ambitions. So when *Saturday Night Live* set out after both George W. Bush and Al Gore Jr. during the presidential campaign season of 2000, the parodies of these men rang true. Voters were left to choose between what was portrayed as a moronic mangler of the English language and a pompous, preening windbag. Does such humor have an effect on voting? Maybe.

Humor plays a large role, too, in arguments of character. If you want audiences to like you, make them laugh. It is no accident that all but the most serious speeches begin with a few jokes or stories. The humor puts listeners at ease and helps them identify with the speaker. In fact, a little self-deprecation can endear writers or speakers to the toughest audiences. You'll listen to people who are confident enough to make fun of themselves because they seem clever and yet aware of their own limitations. No one likes a stuffed shirt.

Humor also works because a funny remark usually contains, at its core, an element of truth:

Clothes make the man. Naked people have little or no influence in society.
—Samuel Clemens

Fame changes a lot of things, but it can't change a light bulb.

–Gilda Radner

Some humor may even involve looking at a subject a little too logically. Dave Barry, for example, analyzes precisely why Florida failed to solve the problems it had counting votes in the 2000 presidential election when it tried again in 2002 (Barry's full piece is reprinted at the end of this chapter):

THE PROBLEM: Voters had trouble understanding a balloting system that required them to punch holes in a piece of cardboard.

SOLUTION A: Use an even simpler system.
SOLUTION B: Use a more complicated system.

Pretty much any life form with a central nervous system, including a reasonably bright squid, would choose Solution A. So naturally our election officials went with Solution B. Yes. Having seen that South Florida voters—people who have yet to figure out how an automobile turn signal works—were baffled by pieces of cardboard, our leaders decided to confront them with . . . computers! And we all know how easy it is to figure out unfamiliar computer systems! That's why the expression "As easy as figuring out an unfamiliar computer system" is so common.

–Dave Barry, "How to Vote in One Easy Step: Use Chisel, Tablet"

Many forms of humor, especially satire and parody, get their power from just such twists of logic. When Jonathan Swift in the eighteenth century suggested in "A Modest Proposal" that Ireland's English rulers consider a diet of fricasseed Irish toddlers, he gambled on readers seeing the parallel between his outrageous proposal and the brutal policies of an oppressive English colonial government. The satire works precisely because it is perfectly logical, given the political facts of Swift's time—though some of his contemporaries missed the joke.

I profess, in the sincerity of my heart, that I have not the least personal interest in endeavoring to promote this necessary work, having no other motive but the public good of my country, by advancing our trade, providing for infants, relieving the poor, and giving some pleasure to the rich.

–Jonathan Swift, "A Modest Proposal"

In our own era, columnist Molly Ivins ridicules opponents of gun control by seeming to agree with them and then adding a logical twist that makes her real point:

I think that's what we need: more people carrying weapons. I support the [concealed gun] legislation but I'd like to propose one small amendment. Everyone should be able to carry a concealed weapon. But everyone who carries a weapon should be required to wear one of those little beanies on their heads with a little propeller on it so the rest of us can see them coming.

– Molly Ivins

CHARACTERIZING KINDS OF HUMOR

It's possible to write whole books about comedy, exploring its many forms such as satire, parody, burlesque, travesty, pastiche, lampoon, caricature, farce, and more. Almost all types of humor involve some kind of argument because laughter can make people think, even while they are having a good time. As we've noted, not all such purposes are praiseworthy; schoolyard bullies and vicious editorial cartoonists may use their humor just to hurt or humiliate their targets. But laughter can also expose hypocrisy or break down barriers of prejudice and thereby help people see their worlds differently. When it is robust and honest, humor is a powerful rhetorical form.

Humor

Humor can contribute to almost any argument, but you have to know when to use it—especially in academic writing. You'll catch a reader's attention if you insert a little laughter to lighten the tone of a serious or dry piece. Here, for example, is the African American writer Zora Neale Hurston addressing the very real issue of discrimination, with a nod and a wink:

> Sometimes I feel discriminated against, but it does not make me angry. It merely astonishes me. How can any deny themselves the pleasure of my company? It's beyond me.
>
> –Zora Neale Hurston, "How It Feels to Be Colored Me"

You might use a whole sequence of comic examples and anecdotes to keep readers interested in a serious point. How might you, for example, make the rather academic point that nurture and socialization alone can't account for certain differences between girls and boys? Here's how Prudence Makintosh, mother of three sons, defends that claim:

> How can I explain why a little girl baby sits on a quilt in the park thoughtfully examining a blade of grass, while my baby William uproots grass by handfuls and eats it? Why does a mother of very

bright and active daughters confide that until she went camping with another family of boys, she feared that my sons had a hyperactivity problem? I am sure there are plenty of noisy, rowdy little girls, but I'm not just talking about rowdiness and noise. I'm talking about some sort of primal physicalness that causes the walls of my house to pulsate on rainy days. I'm talking about something inexplicable that makes my sons fall into a mad, scrambling, pull-your-ears-off-kick-your-teeth-in heap just before bedtime, when they're not even mad at each other. I mean something that causes them to climb the doorjamb with honey and peanut butter on their hands while giving me a synopsis of *Star Wars* that contains only five unintelligible words. . . . When Jack and Drew are not kicking a soccer ball or each other, they are kicking the chair legs, the cat, the baby's silver rattle, and inadvertently, Baby William himself, whom they have affectionately dubbed "Tough Eddy."

–Prudence Makintosh, "Masculine/Feminine"

In reading these words, you can just about feel the angst of a mother who thought she could raise her boys to be different. Most readers will chuckle at little William eating grass, the house pulsating, doorjambs sticky with peanut butter—and appreciate Makintosh's point, whether they agree with it or not. Her intention, however, is not so much to be funny as to give her opinion presence. And, of course, she exaggerates. But exaggeration is a basic technique of humor. We make a situation bigger than life so we can see it better.

Satire

Most of the humor college students write is either satire or parody, which is discussed in the next section. Type "college humor magazines" into the search engine Google and you will find Web sites that list dozens of journals such as the University of Michigan's *Gargoyle*, Penn State's *Phroth*, UC Berkeley's *The Heuristic Squelch*, and Ohio State's *The Shaft*. In these journals you will find humor of all kinds, some pretty raunchy, but much of it aimed at the oddities of college life ranging from unsympathetic administrations to crummy teachers and courses. There is lots of grousing, too, about women and men and campus parking. Much of this material is satire, a genre of writing that uses humor to unmask problems and then suggest (not always directly) how they might be fixed. The most famous piece of satire in English literature is probably Jonathan Swift's *Gulliver's Travels*, which pokes fun at all human shortcomings, targeting especially politics, religion, science, and sexuality. For page after page, Swift argues for change in human character and institutions. In a much different way, so do campus humor magazines.

You'll find social and political satire in television programs such as *The Simpsons* and *Saturday Night Live* and movies such as *This Is Spinal Tap, Dr. Strangelove*, and *Election*. Most editorial cartoons are also satiric when they highlight a problem in society that the cartoonist feels needs to be remedied.

Satire often involves a shift in perspective that asks readers to look at a situation in a new way. In *Gulliver's Travels*, for example, we see human society reduced in scale (in Lilliput), exaggerated in size (in Brobdingnang), even through the eyes of a superior race of horses (the Houyhnhnms). In the land of the giants, Gulliver notices that, up close, women aren't as beautiful as they once seemed to him:

> **Their skins appeared so coarse and uneven, so variously coloured, when I saw them near, with a mole here and there as broad as a trencher, and hairs hanging from it thicker than pack-threads, to say nothing further concerning the rest of their persons.**
> **–Jonathan Swift, *Gulliver's Travels***

So much for human beauty. You'll note that there's nothing especially funny in Gulliver's remarks. That's because satire is sometimes more clever than funny, the point of some satire being to open readers' eyes rather than to make them laugh out loud.

The key to writing effective satire may be finding a humorous or novel angle on a subject and then following through. In other words, you say "What if?" and then employ a kind of mad logic, outlining in great detail all that follows from the question. For example, to satirize groups that believe homosexuals are using the nation's public schools to recruit children to their lifestyle, *The Onion* asks its readers to consider that the charge might be true. For paragraph after paragraph, the satirists let the idea unfold using all the logic and apparatus of a news story happily reporting on the campaign, complete with a graph. You can see from just a few paragraphs how satire of this kind works by making the implausible seem comically real (see Figure 13.2).

Parody

Like satire, parody also offers an argument. What distinguishes the two forms is that parody makes its case by taking something familiar—be

FIGURE 13.2   THE COMPLETE STORY APPEARS IN *THE ONION*, JULY 30, 1998.

⌀ the ONION®

| VOLUME 33 ISSUE 26 | AMERICA'S FINEST NEWS SOURCE™ | 30 JULY–5 AUGUST 1998 |

'98 Homosexual-Recruitment Drive Nearing Goal

SAN FRANCISCO—Spokespersons for the National Gay & Lesbian Recruitment Task Force announced Monday that more than 288,000 straights have been converted to homosexuality since Jan. 1, 1998, putting the group well on pace to reach its goal of 350,000 conversions by the end of the year.

"Thanks to the tireless efforts of our missionaries nationwide, in the first seven months of 1998, nearly 300,000 heterosexuals were ensnared in the Pink Triangle," said NGLRTF co-director Patricia Emmonds. "Clearly, the activist homosexual lobby is winning."

Emmonds credited much of the recruiting success to the gay lobby's infiltration of America's public schools, where programs promoting

phia's Lakeside Elementary School, one of thousands of public schools nationwide that actively promote the homosexual agenda. "I don't want to have a family or go to church."

"Straight people don't have any fun," said Teddy Nance, 11, after watching *Breeders Are Boring!*, an anti-heterosexual filmstrip, in his fifth-grade class at Crestwood Elementary School in Roanoke, VA. "Gay people get to do whatever they want."

In addition to school programs that target youths, the NGLRTF launched a $630 million advertising campaign this year in an effort to convert adults to homosexuality. The campaign, which features TV and radio spots, as well as print advertising in major national magazines, has

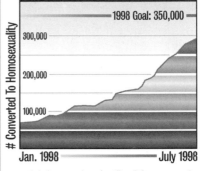

constantly had to worry about things like taking the kids to Little League practice, paying

"For all the progress we've made, America is still overwhelmingly heterosexual,"

---

it songs, passages of prose, TV shows, poems, films, even people—and turning it into something new. The argument sparkles in the tension between the original work and its imitation. That's where the humor lies, too.

Needless to say, parodies work best when audiences make that connection. For instance, you wouldn't entirely appreciate the film *Galaxy Quest* unless you knew the *Star Trek* series, and you could probably name a dozen films that work the same way. A parody of the sitcom *Friends* will likely be pointless fifty years from now unless it has the staying power of *I Love Lucy*. Even today, allusions to President Gerald Ford's clumsiness make sense mostly to those who remember comedian Chevy Chase poking merciless fun at him. Younger people would prefer to laugh at Bill Clinton and George Bush.

Even if the half-life of parody is brief, the form is potent in its prime. Just a few years ago, when a men's movement danced briefly in the national consciousness, Joe Bob Briggs brought the fragile trend to its

FIGURE **13.3**   THE COVER OF THIS COLLEGE HUMOR MAGAZINE MIGHT SEEM PUZZLING
UNLESS YOU RECOGNIZE THAT IT PARODIES SUPERMARKET TABLOIDS.

knees with a ruthless parody of Wild Man weekends, when boorish males
finally got in touch with their inner selves:

> I'll never forget it. I sweated a lot. I cried. I sweated while I was crying.
> Of course, I was crying because they made me sweat so much. We had

> this one part of the weekend where we went into a giant sauna and turned it up to about, oh, 280, until everybody's skin turned the color of strawberry Jell-O and the veins of our heads started exploding, and it turned into this communal out-of-body male thing, where everybody was screaming, "I want out of my body!"
>
> —Joe Bob Briggs, "Get in Touch with Your Ancient Spear"

When a subject or work becomes the object of a successful parody, it's never seen in quite the same way again.

DEVELOPING HUMOROUS ARGUMENTS

It's doubtful anyone can offer a formula for being funny; some would suggest that humor is a gift. But at least the comic perspective is a trait widely distributed among the population. Most people can be funny, given the right circumstances.

However, the stars may not always be aligned when you need them in composing an argument. And just working hard may not help: laughter arises from high-spirited, not labored, insights. Yet once you strike the spark, a blaze usually follows.

Look for humor in obvious situations. Bill Cosby began a stellar career as a humorist with a comedy album that posed the rather simple question: *Why Is There Air?* The late columnist and author Erma Bombeck, too, endeared herself to millions of people by pointing out the humor in daily routines.

Look for humor in incongruity or in "what if?" situations, and then imagine the consequences. *What if men had monthlies? What if reading caused flatulence? What if students hired special prosecutors to handle their grade complaints? What if broccoli tasted like chocolate? What if politicians always told the truth? What if the Pope wasn't Catholic?*

Don't look for humor in complicated ideas. You're more apt to find it in simple premises, for instance, a question Dave Barry once asked: "How come guys care so much about sports?" There are, of course, serious answers to the question. But the humor practically bubbles up on its own once you think about men and their games. You can write a piece of your own just by listing details: *Monday Night Football, sports bars, beer commercials, sagging couches, fantasy camps, 50-inch plasma-screen TVs, Little League, angry wives.* Push a little further, relate such items to personal insights and experiences, and you are likely to discover some of the incongruities and implausibilities at the heart of humor.

Let us stress detail. Abstract humor probably doesn't work for anyone except German philosophers and drunken graduate students. Look for humor in concrete and proper nouns, in people and places readers will recognize but not expect to find in your writing. Consider the technique Dave Barry uses in the following passage defending himself against those who might question his motives for attacking "sports guys":

> **And before you accuse me of being some kind of sherry-sipping ascot-wearing ballet-attending MacNeil-Lehrer-NewsHour-watching wussy, please note that I am a sports guy myself, having had a legendary athletic career consisting of nearly a third of the 1965 season on the track team at Pleasantville High School ("Where the Leaders of Tomorrow Are Leaving Wads of Gum on the Auditorium Seats of Today").**
> **–Dave Barry, "A Look at Sports Nuts—And We Do Mean Nuts"**

Remove the lively details from the passage, and this is what's left:

> **And before you accuse me of being some kind of wussy, please note that I am a sports guy myself, having had an athletic career on the track team at Pleasantville High School.**

Enough said?

KEY FEATURES OF HUMOROUS ARGUMENTS

Drafting humor and revising humor are yin-yang propositions—opposites that complement each other. Think Democrats and Republicans.

Creating humor is, by nature, a robust, excessive, and egotistical activity. It requires assertiveness, courage, and often a (temporary) suspension of good judgment and taste. Whereas drafting more material than necessary usually makes good sense for writers, you can afford to be downright prodigal with humor. Pile on the examples and illustrations. Take all the risks you can with language. Indulge in puns. Leap into innuendo. Be clever, but not childishly obscene. Push your vocabulary. Play with words and have fun.

Then, when you revise, do the opposite. Recall that Polonius in Shakespeare's *Hamlet* is right about one thing: "Brevity is the soul of wit." Once you have written a humorous passage, whether a tooting horn or a full symphonic parody, you must pare your language to the bone. Think: less is more. Cut, then cut again.

That's all there is to it.

Finding a Topic

You may use humor in an argument to

- point out flaws in a policy, proposal, or argument
- suggest a policy of your own
- set people in a favorable frame of mind
- admit weaknesses or deflect criticism
- satirize or parody a position, point of view, or style

Opportunities to use humor in daily life are too numerous to list, but they are much rarer in academic and professional writing. You can find amusing topics everywhere if you think about the absurdities of your job, home life, or surrounding culture. Try to see things you take for granted from radically different perspectives. Or flip-flop the normal order of affairs: Make a small issue cosmic; chop a huge matter to fritters.

Researching Your Topic

You can't exactly research a whimsical argument, but humor does call for some attention to detail. Satires and parodies thrive on actual events, specific facts, telling allusions, or memorable images that can be located in sources or recorded in discussions and conversations. Timeliness is a factor, too; you need to know whom or what your readers will recognize and how they might respond. Seek inspiration for humor in these sources:

- popular magazines, especially weekly journals (for current events)
- TV, including commercials (especially for material about people)
- classic books, music, films, artwork (as inspiration for parodies)
- comedians (to observe how they make a subject funny)

Formulating a Claim

With humorous arguments, satires, and parodies, you won't so much develop a thesis as play upon a theme. But humor of the sort that can grow for several pages does need a focal point, a central claim that requires support and evidence—even if that support strains credulity. (In fact, it probably should.) Here are lines to kick-start a humorous argument:

- What if . . . ?
- What would happen if . . . ?
- Why is it that . . . ?

- How come . . . never happens to . . . ?
- When was the last time you tried to . . . ?
- Why is it that men/women . . . ?
- Can you believe that . . . ?

Preparing a Proposal

If your instructor asks you to prepare a proposal for a satire, parody, or other humorous argument, here's a format you might use (or parody!).

Explain the focus of your project.

Articulate the point of your humor. What is at stake? What do you hope to accomplish?

Specify any models you have for your project. Who or what are you trying to emulate? If you are writing a parody, what is your target or inspiration?

Explain whom you hope to reach by your humor and why this group of readers will be amused.

Briefly discuss the key challenges you anticipate: Defining a point? Finding comic ideas?

Identify the sources you expect to consult. What facts might you have to establish?

Determine the format you expect to use for your project. A conventional paper? A letter to the editor? A Web page?

Thinking about Organization

Humorous arguments can be structured exactly like more serious ones—with claims, supporting reasons, warrants, evidence, qualifiers, and rebuttals. In fact, humor has its own relentless logic. Once you set an argument going, you should press it home with the same vigor you apply in serious pieces.

If you write a parody, you need to be thoroughly familiar with the work on which it is based, particularly its organization and distinctive features. In parodying a song, for example, you've got to be sure listeners recognize familiar lines or choruses. In parodying a longer piece, boil it down to essential elements—the most familiar actions in the plot, the most distinctive characters, the best-known passages of dialogue—and then arrange those elements within a compact and rapidly moving design.

Getting and Giving Response

All arguments can benefit from the scrutiny of others. Your instructor may assign you to a peer group for the purpose of reading and responding to each other's drafts; if not, go out of your way to get some careful response. You can use the following questions to evaluate your own draft, to secure response to it from others, or to prepare a response to a colleague's work. If you are evaluating someone else's draft, be sure to supply examples to illustrate your points. Most writers respond better to specific comments than to general observations.

Focus

- Is the argument funny? Would another approach to the topic — even a serious one — be more effective?
- Does the humor make a clear argumentative point? Is its target clear?
- If the piece is a satire, does it suggest a better alternative to the present situation? If not, does it need to?

Logic, Organization, and Format

- Is there logic to the humor? If so, will readers appreciate it?
- Are the points in the argument clearly connected? Are additional or clearer transitions needed?
- Does the humor build toward a climax? If not, would saving the best laughs for last be more effective?
- Is the piece too long, making the humor seem belabored? If so, how might it be cut?
- Does the format of the piece contribute to the humor? Would it be funnier if it were formatted to look like a particular genre — an advertisement, an email message, a sports column, a greeting card? If you've used illustrations, do they enhance the humor? If there are no illustrations, would adding some help?

Style and Detail

- Is the humor too abstract? Does it need more details about specific people, events, and so on?
- If the piece is a parody, does it successfully imitate the features and language of whatever is being parodied?
- Are the sentences wordy or too complex for the type of humor being attempted?
- Are there any problems with spelling, grammar, punctuation, or mechanics?

RESPOND ●

1. For each of the following items, list particular details that might contribute to a humorous look at the subject.

   zealous environmentalists

   clueless builders and developers

   aggressive drivers

   violent Hollywood films

   anti-war or hemp activists

   drivers of lumbering recreational vehicles

   Martha Stewart

   high school coaches

   college instructors

   malls and the people who visit them

2. Spend some time listening to a friend who you think is funny. What kind of humor does he or she use? What sorts of details crop up in it? Once you've put in a few days of careful listening, try to write down some of the jokes and stories just as your friend told them. Writing humor may be excruciating at first, but you might find it easier with practice.

   After you've written a few humorous selections, think about how well they translate from the spoken word to the written. What's different? Do they work better in one medium than in another? Show your written efforts to your funny friend and ask for comments. How would he or she revise your written efforts?

3. Using Internet search tools, find a transcript of a funny television or radio show. Read the transcript a few times, paying attention to the places where you laugh the most. Then analyze the humor, trying to understand what makes it funny. This chapter suggests several possible avenues for analysis, including normality, incongruity, simplicity, and details. How does the transcript reflect these principles? Or does it operate by a completely different set of principles? (Some of the best humor is funny because it breaks all the rules.)

TWO SAMPLE HUMOROUS ARGUMENTS

Texas Nerds Celebrate "Geek Week"

TREVOR ROSEN

Geek Week obviously parodies the Greek weeks common on some campuses.

The humor is in the details here.

CAMPUS—Dorks, dweebs and gaywads from all areas of the UT community will come together this week for the first Annual Texas Geek Week, a celebration of hyperintellectual fetishism and bad fashion sense representing the widely diverse population of lame-o's at the nation's largest University. "We really felt that the campus needed to hear more about the achievements of Texas Geeks," said Fred Sawser, physics sophomore and Texas Geek Week co-chair. "The great things that we do in the fields of role-playing/strategy games and as TAs in engineering classes go largely unheralded, but we'd really like to change all that." Sawser expressed optimism about Texas Geek Week's impact on the other more socially and sexually experienced members of the UT community. "I think that they'll really start to appreciate us—some of us might even get laid." Sawser then laughed through his nose several times in quick succession before characterizing such a possibility as being "freakin' awesome."

Among the events to be held on the West Mall are: a comparison of the relative merits of Lieutenant Uhura and Counselor Troi—of *Star Trek* and *Star Trek: The Next Generation*, respectively, an exhibit on the evolution of the Devorak keyboard, and an interactive rodent-powered robot named JoJo that makes cup after cup of rich, delicious, healthy chocolate Ovaltine.

"I've never seen anything like this," exclaimed wideeyed super geek Winston Morris, taking off his electrical-

---

Trevor Rosen wrote this parody of Greek week activities while editor-in-chief of *The Texas Travesty*, the humor magazine at the University of Texas, Austin. In the essay, Rosen pokes fun at both nerds and Greeks, though the former bear the brunt of his humor. But at least nerds go on to be university presidents.

taped glasses in order to blow his nose on his caffeine molecule t-shirt. "This week just for us is great for Geek publicity. I mean, people have a really bad idea of who geeks are and what they stand for. They think that we're just all about school and D&D and Renaissance Fairs and getting drunk as a duck at our hard-core parties where we smoke out on grape vine and have wild cyber sex—but that's not all we are. Geeks have a rich cultural heritage that goes well beyond stuff like that. Most people think that Geeks are simple, but if anything, we're multifarious. Think hexadecimal, not binary."

The piece pokes fun, too, at campus events celebrating different cultures.

President Faulkner took a time-out from teaching his informal break-dancing class to weigh in with his opinion on Geek Week: "I'm very excited to see that students are taking an interest and reforming the stereotypes that surround geek culture. Where do you think that the people who make the money in this country come from? Look at me, I've got a Ph.D. in chemistry—but love of the covalent bonds didn't hurt me none, did it? I make the mad Benjamins runnin' this piece—probably more in a year than you'll see in a decade. Geek power!"

How to Vote in One Easy Step: Use Chisel, Tablet

DAVE BARRY

Friday, Sept. 13, 2002

The question you're asking yourself is: Does South Florida contain the highest concentration of morons in the entire world? Or just in the United States?

The reason you're asking this, of course, is South Florida's performance in Tuesday's election. This election was critical to our image, because of our performance in the 2000 presidential election—the one that ended up with the entire rest of the nation watching, impatiently, as clumps of sleep-deprived South Florida election officials squinted at cardboard ballots, trying to figure out what the hell the voters were thinking when they apparently voted for two presidents, or no presidents, or part of a president, or, in some cases, simply drooled on the ballot.

Before it was over, we had roughly 23 million lawyers down here—nearly a quarter of the nation's lawyer supply—filing briefs and torts and arguing in endless televised hearings, until finally the whole mess wound up in the U.S. Supreme Court, which declared George W. Bush the winner, but only because it would have been unconstitutional to apply the more logical remedy, which would be to kick Florida out of the union. We were a national joke. The phrase "Florida voter" became a standard comedy-routine synonym for "idiot."

And thus there was a lot of pressure on Florida, and particularly South Florida, to redeem itself in Tuesday's election. We knew that we could not afford to repeat the 2000 fiasco, and our election officials had more than a year and a half to develop, and test, a voting procedure that even we could not screw up.

So what did our election officials do? Let's examine the problem, and two possible solutions:

THE PROBLEM: Voters had trouble understanding a balloting system that required them to punch holes in a piece of cardboard.

SOLUTION A: Use an even simpler system.
SOLUTION B: Use a more complicated system.

Dave Barry is a syndicated columnist and the author of numerous books, including *Dave Barry's Complete Guide to Guys: A Fairly Short Book* (1995), *Dave Barry Is from Mars and Venus* (1997), and *Dave Barry Talks Back* (1991). Barry resides in Florida, so his comments on the 2002 election primaries in that state are especially pointed. As you'll see, his satire is also a proposal argument (see Chapter 12).

Pretty much any life form with a central nervous system, including a reasonably bright squid, would choose Solution A. So naturally our election officials went with Solution B. Yes. Having seen that South Florida voters—people who have yet to figure out how an automobile turn signal works—were baffled by pieces of cardboard, our leaders decided to confront them with . . . computers! And we all know how easy it is to figure out unfamiliar computer systems! That's why the expression "As easy as figuring out an unfamiliar computer system" is so common.

So Miami-Dade County spent $24.5 million on 7,200 computerized voting machines. Broward spent $17.2 million on 5,200 of the same machines. The particular model that we bought is called the "iVotronic."

TIP FOR CONSUMERS: Never buy a product whose manufacturer does not understand the basic rules of capitalization.

But confronting voters with unfamiliar machines does not, by itself, ensure that your election will be a mess. No, to GUARANTEE failure, you need to take additional precautions, such as: (1) Not training poll workers adequately; (2) Providing confusing instructions; (3) Not having enough technical support; (4) Changing the voting-machine software at the last minute.

We managed to make all of these mistakes, and more, which is why today, days later, we are still not 100 percent certain which candidates won on Tuesday. I would not completely rule out Pat Buchanan.

And so once again, South Florida is making life easy for Leno and Letterman. What is the solution? How can we avoid being international laughingstocks in the next election?

My suggestion—call me crazy—is that we print the ballot on paper, with a box next to each candidate's name. We instruct the voters to put an "X" in their candidate's box. Then we have human beings count the "X"s, and the candidate with the most votes wins.

I realize this is a radical system, but I believe that it would be difficult for even South Floridians to screw it up.

We could get our elections over within a single day, like everybody else, and we would have more time to enjoy the pleasures of South Florida.

Such as scuba diving. On our new artificial reef.

Formed by 12,400 iVotronics.

PART 4

STYLISH argument

chapter fourteen

Figurative Language and Argument

Look at any magazine or Web site and you will see figurative language working on behalf of arguments. When the writer of a letter to the editor complains that "Donna Haraway's supposition that because we rely on cell phones and laptops we are cyborgs is [like] saying the Plains Indians were centaurs because they relied on horses," he is using an analogy to rebut (and perhaps ridicule) Haraway's claim. When another writer says that "the digital revolution is whipping through our lives like a Bengali typhoon," she is making an implicit argument about the speed and strength of the digital revolution. When still another writer calls Disney World a "smile factory," she begins a stinging critique of the way pleasure is "manufactured" there.

Just what is figurative language? Traditionally, the terms *figurative language* and *figures of speech* refer to language that differs from the ordinary—language that calls up, or "figures," something else. But in fact, all language could be said to call up something else. The word *table*, for example, is not itself a table; rather, it calls up a table in our imaginations. Thus, just as all language is by nature argumentative, so too is it all figurative. Far from being mere decoration or embellishment (something like icing on the cake of thought), figures of speech are indispensable to language use.

More specifically, figurative language brings two major strengths to arguments. First, it often aids understanding by likening something unknown to something known. For example, in arguing for the existence of DNA as they had identified and described it, scientists Watson and Crick used two familiar examples—a helix (spiral) and a zipper—to make their point. Today, arguments about new computer technologies are filled with similar uses of figurative language. Indeed, Microsoft's entire word-processing system depends on likening items to those in an office (as in Microsoft Office) to make them more understandable and familiar to users. Second, figurative language can be helpful in arguments because it is often extremely memorable. Someone arguing that slang should be used in formal writing turns to this memorable definition for support: "Slang is language that takes off its coat, spits on its hands, and gets to work." In a brief poem that carries a powerful argument, Langston Hughes (see Figure 14.1) uses figurative language to explore the consequences of unfulfilled dreams:

What happens to a dream deferred?
Does it dry up
Like a raisin in the sun?
Or fester like a sore—
And then run?
Does it stink like rotten meat?
Or crust and sugar over—
Like a syrupy sweet?
Maybe it just sags
Like a heavy load.
Or does it explode?

—Langston Hughes, "Harlem—A Dream Deferred"

FIGURE 14.1 WRITER LANGSTON HUGHES

In 1963, Martin Luther King Jr. used figurative language to make his argument for civil rights unmistakably clear as well as memorable:

> In a sense we have come to our nation's capital to cash a check. When the architects of our republic wrote the magnificent words of the Constitution and the Declaration of Independence, they were signing a promissory note to which every American was to fall heir. This note was a promise that all men would be guaranteed the unalienable rights of life, liberty, and the pursuit of happiness.
>
> It is obvious today that America has defaulted on this promissory note insofar as her citizens of color are concerned. Instead of honoring

> this sacred obligation, America has given the Negro people a bad check; a check which has come back marked "insufficient funds." But we refuse to believe that the bank of justice is bankrupt. We refuse to believe that there are insufficient funds in the great vaults of opportunity in this nation. So we have come to cash this check—a check that will give us upon demand the riches of freedom and the security of justice.
>
> —Martin Luther King Jr., "I Have a Dream"

The figures of the promissory note and the bad check are especially effective in this passage because they suggest financial exploitation, which fits perfectly with the overall theme of King's speech.

You may be surprised to learn that during the European Renaissance, schoolchildren sometimes learned and practiced using as many as 180 figures of speech. Such practice seems more than a little excessive today, especially because figures of speech come so naturally to native speakers of the English language; you hear of "chilling out," "taking flak," "nipping a plot in the bud," "getting our act together," "blowing your cover," "marching to a different drummer," "seeing red," "smelling a rat," "being on cloud nine," "throwing in the towel," "tightening our belts," "rolling in the aisles," "turning the screws"—you get the picture. In fact, you and your friends no doubt have favorite figures of speech, ones you use every day. Why not take a quick inventory during one day—just listen to everything that's said around you and take down any figurative language you hear.

We can't aim for a complete catalog of figures of speech here, much less for a thorough analysis of the power of figurative language. What we can offer, however, is a brief listing—with examples—of some of the most familiar kinds of figures, along with a reminder that they can be used to extremely good effect in the arguments you write.

Figures have traditionally been classified into two main types: *tropes*, which involve a change in the ordinary signification, or meaning, of a word or phrase; and *schemes*, which involve a special arrangement of words. Here are the most frequently used figures in each category, beginning with the familiar tropes of metaphor, simile, and analogy.

TROPES

Metaphor

One of the most pervasive uses of figurative language, metaphor offers an implied comparison between two things and thereby clarifies and enlivens many arguments. In the following passage, bell hooks uses the metaphor of the hope chest to enhance her argument that autobiography involves a special kind of treasure hunt:

> Conceptually, the autobiography was framed in the manner of a hope chest. I remembered my mother's hope chest, with its wonderful odor of cedar, and thought about her taking the most precious items and placing them there for safekeeping. Certain memories were for me a similar treasure. I wanted to place them somewhere for safekeeping. An autobiographical narrative seemed an appropriate place.
>
> –bell hooks, *Bone Black*

In another argument, a *New York Times* editorial, calling on the Augusta National Golf Club to admit women members, says, "If next year's gathering becomes a battlefield for women's rights, as seems likely, the Masters will be an embarrassment for the corporate crowd, for CBS and for the nation's top golfers." Here the writer uses the metaphor of a battlefield to describe a famous golf tournament and suggests how transforming the Augusta course into a scene of warfare will have negative consequences.

English language use is so filled with metaphors that these powerful, persuasive tools often zip by unnoticed, so be on the lookout for effective metaphors in everything you read. For example, when a reviewer of new software that promises complete filtering of advertisements on the World Wide Web refers to the product as "a weedwhacker for the Web," he is using a metaphor to advance an argument about the nature and function of that product.

Simile

A direct comparison between two things, simile is pervasive in written and spoken language. You may even have your own favorites: someone's hair is "plastered to him like white on rice," for instance, or, as one of our grandmothers used to say, "prices are high as a cat's back," or, as a special compliment, "you look as pretty as red shoes." Similes are also at work in many arguments, as you can see in this excerpt from a brief *Wired* magazine review of a new magazine for women:

> Women's magazines occupy a special niche in the cluttered infoscape of modern media. Ask any *Vogue* junkie: no girl-themed Web site or CNN segment on women's health can replace the guilty pleasure of slipping a glossy fashion rag into your shopping cart. Smooth as a pint of chocolate Häagen-Dazs, feckless as a thousand-dollar slip dress, women's magazines wrap culture, trends, health, and trash in a single, decadent package.

But like the diet dessert recipes they print, these slick publications can leave a bad taste in your mouth.

—Tiffany Lee Brown, "En Vogue"

Here three similes are in prominent display: "smooth as a pint of chocolate Häagen-Dazs" and "feckless as a thousand-dollar slip dress" in the third sentence, and "like the diet dessert recipes" in the fourth. Together, the similes add to the image the writer is trying to create of mass-market women's magazines as a mishmash of "trash" and "trends."

In another use of simile, Lerone Bennett Jr. argues that Chicago needs to return to the ideals of its founder, Jean Baptiste Point DuSable:

[A]s Chicago turned the corner of the 200th-plus year since the Black Founding, it was as clear as the Sears Tower that the city cannot reach its full height or fulfill its destiny without a continuing confrontation with DuSable's dream and the fact that all Chicagoans—Black, White, Brown, African, Irish, Polish, Italian—are DuSable's children and debtors.

—Lerone Bennett Jr.

Analogy

Analogies compare two different or dissimilar things for special effect, arguing that if two things are alike in one way they are probably alike in other ways as well. Often extended to several sentences, paragraphs, or even whole essays, analogies can help clarify and emphasize points of comparison. The Web in Motion site contains a list of "web analogies," including this one, contributed by Jill W:

People who think they can build a stellar website because they bought a copy of *FrontPage* are probably the same people who would think that they can be a best-selling author after buying a pen.

And in an argument about the failures of the aircraft industry, another writer uses an analogy for potent contrast:

If the aircraft industry had evolved as spectacularly as the computer industry over the past twenty-five years, a Boeing 767 would cost five hundred dollars today, and it would circle the globe in twenty minutes on five gallons of fuel.

Signifying

One distinctive trope found extensively in African American English is *signifying*, in which a speaker cleverly and often humorously needles the listener. In the following passage, two African American men (Grave Digger and Coffin Ed) signify on their white supervisor (Anderson), who ordered them to discover the originators of a riot:

"I take it you've discovered who started the riot," Anderson said.

"We knew who he was all along," Grave Digger said.

"It's just nothing we can do to him," Coffin Ed echoed.

"Why not, for God's sake?"

"He's dead," Coffin Ed said.

"Who?"

"Lincoln," Grave Digger said.

"He hadn't ought to have freed us if he didn't want to make provisions to feed us," Coffin Ed said.

"Anyone could have told him that."

–Chester Himes, Hot Day, Hot Night

Coffin Ed and Grave Digger demonstrate the major characteristics of effective signifying: indirection, ironic humor, fluid rhythm—and a surprising twist at the end. Rather than insulting Anderson directly by pointing out that he's asked a dumb question, they criticize the question indirectly by ultimately blaming a white man (and not just any white man, but one they're all supposed to revere). This twist leaves the supervisor speechless, teaching him something and giving Grave Digger and Coffin Ed the last word—and the last laugh.

You will find examples of signifying in the work of many African American writers. You may also hear signifying in NBA basketball, for it is an important element of trash talking; what Grave Digger and Coffin Ed do to Anderson, Allen Iverson regularly does to his opponents on the court.

Take a look at the example of signifying from a *Doonesbury* cartoon (see Figure 14.2). Note how Thor satirizes white attitudes about Black language, first by giving a mini-lecture in "standard" academic English and then underscoring his point (and putting down Mike) by reverting to "sho 'nuff."

Other Tropes

Several other tropes deserve special mention.

Hyperbole is the use of overstatement for special effect, a kind of pyrotechnics in prose. The tabloid papers whose headlines scream at shoppers in the grocery checkout line probably qualify as the all-time champions of hyperbole (journalist Tom Wolfe once wrote a satirical review of a *National Enquirer* writers' convention that he titled "Keeps His Mom-in-Law in Chains Meets Kills Son and Feeds Corpse to Pigs"). Everyone has seen these overstated arguments and, perhaps, marveled at the way they seem to sell.

FIGURE 14.2 *DOONESBURY* CARTOON

Hyperbole is also the trademark of more serious writers. In a column arguing that men's magazines fuel the same kind of neurotic anxieties about appearance that have plagued women for so long, Michelle Cottle uses hyperbole and humor to make her point:

> What self-respecting '90s woman could embrace a publication that runs such enlightened articles as "Turn Your Good Girl Bad" and "How to Wake Up Next to a One-Night Stand"? Or maybe you'll smile and wink knowingly: What red-blooded hetero chick wouldn't love all those glossy photo spreads of buff young beefcake in various states of undress, ripped abs and glutes flexed so tightly you could bounce a check on them? Either way you've got the wrong idea. My affection for *Men's Health* is driven by pure gender politics. . . . With page after page of bulging biceps and Gillette jaws, robust hairlines and silken skin, *Men's Health* is peddling a standard of male beauty as unforgiving and unrealistic as the female version sold by those dewy-eyed pre-teen waifs draped across covers of *Glamour* and *Elle*.
>
> –Michelle Cottle, "Turning Boys into Girls"

As you can well imagine, hyperbole of this sort can easily backfire, so it pays to use it sparingly and for an audience whose reactions you believe you can effectively predict. American journalist H. L. Mencken ignored this advice in 1921 when he used hyperbole to savage the literary style of President Warren Harding—and note that in doing so he says that he is offering a "small tribute," making the irony even more notable:

> I rise to pay my small tribute to Dr. Harding. Setting aside a college professor or two and half a dozen dipsomaniacal newspaper reporters, he takes the first place in my Valhalla of literati. That is to say, he writes the worst English that I have ever encountered. It reminds me of a string of wet sponges; it reminds me of tattered washing on the line; it reminds me of stale bean-soup, of college yells, of dogs barking idiotically through endless nights. It is so bad that a sort of grandeur creeps into it. It drags itself out of the dark abysm (I was about to write abcess!) of pish, and crawls insanely up the topmost pinnacle of posh. It is rumble and bumble. It is flap and doodle. It is balder and dash.
>
> —H. L. Mencken, *The Evening Sun*

Understatement, on the other hand, requires a quiet, muted message to make its point effectively. In her memoir, Rosa Parks—a civil rights activist who made history in 1955 by refusing to give up her bus seat to a white passenger—uses understatement so often that it might be said to be characteristic of her writing, a mark of her ethos. She refers to Martin Luther King Jr. simply as "a true leader," to Malcolm X as a person of "strong conviction," and to her own lifelong efforts as simply a small way of "carrying on."

As the examples from Rosa Parks suggest, quiet understatement can be particularly effective in arguments. When Watson and Crick published their first article on the structure of DNA, they felt that they had done nothing less than discover the secret of life. (Imagine what the *National Enquirer* headlines might have been for this story!) Yet in an atmosphere of extreme scientific competitiveness they chose to close their article with a vast understatement, using it purposely to gain emphasis: "It has not escaped our notice," they wrote, "that the specific pairing we have postulated immediately suggests a possible copying mechanism for the genetic material." Forty-some years later, considering the profound developments that have taken place in genetics, including the cloning of animals, the power of this understatement resonates even more strongly.

Rhetorical questions don't really require answers. Rather, they are used to help assert or deny something about an argument. Most of us use rhetorical questions frequently; think, for instance, of the times you have said "Who cares?" or "Why me?" or "How should I know?"—rhetorical questions all. Rhetorical questions also show up in written arguments. In a review of a book-length argument about the use and misuse of power in the Disney dynasty, the reviewer uses a series of rhetorical questions to sketch in part of the book's argument:

> If you have ever visited one of the Disney theme parks, though, you have likely wondered at the labor—both seen and unseen—necessary to maintain these fanciful environments. How and when are the grounds tended so painstakingly? How are the signs of high traffic erased from public facilities? What keeps employees so poised, meticulously groomed, and endlessly cheerful?
> —Linda S. Watts, review of *Inside the Mouse*

And here is Debra Saunders, opening an argument for the legalization of medical marijuana, with a rhetorical question: "If the federal government were right that medical marijuana has no medicinal value, why have so many doctors risked their practices by recommending its use for patients with cancer or AIDS?"

Antonomasia is probably most familiar to you from the sports pages: "His Airness" still means Michael Jordan; "The Great One," Wayne Gretzky; "The Sultan of Swat," Babe Ruth; "The Swiss Miss," Martina Hingis. And "The Answer" is Allen Iverson. Such shorthand substitutions of a descrip-

FIGURE 14.3   ALLEN "THE ANSWER" IVERSON

tive word or phrase for a proper name can pack arguments into just one phrase. What does calling Jordan "His Airness" argue about him?

Irony, the use of words to convey a meaning in tension with or opposite to their literal meanings, also works powerfully in arguments. One of the most famous sustained uses of irony in literature occurs in Shakespeare's *Julius Caesar*, as Mark Antony punctuates his condemnation of Brutus with the repeated ironic phrase "But Brutus is an honourable man." You may be a reader of *The Onion*, noted for its ironic treatment of politics. Another journal, the online *Ironic Times*, devotes itself to irony. Take a look at one front page:

FIGURE 14.4   FRONT PAGE OF THE *IRONIC TIMES*

Ironic Times

NO. 115   *"Expect the Ironic"*   NOV 25 - DEC 1, 2002

| Nov 18 | ... In first act, Ridge orders all copies of '1984' destro | Dec 2 |

WHY WE LIKE THANKSGIVING

34% Opportunity to put on a few pounds.

28% Excitement of traveling during the busiest travel days of the year.

21% Chance to see relatives we would not otherwise choose to see.

10% Chance to eat foods we would not otherwise choose to eat.

7% Animal slaughter.

WORLD NEWS
> **New Book Says U.S. Bought Warlords' Loyalty in Afghanistan**
Gave them $70 million in Enron stock options.

U. S. NEWS
> **White House Prepares for "Unthinkable" Worst-Case Scenario**
Emergency contingency disaster plan in place should Iraq comply with UN inspectors.
> **Homeland Security Bill Passes**
Watch what you say.
> **White House Tightens Dirty Air Rules**
Coal-firing plants ordered to pollute more or face fines.

REMINDER
Rome didn't fall in a day.

> **New York City Mulls Putting Homeless on Cruise Ships**
Would sleep on deck, outside passengers' cabins.
> **Eight Cubans Fly Into Key West, Seek Asylum**
Want to live here, open Haitian restaurant.

BUSINESS
> **Air of Optimism Pervades Wall Street**

SCHEMES

Schemes, figures that depend on word order, can add quite a bit of syntactic "zing" to arguments. Here we present the ones you are likely to see most often.

Parallelism uses grammatically similar words, phrases, or clauses for special effect:

> **The Wild Man process involves five basic phases: Sweating, Yelling, Crying, Drum-Beating, and Ripping Your Shirt off Even If It's Expensive.**
>
> –Joe Bob Briggs, "Get in Touch with Your Ancient Spear"

> **Infertility is not a modern problem, but it has created a modern industry.**
>
> –Jessica Cohen, "Grade A: The Market for a Yale Woman's Eggs"

> **The laws of our land are said to be "by the people, of the people, and for the people."**

Antithesis is the use of parallel structures to mark contrast or opposition:

> **That's one small step for a man, one giant leap for mankind.**
>
> –Neil Armstrong

> **Marriage has many pains, but celibacy has no pleasures.**
>
> –Samuel Johnson

> **Those who kill people are called murderers; those who kill animals, sportsmen.**

Inverted word order, in which the parts of a sentence or clause are not in the usual subject-verb-object order, can help make arguments particularly memorable:

> **Into this grey lake plopped the thought, I know this man, don't I?**
>
> –Doris Lessing

> **Hard to see, the dark side is.**
>
> –Yoda

> **Good looking he was not; wealthy he was not; but brilliant—he was.**

As with anything else, however, too much of such a figure can quickly become, well, too much.

Anaphora, or effective repetition, can act like a drumbeat in an argument, bringing the point home. In an argument about the future of Chicago, Lerone Bennett Jr. uses repetition to link Chicago to innovation and creativity:

> [Chicago]'s the place where organized Black history was born, where gospel music was born, where jazz and the blues were reborn, where the Beatles and the Rolling Stones went up to the mountaintop to get the new musical commandments from Chuck Berry and the rock'n'roll apostles.
>
> –Lerone Bennett Jr., "Blacks in Chicago"

And speaking of the Rolling Stones, here is Dave Barry using repetition in his comments on their 2002 tour:

> Recently I attended a Rolling Stones concert. This is something I do every two decades. I saw the Stones in the 1960s, and then again in the 1980s. I plan to see them next in the 2020s, then the 2040s, then the 2060s, at their 100th anniversary concert.
>
> –Dave Barry, "OK, What Will Stones Do for 100th Anniversary?"

Reversed structures for special effect have been used widely in political argumentation since President John F. Kennedy's inaugural address in 1961 charged citizens, "Ask not what your country can do for you; ask what you can do for your country." Like the other figures we have listed here, this one can help make arguments memorable:

> The Democrats won't get elected unless things get worse, and things won't get worse until the Democrats get elected.
>
> –Jeanne Kirkpatrick

> Your manuscript is both good and original. But the part that is good is not original, and the part that is original is not good.
>
> –Samuel Johnson

> When the going gets tough, the tough get going.

DANGERS OF UNDULY SLANTED LANGUAGE

Although all arguments depend on figurative language to some degree, if the words used call attention to themselves as "stacking the deck" in unfair ways, they will not be particularly helpful in achieving the goals of the argument. In preparing your own arguments, you will want to pay special attention to the connotations of the words you choose—those associations that words and phrases always carry with them. The choices

CULTURAL CONTEXTS FOR ARGUMENT

Style is always affected by language, culture, and rhetorical tradition. What constitutes effective style, therefore, varies broadly across cultures and depends on the rhetorical situation—purpose, audience, and so on. There is at least one important style question to consider when arguing across cultures: what level of formality is most appropriate? In the United States a fairly informal style is often acceptable, even appreciated. Many cultures, however, tend to value more formality. If you are in doubt, therefore, it is probably wise to err on the side of formality, especially in communicating with elders or with those in authority.

- Take care to use proper titles as appropriate—*Ms., Mr., Dr.,* and so on.
- Do not use first names unless invited to do so.
- Steer clear of slang. Especially when you're communicating with members of other cultures, slang may not be understood—or it may be seen as disrespectful.

Beyond formality, stylistic preferences vary widely. When arguing across cultures, the most important stylistic issue might be clarity, especially when you're communicating with people whose native languages are different from your own. In such situations, analogies and similes almost always aid in understanding. Likening something unknown to something familiar can help make your argument forceful—and understandable.

you make will always depend on the purpose you have in mind and those to whom you wish to speak. Should you choose *skinny* or *slender* in describing someone? Should you label a group *left-wing agitators, student demonstrators*—or *supporters of human rights?*

The lesson for writers of arguments is a simple one that can be devilishly hard to follow: know your audience and be respectful of them, even as you argue strenuously to make your case.

RESPOND ●

1. Identify the types of figurative language used in the following advertising slogans—metaphor, simile, analogy, hyperbole, understatement, rhetorical question, antonomasia, irony, parallelism, antithesis, inverted word order, anaphora, or reversed structure.

"Good to the last drop." (Maxwell House coffee)

"It's the real thing." (Coca-Cola)

"Melts in your mouth, not in your hands." (M&M's)

"Be all that you can be." (U.S. Army)

"Got Milk?" (America's Milk Processors)

"Breakfast of champions." (Wheaties)

"Double your pleasure; double your fun." (Doublemint gum)

"Let your fingers do the walking." (the Yellow Pages)

"Think small." (Volkswagen)

"Like a Rock." (Chevy Trailblazer)

"Real bonding, real popcorn, real butter, real good times." (Pop-Secret Popcorn)

2. We mentioned in this chapter that during the Renaissance, students would memorize and practice more than a hundred figures of speech. As part of their lessons, these students would be asked to write whole paragraphs using each of the figures *in order*, in what might be called "connected discourse": The paragraph makes sense, and each sentence builds on the one that precedes it. Use the following list of figures to write a paragraph of connected discourse on a topic of your choice. Each sentence should use a different figure, starting with simile and ending with antonomasia.

   simile

   irony

   parallelism

   analogy

   antithesis

   hyperbole

   inverted word order

   understatement

   anaphora

   rhetorical question

   reversed structure

   antonomasia

   Now rewrite the paragraph, still on the same topic but using the list of figures in *reverse order*. The first sentence should use antonomasia and the last should use simile.

3. Some public speakers are well known for their use of tropes and schemes. (Jesse Jackson comes to mind, as does George W. Bush, who employs folksy sayings to achieve a certain effect.) Using the Internet, find the text of a recent speech by a speaker who uses figures liberally. Pick a paragraph that seems particularly rich in figures and rewrite it, eliminating every trace of figurative language. Then read the two paragraphs—the original and your revised version—aloud to your class. With the class's help, try to imagine rhetorical situations in which the figure-free version would be most appropriate.

Now find some prose that seems dry and pretty much non-figurative. (A technical manual, instructions for operating appliances, or a legal document might serve.) Rewrite a part of the piece in the most figurative language you can muster. Then try to list rhetorical situations in which this newly figured language might be most appropriate.

chapter fifteen

Visual Arguments

You know you shouldn't buy camping gear just because you see it advertised on TV. But what's the harm in imagining yourself on that Arizona mesa with the sun setting, the camp stove open, the tent up and ready? That could be you reminiscing about the rugged trek that got you there, just like the tanned campers in the ad. Now what's that brand name again, and what's its URL?

A student government committee is meeting to talk about campus safety. One member has prepared a series of graphs showing the steady increase in the number of on-campus attacks over the last five years, along with several photographs that bring these crimes vividly to life.

It turns out that the governor and now presidential candidate who claims to be against taxes actually raised taxes in his home state — according to his opponent, who is running thirty-second TV spots to make that point. The ads feature a plainly dressed woman who sure looks credible; she's got to be a real person, not an actor, and she says he raised taxes. She wouldn't lie — would she?

You've never heard of the trading firm. But the letter, printed on thick bond with smart color graphics, is impressive — and hey, the company CEO is offering you $75 just to open an online account. The $75 check is right at the top of the letter, and it looks real enough. The company's Web site seems quite professional — quick-loading and easy to navigate. Somebody's on the ball. Perhaps you should sign up?

A shiny black coupe passes you effortlessly on a steep slope along a curving mountain interstate. It's moving too fast for you to read the nameplate, but on the trunk lid you see a three-pointed star. Hmmmm . . . Maybe after you graduate from law school and your student loans are paid off . . .

FIGURE 15.1 A VISUAL ARGUMENT ON WHEELS

THE POWER OF VISUAL ARGUMENTS

We don't need to be reminded that visual images have clout. Just think for a moment of where you were on September 11, 2001, and what you remember of the events of that day: almost everyone we know still reports being able to see the hijacked planes slamming into the World Trade Towers as though that image were forever etched in some inner eye.

What other potent images are engraved in your memory? Even in mundane moments, not memorable in the way an event like 9/11 is, visual images still surround us, from T-shirts to billboards to computer screens. It seems everyone is trying to get our attention, and they are doing it with images as well as words. In fact, several recently published books argue that images today pack more punch than words. As technology makes it easier for people to create and transmit images, those images are more compelling than ever, brought to us via DVD and HDTV on our computers, on our walls, in our pockets, even in our cars.

FIGURE 15.2 LEONARD SHLAIN'S BOOK EXAMINES
THE GROWING INFLUENCE OF IMAGES.

But let's put this in perspective. Visual arguments weren't invented by Bill Gates, and they've always had power. The pharaohs of Egypt lined the Nile with statues of themselves to assert their authority, and Roman emperors stamped their portraits on coins for the same reason. Some thirty thousand years ago people in the south of France created magnificent cave paintings, suggesting that people have indeed always used images to celebrate and to communicate.

FIGURE 15.3 CEILING OF THE LASCAUX CAVES

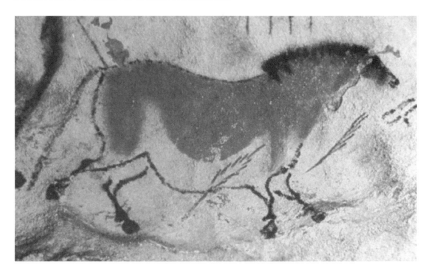

In our own era, two events marked turning points in the growing power of media images. The first occurred in 1960, when presidential candidates John F. Kennedy and Richard M. Nixon met in a nationally televised debate. Kennedy, robust and confident in a dark suit, faced a pale and haggard Nixon barely recovered from an illness. Kennedy looked cool and "presidential"; Nixon did not. Many viewers believe that the contrasting images Kennedy and Nixon presented on that evening radically changed the direction of the 1960 election campaign, leading to Kennedy's narrow victory. For better or worse, the debate also established television as the chief medium for political communication in the United States.

The second event is more recent—the introduction in the early 1980s of personal computers with graphic interfaces. These machines, which

FIGURE **15.4**   RICHARD NIXON AND JOHN KENNEDY BEFORE A TELEVISED DEBATE, 1960

initially seemed strange and toylike, operated with icons and pictures rather than through arcane commands. Subtly at first, and then with the smack of a tsunami, graphic computers (the only kind we use now) moved people away from an age of print into an era of electronic, image-saturated communications.

So that's where we are in the opening decade of a new millennium. People today are adjusting rapidly to a world of seamless, multichannel communications. The prophet of this time is Marshall McLuhan, the guru of *Wired* magazine who proclaimed some forty years ago that "the medium is the massage," with the play on words (*message/massage*) definitely intentional. Certainly images "massage" us all the time, and anyone reading and writing today has to be prepared to deal with arguments that shuffle more than words.

SHAPING THE MESSAGE

Images make arguments of their own. A photograph, for example, isn't a faithful representation of reality; it's reality shaped by the photographer's point of view. You can see photographic and video arguments at work everywhere, but perhaps particularly so during political campaigns. Staff photographers work to place candidates in settings that will show them in the best possible light—shirtsleeves rolled up, surrounded by smiling children and red-white-and-blue bunting—whereas their opponents look for opportunities to present them in a bad light. Closer to home, you may well have chosen photographs that showed you at your best to include in your college applications.

One of the most often reprinted photographs appearing in the wake of the September 11, 2001, terrorist attacks was shot by Thomas Franklin and shows three firefighters struggling to hoist the American flag as dust settles all around them. This photo, and others like Bridget Besaw Gorman's shown in Figure 15.5, immediately brought another famous photo to the minds of many Americans: Joe Rosenthal's photo of U.S. Marines raising the flag on Iwo Jima in 1945 (see Figure 15.6).

FIGURE 15.5 BRIDGET BESAW GORMAN'S 2001 PHOTO

FIGURE **15.6** JOE ROSENTHAL'S 1945 PHOTO

Take a look at the two photos and consider how they are composed—what attracts your attention, how your eyes move over the image, what immediate impression they create. What do you read in these images—heroism, endurance, character, conviction, hope? Gorman's and Rosenthal's skill as photographers enables viewers to take a lot of meaning from these images; they are ones viewers come back to again and again.

Even if those who produce images shape the messages those images convey, those of us who "read" them are by no means passive. Human vision is selective: to some extent, we actively shape what we see. Much of what we see is laden with cultural meanings, too, and we must have "learned" to see things in certain ways. Consider the Statue of Liberty welcoming immigrants to America's shores—and then imagine her instead as Bellona, the goddess of war, guarding New York Harbor with a blazing torch. For a moment, at least, she'd be a different statue.

FIGURE 15.7 STATUE OF LIBERTY

Of course, we don't always see things the same way, which is one reason eyewitnesses to the same event often report it differently. Or why
even instant replays don't always solve disputed calls on football fields.

The visual images that surround us today—and that argue forcefully for our attention and often for our time and money—are constructed to invite, perhaps even coerce, us into seeing them in just one way. But each of us has our own powers of vision, our own frames of reference that influence how we see. So visual arguments might best be described as a give-and-take, a dialogue, or even a tussle.

ACHIEVING VISUAL LITERACY

Why take images so seriously? Because they matter. Images change lives and shape behavior. When advertisements for sneakers are powerful enough to lead some kids to kill for the coveted footwear, when five- and ten-second images and sound bites are deciding factors in presidential elections, when the image of Joe Camel is credibly accused of enticing youngsters to smoke, or when a cultural icon like Oprah Winfrey can sell more books in one TV show than a hundred writers might do—it's high time to start paying careful attention to visual elements of argument.

How text is presented affects how it is read—whether it is set in fancy type, plain type, or handwritten; whether it has illustrations or not; whether it looks serious, fanciful, scholarly, or commercial. Figure 15.8 shows information about a peer-tutoring service presented visually in three different ways—as an email message, as a flyer with a table, and as a flyer with a visual (this is how it actually exists). Look at the three different versions of this text and consider in each case how the presentation affects how you perceive the information. Does the photograph and play on the movie *The Usual Suspects*, for example, make you more or less likely to use this tutoring service? The point, of course, is that as you read any text, you need to consider its presentation—a crucial element in any written argument.

ANALYZING VISUAL ELEMENTS OF ARGUMENTS

We've probably said enough to suggest that analyzing the visual elements of argument is a challenge, one that's even greater as we encounter multimedia appeals as well, especially on the Web. Here are some questions that can help you recognize—and analyze—visual and multimedia arguments:

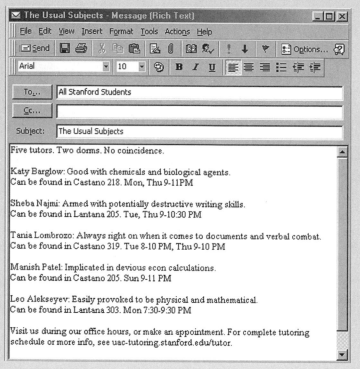

a

THE USUAL SUBJECTS

Five tutors. Two dorms. No coincidence.

Katy Barglow	Sheba Najmi	Tania Lombrozo	Manish Patel	Leo Alekseyev
Good with chemicals and biological agents.	Armed with potentially destructive writing skills.	Always right on when it comes to documents and verbal combat.	Implicated in devious econ calculations.	Easily provoked to be physical and mathematical.
Can be found in: Castano 218 Mon, Thu 9–11 PM	Can be found in: Lantana 205 Tue, Thu 9–10:30 PM	Can be found in: Castano 319 Tue 8–10 PM Thu 9–10 PM	Can be found in: Castano 205 Sun 9–11 PM	Can be found in: Lantana 303 Mon 7:30–9:30 PM

Visit us during our office hours, or make an appointment. For complete tutoring schedule or more info, see uac-tutoring.stanford.edu/tutor.

b

six tutors. two dorms. no coincidence

6'6"
6'0"
5'6"
5'0"
4'6"
4'

The Usual Subjects

Katy Barglow	Sheba Najmi	Tania Lombrozo	Manish Patel	Leo Alekseyev
Good with chemicals and biological agents.	Armed with potentially destructive writing skills.	Always right on when it comes to documents and verbal combat.	Implicated in devious econ calculations.	Easily provoked to be physical and mathematical.
Can be found in:	*Can be found in:*	*Can be found in:*	*Can be found in:*	*Can be found in:*
Castano 218 *Mon, Thu* 9 – 11 PM	Lantana 205 *Tue, Thu* 9 – 10:30 PM	Castano 319 *Tue* 8 – 10 PM *Thu* 9 – 10 PM	Castano 205 *Sun* 9 – 11 PM	Lantana 303 *Mon* 7:30 – 9:30 PM

Visit us during our office hours, or make an appointment.

For complete tutoring schedule or more info, see

uac-tutoring.stanford.edu/tutor

c

ABOUT THE CREATORS/AUTHORS

- Who created this visual text?
- What can you find out about this person(s), and what other work they have done?
- What does the creator's attitude seem to be toward the visual image?
- What do the creators intend its effects to be?

ABOUT THE MEDIUM

- Which media are used for this visual text? Images only? Words and images? Sound, video, graphs, charts?
- What effect does the choice of medium have on the message of the visual text? How would the message be altered if different media were used?
- What is the role of words that may accompany the visual text? How do they clarify or reinforce (or blur or contradict) the message?

ABOUT VIEWERS/READERS

- What does the visual text assume about its viewers—and about what they know and agree with?
- What overall impression does the visual text create in you?
- Does the visual evoke positive—or negative—feelings about individuals, scenes, or ideas?

ABOUT CONTENT AND PURPOSE

- What argumentative purpose does the visual text convey? What is it designed to convey?
- What cultural values or ideals does the visual evoke or suggest? The good life? Love and harmony? Sex appeal? Youth? Adventure? Economic power or dominance? Freedom? Does the visual reinforce these values or question them? What does the visual do to strengthen the argument?
- What emotions does the visual evoke? Which ones do you think it intends to evoke? Desire? Envy? Empathy? Shame or guilt? Pride? Nostalgia? Something else?

ABOUT DESIGN

- How is the visual text composed? What is your eye drawn to first? Why?
- What is in the foreground? In the background? What is in or out of focus? What is moving? What is placed high, and what is placed low?

What is to the left, in the center, and to the right? What effect do these placements have on the message?

- Is any particular information (such as a name, face, or scene) highlighted or stressed in some way to attract your attention?

- How are light and color used? What effect(s) are they intended to have on you? What about video? Sound?

- What details are included or emphasized? What details are omitted or deemphasized? To what effect? Is anything downplayed, ambiguous, confusing, distracting, or obviously omitted? To what ends?

- What, if anything, is surprising about the design of the visual text? What do you think is the purpose of that surprise?

- Is anything in the visual repeated, intensified, or exaggerated? Is anything presented as "supernormal" or idealistic? What effects are intended by these strategies, and what effects do they have on you as a viewer? How do they clarify or reinforce (or blur or contradict) the message?

- How are you directed to move within the argument? Are you encouraged to read further? Click on a link? Scroll down? Fill out a form? Provide your email address? Place an order?

Take a look at the home page of United Colors of Benetton, a company that sells sportswear, handbags, shoes, and more. You might expect a company that sells eighty million items of clothing and accessories annually to feature garments on its home page or to make a pitch to sell you something. And you would find many of those items if you probed the Benetton site more deeply. But on the company's main page (see Figure 15.9) you see the torso of a man, his right arm ending not in a hand but in a prosthetic device attached to a spoon and what looks like a makeshift knife. To the left of this arresting image is the simple heading Food for Life. Clicking on that area takes you to a second page that announces "Food for Life: United Colors of Benetton and World Food Programme Communication Campaign 2003." This campaign is presented on the World Food Programme's Web site, as well (see Figure 15.10). Taken together, these pages make a powerful argument that we should all be concerned about world hunger—and take action to address it.

Even this brief investigation of the Benetton site reveals that this manufacturer of clothing and accessories promotes its wares through an involvement in social activism. So its images challenge viewers to join in—or at least to consider doing so. What effect do these pages have on you?

FIGURE 15.9   UNITED COLORS OF BENETTON HOME PAGE

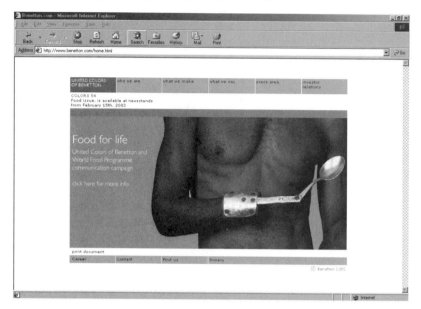

FIGURE 15.10   WORLD FOOD PROGRAMME HOME PAGE

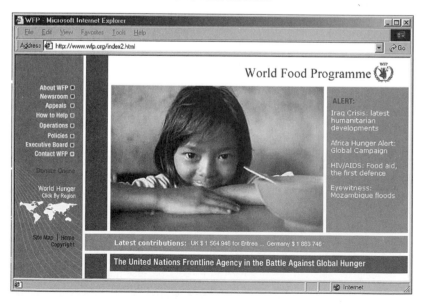

USING VISUALS IN YOUR OWN ARGUMENTS

You too can, and perhaps must, use visuals in your writing. Many college classes now call for projects to be posted on the Web, which almost always involves the use of images. Many courses also require students to make multimedia presentations using software such as PowerPoint, or even good, old-fashioned overhead projectors with transparencies.

Here we sketch out some basic principles of visual rhetoric. To help you appreciate the argumentative character of visual texts, we examine them under some of the same categories we use for written and oral arguments earlier in this book (Chapters 4, 6, and 7), though in a different order. You may be surprised by some of the similarities you will see in visual and verbal arguments.

Visual Arguments Based on Character

What does character have to do with visual argument? Consider two argumentative essays submitted to an instructor. One is scrawled in thick pencil on pages ripped from a spiral notebook, little curls of paper still dangling from the left margin. The other is neatly typed on bond paper and in a form the professor likely regards as "professional." Is there much doubt about which argument will (at least initially) get the more sympathetic reading? You might object that appearances shouldn't count for so much, and you would have a point. The argument scratched in pencil could be the stronger piece, but it faces an uphill battle because its author has sent the wrong signals. Visually, the writer seems to be saying, "I don't much care about this message or the people to whom I am sending it."

There may be times when you want to send exactly such a signal to an audience. Some TV advertisements aimed at young people are deliberately designed to antagonize older audiences with their blaring soundtracks, MTV-style quick cuts, and in-your-face style. The point is that the visual rhetoric of any piece you create ought to be a deliberate choice, not an accident. Also keep control of your own visual image. In most cases, when you present an argument, you want to appear authoritative and credible.

Look for images that reinforce your authority and credibility.

For a brochure about your new small business, for instance, you would need to consider images that prove your company has the resources to do its job. Consumers might feel reassured seeing pictures that show you have an actual office, up-to-date equipment, and a competent staff. Similarly, for a Web site about a company or organization you represent, you would consider including its logo or emblem. Such emblems have authority and weight. That's why university Web sites so often include the seal of the institution somewhere on the home page, or why the president of the United States always travels with a presidential seal to hang upon the speaker's podium. The emblem or logo, like the hood ornament on a car, can convey a wealth of cultural and historical implications.

FIGURE 15.11 THREE IMAGES: THE U.S. PRESIDENTIAL SEAL, THE MCDONALD'S LOGO, AND THE BMW ORNAMENT

Consider how design reflects your character.

Almost every design element sends signals about character and ethos, so be sure you think carefully about them. For example, the type fonts you select for a document can mark you as warm and inviting or efficient and contemporary. The warm and readable fonts often belong to a family called *serif*. The serifs are those little flourishes at the ends of their strokes that make the fonts seem handcrafted and artful:

warm and readable (Bookman Old Style)

warm and readable (Times New Roman)

warm and readable (Bookman)

Cleaner, modern fonts go without those little flourishes and are called *sans serif*. These fonts are cooler and simpler — and, some argue, more readable on a computer screen (depending on screen resolution):

efficient and contemporary (Helvetica)

efficient and contemporary (Arial Black)

efficient and contemporary (Arial)

You may also be able to use decorative fonts. These are appropriate for special uses, but not for extended texts:

decorative and special uses (Zapf Chancery)

decorative and special uses (Goundy Handtooled BT)

Other typographic elements shape your ethos as well. The size of type, for one, can make a difference. You'll seem to be shouting if your headings or text is boldfaced and too large. Tiny type might make you seem evasive:

Lose weight! Pay nothing!*

*Excludes the costs of enrollment and required meal purchases. Minimum contract: 12 months.

Similarly, your choice of color—especially for backgrounds—can make a statement about your taste, personality, and common sense. For instance, you'll make a bad impression with a Web page whose background colors or patterns make reading difficult. If you want to be noticed, you might use bright colors—the same sort that would make an impression in clothing or cars. But more subtle shades might be a better choice in most situations.

Don't ignore the impact of illustrations and photographs. Because they reveal what you visualize, images can send powerful signals about your preferences, sensitivities, and inclusiveness—and it's not always easy. Conference planners designing a program, for example, wanted to make sure to include pictures that represent the members who will be attending; as a result, they double-checked to make sure that they didn't show only women in their photos, or only men, or only members of one race or ethnic group.

Even your choice of medium says something important about you. If you decide to make an appeal on a Web site, you send signals about your technical skills and contemporary orientation as well as about your personality. Take a look at the Web site of undergraduate student Dennis Tyler (see Figure 15.12). What can you deduce about Tyler from this page—his personality, his values, and so on?

A presentation that relies on an overhead projector gives a different impression from one presented on an LCD projector with software—or one presented with a poster and handouts. If you are reporting on a children's story you're writing, the most effective medium of presentation might be old-fashioned cardboard and paper made into an oversized book and illustrated by hand.

FIGURE 15.12 DENNIS TYLER'S WEB SITE

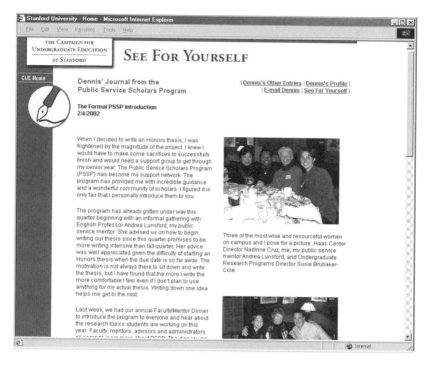

Follow required design conventions.

Many kinds of writing have required design conventions. When that's the case, follow them to the letter. It's no accident that lab reports for science courses are sober and unembellished. Visually, they reinforce the serious character of scientific work. The same is true of a college research paper. You might resent the tediousness of placing page numbers in the right place or aligning long quotations just so, but these visual details help convey your competence. So whether you are composing a term paper, résumé, screenplay, or Web site, look for authoritative models and follow them. Here is Dennis Tyler's résumé. Note that its look is serious: The type is clear and easy to read; the black on white is simple and no-nonsense; the headings call attention to Tyler's accomplishments.

FIGURE 15.13 DENNIS TYLER'S RÉSUMÉ

DENNIS TYLER JR.

CURRENT ADDRESS
P.O. Box 12345
Stanford, CA 94309
Phone: (650) 498-4731
Email: dtyler@yahoo.com

PERMANENT ADDRESS
506 Chanelle Court
Baton Rouge, LA 70128
Phone: (504) 246-9847

CAREER OBJECTIVE   Position on editorial staff of a major newspaper

---

EDUCATION

9/98–6/02   **Stanford University**, Stanford, CA
                   B.A., ENGLISH AND AMERICAN STUDIES, June 2002

9/00–12/00   **Morehouse College**, Atlanta, GA
                   STANFORD STUDY EXCHANGE PROGRAM

EXPERIENCE

6/01–9/01   **Business Scholar Intern**, Finance, AOL Time Warner, New
                   York, NY
                   Responsible for analyzing data for strategic marketing
                   plans. Researched the mergers and acquisitions of compa-
                   nies to which Time Inc. sells advertising space.

1/00–6/01   **Editor-in-Chief**, *Enigma* (a literary journal), Stanford
                   University, CA
                   Oversaw the entire process of Enigma. Edited numerous cre-
                   ative works: short stories, poems, essays, and interviews.
                   Selected appropriate material for the journal. Responsible
                   for designing cover and publicity to the greater community.

8/00–12/00   **Community Development Intern**, University Center
                   Development Corporation (UCDC), Atlanta, GA
                   Facilitated workshops and meetings on the importance of
                   home buying and neighborhood preservation. Created
                   UCDC brochure and assisted in the publication of the cen-
                   ter's newsletter.

6/00–8/00   **News Editor**, *Stanford Daily*, Stanford University, CA
                   Responsible for editing stories and creating story ideas for
                   the newspaper. Assisted with the layout for the newspaper
                   and designs for the cover.

SKILLS AND HONORS

- Computer Skills: MS Word, Excel, PageMaker, Microsoft
  Publisher; Internet research
- Language: Proficient in Spanish
- Trained in making presentations, conducting research,
  acting, and singing
- Mellon Fellow, Gates Millennium Scholar, Public Service
  Scholar, National Collegiate Scholar
- Black Community Service Arts Award. 2001–2002

REFERENCES   Available upon request

Visual Arguments Based on Facts and Reason

We tend to associate facts and reason with verbal arguments, but here too visual elements play an essential role. Indeed, it is hard to imagine a compelling presentation these days that doesn't rely, to some degree, on visual elements to enhance or even make the argument.

Many readers and listeners now expect ideas to be represented graphically. Not long ago, media critics ridiculed the colorful charts and graphs in newspapers like *USA Today*. Today, comparable features appear in even the most traditional publications because they work. They convey information efficiently.

Organize information visually.

A design works well when readers can look at an item and understand what it does. A brilliant, much-copied example of such an intuitive design is a seat adjuster invented many years ago by Mercedes-Benz. It is shaped like a tiny seat. Push any element of the control, and the real seat moves the same way—back and forth, up and down. No instructions are necessary.

Good visual design can work the same way in an argument, conveying information without elaborate instructions. Titles, headings, subheadings, pull quotes, running heads, boxes, and so on are some common visual signals. When you present parallel headings in a similar type font, size, and color, you make it clear that the information under these headings is in some way related. So in a conventional term paper, you should use headings and subheadings to group information that is connected or parallel. Similarly, on a Web site, you might create two or three types of headings for groups of related information.

Use headings when they will help guide your readers through the document you are presenting. For more complex and longer pieces, you may choose to use both headings and subheadings.

You should also make comparable inferences about the way text should be arranged on a page: look for relationships among items that should look alike. In this book, for example, bulleted lists are used to offer specific guidelines while boxes mark sections on "Cultural Contexts for Argument." You might use a list or a box to set off information that should be treated differently from the rest of the presentation, or you might visually mark it in other ways—by shading, color, or typography.

An item presented in large type or under a larger headline should be more important than one that gets less visual attention. Place illustrations carefully: what you position front and center will appear more

FIGURE 15.14 THE SERVICE EMPLOYEES INTERNATIONAL UNION'S WEB SITE USES VARIOUS HEADINGS TO GROUP DIFFERENT KINDS OF INFORMATION.

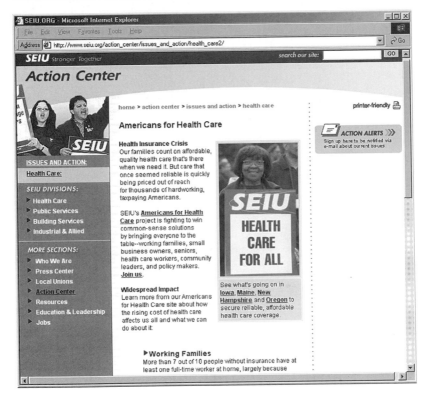

important than items in less conspicuous places. On a Web site, key headings should usually lead to subsequent pages on the site.

Needless to say, you take a risk if you violate the expectations of your audience or if you present a visual text without coherent signals. Particularly for Web-based materials that may be accessible to people around the world, you can't make many assumptions about what will count as "coherent" across cultures. So you need to think about the roadmap you are giving viewers whenever you present them with a visual text. Remember that design principles evolve and change from medium to medium. A printed text or an overhead slide, for example, ordinarily works best when its elements are easy to read, simply organized, and surrounded by restful white space. But some types of Web pages seem to thrive on visual clutter,

attracting and holding audiences' attention through the variety of information they can pack onto a relatively limited screen. Check out the way
the opening screens of most search engines assault a viewer with entice-
ments. Yet look closely, and you may find the logic in these designs.

One group that regularly analyzes Web sites, the Stanford Persuasive
Technology Lab, recently concluded that Google News may soon become
the most credible Web site of all. Here are just a few of the Lab's points
about what makes Google News credible: It's easy to navigate; it provides
a diversity of viewpoints; it has a reputation for outstanding performance
in other areas; it has no broken links, typos, and so on; it provides clear
information about the site; it has an easy-to-understand structure; it dis-
closes information about the organization; and it has no ads. Take a look
at Google News yourself: do you agree that it is a fairly credible site?

FIGURE 15.15 GOOGLE NEWS SITE

Use visuals to convey information efficiently.

Words are immensely powerful and capable of enormous precision and
subtlety. But the simple fact is that some information is conveyed more
efficiently by charts, graphs, drawings, maps, or photos than by words.
When making an argument, especially to a large group, consider what
information should be delivered in nonverbal form.

A *pie chart* is an effective way of comparing a part to the whole. You might use a pie chart to illustrate the ethnic composition of your school, the percentage of taxes paid by people at different income levels, or the consumption of energy by different nations. Pie charts depict such information memorably, as Figure 15.16 shows:

FIGURE 15.16 HISPANIC POPULATION, BY TYPE OF ORIGIN, 1996 (IN PERCENT)

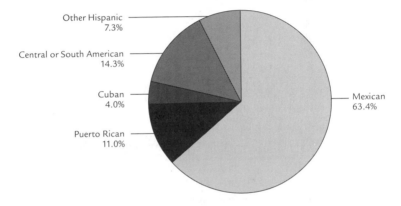

Source: U.S. Census Bureau, Current Population Survey. "The Hispanic Population." *1997 Population Profile of the United States.* Ed. John M. Reed. Washington: U.S. Department of Commerce, September 1998.

A *graph* is an efficient device for comparing items over time or according to other variables. You could use a graph to trace the rise and fall of test scores over several decades, or to show college enrollment for men and women, as in Figure 15.17.

Diagrams or drawings are useful for drawing attention to details. You can use drawings to illustrate complex physical processes or designs of all sorts. After the attack on the World Trade Center, for example, engineers used drawings and diagrams to help citizens understand precisely what led to the total collapse of the buildings.

You can use *maps* to illustrate location and spatial relationships — something as simple as the distribution of office space in your student union or as complex as the topography of Utah. Such information would probably be far more difficult to explain using words alone.

FIGURE 15.17 COLLEGE ENROLLMENT FOR MEN AND WOMEN BY AGE, 1998 (IN MILLIONS)

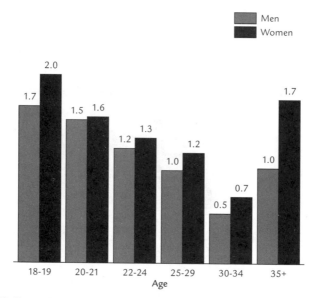

Source: U.S. Census Bureau, Current Population Survey, October 1998. "Scholars of All Ages: School Enrollment, 1998." 1998 Population Profile of the United States. Washington: U.S. Department of Commerce, March 2001.

Follow professional guidelines for presenting visuals.

Charts, graphs, tables, and illustrations play such an important role in many fields that professional groups have come up with specific guidelines for labeling and formatting these items. You need to become familiar with those conventions as you advance in a field. A guide such as the *Publication Manual of the American Psychological Association* (5th edition) or the *MLA Style Manual and Guide to Scholarly Publishing* (6th edition) describes these rules in detail.

Remember to check for copyrighted material.

You also must be careful to respect copyright rules when you use visual items created by someone else. It is relatively easy these days to download visual texts of all kinds from the Web. Some of these items—such as clip art or government documents—may be in the public domain, meaning that you are free to use them without requesting permission or paying a royalty. But other visual texts may require permission, especially if you intend to publish your work or use the item commercially. And remember: anything you place on a Web site is considered "published." (See Chapter 20 for more on intellectual property.)

Visual Arguments That Appeal to Emotion

To some extent, we tend to be suspicious of arguments supported by visual and multimedia elements because they can seem to manipulate our senses. And many advertisements, political documentaries, rallies, marches, and even church services do in fact use visuals to trigger our emotions. Who has not teared up at a funeral when members of a veteran's family are presented with the American flag, with a bugler blowing taps in the distance? Who doesn't remember being moved emotionally by a powerful film performance accompanied by a heart-wrenching musical score? But you might also have seen or heard about *Triumph of the Will*, a Nazi propaganda film from the 1930s that powerfully depicts Hitler as the benign savior of the German people, a hero of Wagnerian dimensions. It is a chilling reminder of how images can be manipulated and abused.

Yet you cannot flip through a magazine without being cajoled or seduced by images of all kinds—most of them designed in some way to attract your eye and attention. Not all such seductions are illicit, nor should you avoid using them when emotions can support the legitimate claims you hope to advance. What is the effect of the image presented in Figure 15.18?

FIGURE 15.18 SOMALI CHILD, 1992

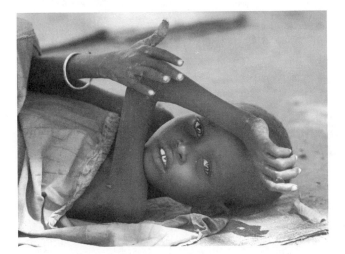

Appreciate the emotional power of images.

Images can bring a text or presentation to life. Sometimes the images have power in and of themselves to persuade. This was the case with images in the 1960s that showed civil rights demonstrators being assaulted by police dogs and water hoses, and with horrifying images in 2001 of dead Afghani children, which led many people to contribute to relief for Afghanistan.

Images you select for a presentation may be equally effective if the visual text works well with other components of the argument. Indeed, a given image might support many different kinds of arguments. Take, for example, the famous *Apollo 8* photograph of our planet as a big blue mar-

FIGURE 15.19   EARTH SHINING OVER THE MOON

ble hanging above the horizon of the moon. You might use this image to introduce an argument about the need for additional investment in the space program. Or it might become part of an argument about the need to preserve our frail natural environment, or part of an argument against nationalism: *from space, we are one world.* You could, of course, make any of these claims without the image. But the photograph—like most images—might touch members of your audience more powerfully than words alone could.

Appreciate the emotional power of color.

Consider the color red. It attracts hummingbirds—and cops. It excites the human eye in ways that other colors don't. You can make a powerful statement with a red dress or a red car—or red shoes. In short, red evokes emotions. But so do black, green, pink, and even brown. That we respond to color is part of our biological and cultural makeup. So it makes sense to consider carefully what colors are compatible with the kind of argument you are making. You might find that the best choice is black on a white background.

In most situations, you can be guided in your selection of colors by your own good taste (guys—check your ties), by designs you admire, or by the advice of friends or helpful professionals. Some design and presentation software will even help you choose colors by offering you dependable "default" shades or by offering an array of preexisting designs and compatible colors—for example, of presentation slides.

The colors you choose for a design should follow certain common-sense principles. If you are using background colors on a poster, Web site, or slide, the contrast between words and background should be vivid enough to make reading easy. For example, white letters on a yellow background will likely prove illegible. Any bright background color should be avoided for a long document. Indeed, reading seems easiest with dark letters against a light or white background. Avoid complex patterns, even though they might look interesting and be easy to create. Quite often, they interfere with other, more important elements of your presentation.

As you use visuals in your college projects, test them on prospective readers. That's what professionals do because they appreciate how delicate the choices about visual and multimedia texts can be. These responses will help you analyze your own arguments as well as improve your success with them.

1. The December 2002 issue of the *Atlantic Monthly* included the following poem, along with the photograph that may have inspired it, shown in Figure 15.20. Look carefully at the image and then read the poem several times, at least once aloud. Working with another person in your class, discuss how the words of the poem and the image interact with one another. What difference would it make if the image had not accompanied this text? Write a brief report of your findings, and bring it to class for discussion.

The Launching Chains of The Great Eastern (By Robert Howlett, 1857)

JOHN SPAULDING

A waterfall of black chains
looms behind the man in the stovepipe hat.
Cigar. Wrinkled clothes. This is
Isambard Kingdom Brunel.
Who could not stop working. Slept
and ate at the shipyard.
The largest ship in the world.
Driven to outdo himself.
Fashioned from iron plate and
powered by three separate means.
Able to sail to Ceylon and back
without refueling. Fated
to lay the Atlantic cable, the India cable.
Untouched in size for forty years.
The Great Leviathan. The Little Giant,
Isambard Kingdom Brunel.
Builder of tunnels, ships, railroads, bridges.
Engineer and Genius of England.
He should have built churches, you know.
Everything he prayed for came true.

FIGURE **15.20** THIS PHOTOGRAPH OF ISAMBARD KINGDOM BRUNEL WAS TAKEN BY ROBERT HOWLETT AND IS INCLUDED IN THE NATIONAL PORTRAIT GALLERY'S COLLECTION IN LONDON.

2. Find an advertisement with both verbal and visual elements. Analyze the ad's visual argument by answering some of the questions on pp. 312–13, taking care to "reread" its visual elements just as carefully as you would its words. After you've answered each question as thoroughly as possible, switch ads with a classmate and analyze the new argument in the same way. Then compare your own and your classmate's responses to the two advertisements. If they are different — and there is every reason to expect they will be — how do you account for the differences? What is the effect of audience on the argument's reception? What are the differences between your own active reading and your classmate's?

3. If you have used the World Wide Web, you have no doubt noticed the relationships between visual design and textual material. In the best Web pages, the elements work together rather than simply competing for space. In fact, even if you have not used the Web, you still know a great deal about graphic design: newspapers, magazines, and your own college papers make use of design principles to create effective texts.

Find three or four Web or magazine pages that you think exemplify good visual design — and then find just as many that do not. When you've picked the good and bad designs, draw a rough sketch of their physical layout. Where are the graphics? Where is the text? What are the relative size and relationship of text blocks to graphics? How is color used? Can you discern common principles among the pages, or does each good page work well in its own way? Write a brief explanation of what you find, focusing on the way the visual arguments influence audiences.

4. If you have access to the Internet, go to the Pulitzer Prize Archives at <pulitzer.org>. Pick a year to review, and then study the images of the winners in three categories: editorial cartooning, spot news photography, and feature photography. (Click on "Works" to see the images.) From among the images you review, choose one you believe makes a strong argument. Then, in a paragraph, describe that image and the argument it makes.

5. Choose one chapter of this textbook, and then spend some time looking at its design and use of visual images. Note the use of white space and margins as well as color, font and type size — and all images. How effective do you find the design of this chapter? What recommendations would you make for improving the design?

chapter sixteen

Arguments in Electronic Environments

A student who has just loaded a new Web browser goes looking for online sources to develop a research assignment about a contemporary political issue. Looking for newsgroups, she notices that the default service on the browser offers many discussion groups sponsored by a big software company. But many of the groups she ordinarily consults don't seem to be available. She contemplates writing her research paper on the way commercial interests can shape and limit political discussion on the Web.

You send email to a friend questioning the integrity of your state's high school competency examinations. You mention irregularities you yourself have witnessed in testing procedures. A week later, you find passages from your original email circulating in a listserv. The remarks aren't attributed to you, but they sure are stirring up a ruckus.

A group of students on your campus have tried to disrupt a lecture by a controversial writer, shouting questions and insults throughout her talk until she finally walks off stage. The incident is reported in your campus newspaper—which includes an electronic version. You send a link to the online story to your favorite Web logger, who posts it. The attempt to suppress free speech on your campus becomes a national issue, putting pressure on your school's administration to take action against those who disrupted the lecture.

One of the news-talk channels is exploring the issue of genetically engineered foods. Unfortunately, the experts being interviewed have to squeeze in their opinions among interruptions from two aggressive hosts, questions from generally hostile callers, and commercials for Viagra. Meanwhile, the hosts are urging viewers to participate in an online poll on the subject posted on the network's Web site. The results, they admit, are unscientific.

You've been discussing gender roles on a MOO with a woman who calls herself Taurean. She sure seems to have your number, almost anticipating the arguments you make. Even though you find her positions untenable, you admire her intuition and perception. Then you discover that Taurean is really your roommate Julio! He says he has enjoyed playing with your mind.

■ ■ ■

Within the last decade or so, computers have created new environments where ideas can be examined, discussed, and debated in shapes many might never have imagined—some custom-fitted to the give-and-take of argument. Serious thinkers and determined advertisers alike are still learning how (and when) to use these new media, which users can tap into through a growing array of increasingly integrated devices. Cell phones and wireless PDAs can now download images, email, and even Internet services, while powerful laptop computers can crunch huge image files fed to them by mega-pixel digital cameras. Is there a special rhetoric of argument for such environments, a way of making effective and honest claims in this brave new world where each of us controls such powerful tools? Clearly there is, but it remains a work in progress, evolving gradually as people learn to cross boundaries among written, aural, and visual texts.

It's an exciting time for extending the reach of the human mind. What follows are some observations and speculations about the play of argument online, including Web logs and Web pages, email and discussion groups, and synchronous communications.

WEB LOGS

Web logs have recently exploded into public consciousness, though they have evolved from Internet-based magazines such as <Slate.com>, news services such as <drudgereport.com>, and the give-and-take of listservs and news groups. A Web log—or blog, for short—is an interactive Web site maintained by an individual who updates it frequently, often daily, posting items and links related to the theme of the site. Bloggers frequently link to information on other Web logs, creating an active community of writers and readers, able in some cases to reach remarkably large audiences in a short time.

There are at least a half-million Web logs on the Web now, covering every subject and interest you could imagine. Some blogs are highly personal, specialized, and even eccentric. But the most influential and interesting as examples of argument tend to be political sites such as <andrewsullivan.com>, <InstaPundit.com>, and <talkingpointsmemo.com> visited by hundreds of thousands of readers a day. These and many similar blogs provide forums for the political opinions of their hosts; the daily, even hourly, postings are like long-running national bull sessions—at varying levels of quality—keeping the more prestigious traditional media on their toes. Some of the bloggers, for example, enjoy pointing out errors or biases in the *New York Times* or *Washington Post* or national TV networks. But the bloggers also create news on their own, focusing on local issues or small stories ignored by the mainstream press—at least until the drumbeat of attention from the Web forces a topic into wider circulation. In fact, it is the bloggers' sense of community that is one of their most appealing features. Almost every site includes links to pages of other favorite Web loggers. Visit any site and you are well on your way to finding many more. Or you could go to a blog directory such as <GlobeofBlogs.com>, <Portal.Eatonweb.com>, or the Pepys Project at < pepys.akacooties.com>.

FIGURE 16.1 PATRICK RUFFINI OFFERS A CONSERVATIVE POINT OF VIEW ON HIS WEB
LOG AT <PATRICKRUFFINI.COM>.

By their nature, blogs favor compressed forms of argument—
paragraphs rather than extended essays, although bloggers like Andrew
Sullivan (often cited in this book) and Virginia Postrel at <dynamist.com>
will link to their articles published elsewhere. Bloggers pay attention, too,
to facts and information, linking frequently to data or online archives to
support or refute claims. Pity politicians these days who switch their positions to serve new ends, hoping the general public won't notice. If their
earlier words are on record, a blogger will find them and send the awk-
ward quotations scurrying around the "blogosphere"—the informal net-

FIGURE 16.2 JERLYNN MERRITT RUNS TALKLEFT, A BLOG ABOUT CRIME THAT
ANNOUNCES OPENLY THAT IT IS "NOT A NEUTRAL SITE." IT IS AT <TALKLEFT.COM>.

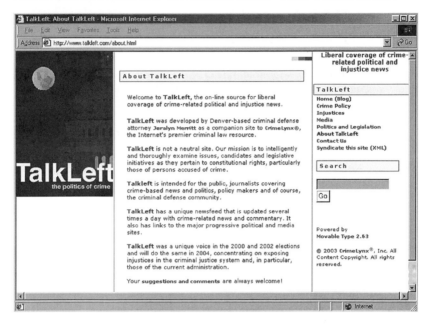

work of active Web loggers. Bloggers are fond, too, of what InstaPundit author Glenn Reynolds calls a "fisking": an almost line-by-line, often sarcastic or humorous, refutation of an argument considered inaccurate or rhetorically suspect. You can learn a lot about argument from these close analyses, recognizing always that the blogger is almost certainly grinding an axe. But that's one of the defining features of Web logs: they are usually upfront about their distinctive points of view.

Here's Australian blogger Tim Blair <timblair.blogspot.com> fisking the opening paragraphs of a book on 9/11, one that Blair obviously finds pretentious and shallow. Following a blogger convention, the lines Blair is critiquing are indented and italicized. On the Web site, the underlined words link to other pages.

> DR. JOHN CARROLL is a reader in sociology at Melbourne's La Trobe University. That is to say, he is paid to educate young adults.
>
> This bland statement of fact may mean nothing to you now, but let's see how you feel after we've finished examining the highlights from

chapter one of Carroll's <u>awesomely pretentious and imbecilic new book</u>, Terror: A Meditation on the Meaning of September 11 . . .

> *The highjacked planes were flown through the bright early-morning American east-coast sky. This is the hour of Apollo, the sun god, who presided over ancient Delphi. His oracle dwelt high on the side of the sacred mountain, with two mottos carved over its portal. Two sayings watched over the foundation of our civilization, in exhortation and warning: "Know Thyself!" and "Nothing Too Much!"*

Not to mention "Nothing Over 99 Cents!" and "Si habla Espanol!"

> *Ignorantly and flagrantly, the modern West has violated both.*

As will shortly be revealed, <u>Carroll</u> follows a combination of both: "Know Nothing!"

> *We all know the story—about the events of September 11 and their aftermath. We all share the shock, surreal image of the second plane slicing through the World Trade Center tower like . . .*

All together now . . .

> *. . . a knife through butter. We will take to our graves the slow-motion horror of watching, many of us as it happened, the tallest skyscrapers in the world crumpling, one after the other . . .*

The World Trade Center towers weren't even the <u>tallest skyscrapers in the United States</u>.

> *. . . each no more substantial than a child's house of cards. Nothing was left of where 50,000 people had once worked but dust and smoke, numb pain for those trapped inside, and speechless awe at the power that had done this.*

Nothing was left? Then how come it took eight months to clear all that nothing away? Lazy teamsters!

> *These, however, are surface facts. The heart of the matter lies deep beneath. This is a story that is hard to read, essential to read.*

He's got that half right.

> *Our culture has developed the shrug of the shoulders into a cosy reflex while we pour another drink, switch on the amusement parade, and wait for the house prices and stock market to rise.*

"Honey, I'm home! Get me a Scotch and switch on the amusement parade!"

> *Will this culture be able to relearn how to take itself seriously?*

<u>Carroll</u> isn't making it very easy.

Will anyone again choose to work in a skyscraper?

Beats me. I guess you could ask all the people worldwide who work in them every day.

Which insurance company will cover a landmark tower?

Er . . . the ones that *do?*

Indeed, were the twin 110-storey towers to be rebuilt they would stand like pyramids, colossal empty tombs, in memoriam to a lost civilization.

I'm no architect, but I'm pretty sure that rebuilt towers would stand like *towers.* Pyramids are lots more pointy and triangly. Here's a picture.

And if the age of the skyscraper is over, so is that of New York. Nothing big is safe anymore. Icarus never flew twice.

Icarus's problem was that he flew too close to the sun. New York's problem was that scum flew too close to it. Slight difference.

Web logs, of course, are not edited, nor do they subscribe to any journalistic standards except those enforced by the bloggers themselves. You should read blogs at least as critically as anything else you encounter on the Web. But you can learn a great deal about argument by participating in these sites either as a reader or as a blogger yourself. In fact, you can find just about everything you need to know about setting up your own Web log (at modest cost) at <blogspot.com/>.

WEB SITES

The Web supports many traditional components of argument, but it complicates them too. For example, a Web site for a political or special interest group might include many conventional claims supported with evidence and good reasons. But instead of merely summarizing the evidence and providing a source citation as you might in a conventional paper, a Web author might furnish links to the primary evidence itself—to statistics borrowed directly from a government Web site or to online documents at a university library. Indeed, the links within a Web page can be a version of documentation, leading to the very material the original author examined, full and complete.

A site might also provide links to other sites dealing with the same issue, connect readers to discussion groups about it, or even support chatrooms where anyone can offer an opinion in real time. And, of course, a Web site can incorporate visual and aural elements of all sorts into its argument, not as embellishments but as persuasive devices. For this reason, writers today need to learn new techniques of document design if they expect to communicate in this complex medium.

When crafting a Web site designed to present an argument of your own, you will want not only to take full advantage of the electronic medium but also to meet its distinctive challenges. Your pages need to be graphically interesting to persuade readers to enter your site and to encourage them to read your lengthier arguments (see Chapter 15). If you just post a traditional argument, thick with prose paragraphs that have to be scrolled endlessly, readers might ignore it. Check out the way online periodicals—whether newspapers or magazines—arrange their articles

FIGURE 16.3 THE ASPCA SITE OFFERS PLENTY OF LINKS AND VISUALS TO HELP ARGUE ITS CASE.

to make them Web readable, or examine the design of other sites you find especially effective in presenting an argument.

Because the Web encourages browsing and surfing, you also need to consider how to cluster ideas so that they retain their appeal. In a traditional print argument, though you can't prevent readers from skipping around and looking ahead, you can largely control the direction they take through your material, from claim to warrant to evidence. On a Web page, however, readers usually want to choose their own paths. Inevitably that means they will play a larger role in constructing your argument. You lose

FIGURE 16.4 THE WEB SITE FOR FIRE CLUSTERS IDEAS EFFECTIVELY AND PROVIDES LINKS TO ADDITIONAL NEWS SOURCES.

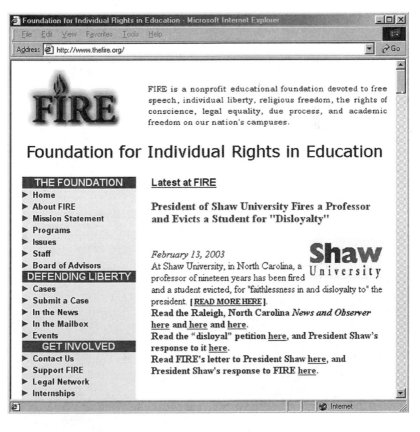

an element of control, but your argument gains a new dimension, particularly if you provide links that help readers understand how you came to your conclusions. Sometimes that may mean including links to sites that don't necessarily support your views. But you enhance your credibility by recognizing a full range of ideas, hoping that, on their own, readers will reach the same conclusions you have reached.

EMAIL AND DISCUSSION GROUPS

Email, Usenet groups, and listservs all transmit electronic messages via the Internet from person to person. Sometimes the messages go from one individual to another; in other cases, they are distributed to groups or to anyone with Internet access. As you'll see, this rapid communication has changed more than the speed by which individuals can share ideas.

Email

Everyone does email today. Of course, an email message can be a private communication to one person or a message distributed among groups, large and small, creating communities linked by information. Unlike regular ("snail") mail, email makes back-and-forth discussions easy and quick: people can speak their minds, survey opinion, or set agendas for face-to-face meetings. And they can meet at all hours, since electronic messages arrive whenever a server routes them. Increasingly, email communication is going wireless, available via cell phone, PDA, or other mobile devices.

An email message has a character of its own, halfway between the formality of a letter and the intimacy of a telephone call. It can feel less pushy than a phone call, yet at the same time be more insistent—the person too shy to say something in person or on the phone may speak up boldly in email. Like a letter, email preserves a written record of all thoughts and comments, which can be an advantage in many situations. Yet because it is less formal than a business letter, many readers tend to ignore or forgive slips in email (misspellings, irregular punctuation and capitalization) that might disturb them in another type of message.

Arguments in email operate by some relatively new conventions. First, they tend to be "dialogic," with a rapid back-and-forth of voices in conversation. When you send an email, you can usually anticipate a quick reply. Second, the very speed of response in email invites answers that may be less carefully considered than those sent by snail mail. Third, because email can be easily forwarded, your arguments may travel well beyond your intended audience, a factor to consider before clicking on "send."

Much advice about email is obvious once you've used it for a while. For one thing, although email messages can be quite long, most people won't read an argument that asks them to scroll through page after page of single-spaced print. You'll make a stronger impression with a concise claim, one that fits on a single screen if possible. And when replying to an email message, send back just enough of the original posting so that your reader knows what you are responding to; this will set your claim within its context.

Remember, too, that your email messages need to be verbally powerful. You can highlight your ideas by skipping lines between paragraphs to open some white space, bulleting key ideas or short lists, drawing lines, and using boldface and italic type as appropriate. In general, don't use all capital letters, LIKE THIS, for emphasis. The online equivalent of shouting, it will alienate many readers—as will using all lowercase letters, which makes text harder to read. You can attach photographs and other images to email messages, but don't clog your readers' mailboxes with five million–pixel jpegs.

Your email signature, known as a .sig file, can influence readers, too. Automatically attached to the bottom of every email you send (unless you switch this function off), your .sig file might include your address, phone numbers, fax numbers, and professional credentials. You can use the signature as a way to reinforce your credibility by explaining who you are and what you do. Here is an example:

Celia Garcia

Executive Secretary

Students for Responsive Government

University of Texas at San Antonio

Usenet Newsgroups and Listservs

Usenet is an electronic network that provides access to thousands of newsgroups, which are interactive discussion forums grouped by subject and open to anyone with email access to the network. Listservs also use the Internet to bring together people with common interests, but they are more focused: you have to subscribe to a particular listserv to receive its messages. In both newsgroups and listservs, messages consist of email-like postings that can be linked to form threads exploring particular subjects.

Newsgroups and listservs would seem to be great places for productive arguments—where knowledgeable people worldwide can exchange their ideas. Unfortunately, not all group discussions live up to this potential. Some people in these groups don't behave like good citizens: they forget the importance of their own character in making an argument (see Chapter 6). The result has been a dumbing down of many discussions, especially in newsgroups with the less-regulated "alt." designation. And because postings are so easy in either type of forum, even more responsible groups can be spammed with pointless messages, unwanted advertisements, and worse.

Nevertheless, newsgroups and listservs can be stimulating places for interchanges, particularly where the subject matter is specialized enough to attract informed and interested participants. Before posting, you owe it to the group to learn something about it, either by reading some messages already posted in a newsgroup or by subscribing to a listserv and lurking for enough time to gain a feel for the way issues are introduced, discussed, and debated. If a group offers a file of frequently asked questions (known as FAQs), read what it has to say about the group's rules of discourse and print it out for later reference.

When you decide to join in a conversation, be sure your posting contains enough information to make a smooth transition between the message to which you are responding and your own contribution to the group. If you have little to contribute, don't bother posting. A comment such as "I agree" wastes the time of everyone in the group who bothers to download your item—as some of the members may tell you in none-too-polite terms. In fact, if you are new to the Internet, you may be surprised at the temper of some online conversation participants. You can get flamed—bombarded with email—for asking a question that has already been asked and answered repeatedly by other members, for veering too far from the topic of discussion, or just for sending a message someone doesn't like. Flaming is unfortunate, but it is also a reality of newsgroups and listservs.

As sources for academic work, listservs are probably more reliable than newsgroups, though both forums can help you grasp the range of opinion on an issue. In fact, the range expressed in some groups may be startling. You'll likely discover much information too, including the names of reputable authorities, the titles of useful books and articles, and guidance to other groups or Web sites concerned with related topics. But don't quote facts, figures, statistics, or specific claims from newsgroups or listservs

FIGURE **16.5** TO LOCATE AND SEARCH NEWSGROUPS, YOU CAN CLICK ON THE
"GROUPS" BUTTON AT <GOOGLE.COM>.

unless you cross-check them with more conventional sources, such as
library reference material. Remember, too, that you can usually query
individual members of a group by going "off list" to find out more information. In effect you have an email exchange with one person rather than
with the whole group.

REAL-TIME COMMUNICATION: IRCS AND MOOS

Newsgroups and listservs operate like email, with a delay between the
time a message is typed and the time it is received. The senders and
receivers of email messages need not even be at their computers at the
same time; in fact, the mailbox metaphor common to email systems
assumes they are not. Now imagine an electronic conversation in which
multiple participants are all online at the same time, although in different
places, all receiving messages almost instantaneously as others are typing
them—just like a conference call, except that the communication is in
words that appear on computer screens. That's the basic shape of Internet

relay chat (IRC) and MUD object-oriented (MOO) environments, examples of synchronous communication—communication in real time—on the Internet.

IRCs

IRCs are chatrooms that allow for relatively straightforward online conversations among people gathered together electronically to discuss particular subjects or topics. Typically, IRCs involve people in different and distant locations, but some schools provide local IRC networks to encourage students to participate in online class discussions. Once a topic is established, members of the IRC group begin typing in their comments and responding to one another.

As you might guess, an IRC environment can create a conversational free-for-all as opinions come rolling in. Their sequence can feel frustratingly random, especially to outsiders reading a transcript of such exchanges. After all, by the time a participant responds to a particular message, a dozen more may have appeared on the screen. In such an environment it is difficult to build or sustain complex arguments, especially because the rapid pace of the conversation favors witty or sharp remarks. A chatroom working at its best keeps writers on their toes. Indeed, it can be a form of dialogic freewriting, with writers pouring out their thoughts and watching as they receive almost instantaneous feedback. Since participants can be spread all over the world, IRCs also can support diverse conversations. So IRCs might work well as tools of invention for other, more conventional forms of argument. A good exercise is to print out an IRC transcript and highlight its best comments or exchanges for future reference.

MOOs

MOOs resemble IRCs in that participants communicate online in real time. But MOOs, unlike IRCs, have a spatial dimension: participants enter an imaginary place, take on assumed characters, and follow specified routines.

Arguments in MOOs can involve powerful stretches of the imagination because a participant can be anyone he or she wants to be. Thus the environment encourages writers to create an ethos self-consciously and to experience what it is like to be someone else—rich rather than poor, powerful rather than powerless, female rather than male. Imaginary situations are crafted, too, making participants unusually sensitive to the contexts in which their words and ideas exist. Indeed, MOOs reflect the power of words to shape one's reality. As such, they raise interesting and powerful questions about the nature of the world "outside."

Not everyone takes MOOs seriously. There's a learning curve for those entering such environments, and to some they remain games—hardly worth serious attention. But game or not, MOOs are an environment for argument that is out there, open for anyone willing to experiment with something new.

KEY POINTS TO REMEMBER IN ARGUING ELECTRONICALLY

EMAIL

- Keep your remarks short and pertinent.
- Think twice before replying immediately to an argumentative message. Don't lose your cool.
- Remember that email is easily forwarded. Your actual audience may prove to be much larger than you initially intended.

NEWSGROUPS, LISTSERVS, IRCS, AND MOOS

- Get a feel for groups before posting to them.
- Post concise messages directly related to the interests of the group.
- Consider whether your posting should go to everyone on the list. Would an individual email message be more appropriate?
- Resist the temptation to flame or be impolite, especially when an argument heats up.

WEB SITES AND WEB LOGS

- Plan your site carefully. Use your home page to direct readers to more detailed information within the site.
- Think of design in terms of pages. When you can, chunk a claim to fit within a single page. If your argument is highly readable, readers won't mind some scrolling, but don't expect them to advance through more than four or five screens' worth of material.
- Shape pages according to their purpose. A page of useful links will differ in arrangement from a page of prose argument.
- When your argument requires a lot of text, break it up with concise, helpful headings and white space.

- At the bottom of the home page, include your name, your contact information, and the date you created or last updated the site. This information will help other readers cite your work or reach you one-on-one to continue a discussion.

GRAPHICS

- Use graphics purposefully to support an argument. Images should make points you can't convey as effectively in prose.
- Keep graphics to a minimum. It takes time to download pages heavy in graphics — time readers might not have.
- Avoid images that pulse, rotate, or blink. Such glitz will likely distract readers from your argument.
- Graphics taken from the Web may be copyrighted items. Be sure to request permission from and to credit the source for any materials you import into your own pages. See Chapter 20, pages 408–409.

LINKS

- Use links to guide readers to evidence that explains your ideas.
- Be sure your links are diverse. You'll gain credibility by acknowledging alternative views.
- Be sure readers can understand from the context what the links you create will do or where they will lead.

RESPOND •

1. Begin with a single political Web log that is regularly updated, and read it for several days to gain a sense of its focus and methods (a good directory to these is <GlobeofBlogs.com>). Also note how it often leads you to other blogs and sites. Does it ever take you to sites that provide significantly different perspectives? Does it encourage you to participate in the discussions?

2. Take a copy of an argumentative paper you've written for any class — it should be longer than two pages — and literally cut it up into separate paragraphs. Shuffle the stack of paragraphs so that they are completely reordered. Then read the paragraphs in their new order, from top to bottom. How is the argument affected? Is your claim still clear? Is your evidence powerful?

   Now imagine that those paragraphs were separate pages on a Web site that readers could browse through in any order. Would the site's argument be effective? If not, how could you rearrange the argument so that readers could move among its sections without being confused? Try to make an arrangement that could translate well to the Web's hypertextual environment. You might need to create headings that point readers in appropriate directions, or you might need to write transitions that help readers make decisions about what to read next.

3. Newcomers to a newsgroup or listserv normally lurk for a while, reading postings and getting to know the people who participate in the group, before entering the conversation themselves. Over the next several days, pick a group that interests you—there are thousands to choose from—and read as many of its postings as you can. For some groups, this might entail a tremendous amount of work, so limit your reading to those threads (topics within a group) that interest you.

   When you have a sense of the direction of the group, pick a single thread and follow the postings on that topic. Read all the postings that you can, making special note of quoting techniques—how writers refer to previous postings—and other interplay among writers. On the basis of the small evidence that you have (the group may have existed for several years), try to reconstruct the "conversation" on this thread that went on before you arrived. Who were the most frequent writers? What did they claim? How did others respond to those claims? What is the current state of the conversation? Are people in general agreement or disagreement?

4. FAQs can tell a careful reader a lot about a particular newsgroup or listserv and its contributors. Find the FAQs of three different groups and read them carefully. What suppositions about audience are inherent in these texts? Write an audience analysis of each FAQ, based on the kinds of questions and answers you see there, their tone, and their length. Who are the FAQs' intended readers? What kinds of rules about argument does each FAQ offer?

5. Find several Web sites that make explicit argumentative claims, and evaluate them on the basis of a set of criteria you develop. What constitutes a good Web-based argument? What are the characteristics of effective Web rhetoric? Do these sites exhibit those characteristics? How does the nonlinear nature of the site affect your reading or its persuasiveness? If your instructor requests, make a presentation to the class, showing printouts of the site (or directing the class to look at it if you are in a networked classroom) and explaining why the Web-based arguments are effective or ineffective.

chapter seventeen

Spoken Arguments

In the wake of a devastating hurricane, local ministers search for just the right words to offer comfort and inspire hope in their congregations.

At a campus rally, student leaders call for the administration to provide a living wage for campus workers.

A customer looking for a good buy on a new car settles in for some tough negotiations with the salesperson and manager.

At the half, the team is down by ten. In the locker room, the captain calls on all her persuasive powers to rebuild morale and help seize the momentum.

For a course in psychology, a student gives a multimedia presentation on the work of neuroscientist Constance Pert.

During their wedding, a couple exchanges the special vows they have worked together to create.

■ ■ ■

As these examples suggest, people are called on every day to present spoken arguments of one kind or another. Successful speakers point to several crucial elements in that success:

- They have thorough knowledge of their subjects;
- They pay very careful attention to the values, ideas, and needs of their listeners;
- They use structures and styles that make their spoken arguments easy to follow;
- They keep in mind the interactive nature of spoken arguments (live audiences can argue back!);
- They realize that most oral presentations involve visuals of some sort, and they plan accordingly for the use of presentation software, illustrations, and so on;
- They practice, practice—and then practice some more.

SPOKEN ARGUMENTS IN DISCUSSIONS

Perhaps the most common context for spoken argument takes place in ordinary discussions, whether you're trying to persuade your parents that you need a new computer for your college work, to explore the meaning of a poem in class, or to make a decision about a new company health plan. In such everyday contexts, many people automatically choose the tone of voice, kind of evidence, and length of speaking time to suit the situation. You can improve your own performance in such contexts by observing closely other speakers you find effective and by joining in on conversations whenever you possibly can: the more you participate in lively discussions, the more comfortable you will be doing so. To make sure your in-class comments count, follow these tips:

- Be well prepared so that your comments will be relevant to the class;
- Listen with a purpose, jotting down important points;
- Ask a key question—or offer a brief analysis or summary of the points that have already been made, to make sure you and other students (and the instructor) are "on the same page";
- Respond to questions or comments by others in specific rather than vague terms;
- Offer a brief analysis of an issue or text that invites others to join in and build on your comments.

CULTURAL CONTEXTS FOR ARGUMENT

Speaking up in class is viewed as inappropriate or even rude in some cultures. In the United States, however, doing so is expected and encouraged. Some instructors even assign credit for such class participation.

FORMAL PRESENTATIONS

You have probably already been asked to make a formal presentation in some of your classes or on the job. In such cases, you need to consider the full context carefully. Note how much time you have to prepare and how long the presentation should be. You want to use the allotted time effectively, while not infringing on the time of others. Consider also what visual aids, handouts, or other materials might help make the presentation successful. Will you have an overhead projector? Can you use PowerPoint or other presentation software? A statistical pie chart may carry a lot of weight in one argument whereas photographs will make your point better in another. (See Chapter 15.)

Think about whether you are to make the presentation alone or as part of a group—and plan and practice accordingly. Especially with a group, turn-taking will need to be worked out carefully. Check out where your presentation will take place—in a classroom with fixed chairs? A lecture or assembly hall? An informal sitting area? Will you have a lectern? An overhead projector? Will you sit or stand? Remain in one place or move around? What will the lighting be, and can you adjust it? Finally, note any criteria for evaluation: how will your spoken argument be assessed?

Whenever you make a formal presentation, you need to consider several key elements:

Purpose

- Determine your major argumentative purpose. Is it to inform? Convince or persuade? Explore? Make a decision? Entertain? Something else?

Audience

- Who is your audience? What will be the mix of age groups, men and women, and so on: think carefully about what they will know about your topic and what opinions they are likely to hold. If your audience is an academic one, your instructor may be one important member, in addition to other class members. Can you count on the audience being interested in your topic? If not, how can you capture their interest and attention?

Stance

- Consider your own stance toward your topic and audience. Are you an expert? Novice? Fairly well informed? Interested observer? Peer?

Support

- Make sure that you have plenty of support—examples, facts, anecdotes, statistics, testimony of authorities—for your argument.

Structure

- Structure your presentation to make it easy to follow, and remember to take special care to plan an introduction that gets the audience's attention and a conclusion that makes your argument memorable. You'll find more help with structure on page 353.

ARGUMENTS TO BE HEARD

Even if you work from a printed text in delivering a presentation, that text must be written to be *heard* rather than read. Such a text—whether in the form of an overhead list, note cards, or a fully written-out text—should feature a strong introduction and conclusion, a clear organization with helpful signposts and structures, straightforward syntax, and concrete diction.

Introductions and Conclusions

Like readers, listeners tend to remember beginnings and endings most readily. Work hard, therefore, to make these elements of your spoken argument especially memorable. Consider including a provocative or puzzling statement, opinion, or question; a memorable anecdote; a powerful quotation; or a vivid visual image. If you can refer to the interests or experiences of your listeners in the introduction or conclusion, do so.

Look at the introduction in Toni Morrison's acceptance speech to the Nobel Academy when she won the Nobel Prize for Literature:

> "Once upon a time there was an old woman. Blind but wise." Or was it an old man? A guru, perhaps. Or a griot soothing restless children. I have heard this story, or one exactly like it, in the lore of several cultures.
>
> "Once upon a time there was an old woman. Blind. Wise."
>
> – Toni Morrison

Here Morrison uses a storytelling strategy, calling on the traditional "Once upon a time" to signal to her audience that she is doing so. Note also the use

FIGURE 17.1   TONI MORRISON ACCEPTING THE NOBEL PRIZE FOR LITERATURE IN 1993

of repetition and questioning. These strategies raise interest and anticipation in her audience: how will she use this story in accepting the Nobel Prize?

Structures and Signposts

For a spoken argument, you want your organizational structure to be crystal clear. Offer an overview of your main points toward the beginning of your presentation, and make sure that you have a clearly delineated beginning, middle, and end to the presentation. Throughout, remember to pause between major points and to use helpful "signposts" to mark your movement from one topic to the next. Such signposts act as explicit transitions in your spoken argument and thus should be clear and concrete: *The second crisis point in the breakup of the Soviet Union occurred hard on the heels of the first*, rather than *The breakup of the Soviet Union came to another crisis*. In addition to such explicit transitions as *next, on the contrary*, or *finally*, you can offer signposts to your listeners by repeating key words and ideas as well as by carefully introducing each new idea with concrete topic sentences.

Diction and Syntax

Avoid long, complicated sentences, and use straightforward syntax (subject-verb-object, for instance, rather than an inversion of that order) as much as possible. Remember, too, that listeners can hold onto concrete verbs and nouns more easily than they can grasp a steady stream of abstractions. So when you need to deal with abstract ideas, try to illustrate them with concrete examples.

Take a look at the following paragraph from an essay that student Ben McCorkle wrote on the Simpsons, first as he wrote it for his essay and then for an oral presentation:

Written Version

The Simpson family has occasionally been described as a "nuclear" family, which obviously has a double meaning: first, the family consists of two parents and three children, and, second, Homer works at a nuclear power plant with very relaxed safety codes. The overused label *dysfunctional*, when applied to the Simpsons, suddenly takes on new meaning. Every episode seems to include a scene in which son Bart is being choked by his father, the baby is being neglected, or Homer is sitting in a drunken stupor transfixed by the television screen. The comedy in these scenes comes from the exaggeration of commonplace household events (although some talk shows and news programs would have us believe that these exaggerations are not confined to the madcap world of cartoons).

–Ben McCorkle, "The Simpsons: A Mirror of Society"

Spoken Version (with a visual illustration)

What does it mean to describe the Simpsons as a *nuclear* family? Clearly, a double meaning is at work. First, the Simpsons fit the dictionary meaning—a family unit consisting of two parents and some children. The second meaning, however, packs more of a punch. You see, Homer works at a nuclear power plant [pause here] with *very* relaxed safety codes!

Still another overused family label describes the Simpsons. Did everyone guess I was going to say *dysfunctional*? And like "nuclear," when it comes to the Simpsons, "dysfunctional" takes on a whole new meaning.

Remember the scene when Bart is being choked by his father?

How about the many times the baby is being neglected?

Or the classic view—Homer sitting in a stupor transfixed by the TV screen!

My point here is that the comedy in these scenes often comes from double meanings—and from a lot of exaggeration of everyday household events.

FIGURE 17.2   HOMER SIMPSON IN A TYPICAL POSE

Note that the revised paragraph presents the same information, but this time it is written to be heard. See how the revision uses helpful signposts, some repetition, a list, italicized words to prompt the speaker to give special emphasis, and simple syntax to help make it easy to listen to.

ARGUMENTS TO BE REMEMBERED

You can probably think of spoken arguments that still stick in your memory—a song like Bruce Springsteen's "Born in the USA," for instance. Such arguments are memorable in part because they call on the power of figures of speech and other devices of language. In addition, careful repetition can make spoken arguments memorable, especially when linked with parallelism and climactic order. (See Chapter 14 for more on using figurative language to make arguments more vivid and memorable.)

FIGURE 17.3 **BRUCE SPRINGSTEEN**

Repetition, Parallelism, and Climactic Order

Whether they are used alone or in combination, repetition, parallelism, and climactic order are especially appropriate for spoken arguments that sound a call to arms or that seek passionate engagement from the audience. Perhaps no person in the twentieth century used them more effectively than Martin Luther King Jr., whose sermons and speeches helped to spearhead the civil rights movement. Standing on the steps of the Lincoln Memorial in Washington, D.C., on August 28, 1963, with hundreds of thousands of marchers before him, King called on the nation to make good on the promissory note represented by the Emancipation Proclamation.

FIGURE 17.4 MARTIN LUTHER KING JR., SPEAKING AT THE LINCOLN MEMORIAL

Look at the way King uses repetition, parallelism, and climactic order in the following paragraph to invoke a nation to action (emphasis added):

> It is obvious today that America has defaulted on this promissory note insofar as her citizens of color are concerned. Instead of honoring this sacred obligation, America has given the Negro people a bad check which has come back marked "insufficient funds." But *we refuse* to believe that the bank of justice is bankrupt. *We refuse* to believe that there are insufficient funds in the great vaults of opportunity of this nation. So *we have come* to cash this check—a check that will give us upon demand the riches of freedom and the security of justice. *We have also come* to this hallowed spot to remind America of the fierce urgency of now. This is *no time* to engage in the luxury of cooling off or to take the tranquilizing drug of gradualism. *Now is the time* to rise from the dark and desolate valley of segregation to the sunlit path of racial justice. *Now is the time* to open the doors of opportunity to all of God's children. *Now is the time* to lift our nation from the quicksands of racial injustice to the solid rock of brotherhood.
>
> —Martin Luther King Jr., "I Have a Dream"

The italicized words highlight the way King uses repetition to drum home his theme. But along with that repetition, King sets up a powerful set of parallel verb phrases, calling on all "to rise" from the "dark and desolate valley of segregation" to the "sunlit path of racial justice" and "to open the doors of opportunity" for all. The final verb phrase ("to lift") leads to a strong climax, as King moves from what each individual should do to what the entire nation should do: "to lift our nation from the quicksands of racial injustice to the solid rock of brotherhood." These stylistic choices, together with the vivid image of the "bad check," help to make King's speech powerful, persuasive—and memorable.

Thank goodness you don't have to be as highly skilled as Dr. King to take advantage of the power of repetition and parallelism: simply repeating a key word in your argument can help impress it on your audience, as can arranging parts of sentences or items in a list in parallel order.

THE ROLE OF VISUALS AND MULTIMEDIA

Visuals often play an important part in spoken arguments, and they should be prepared with great care. Don't think of them as add-ons but rather as a major means of getting across your message and supporting the claims you are making. In this regard, a visual—like a picture—can be worth a thousand words, helping your audience see examples or illustrations or other data that make your argument compelling. Test the effectiveness of your visuals on classmates, friends, or family members, asking them to judge whether the visuals help advance your argument.

Whatever visuals you use—charts, graphs, photographs, summary statements, sample quotations, lists—must be large enough to be readily seen by your audience. If you use slides or overhead projections, be sure that the information on each frame is simple, clear, and easy to read and process. In order for audience members to read information on a transparency, this means using 36 point type for major headings; 24 point for subheadings; and at least 18 point for all other text. For slides, use 24 point for major headings; 18 point for subheadings; and at least 14 point for other text.

The same rule for clarity and simplicity holds true for posters, flip charts, or a chalkboard. And remember not to turn your back on your audience while you refer to any of these visuals. Finally, if you prepare supplementary materials for your audience—bibliographies or other handouts—distribute these at the moment the audience will need them or at the end of the presentation so that they will not distract the audience from your spoken argument.

If you plan to use PowerPoint or other presentation software, take care with the colors you choose for background and for text and illustrations. Light text on a dark background is particularly hard to read, so as a general rule you'll be better off to use white or light cream-colored backgrounds. If you've seen many PowerPoint presentations, you are sure to have seen some really bad ones: the speaker just stands up and reads off what is on each slide. Nothing can be more deadly boring than that. So in your own use of PowerPoint or other presentation slides, make sure that they provide an overview of what you are talking about, but do not repeat word for word what you are saying.

For a talk about how best to make an effective oral presentation, one writer used the PowerPoint slides shown in Figure 17.5. Note how easy these slides are to read. The first one introduces the topic simply and clearly. Subsequent slides provide an overview of major points and an easy-to-read graph, clearly labeled. All are uncluttered and simple.

The best way to test the effectiveness of all your visuals is to try them out on friends, classmates, or roommates. If they don't get the meaning of the visuals right away, revise and try again.

Finally, remember that visuals can help you be sure your presentation is accessible: some members of your audience may not be able to see your

FIGURE 17.5   SLIDES FROM A POWERPOINT PRESENTATION

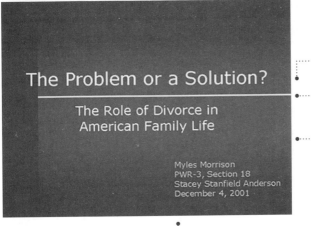

The Problem or a Solution?

The Role of Divorce in
American Family Life

Myles Morrison
PWR-3, Section 18
Stacey Stanfield Anderson
December 4, 2001

⋯ Heading in large,
easy-to-read type

⋯ Design adapted from
PowerPoint design
template

⋯ Clear contrast
between light-colored
type and dark back-
ground

⋯ Presenter, course,
instructor, and date
are identified

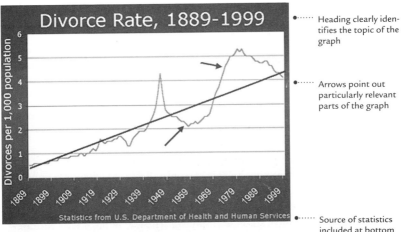

Divorce Rate, 1889–1999

⋯ Heading clearly iden-
tifies the topic of the
graph

⋯ Arrows point out
particularly relevant
parts of the graph

Statistics from U.S. Department of Health and Human Services

⋯ Source of statistics
included at bottom
of graph

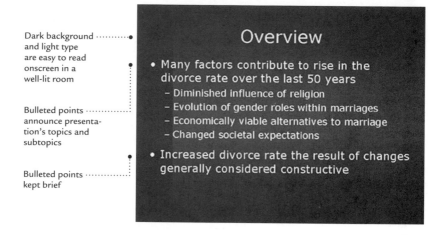

Dark background and light type are easy to read onscreen in a well-lit room

Bulleted points announce presentation's topics and subtopics

Bulleted points kept brief

Overview

- Many factors contribute to rise in the divorce rate over the last 50 years
  - Diminished influence of religion
  - Evolution of gender roles within marriages
  - Economically viable alternatives to marriage
  - Changed societal expectations
- Increased divorce rate the result of changes generally considered constructive

presentation or may have trouble hearing it. Here are a few key rules to remember:

- Don't rely on color or graphics alone to get across information: use words along with them.

- Consider providing a written overview of your presentation, or put the text on an overhead projector—for those who learn better by reading *and* listening.

- If you use video, label sounds that won't be audible to some audience members. (Be sure your equipment is caption capable.)

THE IMPORTANCE OF DELIVERY

When a famous orator in ancient times was asked to rank the most important parts of effective rhetoric, he said, "Delivery, delivery, delivery." Indeed, most effective spoken arguments are performances that call on you to pay very careful attention to the persuasive effects your clothing, body language, voice, and so on will have on the audience. Many practiced speakers say that they learned to improve the performance of spoken arguments through extensive practice. To make this advice work for you, get together a draft of your presentation, including all visuals, enough in advance to allow for several run-throughs. Some speakers audiotape or videotape these rehearsals and then revise the argument and the performance based on a study of the tapes. Others practice in front of a mirror, watching every movement with a critical eye. Still others practice in front of friends. Any of these techniques can work; the main thing is to practice.

One point of all that practice is to make sure you can be heard clearly. Especially if you are at all soft-spoken, you will need to concentrate on projecting your voice. Or you may need to practice lowering the pitch or speaking more slowly or enunciating each word more clearly. Tone of voice can dispose audiences for—or against—speakers. Those who sound sarcastic, for instance, usually win few friends. For most spoken arguments, you want to develop a tone that conveys interest and commitment to your position as well as respect for your audience.

The way you dress, the way you move, as well as the sound of your voice make arguments of their own that can either add to or detract from the main one you are trying to make. How to dress for an effective presentation, of course, depends on what is appropriate for your topic, audience, and setting, but most experienced speakers like to wear clothes that are simple and comfortable and that allow for easy movement—but that are not overly casual: "dressing up" a little indicates that you take pride in your appearance, that you have confidence in your argument, and that you respect your audience.

Most speakers make a stronger impression standing than sitting. Stand with your hands resting lightly on the lectern or at your side (don't fidget with anything) and with both feet solidly on the floor—and move about a little, even if you are using a lectern. Moving a bit may also help you make good eye contact with members of your audience. According to several studies, making eye contact is especially important for spoken arguments, since audiences perceive those who look at them directly to be more honest, friendly, and informed than others who do not.

Last but not at all least: time your presentation carefully to make sure you will stay within the allotted time. If you are working from a written text, a good rule of thumb is to allow roughly two and a half minutes for every double-spaced $8\frac{1}{2} \times 11$-inch page of text (or one and a half minutes for every 5×7-inch card). The only way to make sure of your time, however, is to set a clock and time the presentation precisely. Preparing so that you will not intrude on the time allotted to other speakers not only signals your respect for their presentations but will also help you relax and gain self-confidence; and when your audience senses your self-confidence, they will become increasingly receptive to your message.

Some Helpful Presentation Strategies

In spite of your best preparation, you may feel some anxiety before your presentation. (According to one Gallup poll, Americans often identify public speaking as a major fear, scarier than attacks from outer space!) Experienced speakers say they have strategies for dealing with anxiety—and even that a little anxiety (and accompanying adrenaline) can act to a speaker's advantage.

The most effective strategy seems to be knowing your topic and material through and through. Confidence in your own knowledge goes a long way toward making you a confident speaker. In addition to being well prepared, you may wish to try some of the following strategies:

- Visualize your presentation. Go over the scene of the presentation in your mind, and think it through completely.

- Get some rest before the presentation, and avoid consuming excessive amounts of caffeine.

- Concentrate on relaxing. Consider doing some deep-breathing exercises right before you begin.

- Pause before you begin, concentrating on your opening lines.

- Remember to interact with the audience whenever possible; doing so will often help you relax and even have some fun.

Finally, remember to allow time for audience members to respond and ask questions. Try to keep your answers brief so that others may get in on the conversation. And at the very end of your presentation, thank your audience for attending so generously to your arguments.

RESPOND●

1. Take a brief passage—three or four paragraphs—from an essay you've recently written. Then, following the guidelines in this chapter, rewrite the passage to be *heard*. Finally, make a list of every change you made.

2. Look in the TV listings for a speech or oral presentation you'd like to hear. Check out c-span or Sunday morning news shows such as *Meet the Press*. Watch and listen to the presentation, making notes of the strategies the speaker uses to good effect—signpost language, repetition, figurative language, and so on.

3. Attend a lecture or presentation on your campus and observe the speaker's delivery very carefully. Note what strategies the speaker uses to capture and hold your attention (or not). What signpost language and other guides to listening can you detect? How well are any visuals integrated into the presentation? What aspects of the speaker's tone, dress, eye contact, and movement affect your understanding and appreciation (or lack of it)? What is most memorable about the presentation and why? Finally, write up an analysis of this presentation's effectiveness.

CONVENTIONS OF argument

chapter eighteen

What Counts as Evidence

A downtown office worker who can never find a space in the company lot to park her motorcycle decides to argue for a designated motorcycle parking area. In building her argument, she conducts a survey to find out exactly how many employees drive cars to work and how many ride motorcycles.

A business consultant wants to identify characteristics of effective teamwork so that he can convince his partners to adopt these characteristics as part of their training program. To begin gathering evidence for this argument, the consultant decides to conduct on-site observations of three effective teams, followed by in-depth interviews with each member.

For an argument aimed at showing that occupations are still often unconsciously thought of as either masculine or feminine, a student decides to carry out an experiment: she will ask fifty people chosen at random to draw pictures of a doctor, a police officer, a nurse, a CEO, a lawyer, and a secretary—and see which are depicted as men, which as women. The results of this experiment will become evidence for (or against) the argument.

Trying to convince her younger brother to invest in a PC laptop, a college student mentions her three years of personal experience using a similar computer for her college coursework.

In arguing that virtual reality technology may lead people to ignore or disregard the most serious of "real" world problems, a student writer provides evidence for this claim in part by citing sixteen library sources that review and critique cyberspace and virtual reality.

■ ■ ■

EVIDENCE AND THE RHETORICAL SITUATION

As the examples above demonstrate, people use all kinds of evidence in making and supporting claims. But this evidence doesn't exist in a vacuum; instead, it becomes part of the larger context of the argument and its rhetorical situation: when, where, and to whom it is made. Remembering the rhetorical situation that evidence becomes a part of leads to an important point regarding argumentative evidence: It may be persuasive in one time and place but not in another; it may convince one kind of audience but not another; it may work with one genre of discourse but not another.

To be most persuasive, then, evidence should match the time and place in which you make your argument. For example, arguing that a military leader should employ a certain tactic because that very tactic worked effectively for George Washington is likely to fail if Washington's use of the tactic is the only evidence provided. After all, a military tactic that was effective in 1776 is more than likely an *ineffective* one today. In the same way, a writer may achieve excellent results by using her own experience as well as an extensive survey of local leaders and teenagers as evidence to support a proposal for a new teen center in her small-town community—but she may have far less success in arguing for the same thing in a distant, large inner-city area.

Careful writers also need to consider the disciplinary context in which they plan to use evidence, since some disciplines privilege certain kinds of evidence and others do not. Observable, quantifiable data may constitute the best evidence in, say, experimental psychology, but the same kind of data may be less appropriate—or impossible to come by—in a historical study. As you become more familiar with a particular discipline or area of study, you will gain a sense of just what it takes to prove a point or support a claim in that field. The following questions will help you begin understanding the rhetorical situation of a particular discipline:

- How do other writers in the field use precedence—examples of actions or decisions that are very similar—and authority as evidence? What or who counts as an authority in this field? How are the credentials of authorities established?

- What kinds of data seem to be preferred as evidence? How are such data gathered and presented?

- How are statistics or other numerical information used and presented as evidence? Are tables, charts, or graphs commonly used? How much weight do they carry?

- How are definitions, causal analyses, evaluations, analogies, and examples used as evidence?

- How does the field use firsthand and secondhand sources as evidence?

- How is personal experience used as evidence?

- How are quotations used as part of evidence?

- How are images used as part of evidence, and how closely are they related to the verbal parts of the argument being presented?

As these questions suggest, evidence may not always travel well from one field to another. As you consider the kinds of evidence surveyed in the rest of this chapter, consider in which contexts or rhetorical situations each kind of evidence would be most (or least) effective.

FIRSTHAND EVIDENCE AND RESEARCH

Firsthand evidence comes from research you have carried out or been closely involved with, and much of this kind of research requires you to collect and examine data. Here we will discuss the kinds of firsthand research most commonly conducted by student writers.

Observations

"What," you may wonder, "could be any easier than observing something?" You just choose a subject, look at it closely, and record what you see and hear. If observing were so easy, eyewitnesses would all provide reliable accounts. Yet experience shows that several people who have observed the same phenomenon generally offer different, sometimes even contradictory, evidence on the basis of those observations. Trained observers say that getting down a faithful record of an observation requires intense concentration and mental agility.

Before you begin an observation, then, decide exactly what you want to find out and anticipate what you are likely to see. Do you want to observe an action repeated by many people (such as pedestrians crossing a street, in relation to an argument for putting in a new stoplight), a sequence of actions (such as the stages involved in student registration, which you want to argue is far too complicated), or the interactions of a group (such as meetings of the campus Young Republicans, which you want to see adhere to strict parliamentary procedures)? Once you have a clear sense of what you will observe and what questions you wish to answer through the observation, use the following guidelines to achieve the best results:

- Make sure the observation relates directly to your claim.

- Brainstorm about what you are looking for, but don't be rigidly bound to your expectations.

- Develop an appropriate system for collecting data. Consider using a split notebook or page: On one side, record the minute details of your observations directly; on the other, record your thoughts or impressions.

- Be aware that the way you record data will affect the outcome, if only in respect to what you decide to include in your observational notes and what you leave out.

- Record the precise date, time, and place of the observation.

In the following excerpt, Pico Iyer uses information drawn from minute and prolonged observation in an argument about what the Los Angeles International Airport (LAX) symbolizes about America:

LAX is, in fact, a surprisingly shabby and hollowed-out kind of place, certainly not adorned with the amenities one might expect of the world's strongest and richest power. When you come out into the Arrivals area in the International Terminal, you will find exactly one tiny snack bar, which serves nine items; of them, five are identified as Cheese Dog, Chili Dog, Chili Cheese Dog, Nachos with Cheese, and Chili Cheese Nachos. There is a large panel on the wall offering rental-car services and hotels, and the newly deplaned American dreamer can choose between the Cadillac Hotel, the Banana Bungalow . . . and the Backpacker's Paradise.

–Pico Iyer, "Where Worlds Collide"

FIGURE **18.1** LOS ANGELES INTER-NATIONAL AIRPORT

Interviews

Some evidence is best obtained through direct interviews. If you can talk with an expert—in person, on the phone, or online—you might get information you could not have obtained through any other type of research. In addition to getting expert opinion, you might ask for firsthand accounts, biographical information, or suggestions of other places to look or other people to consult. The following guidelines will help you conduct effective interviews:

* Determine the exact purpose of the interview, and be sure it is directly related to your claim.

* Set up the interview well in advance. Specify how long it will take, and if you wish to tape-record the session, ask permission to do so.

* Prepare a written list of both factual and open-ended questions. (Brainstorming with friends can help you come up with good questions.) Leave plenty of space for notes after each question. If the interview proceeds in a direction that you had not expected but that seems promising, don't feel you have to cover every one of your questions.

- Record the subject's full name and title, as well as the date, time, and place of the interview.

- Be sure to thank those you interview, either in person or with a follow-up letter or email message.

In arguing that the Gay Games offer a truly inclusive alternative — rather than a parallel — to the Olympics, Caroline Symons uses data drawn from extensive interviews with organizers and participants in the Gay Games:

> Out of twenty-four in-depth interviews I conducted with gay men involved in the Gay Games as organizers, over half indicated that they had sufficiently alienating experiences with sport during childhood and adolescence to be put off participating until the advent of gay sports organizations and events. . . . Gay men in particular have found a safe and welcoming environment to engage in sport through the emergence of gay sports organizations and the Gay Games.
>
> —Caroline Symons, "Not the Gay Olympic Games"

FIGURE 18.2 THE GAY GAMES WEB SITE

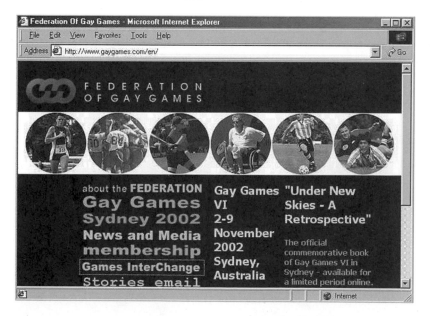

Surveys and Questionnaires

Surveys usually require the use of questionnaires. On any questionnaire, the questions should be clear, easy to understand, and designed so that respondents' answers can be analyzed easily. Questions that ask respondents to say "yes" or "no" or to rank items on a scale (1 to 5, for example, or "most helpful" to "least helpful") are particularly easy to tabulate. Here are some guidelines to help you prepare for and carry out a survey:

- Write out your purpose in conducting the survey, and make sure its results will be directly related to your claim.

- Brainstorm potential questions to include in the survey, and ask how each relates to your purpose and claim.

- Figure out how many people you want to contact, what the demographics of your sample should be (men in their twenties, or an equal number of men and women?), and how you plan to reach these people.

- Draft questions, making sure that each calls for a short, specific answer.

- Think about possible ways respondents could misunderstand you or your questions, and revise with these points in mind.

- Test the questions on several people, and revise those questions that are ambiguous, hard to answer, or too time-consuming to answer.

- If your questionnaire is to be sent by mail or email or posted on the Web, draft a cover letter explaining your purpose and giving a clear deadline. For mail, provide an addressed, stamped return envelope.

- On the final draft of the questionnaire, leave plenty of space for answers.

- Proofread the final draft carefully; typos will make a bad impression on those whose help you are seeking.

- Finally, you will need to tabulate the responses to your survey. Because tabulation can take time and effort, limit the number of questions you ask (people often resent being asked to answer more than about twenty questions, especially online). After you have done your tabulations, set out your findings in a clear, easily readable fashion, using a chart or spreadsheet if possible.

In an argument about whether the government should label genetically modified foods, analyst Gary Langer draws on data from a recent ABC News Poll asking Americans what they thought about such food:

Nearly everyone—93 percent—says the federal government should require labels on food saying whether it's been genetically modified, or "bio-engineered" (this poll used both phrases). Such near-unanimity in public opinion is rare.

Fifty-seven percent also say they'd be less likely to buy foods labeled as genetically modified. That puts the food industry in a quandary: By meeting consumer demand for labeling, it would be steering business away from its genetically modified products.

—Gary Langer, "Behind the Label: Many Skeptical of Genetically Modified Foods"

Experiments

Some arguments may be supported by evidence gathered through experiments. In the sciences, experimental data are highly valued—if the experiment is conducted in a rigorously controlled situation. For other kinds of writing, "looser" and more informal experiments can be acceptable, especially if they are intended to provide only part of the support for an argument. If you want to argue that the recipes in *Gourmand* magazine are impossibly tedious to follow and take far more time than the average person wishes to spend, you might ask five or six people to conduct a little experiment with you: following two recipes apiece from a recent issue, and recording and timing every step. The evidence you gather from this informal experiment could provide some concrete support—by way of specific examples—for your contention. But such experiments should be taken with a grain of salt; they may not be effective with certain audiences, and if they can easily be attacked as skewed or sloppily done ("The people you asked to make these recipes couldn't cook their way out of paper bags!"), then they may do more harm than good.

In an essay about computer hackers and the threats they pose to various individuals and systems, Winn Schwartau reports on an experiment performed by a former hacker he knows. One afternoon in Newport Beach, Jesse [the former hacker] carried out an experiment aimed at showing how easy it was to rob a bank. The experiment Schwartau describes makes his claim about bank security more believable.

> Jesse took his audience to a trash bin behind Pacific Bell, the Southern California Baby Bell service provider. Dumpster diving proved to be an effective means of social engineering because within minutes, an internal telephone company employee list was dredged out of the garbage. On it, predictably, were handwritten notes with computer passwords.

In the neighborhood was a bank, which shall go nameless. After some more dumpster diving, financial and personal profiles of wealthy bank customers surfaced. That was all Jesse said he needed to commit the crime.

At a nearby phone booth, Jesse used a portable computer with an acoustic modem to dial into the telephone company's computer. Jesse knew a lot about the telephone company's computers, so he made a few changes. He gave the pay phone a new number, that of one of the wealthy clients about whom he now knew almost everything. He also turned off the victim's phone with that same number. Jesse then called the bank and identified himself as Mr. Rich, an alias.

"How can we help you, Mr. Rich?"

"I would like to transfer $100,000 to this bank account number."

"I will need certain information."

"Of course."

"What is your balance?"

"About ____," he supplied the number accurately.

"What is your address?"

Jesse gave the address.

"Are you at home, Mr. Rich?"

"Yes."

"We'll need to call you back for positive identification."

"I understand. Thank you for providing such good security."

In less than a minute the phone rang.

"Hello, Rich here."

The money was transferred, then transferred back to Mr. Rich's account again, to the surprise and embarrassment of the bank. The money was returned and the point was made.

–Winn Schwartau, "Hackers: The First Information Warriors"

Personal Experience

Personal experience can serve as powerful evidence when it is appropriate to the subject, to your purpose, and to the audience. Remember that if it is your *only* evidence, however, personal experience probably will not be sufficient to carry the argument. Nevertheless, it can be especially effective for drawing listeners or readers into an argument, as Gloria Naylor demonstrates early in an argument about language and racism:

> I remember the first time I heard the word "nigger." In my third-grade class, our math tests were being passed down the rows, and as I handed the papers to a little boy in back of me, I remarked that once again he had received a much lower mark than I did. He snatched his

test from me and spit out that word. Had he called me a nymphomaniac or a necrophiliac, I couldn't have been more puzzled. I didn't know what a nigger was, but I knew that whatever it meant, it was something he shouldn't have called me. This was verified when I raised my hand, and in a loud voice repeated what he had said and watched the teacher scold him for using a "bad" word. I was later to go home and ask the inevitable question that every black parent must face—"Mommy, what does 'nigger' mean?"

–Gloria Naylor, "Mommy, What Does 'Nigger' Mean?"

CULTURAL CONTEXTS FOR ARGUMENT

Personal experience counts in making academic arguments in some but not all cultures. Showing that you have personal experience with a topic can carry strong persuasive appeal with many English-speaking audiences, however, so it will probably be a useful way to argue a point in the United States. As with all evidence used to make a point, evidence based on your own experience must be pertinent to the topic, understandable to the audience, and clearly related to your purpose and claim.

SECONDHAND EVIDENCE AND RESEARCH

Secondhand evidence comes from sources beyond yourself—books, articles, films, online documents, and so on.

Library Sources

Your college library has not only a great number of print materials (books, periodicals, reference works) but also computer terminals that provide access to electronic catalogs and indexes as well as to other libraries' catalogs via the Internet. Although this book isn't designed to give a complete overview of library resources, we can offer some important distinctions and pose a few key questions that can help you use the library most efficiently.

TWO IMPORTANT DISTINCTIONS

- Remember the distinction between the library databases and the Internet/Web. Your library computers hold important resources that are either not available on the Web at all or are not easily accessible to you except through the library's own system. The most important of these resources is the library's own catalog of its holdings (mostly books), but college libraries also pay to subscribe to a large number of scholarly databases—guides to journal and magazine articles, the Lexis/Nexis database of news stories and legal cases, and compilations of statistics, for example—that you can use for free. You'll be wise, then, to begin research using the electronic sources available to you through your college library before turning to the Web.

- Remember the distinction between subject headings and keywords. The library catalog and databases usually index contents by author, by title, by publication date, and by subject headings—a standardized set of words and phrases used to classify the subject matter of books and articles. When you do a subject search of the catalog, then, you are searching only one part of the electronic record of the library's books, and you will need to use the exact wording of the *Library of Congress Subject Headings* (LCSH) classifications. Searches using keywords, on the other hand, make use of the computer's ability to look for any term in any field of the electronic record. Keyword searching is less restrictive, but it requires you to think carefully about your search terms in order to get good results. In addition, you need to learn to use the techniques for combining keywords with the words *and*, *or*, and *not* and with parentheses and quotation marks to limit (or expand) your search.

SOME QUESTIONS FOR BEGINNING RESEARCH

- What kinds of sources do you need to consult? Check your assignment to see whether you are required to consult different kinds of sources. If you will use print sources, find out whether they are readily available in your library or whether you must make special arrangements (such as an interlibrary loan) to use them. If you need to locate nonprint sources, find out where those are kept and whether you need special permission to examine them.

- How current do your sources need to be? If you must investigate the very latest findings about, say, a new treatment for Alzheimer's, you will probably want to check periodicals, medical journals, or the Web. If you want broader, more detailed coverage and background information, you may need to depend more on books. If your argument deals with a specific time period, you may need to examine newspapers, magazines, or books written during that period.

- How many sources should you consult? Expect to look over many more sources than you will end up using. The best guideline is to make sure you have enough sources to support your claim.

- Do you know your way around the library? If not, ask a librarian for help in locating the following resources in the library: general and specialized encyclopedias; biographical resources; almanacs, yearbooks, and atlases; book and periodical indexes; specialized indexes and abstracts; the circulation computer or library catalog; special collections; audio, video, and art collections; the interlibrary loan office.

- Do you know how to conduct subject heading searches about your topic? Consult the *Library of Congress Subject Headings* (LCSH) for a list of standard subject headings related to your topic. This reference work, available in print and online, is a helpful starting point because it lists the subject headings used in most library catalogs and indexes.

Online Sources

Many important resources for argument are now available in databases, either online or on CD-ROM. But the Internet has no overall index such as the *Library of Congress Subject Headings*—at least not yet. Like library catalogs and databases, however, the Internet and Web offer two basic ways to search for sources related to your argument: one using subject categories and one using keywords. A subject directory organized by categories allows you to choose a broad category like "Entertainment" or "Science" and then click on increasingly narrow categories like "Movies" or "Astronomy" and then "Thrillers" or "The Solar System" until you reach a point where you are given a list of Web sites or the opportunity to do a keyword search. With the second kind of Internet search option, a search engine, you start right off with a keyword search. Because the Internet contains vastly more material than even the largest library catalog or database, searching it with a search engine requires even more thought and care in the choice and combination of keywords. For an argument about the fate of the hero in contemporary films, for example, you might find that *film* and *hero* produce far too many possible matches, or "hits." You might further narrow the search by adding a third keyword, say, *American* or *current*.

In doing such searches, you will need to observe the search logic for a particular database. Using *and* between keywords (*movies and heroes*) usually indicates that both terms must appear in a file for it to be called up. Using *or* between keywords usually instructs the computer to locate every file in which either one word or the other shows up, whereas using *not* tells the computer to exclude files containing a particular word from the search results (*movies not heroes*).

Software programs called browsers enable you to navigate the contents of the Web and to move from one Web site to another. Today, most browsers—such as Netscape Navigator, Safari, and Microsoft Explorer—are graphics browsers that display both text and visual images.

Web-based search engines can be used to carry out keyword searches or view a list of contents available in a series of directories. Here are a few of the most popular search engines:

Search Tools

AltaVista <altavista.digital.com> lets you search the entire Web using either a single keyword or multiple keywords.

Excite <excite.com> allows you to do keyword and subject directory searches.

Google <google.com> is a popular search tool that is a favorite of many students. Allows subject directory and keyword searches.

HotBot <hotbot.com> lets you search for individual words or phrases, names, or URLs in millions of Web sites and narrow the search to specific dates, media, and other criteria. Allows keyword and subject directory searches.

Lycos <lycos.com> allows you to search a huge catalog of Web sites and includes multimedia documents. Allows keyword and subject directory searches.

Magellan <magellan.com> allows you to search the entire Web or Web sites that have been evaluated for the quality of their content and organization. Allows keyword and subject directory searches.

WebCrawler <webcrawler.com> lets you search millions of Web sites with an easy-to-use procedure that is especially helpful for those new to keyword searching. Also allows for subject directory searches.

Yahoo! <yahoo.com> allows you either to search directories of sites related to particular subjects (such as entertainment or education) or to enter keywords that Yahoo! gives to a search engine (Google), which sends back the results.

USING EVIDENCE EFFECTIVELY

You may gather an impressive amount of evidence on your topic—from firsthand interviews, from careful observations, and from intensive library and online research. But until that evidence is woven into the fabric of your own argument, it is just a pile of data. Using your evidence effectively calls for turning data into information that will be persuasive to your intended audience.

Considering Audiences

The ethos you bring to an argument is crucial to your success in connecting with your audience. Of course, you want to present yourself as reliable and credible, but you also need to think carefully about the way your evidence relates to your audience. Is it appropriate to this particular group of readers or listeners? Does it speak to them in ways they will understand and respond to? Does it acknowledge and appeal to where they are "coming from"? It's hard to give any definite advice for making sure that your evidence is appropriate to the audience. But in general, timeliness is important to audiences: the more up-to-date your evidence, the better. In addition, evidence that is representative is usually more persuasive than evidence that is extreme or unusual. For example, in arguing for a campus-wide escort service after 10 P.M., a writer who cites numbers of students frightened, threatened, or attacked on their way across campus after dark and numbers of calls for help from campus phone boxes will be in a stronger position than one who cites only an attack that occurred four years ago.

Building a Critical Mass

Throughout this chapter we have stressed the need to discover as much evidence as possible in support of your claim. If you can find only one or two pieces of evidence, only one or two reasons to back up your contention, then you may be on weak ground. Although there is no magic number, no definite way of saying how much is "enough" evidence, you should build toward a critical mass, with a number of pieces of evidence all pulling in the direction of your claim. Especially if your evidence relies heavily on personal experience or on one major example, you should stretch your search for additional sources and good reasons to back up your claim.

CULTURAL CONTEXTS FOR ARGUMENT

How do you decide what evidence will best support your claims? The answer depends, in large part, on how you define evidence. Differing notions of what counts as evidence can lead to arguments that go nowhere fast.

Many examples of such failed arguments occurred during the 2003 war with Iraq. Even before the war began, members of the United Nations were less than satisfied with the evidence that Iraq represented a clear and present danger. What was completely persuasive to the U.S. government—pictures of convoys that could be moving around chemical weapons, for example—was not at all persuasive to others; they did not count as adequate evidence. Journalists are often called on to interview those whose view of what constitutes effective evidence differs markedly from their own. When Italian journalist Oriana Fallaci interviewed the Ayatollah Khomeini in 1971, for example, she argued in a way that is common in North American and Western European cultures: she presented what she considered adequate assertions backed up with facts ("Iran denies freedom to people. . . . Many people have been put in prison and even executed, just for speaking out in opposition"). In response, Khomeini relied on very different kinds of evidence: analogies ("Just as a finger with gangrene should be cut off so that it will not destroy the whole body, so should people who corrupt others be pulled out like weeds so they will not infect the whole field") and, above all, the authority of the Qur'an. Partly because of these differing beliefs about what counts as evidence, the interview ended unsuccessfully.

People in the United States tend to give great weight to factual evidence, but as this example shows, the same is not true in some other parts of the world. In arguing across cultures, you need to think carefully about how you are accustomed to using evidence—and to pay attention to what counts as evidence to members of other cultures.

- Do you rely on facts? Examples? Firsthand experience?
- Do you include testimony from experts? Which experts are valued most (and why)?
- Do you cite religious or philosophical texts? Proverbs or everyday wisdom?
- Do you use analogies as evidence? How much do they count?

Once you determine what counts as evidence in your own arguments, ask these same questions about the use of evidence by members of other cultures.

Arranging Evidence

You can begin to devise a plan for arranging your evidence effectively by producing a rough outline or diagram of your argument, a series of hand-written or computer note cards that can be grouped into categories, or anything else that makes the major points of the argument very clear. Then review your evidence, deciding which pieces support which points in the argument. In general, try to position your strongest pieces of evidence in key places—near the beginning of paragraphs, at the end of the introduction, or where you build toward a powerful conclusion. In addition, try to achieve a balance between, on the one hand, your own argument and your own words, and on the other hand, the sources you use or quote in support of the argument. The sources of evidence are important props in the structure, but they should not overpower the structure (your argument) itself.

RESPOND●

1. What counts as evidence depends in large part on the rhetorical situation. One audience might find personal testimony compelling in a given case, whereas another might require data that only experimental studies can provide.

    Imagine that you want to argue for a national educational campaign for ending spousal and partner abuse, composed of television ads to air before and during the Super Bowl—and you want the National Football League to pay for those ads. Make a list of reasons and evidence to support your claim, aimed at NFL executives. What kind of evidence would be most compelling to that group? How would you rethink your use of evidence if you were writing for the newsletter of a local women's shelter? This is not an exercise in pulling the wool over anyone's eyes; your goal is simply to anticipate the kind of evidence that different audiences would find persuasive given the same case.

2. Finding, evaluating, and arranging evidence in an argument is often a *discovery* process: sometimes you're concerned not only with digging up support for an already established claim but also with creating and revising tentative claims. Surveys and interviews can help you figure out what to argue, as well as provide evidence for a claim.

    Interview a classmate with the goal of writing a brief proposal argument about his or her career goals. The claim should be *My classmate should be doing X five years from now.* Limit yourself to ten questions; write them ahead of time and do not deviate from them. Record the results of the interview (written notes are fine—you don't need a tape recorder).

Then interview another classmate, with the same goal in mind. Ask the same first question, but this time let the answer dictate the rest of the questions. You still get only ten questions.

Which interview gave you more information? Which one helped you learn more about your classmate's goals? Which one better helped you develop claims about his or her future?

3. Imagine that you're trying to decide whether to take a class with a particular professor, but you don't know if he or she is a good teacher. You might already have an opinion, based on some vaguely defined criteria and dormitory gossip, but you're not sure if that evidence is reliable. You decide to observe a class to inform your decision.

    Visit a class in which you are not a student, and make notes on your observations following the guidelines in this chapter (p. 370). You probably only need a single day's visit to get a sense of the note-taking process, though you would, of course, need much more time to write a thorough evaluation of the professor.

    Write a short evaluation of the professor's teaching abilities on the basis of your observations. Then write an analysis of your evaluation. Is it honest? Fair? What other kinds of evidence might you need if you wanted to make an informed decision about the class and the teacher?

chapter nineteen

Fallacies of Argument

"That villainous abominable misleader of youth . . . that old white-bearded Satan."

"But if I don't get an 'A' in this class, I won't get into medical school."

"Ask not what your country can do for you; ask what you can do for your country."

"Make love, not war."

"All my friends have AOL. I'm the only one who can't get instant messages!"

■ ■ ■

Certain types of argumentative moves are so controversial they have been traditionally classified as *fallacies*, a term we use in this chapter. But you might find it more interesting to think of them as *flashpoints* or *hotspots* because they instantly raise questions about the ethics of argument—that is, whether a particular strategy of argument is fair, accurate, or principled. Fallacies are arguments supposedly flawed by their very nature or structure; as such, you should avoid them in your own writing and challenge them in arguments you hear or read. That said, it's important to appreciate that one person's fallacy may well be another person's stroke of genius.

Consider, for example, the fallacy termed *ad hominem* argument—"to the man." It describes a strategy of attacking the character of people you disagree with rather than the substance of their arguments: *So you think Eminem is a homophobic racist? Well, you're just a thumb-sucking, white-bread elitist.* Everyone has blurted out such insults at some time in their lives.

But there are also situations when someone's character is central to an argument. If that weren't so, appeals based on character would be pointless. The problem arises in deciding when such arguments are legitimate and when they are flashpoints. You are much more likely to think of attacks on people you admire as *ad hominem* slurs, but personal attacks on those you disagree with as reasonable criticisms. Obviously, debates about character can become quite ugly and polarizing. Consider Anita Hill and Clarence Thomas, Eminem and Moby, Pete Rose and major league baseball. (For more on arguments based on character, see Chapter 6.)

FIGURE 19.1 MOBY PERFORMING

It might be wise to think of fallacies not in terms of errors you can detect and expose in someone else's work, but as strategies that hurt everyone (including the person using them) because they make productive argument more difficult. Fallacies muck up the frank but civil conversations people should be able to have—regardless of their differences.

To help you understand flashpoints of argument, we've classified them according to three rhetorical appeals discussed in earlier chapters: emotional arguments, arguments based on character, and logical arguments. (See Chapters 4, 6, and 7.)

FLASHPOINTS OF EMOTIONAL ARGUMENT

Many people deride emotional arguments as "womanish" and, therefore, weak and suspect. But such views are not only close-minded and sexist; they're flat-out wrong. Emotional arguments can be both powerful and suitable in many circumstances, and most writers use them frequently. However, writers who pull on their readers' heartstrings too often can violate the good faith on which legitimate argument depends. Readers won't trust a writer who can't make a point without frightening someone or provoking tears or stirring up hatred.

Scare Tactics

Corrupters of children, the New Testament warns, would be better off dropped into the sea with millstones around their necks. Would that politicians, advertisers, and public figures who peddle their ideas by scaring people and exaggerating possible dangers well beyond their statistical likelihood face similarly stern warnings. Yet scare tactics are remarkably common in everything ranging from ads for life insurance to threats of audits by the Internal Revenue Service. Such ploys work because it is usually easier to imagine something terrible happening than to appreciate its statistical rarity. That may be why so many people fear flying more than driving. Auto accidents occur much more frequently, but they don't have the same impact on our imaginations as do air disasters.

Scare tactics can also be used to stampede legitimate fears into panic or prejudice. People who genuinely fear losing their jobs can be persuaded, easily enough, to mistrust all immigrants as people who might work for less money; people living on fixed incomes can be convinced that even minor modifications of entitlement programs represent dire threats to their standard of living. Such tactics have the effect of closing off thinking because people who are scared seldom act rationally.

Even well-intended fear campaigns—like those directed against drugs or HIV infection—can misfire if their warnings prove too shrill. When health professionals originally overestimated the rate at which AIDS would occur within the heterosexual population in the United States, many people became suspicious of the establishment's warnings and so grew careless about their own sexual behavior, thereby greatly increasing their risk of exposure to infection.

Either-Or Choices

A way to simplify arguments and give them power is to reduce the options for action to only two choices. The preferred option might be drawn in the warmest light, whereas the alternative is cast as an ominous shadow. That's the nature of the choices President George W. Bush offered to the United Nations in its dealings with Iraq in the fall of 2002:

> Events can turn in one of two ways: If we fail to act in the face of danger, the people of Iraq will continue to live in brutal submission. The regime will have new power to bully and dominate and conquer its neighbors, condemning the Middle East to more years of bloodshed and fear. . . . If we meet our responsibilities, if we overcome this danger, we can arrive at a very different future. The people of Iraq can shake off their captivity.
>
> –George W. Bush, September 12, 2002

Sometimes neither of the alternatives is pleasant: that's the nature of many "ultimatums." For instance, the allies in World War II offered the Axis powers only two choices as the conflict drew to a close: either continued war and destruction, or unconditional surrender. No third option was available.

Either-or arguments can be well-intentioned strategies to get something accomplished. Parents use them all the time; they will tell children either to eat their broccoli or they won't get dessert. Such arguments become fallacious when they reduce a complicated issue to excessively simple terms or when they are designed to obscure legitimate alternatives.

For instance, to suggest that Social Security must be privatized or the system will go broke may have rhetorical power, but the choice is too simple. The financial problems of Social Security can be fixed in any number of ways, including privatization. But to defend privatization, falsely, as the *only* possible course of action is to risk losing the support of people who know better.

But then *either-or* arguments—like most scare tactics—are often purposefully designed to seduce those who don't know much about a subject. That's another reason the tactic violates principles of civil discourse. Argument should enlighten people, making them more knowledgeable and more capable of acting intelligently and independently. Very often, we don't have to choose one side over the other. Listen to Bill Clinton make exactly that point in defending the environmental record of his administration [emphasis added]:

> From our inner cities to our pristine wild lands, we have worked hard to ensure that every American has a clean and healthy environment. We've rid hundreds of neighborhoods of toxic waste dumps, and taken the most dramatic steps in a generation to clean the air we breathe. We have made record investments in science and technology to protect future generations from the threat of global warming. We've worked to protect and restore our most glorious natural resources, from the Florida Everglades to California's redwoods to Yellowstone. *And we have, I hope, finally put to rest the false choice between the economy and the environment, for we have the strongest economy perhaps in our history, with a cleaner environment.*
>
> —Bill Clinton, January 11, 2000

Slippery Slope

The slippery slope flashpoint is well named, describing an argument that casts today's tiny misstep as tomorrow's avalanche. Of course, not all arguments aimed at preventing dire consequences are slippery slope fallacies: the parent who corrects a child for misbehavior now is acting sensibly to prevent more serious problems as the child grows older. And like the homeowner who repairs a loose shingle to prevent an entire roof from rotting, businesses and institutions that worry about little problems often prevent bigger ones. The city of New York learned an important lesson in the 1990s about controlling crime by applying what had become known as "the broken window theory": after former mayor Rudolph Giuliani directed police to crack down on petty crimes that make urban life especially unpleasant, major crimes declined as well.

A slippery slope argument becomes a flashpoint when a writer exaggerates the future consequences of an action, usually to frighten readers. As such, slippery slope arguments are also scare tactics. But people encounter them so often that they come to seem almost reasonable. For instance, defenders of free speech often regard even mild attempts to regulate behavior as constitutional matters: for example, a school board's request that a school pupil cut his ponytail becomes a direct assault on the child's First Amendment rights, litigated through the courts. Similarly, opponents of gun control warn that any legislation regulating firearms is just a first step toward the government knocking down citizens' doors and seizing weapons.

Ideas and actions do have consequences, but they aren't always as dire as writers fond of slippery slope tactics would have you believe.

Sentimental Appeals

Sentimental appeals are arguments that use emotions excessively to distract readers from facts. Quite often, such appeals are highly personal and individual—focusing attention on heart-warming or heart-wrenching situations that make readers feel guilty if they challenge an idea, policy, or proposal. Emotions become an impediment to civil discourse when they keep people from thinking clearly.

FIGURE 19.2 SENTIMENTAL IMAGES OF THREATENED SPECIES SUCH AS PANDAS OR WOLVES APPROPRIATE FOR SUPPORT OF ENVIRONMENTAL CAUSES ARE SOMETIMES ATTACHED TO MUCH LESS WORTHY SALES PITCHES.

· Yet sentimental appeals are a major vehicle of television news, where it is customary to convey ideas through personal tales that tug at viewers' heartstrings. For example, a camera might document the day-to-day life of a single mother on welfare whose on-screen generosity, kindness, and tears come to represent the spirit of an entire welfare clientele under attack by callous legislators; or the welfare recipient might be shown driving a new pickup and illegally trading food stamps for money while a lower-middle-class family struggles to meet its grocery budget. In either case, the conclusion the reporter wants you to reach is supported by powerful images that evoke emotions in support of that conclusion. But though the individual stories presented may be genuinely moving, they seldom give a complete picture of a complex social or economic issue.

Bandwagon Appeals

Bandwagon appeals are arguments that urge people to follow the same path everyone else is taking. Curiously, many American parents seem

FIGURE **19.3** JIMMY MARGULIES, EDITORIAL CARTOONIST FOR *THE RECORD*, BLAMES TV CABLE CHANNELS FOR BANDWAGON APPROACHES TO THE NEWS.

endowed with the ability to refute bandwagon appeals. When their kids whine that *Everyone else is going camping overnight without chaperones*, the parents reply instinctively, *And if everyone else jumps off a cliff (or a railroad bridge, or the Empire State Building), you will too?* The children stomp and groan—and then try a different line of argument.

Unfortunately, not all bandwagon approaches are so transparent. Though Americans like to imagine themselves as rugged individualists, they're easily seduced by ideas endorsed by the mass media and popular culture. Such trends are often little more than harmless fashion statements. At other times, however, Americans become obsessed by issues that politicians or the media select for their attention—such as the seemingly endless coverage of Gary Condit in 2001 and Elián Gonzalez the year before. In recent decades, bandwagon issues have included the war on drugs, the nuclear freeze movement, health care reform, AIDS prevention, gun control, drunk driving, tax reform, welfare reform, teen smoking, campaign finance reform, and post 9/11 antiwar movements.

In the atmosphere of obsession, there is a feeling that everyone must be concerned by this issue-of-the-day, and something—*anything*—must be done! More often than not, enough people jump on the bandwagon to achieve a measure of reform. And when changes occur because people have become sufficiently informed to exercise good judgment, then one can speak of "achieving consensus," a rational goal for civil argument.

But sometimes bandwagons run out of control, as they did in the 1950s when some careers were destroyed by "witch hunts" for suspected communists during the McCarthy era and in the late 1980s when concerns over child abuse mushroomed into indiscriminate prosecutions of parents and child care workers. In a democratic society, the bandwagon appeal is among the most potentially serious and permanently damaging flashpoints of argument.

FLASHPOINTS OF ETHICAL ARGUMENT

Not surprisingly, readers give their closest attention to authors whom they respect or trust. So, writers usually want to present themselves as honest, well informed, likable, or sympathetic in some way. But *trust me* is a scary warrant. Not all the devices writers use to gain the attention and confidence of readers are admirable. (For more on appeals of character, see Chapter 6.)

Appeals to False Authority

One of the effective strategies a writer can use to support an idea is to draw on the authority of widely respected people, institutions, and texts. In fact, many academic research papers are essentially exercises in finding and reflecting on the work of reputable authorities. Writers usually introduce these authorities into their arguments through direct quotations, citations (such as footnotes), or allusions. (See Chapter 21 for more on assessing the reliability of sources.)

False authority occurs chiefly when writers offer themselves, or other authorities they cite, as sufficient warrant for believing a claim:

Claim	X is true because I say so.
Warrant	What I say must be true.
Claim	X is true because Y says so.
Warrant	What Y says must be true.

Rarely will you see authority asserted quite so baldly as in these formulas, because few readers would accept a claim stated in either of these ways. Nonetheless, claims of authority drive many persuasive campaigns. American pundits and politicians are fond of citing the U.S. Constitution or Bill of Rights as ultimate authorities, a reasonable practice when the documents are interpreted respectfully. However, as often as not, the constitutional rights claimed aren't in the texts themselves or don't mean what the speakers think they do. And most constitutional matters are quite debatable—as centuries of court records could prove.

Likewise, communities of believers often base their religious beliefs on books or traditions that claim great authority. However, the power of these texts is usually somewhat limited outside that group and, hence, less capable of persuading others solely on the grounds of their authority alone—though arguments of faith often have power on other grounds.

Institutions can be cited as authorities too. Certainly, serious attention should be paid to claims supported by authorities one respects or recognizes—the White House, the FBI, the FDA, the National Science Foundation, the *New York Times*, the *Wall Street Journal*, and so on. But one ought not to accept facts or information simply because they have the imprimatur of such offices and agencies. To quote a Russian proverb made famous by Ronald Reagan, "Trust, but verify."

Dogmatism

A writer who attempts to persuade by asserting or assuming that a particular position is the only one conceivably acceptable within a community is trying to enforce dogmatism. Indeed, dogmatism is a flashpoint of character because the tactic undermines the trust that must exist between those who would make and those who would receive arguments. In effect, people who speak or write dogmatically imply that there are no arguments to be made: the truth is self-evident to those who know better. You can usually be sure you are listening to a dogmatic opinion when someone begins a sentence or phrase with *No rational person would disagree that* . . . or *It is clear to anyone who has thought about it that* . . .

Of course, there are some arguments beyond the pale of civil discourse—positions and claims so outrageous or absurd that they are unworthy of serious attention. For example, attacks on the historical reality of the Holocaust fall into this category. But relatively few subjects in a free society ought to be off the table from the start—certainly none that can be defended with facts, testimony, and good reasons. In general, therefore, when someone suggests that merely raising an issue for debate is somehow "politically incorrect"—whether racist or sexist, unpatriotic or sacrilegious, or insensitive or offensive in some other way—you should be suspicious. It is likely you are dealing with someone more interested in repressing ideas than exploring them.

Moral Equivalence

A fallacy of argument perhaps more common today than a decade ago is moral equivalence—that is, suggesting that serious wrongdoings don't differ in kind from minor offenses. A warning sign that this fallacy is likely to come into play is the retort of the politician or bureaucrat accused of wrongdoing: *But everyone else does it too!* Richard Nixon insisted that the crimes that led to his resignation did not differ from the activities of previous presidents; Bill Clinton made similar claims about the fund-raising and other scandals of his administration. Regardless of the validity of these particular defenses, there is a point at which comparisons become absurd. For example, many readers thought that Joan Jacobs Brumberg and Jacquelyn Jackson reached such a point when they suggested in an article in the *Boston Globe* that American women might not be much better off than women in Afghanistan living under Taliban rule:

> The war on terrorism has certainly raised our awareness of the ways in which women's bodies are controlled by a repressive regime in a faraway land, but what about the constraints on women's bodies here at home, right here in America? . . . Whether it's the dark, sad eyes of a woman in purdah or the anxious darkly circled eyes of a girl with anorexia nervosa, the woman trapped inside needs to be liberated

from cultural confines in whatever form they take. The burka and the bikini represent opposite ends of the political spectrum but each can exert a noose-like grip on the psyche and physical health of girls and women.
      —Joan Jacobs Brumberg and Jacquelyn Jackson, "The Burka and the Bikini"

Moral equivalence can work both ways. You've probably seen arguments in which relatively innocuous activities are raised to the level of major crimes. Some would say that the national campaign against smoking falls into this category — a common and legally sanctioned behavior now given the social stigma of serious drug abuse. And if smoking is almost criminal, should one not be equally concerned with people who use and abuse chocolate — a sweet and fatty food responsible for a host of health problems? You see how easy it is to make an equivalence argument. Yet suggesting that all behaviors of a particular kind — in this case, abuses of substances — are equally wrong (whether they involve cigarettes, alcohol, drugs, or fatty foods) blurs the distinctions people need to make in weighing claims.

Ad Hominem Arguments

Ad hominem (from the Latin for "to the man") arguments are attacks directed at the character of a person rather than at the claims he or she makes. The theory is simple: Destroy the credibility of your opponents, and either you destroy their ability to present reasonable appeals or you distract from the successful arguments they may be offering. Here, for example, is social critic Christopher Hitchens questioning whether former secretary of state Henry Kissinger should be appointed to head an important government commission in 2002: "But can Congress and the media be expected to swallow the appointment of a proven coverup artist, a discredited historian, a busted liar, and a man who is wanted in many jurisdictions for the vilest of offenses?" Not much doubt where Hitchens stands. Critics of Rush Limbaugh's conservative politics rarely fail to note his weight (even after he has lost most of it); critics of Bill Clinton's policies just as reliably still mention his womanizing.

In such cases, *ad hominem* tactics turn arguments into ham-fisted, two-sided affairs with good guys and bad guys. Civil argument resists this destructive nastiness, though the temptation to use such tactics persists even (some would say, especially) in colleges and universities.

Of course, character does matter in argument. People expect the proponent of peace to be civil, the advocate of ecology to respect the environment, the champion of justice to be fair even in private dealings. But it is fallacious to attack an idea by uncovering the foibles of its advocates or attacking their motives, backgrounds, or unchangeable traits.

FLASHPOINTS OF LOGICAL ARGUMENT

You'll encounter a flashpoint in any argument when the claims, warrants, and/or evidence in it are invalid, insufficient, or disconnected. In the abstract, such problems seem easy enough to spot; in practice, they can be camouflaged by a skillful use of words or images. Indeed, logical fallacies pose a challenge to civil argument because they often seem quite reasonable and natural, especially when they appeal to people's self-interests. Whole industries (such as phone-in psychic networks) depend on one or more of the logical fallacies for their existence; political campaigns, too, rely on them to prop up that current staple of democratic interchange— the fifteen-second TV spot.

Hasty Generalization

Among logical fallacies, only faulty causality might be able to challenge hasty generalization for the crown of most prevalent. A hasty generalization is an inference drawn from insufficient evidence: *Because my Honda broke down, all Hondas must be junk.* It also forms the basis for most stereotypes about people or institutions: because a few people in a large group are observed to act in a certain way, one infers that all members of that group will behave similarly. The resulting conclusions are usually sweeping claims of little merit: *Women are bad drivers; men are boors; Scots are stingy; Italians are romantic; English teachers are nit-picking; scientists are nerds.* You could, no doubt, expand this roster of stereotypes by the hundreds.

To draw valid inferences, you must always have sufficient evidence: a random sample of a population, a selection large enough to represent fully the subjects of your study, an objective methodology for sampling the population or evidence, and so on (see Chapter 18). And you must qualify your claims appropriately. After all, people do need generalizations to help make reasonable decisions in life; such claims can be offered legitimately if placed in context and tagged with appropriate qualifiers: *some, a few, many, most, occasionally, rarely, possibly, in some cases, under certain circumstances, in my experience.*

You should be especially alert to the fallacy of hasty generalization when you read reports and studies of any kind, especially case studies based on carefully selected populations. Be alert for the fallacy, too, in the interpretation of poll numbers. Everything from the number of people selected to the time the poll was taken to the exact wording of the questions may affect its outcome.

Faulty Causality

In Latin, the fallacy of faulty causality is described by the expression *post hoc, ergo propter hoc*, which translates word-for-word as "after this, therefore because of this." Odd as the translation may sound, it accurately describes what faulty causality is—the fallacious assumption that because one event or action follows another, the first necessarily causes the second.

Some actions, of course, do produce reactions. Step on the brake pedal in your car, and you move hydraulic fluid that pushes calipers against disks to create friction that stops the vehicle. Or, if you happen to be chair of the Federal Reserve Board, you raise interest rates to increase the cost of borrowing to slow the growth of the economy in order to curb inflation—you hope. Causal relationships of this kind are reasonably convincing because one can provide evidence of relationships between the events sufficient to convince most people that an initial action did, indeed, cause others.

But as even the Federal Reserve example suggests, causality can be difficult to control when economic, political, or social relationships are involved. That's why suspiciously simple or politically convenient causal claims should always be subject to scrutiny.

Begging the Question

There's probably not a teacher in the country who hasn't heard the following argument from a student: *You can't give me a "C" in this course; I'm an "A" student.* The accused felon's version of the same argument goes this way: *I can't be guilty of embezzlement; I'm an honest person.* In both cases, the problem with the claim is that it is made on grounds that cannot be accepted as true because those grounds are in doubt. How can the student claim to be an "A" student when she just earned a "C"? How can the accused felon defend himself on the grounds of honesty when that honesty is now suspect? Setting such arguments in Toulmin terms helps to expose the fallacy:

Claim + *Reason*	**You can't give me a "C" in this course because I'm an "A" student.**
Warrant	**An "A" student is someone who can't receive "C"s.**
Claim + *Reason*	**I can't be guilty of embezzlement because I'm an honest person.**
Warrant	**An honest person cannot be guilty of embezzlement.**

With the warrants stated, you can see why begging the question—that is, assuming as true the very claim that is disputed—is a form of circular argument, divorced from reality. If you assume that an "A" student can't receive "C"s, then the first argument stands. But no one is an "A" student *by definition*; that standing has to be earned by performance in individual courses. Otherwise, there would be no point for a student who once earned an "A" to be taking additional courses; "A" students can only get "A"s, right?

Likewise, even though someone with a record of honesty is unlikely to embezzle, a claim of honesty is not an adequate defense against specific charges. An honest person won't embezzle, but merely claiming to be honest does not make one so. (For more on Toulmin argument, see Chapter 8.)

Equivocation

Both the finest definition and the most famous literary examples of equivocation come from Shakespeare's tragedy *Macbeth*. In the drama three witches, representing the fates, make prophecies that favor the ambitious Macbeth but that prove disastrous when understood more fully. He is told, for example, that he has nothing to fear from his enemies "till Birnam wood / Do come to Dunsinane" (*Mac.* V.v.44–45); but these woods do move when enemy soldiers cut down branches from the forest of Birnam for camouflage and march on Macbeth's fortress. Catching on to the game, Macbeth starts "[t]o doubt the equivocation of the fiend / That *lies like truth*" (V.v.43–44, emphasis added). An equivocation, then, is an argument that gives a lie an honest appearance; it is a half-truth.

Equivocations are usually juvenile tricks of language. Consider the plagiarist who copies a paper word-for-word from a source and then declares—honestly, she thinks—that "I wrote the entire paper myself," meaning that she physically copied the piece on her own. But the plagiarist is using "wrote" equivocally—that is, in a limited sense, knowing that most people would understand "writing" as something more than the mere copying of words. Certainly the most famous equivocation of the last decade was Bill Clinton's "I never had sex with that woman" claim, but many public figures are fond of parsing their words carefully so that no certain meaning emerges.

Non Sequitur

A *non sequitur* is an argument in which claims, reasons, or warrants fail to connect logically; one point does not follow from another. As with other fallacies, children are notably adept at framing *non sequiturs*. Consider this familiar form: *You don't love me or you'd buy me that bicycle!* It might be more evident to harassed parents that no connection exists between love and Huffys if they were to consider the implied warrant:

Claim	**You must not love me**
Reason	**. . . because you haven't bought me that bicycle.**
Warrant	**Buying bicycles for children is essential to loving them.**

A five-year-old might endorse that warrant, but no responsible adult would because love does not depend on buying things, at least not a particular bicycle. Activities more logically related to love might include feeding and clothing children, taking care of them when they are sick, providing shelter and education, and so on.

In effect, *non sequiturs* occur when writers omit a step in an otherwise logical chain of reasoning, assuming that readers agree with what may be a highly contestable claim. For example, it is a *non sequitur* simply to argue that the comparatively poor performance of American students on international mathematics examinations means the country should spend more money on math education. Such a conclusion might be justified if a correlation were known or found to exist between mathematical ability and money spent on education. But the students' performance might be poor for reasons other than education funding, so a writer should first establish the nature of the problem before offering a solution.

Faulty Analogy

Comparisons give ideas greater presence or help clarify concepts. Consider all the comparisons packed into this reference to Jack Kennedy from a tribute to Jacqueline Kennedy by Stanley Crouch:

> The Kennedys had spark and Jack had grown into a handsome man, a male swan rising out of the Billy the Kid version of an Irish duckling he had been when he was a young senator.
>
> —Stanley Crouch, "Blues for Jackie"

When comparisons are extended, they become analogies—ways of understanding unfamiliar ideas by comparing them with something that is already known. Some argue that it is through comparisons, metaphors, and analogies that people come to understand the universe. But useful as such comparisons are, they may prove quite false either on their own or when pushed too far or taken too seriously. At this point they become faulty analogies, inaccurate or inconsequential comparisons between objects or concepts. For instance, to think of a human mind as a garden has charm: Gardens thrive only if carefully planted, weeded, watered, pruned, and harvested; so too the mind must be cultivated, if it is to bear fruit. But gardens also thrive when spread with aged manure. Need we follow the analogy down that path? Probably not.

RESPOND ●

1. Following is a list of political slogans or phrases that may be examples of logical fallacies. Discuss each item to determine what you may know about the slogan and then decide which, if any, fallacy might be used to describe it.

   "It's the economy, stupid." (sign on the wall at Bill Clinton's campaign headquarters)

   "Nixon's the one." (campaign slogan)

   "Remember the Alamo."

   "Make love, not war." (antiwar slogan during the Vietnam War)

   "A chicken in every pot."

   "No taxation without representation."

   "No Payne, your gain." (aimed at an opponent named Payne)

   "Loose lips sink ships."

   "Guns don't kill, people do." (NRA slogan)

   "If you can't stand the heat, get out of the kitchen."

2. We don't want you to argue fallaciously, but it's fun and good practice to frame argumentative fallacies in your own language. Pick an argumentative topic—maybe even one that you've used for a paper in this class—and write a few paragraphs making nothing but fallacious

arguments in each sentence. Try to include all the fallacies of emotional, ethical, and logical argument that are discussed in this chapter. It will be a challenge, since some of the fallacies are difficult to recognize, much less produce. Then revise the paragraphs, removing all traces of fallacious reasoning, rewriting for clarity, and improving the quality of the argument. This may be an even greater challenge — sometimes fallacies are hard to fix.

3. Choose a paper you've written for this or another class, and analyze it carefully for signs of fallacious reasoning. Once you've tried analyzing your own prose, find an editorial, a syndicated column, and a political speech and look for the fallacies in them. Which fallacies are most common in the four arguments? How do you account for their prevalence? Which are the least common? How do you account for their absence? What seems to be the role of audience in determining what is a fallacy and what is not? Did you find what seem to be fallacies other than the kinds discussed in this chapter?

4. Arguments on the Web are no more likely to contain fallacies than are arguments in any other text, but the fallacies can take on different forms. The hypertextual nature of Web arguments and the ease of including visuals along with text make certain fallacies more likely to occur there. Find a Web site sponsored by an organization, business, government entity, or other group (such as the sites of the Democratic and Republican National Committees), and analyze the site for fallacious reasoning. Among other considerations, look at the relationship between text and graphics, and between individual pages and the pages that surround or are linked to them. How does the technique of separating information into discrete pages affect the argument? Then send an email message to the site's creators, explaining what you found and proposing ways the arguments in the site could be improved.

5. Political Web logs such as andrewsullivan.com and InstaPundit.com typically provide quick responses to daily events and detailed critiques of material in other media sites, including national newspapers. Study one active political Web log for a few days to determine whether and how the blogger critiques the material he links to in his or her site. Does the blogger point to flashpoints and fallacies in arguments? Summarize your findings in an oral report to your class on that particular Web log.

chapter twenty

Intellectual Property, Academic Integrity, and Avoiding Plagiarism

On a college campus, a student receives a warning: she has been detected using peer-to-peer music file sharing software. Has she been practicing fair use, or is she guilty of copyright infringement?

A student writing an essay about Title IX's effect on college athletic programs finds some powerful supporting evidence for her argument on a Web site. Can she use this information without gaining permission?

Day care centers around the country receive letters arguing that they will be liable to lawsuit if they use representations of Disney characters without explicit permission or show Disney films "outside the home."

In California, one large vintner sues another, claiming that the second "stole" the idea of a wine label from the first, although a judge later finds that even though the labels were similar, the second was not "copied" from the first.

Musicians argue against other musicians, saying that the popular use of "sampling" in songs amounts to a form of musical "plagiarism."

In cyberspace, the development of digital "watermarks" and other forms of tracking systems have made it possible to trace not only documents printed out but those read online as well; as a result, some lawyers argue that public access to information is being limited in ways that are unconstitutional.

■ ■ ■

In prior ages of agriculture and industrialization, products that could provide a livelihood were likely to be concrete things: crops, tools, machines. But in an age of information such as the current one, ideas (intellectual property) are arguably society's most important products. Hence the growing importance of—and growing controversies surrounding—what counts as "property" in an information age.

Perhaps the framers of the Constitution foresaw such a shift in the bases of the nation's economy. At any rate, they articulated in the Constitution a delicate balance between the public's need for information and the incentives necessary to encourage people to produce work—both material and intellectual. Thus the Constitution empowers Congress "[t]o promote the progress of Science and useful Arts, by securing for limited Times to Authors and Inventors the exclusive Right to their respective Writings and Discoveries" (Article 1, Section 8, Clause 8). This passage allows for limited protection (copyright) of the expression of ideas ("Writings and Discoveries"), and through the years that time limit has been extended to up to lifetime plus seventy-five years (and it may be extended yet again to lifetime plus one hundred years).

Why is this historical information important to student writers? First, because writers need to know that ideas themselves cannot be copyrighted—only the expression of those ideas. Second, this information explains why some works fall out of copyright and are available for students to use without paying a fee (as you have to do for copyright-protected material in a coursepack, for instance). Third, this information is crucial to the current debates over who owns online materials—

FIGURE 20.1 AS A UNIT WITHIN THE LIBRARY OF CONGRESS, THE U.S. COPYRIGHT OFFICE WORKS TO UPHOLD CONSTITUTIONAL COPYRIGHT LAWS.

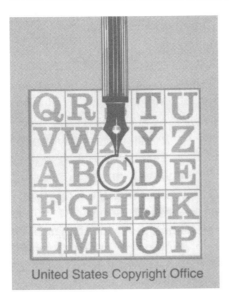

United States Copyright Office

materials that may never take any form of concrete expression. The debate will certainly be raging during and after the publication of this book—and the way in which it is resolved will have many direct effects on students and teachers. For up-to-date information about copyright law, see the Digital Future Coalition site at <dfc.org> or the U.S. Copyright site at <lcweb.loc.gov/copyright/>.

Although you may not have thought much about it, all of your work in college represents a growing bank of intellectual property, and this includes all the writing you do online and off. In fact, such original work is automatically copyrighted, even if it lacks the © symbol. As a result, you should be careful with your passwords and with discs you carry around with you. Whatever method you use for storing your work should be secure; only you should be able to give someone access to that work. In addition, remember that any email you send or any posting you make to a listserv or online forum is public. If you don't want your thoughts and ideas repeated (or forwarded), keep them offline. In turn, remember that you should not use material from email, discussion groups, or other online forums without asking the writer for permission to do so.

CREDITING SOURCES IN ARGUMENTS

Acknowledging your sources and giving full credit is especially important in argumentative writing because doing so helps establish your ethos as a writer. In the first place, saying "thank you" to those who have been of help to you reflects gratitude and openness, qualities that audiences generally respond to very well. Second, acknowledging your sources demonstrates that you have "done your homework," that you know the conversation surrounding your topic and are familiar with what others have thought and said about it, and that you want to help readers find other contributions to the conversation and perhaps join it themselves. Finally, acknowledging sources reminds you to think very critically about your own stance in your argument and about how well you have used your sources. Are they timely and reliable? Have you used them in a biased or overly selective way? Have you used them accurately, double-checking all quotations and paraphrases? Thinking through these questions will improve your overall argument.

CITING SOURCES AND RECOGNIZING PLAGIARISM

In some ways, it is completely true that there is "nothing new under the sun." Indeed, whatever you think or write or say draws on everything you have ever heard or read or experienced. Trying to recall every influence or source of information you have drawn on, even in one day, would take so long that you would have little time left in which to say anything at all. Luckily, people are seldom if ever called on to list every single influence or source of their ideas and writings.

Certainly, recognizing and avoiding plagiarism is a good deal easier and more practical than that. And avoiding plagiarism is very important, for in Western culture *the use of someone else's words or ideas without acknowledgment and as your own is an act of academic dishonesty that can bring devastating results.* Moreover, as we noted above, taking care to cite your sources works to your advantage in an academic setting: it builds your credibility, showing that you have done your homework as a researcher.

FIGURE 20.2 DOONESBURY CARTOON ON INTELLECTUAL PROPERTY

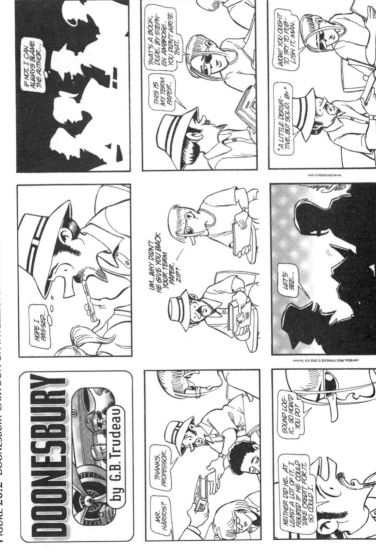

INACCURATE OR INCOMPLETE CITATION OF SOURCES

If you use a paraphrase that is too close to the original wording or sentence structure, if you leave out the parenthetical reference for a quotation (even if you include the quotation marks themselves), or if you don't indicate clearly the source of an idea you obviously didn't come up with on your own, you may be accused of plagiarism—even if that was not your intent. This kind of inaccurate or incomplete citation of sources often results either from carelessness or from not trying to learn how to use citations accurately and fully. Still, because the costs of even unintentional plagiarism can be severe, it's important to understand how it can happen and how you can guard against it.

In a January 2002 article published in *Time* magazine, historian Doris Kearns Goodwin (see Figure 20.3) explains how someone else's writing wound up in her book. The book in question, nine hundred pages long and with thirty-five hundred footnotes, took Goodwin ten years to write. During these ten years, she says, she took most of her notes by hand, organized the notes into boxes, and—once the draft was complete—went back to all her sources to check that all the material from them was correctly cited. "Somehow in this process," Goodwin goes on to say, "a few books were not fully rechecked," and so she omitted some necessary quotation marks in material she didn't acknowledge. Reflecting back on this experience, Goodwin says that discovering such carelessness in her own work was very troubling—so troubling that in the storm of criticism that ensued over the discovery of these failures to cite properly, she resigned from her position as a member of the Pulitzer Prize Committee.

FIGURE 20.3 DORIS KEARNS GOODWIN

CULTURAL CONTEXTS FOR ARGUMENT

Not all cultures accept Western notions of plagiarism, which rest on a belief that language can be owned by writers. Indeed, in many countries, and in some communities within the United States, using the words of others is considered a sign of deep respect and an indication of knowledge—and attribution is not expected or required. In writing arguments in the United States, however, you should credit all materials but those that are common knowledge, that are available in a wide variety of sources, or that are your own findings from field research.

ACKNOWLEDGING YOUR USE OF SOURCES

The safest way to avoid charges of plagiarism is to acknowledge as many of your sources as possible, with the following three exceptions:

- *common knowledge*, a specific piece of information most readers will know (that Bill Clinton won the 1996 presidential election, for instance)
- *facts available from a wide variety of sources* (that the Japanese bombing of Pearl Harbor occurred on December 7, 1941, for example)
- *your own findings from field research* (observations, interviews, experiments, or surveys you have conducted), which should simply be announced as your own

For all other source material you should give credit as fully as possible, placing quotation marks around any quoted material, citing your sources according to the documentation style you are using, and including them in a list of references or works cited. Material to be credited includes all of the following:

- *direct quotations*
- *facts not widely known or arguable statements*
- *judgments, opinions, and claims made by others*
- *images, statistics, charts, tables, graphs, or other illustrations* from any source
- *collaboration, the help provided by friends, colleagues, instructors, supervisors, or others*

(See Chapters 21 and 22 for more on using and documenting sources.)

USING COPYRIGHTED INTERNET SOURCES

If you've done any surfing on the Net, you already know that it opens the doors to worldwide collaborations, as you can contact individuals and groups around the globe and have access to whole libraries of information. As a result, writing (most especially, online writing) seems increasingly to be made up of a huge patchwork of materials that you alone or you and many others weave together. (For a fascinating discussion of just how complicated charges and countercharges of plagiarism can be on the Internet, see <ombuds.org/narrative1.html>, where you can read a description of a mediation involving a Web site that included summaries of other people's work.) But when you use information gathered from Internet sources in your own work, it is subject to the same rules that govern information gathered from other types of sources.

Thus, whether or not the material includes a copyright notice or symbol ("© 2004 by John J. Ruszkiewicz and Andrea A. Lunsford," for example), it is more than likely copyrighted—and you may need to request permission to use part or all of it. Although they are currently in danger, "fair use" laws still allow writers to quote brief passages from published works without permission from the copyright holder if the use is for educational or personal, noncommercial reasons and full credit is given to the source. For personal communication such as email or for listserv postings, however, you should ask permission of the writer before you include any of his or her material in your own argument. For graphics, photos, or other images you wish to reproduce in your text, you should also request permission from the creator or owner (except when you are using them in work only turned in to an instructor, which is "fair use"). And if you are going to disseminate your work beyond your classroom—especially by publishing it online—you must ask permission for any material you borrow from an Internet source.

Here are some examples of student requests for permission:

To: litman@mindspring.com
CC: lunsford.2@stanford.edu
Subject: Request for permission

Dear Professor Litman:

I am writing to request permission to quote from your essay "Copyright, Owners' Rights and Users' Privileges on the Internet: Implied Licences, Caching, Linking, Fair Use, and Sign-on Licences." I want to quote some of your work as part of an essay I am writing for my composition class at Stanford University to explain the complex debates over ownership on the Internet and to argue that students in my class should be participating in these debates. I will give full credit to you and will cite the URL where I first found your work: <msen.com/~litman/dayton/htm>.

Thank you very much for considering my request.

Raul Sanchez <sanchez.32@stanford.edu>

To: fridanet@aol.com
CC: lunsford.2@stanford.edu
Subject: Request for permission

Dear Kimberley Masters:

I am a student at Stanford University writing to request your permission to download and use a photograph of Frida Kahlo in a three-piece suit <fridanet/suit.htm#top> as an illustration in a project about Kahlo that I and two other students are working on in our composition class. In the report on our project, we will cite <members.aol.com/fridanet/kahlo.htm> as the URL, unless you wish for us to use a different source.

Thank you very much for considering our request.

Jennifer Fox <fox.360@stanford.edu>

ACKNOWLEDGING COLLABORATION

We have already noted the importance of acknowledging the inspirations and ideas you derive from talking with others. Such help counts as one form of collaboration, and you may also be involved in more formal kinds of collaborative work—preparing for a group presentation to a class, for example, or writing a group report. Writers generally acknowledge all participants in collaborative projects at the beginning of the presentation, report, or essay—in print texts, often in a footnote or brief prefatory note. The sixth edition of the *MLA Handbook for Writers of Research Papers* (2003) calls attention to the growing importance of collaborative work and gives the following advice on how to deal with issues of assigning fair credit all around:

Joint participation in research and writing is common and, in fact, encouraged in many courses and in many professions. It does not constitute plagiarism provided that credit is given for all contributions. One way to give credit, if roles were clearly demarcated or were unequal, is to state exactly who did what. Another way, especially if roles and contributions were merged and shared, is to acknowledge all concerned equally. Ask your instructor for advice if you are not certain how to acknowledge collaboration.

RESPOND.

1. Not everyone agrees with the concept of intellectual material as property, as something to be protected. Lately the slogan "information wants to be free" has been showing up in popular magazines and on the Internet, often along with a call to readers to take action against forms of protection such as data encryption and further extension of copyright.

   Using a Web search engine, look for pages where the phrase "free information" appears. Find several sites that make arguments in favor of free information, and analyze them in terms of their rhetorical appeals. What claims do the authors make? How do they appeal to their audience? What is the site's ethos, and how is it created? Once you have read some arguments in favor of free information, return to this chapter's arguments about intellectual property. Which do you find more persuasive? Why?

2. Although this text is principally concerned with ideas and their written expression, there are other forms of protection available for intellectual property. Scientific and technological developments are protectable under patent law, which differs in some significant ways from copyright law.

   Find the standards for protection under U.S. copyright law and U.S. patent law. You might begin by visiting the U.S. copyright Web site at <lcweb.loc.gov/copyright/>. Then, imagine that you are the president of a small, high-tech corporation and are trying to inform your employees of the legal protections available to them and their work. Write a paragraph or two explaining the differences between copyright and patent and suggesting a policy that balances employees' rights to intellectual property with the business's needs to develop new products.

3. Define plagiarism in your own terms, making your definition as clear and explicit as possible. Then compare your definition with those of two or three other classmates and write a brief report on the similarities and differences you noted in the definitions.

4. Spend fifteen or twenty minutes jotting down your ideas about intellectual property and plagiarism. Where do you stand, for example, on the issue of music file sharing? On downloading movies free of charge? Do you think these forms of intellectual property should be protected under copyright law? How do you define your own intellectual property, and in what ways and under what conditions are you willing to share it? Finally, come up with your own definition of "academic integrity."

chapter twenty-one

Evaluating and Using Sources

EVALUATING SOURCES

As many examples in this text have shown, the quality of an argument often depends on the quality of the sources used to support or prove it. As a result, careful evaluation and assessment of all your sources is important, including those you gather in libraries or from other print sources, in online searches, or in field research you conduct yourself.

Print Sources

Since you want the information you glean from sources to be reliable and persuasive, it pays to evaluate thoroughly each potential source. The following principles can help you in conducting such an evaluation for print sources:

- *Relevance.* Begin by asking what a particular source will add to your argument and how closely related to your argumentative claim it is. For a book, the table of contents and the index may help you decide. For an article, check to see if there is an abstract that summarizes the contents. And if you can't think of a good reason for using the source, set it aside; you can almost certainly find something better.

- *Credentials of the author.* You may find the author's credentials set forth in an article, book, or Web site, so be sure to look for a description of the author. Is the author an expert on the topic? To find out, you can also go to the Internet to gather information: Just open a search tool such as InfoSeek or AltaVista, and type in the name of the person you are looking for. Still another way to learn about the credibility of an author is to search Google Groups for postings that mention the author or to check the Citation Index to find out how others refer to this author. And if you see your source cited by other sources you are using, look at how they cite it and what they say about it that could provide clues to the author's credibility.

- *Stance of the author.* What is the author's stance on the issue(s) involved, and how does this stance influence the information in the source? Does the author's stance support or challenge your own views?

- *Credentials of the publisher or sponsor.* If your source is from a newspaper, is it a major one (such as the *San Francisco Chronicle* or the *New York Times*) that is known for integrity in reporting, or is it a tabloid? Is it a

FIGURE 21.1   NOTE THE DIFFERENCES BETWEEN THE *PEOPLE* MAGAZINE COVER AND THAT OF A LITERARY JOURNAL.

popular magazine like *People* or a journal sponsored by a professional group, such as the *Journal of the American Medical Association?* If your source is a book, is the publisher one you recognize or can find described on its own Web site?

- *Stance of the publisher or sponsor.* Sometimes the rhetorical stance of a source will be absolutely obvious: A Web site titled "Save the Spotted Owl" strongly suggests that the sponsor will take a pro-environmental stance, whereas the Web site for the Republican National Committee will certainly take a conservative stance. But other times, you need to read carefully between the lines to identify particular stances, so you can see how the stance affects the message the source presents. Start by asking what the source's goals are: what does the sponsoring group want to make happen?

- *Currency.* Check the date of publication of any book or article as well as the date of posting or updating on a Web source. (And remember that the publication dates of Internet sites can often be hard to pin down; most reliable will be those that are updated regularly.) Recent sources are often more useful than older ones, particularly in the sciences. However, in some fields such as history or literature, the most authoritative works can be the older ones.

- *Level of specialization.* General sources can be helpful as you begin your research, but later in the project you may need the authority or currency of more specialized sources. On the other hand, keep in mind that extremely specialized works on your topic may be too difficult for your audience to understand easily.

- *Audience.* Was the source written for a general readership? For specialists? For advocates or opponents?

- *Length.* Is the source long enough to provide adequate detail in support of your claim?

- *Availability.* Do you have access to the source? If it is not readily accessible, your time might be better spent looking elsewhere.

- *Omissions.* What is missing or omitted from the source? Might such exclusions affect whether or how you can use the source as evidence?

Electronic Sources

You will probably find working on the Internet and the World Wide Web both exciting and frustrating, for even though these tools have great potential, they still hold loads of suspect information. As a result, careful researchers look for corroboration before accepting evidence they find online, especially if it comes from a site whose sponsor's identity is less than clear. In such an environment, you must be the judge of how accurate and trustworthy particular electronic sources are. In making these judgments you should rely on the same kind of careful thinking you would use to assess any source. In addition, you may find some of the following questions helpful in evaluating online sources:

• Who has posted the document or message or created the site? An individual? An interest group? A company? A government agency? Does the URL offer any clues? Note especially the final suffix in a domain name: .com (commercial); .org (nonprofit organization); .edu (educational institution); .gov (government agency); .mil (military); .net (network)—or the geographical domains that indicate country of origin, as in .ca (Canada) or .ar (Argentina). The home page or first page of a site should tell you something about the sponsorship of the source, letting you know who can be held accountable for its information. (You may need to click on an "About Us" button.) Finally, links may help you learn how credible and useful the source is. Click on some of them to see if they lead to legitimate and helpful sites.

• What can you determine about the credibility of the author or sponsor? Can the information in the document or site be verified in other sources? How accurate and complete is it?

• Who can be held accountable for the information in the document or site? How well and thoroughly does it credit its own sources?

• How current is the document or site? Be especially cautious of undated materials. Most reliable will be those that are updated regularly.

• How effectively is the document or site designed? How "friendly" is it? Are its links, if any, helpful? What effects do design, visuals, and/or sound have on the message? (See Chapters 15 and 16.)

• What perspectives are represented? If only one perspective is represented, how can you balance or expand this point of view?

At a recent conference, the Stanford Persuasive Technology Lab argued that Google News may soon be the "most credible Web site of them all." The Lab listed twenty-five reasons in support of this conclusion, from the timeliness of the information, to the lack of a single viewpoint or ideology, to the ad-free policy. The next time you log on to Google News, ask yourself what other features of this site help build its credibility.

Field Research

If you have conducted experiments, surveys, interviews, observations, or any other field research in developing and supporting an argument, make sure to review your own results with a critical eye. The following questions can help you evaluate your own field research:

- Have you rechecked all data and all conclusions to make sure they are accurate and warranted?
- Have you identified the exact time, place, and participants in all field research?
- Have you made clear what part you played in the research and how, if at all, your role could have influenced the results or findings?
- If your research involved other people, have you gotten their permission to use their words or other material in your argument? Have you asked whether you could use their names or whether the names should be kept confidential?

USING SOURCES

As you locate, examine, and evaluate sources in support of an argument, remember to keep a careful record of where you have found them. For print sources, you may want to keep a working bibliography on your computer—or a list in a notebook you can carry with you. In any case, make sure you take down the *name of the author*; the *title* of the book or periodical and article, if any; the *publisher* and *city of publication*; the *date of publication*; relevant *volume, issue*, and exact *page numbers*; and any other information you may later need in preparing a works-cited or references list. In addition, for a book, note where you found it—the section of the library, for example, along with the call number for the book.

For electronic sources, you should also keep a careful record of the information you will need in your works-cited or references list—particularly the *name of the database or online source*, the full *electronic address (URL)*, and several potentially important dates: (1) the *date the document was first produced*; (2) the *date the document was published on the Web*—this may be a version number or a revision date; and (3) the *date you accessed the document*. The simplest way to ensure that you have this information is to get a printout of the source, highlighting source information and writing down any other pertinent information.

Signal Words and Introductions

Because your sources are crucial to the success of your arguments, you need to introduce them carefully to your readers. Doing so usually calls for beginning a sentence in which you are going to use a source with a signal phrase of some kind: *According to noted child psychiatrist Robert Coles, children develop complex ethical systems at extremely young ages.* In this sentence, the signal phrase tells readers that you are about to draw on the work of a person named Robert Coles and that this person is a "noted child psychiatrist." Now look at an example that uses a quotation from a source in more than one sentence:

> In *Job Shift*, consultant William Bridges worries about "dejobbing and about what a future shaped by it is going to be like." Even more worrisome, Bridges argues, is the possibility that "the sense of craft and of professional vocation . . . will break down under the need to earn a fee" (228).

The signal verbs "worries" and "argues" add a sense of urgency to the message Bridges offers and suggest that the writer either agrees with—or is neutral about—Bridges's points. Other signal verbs have a more negative slant, indicating that the point being introduced in the quotation is open to debate and that others (including the writer) might disagree with it. If the writer of the passage above had said, for instance, that Bridges "unreasonably contends" or that he "fantasizes," these signal verbs would carry quite different connotations from those associated with "argues." In some cases, a signal verb may require more complex phrasing to get the writer's full meaning across:

> Bridges recognizes the dangers of changes in work yet refuses to be overcome by them: "The real issue is not how to stop the change but how to provide the necessary knowledge and skills to equip people to operate successfully in this New World" (229).

As these examples illustrate, the signal verb is important because it allows you to characterize the author's or source's viewpoint or perspective as well as your own—so choose these verbs with care. Other frequently used signal verbs include *acknowledges, advises, agrees, allows, asserts, believes, charges, claims, concludes, concurs, confirms, criticizes, declares, disagrees, discusses, disputes, emphasizes, expresses, interprets, lists, objects, observes, offers, opposes, remarks, replies, reports, responds, reveals, states, suggests, thinks,* and *writes.*

Quotations

For supporting argumentative claims, you will want to quote—that is, to reproduce an author's precise words—in at least three kinds of situations: when the wording is so memorable or expresses a point so well that you cannot improve it or shorten it without weakening it; when the author is a respected authority whose opinion supports your own ideas particularly well; and when an author challenges or disagrees profoundly with others in the field.

Direct quotations can be effective in capturing your readers' attention—for example, through quoting a memorable phrase in your introduction or quoting an eyewitness account in arresting detail. In an argument, quotations from respected authorities can help build your ethos as someone who has sought out experts in the field. Finally, carefully chosen quotations can broaden the appeal of your argument by drawing on emotion as well as logic, appealing to the reader's mind and heart. A student writing on the ethical issues of bullfighting, for example, might introduce an argument that bullfighting is not a sport by quoting Ernest Hemingway's comment that "the formal bull-fight is a tragedy, not a sport, and the bull is certain to be killed," and might accompany the quotation with an image such as the one below:

FIGURE 21.2 BULLFIGHT

The following guidelines can help you make sure that you quote accurately:

- If the quotation extends over more than one page in the original source, note the placement of page breaks in case you decide to use only part of the quotation in your argument.

- Label the quotation with a note that tells you where and/or how you think you will use it.

- Make sure you have all the information necessary to create an in-text citation as well as an item in your works-cited or references list.

- When you use a quotation in your argument, make sure you have introduced the author(s) of the quotation and that you follow the quotation with some commentary of your own that points out the significance of the quotation.

- Copy quotations carefully, being sure that punctuation, capitalization, and spelling are exactly as they are in the original.

- Enclose the quotation in quotation marks; don't rely on your memory to distinguish your own words from those of your source. If in doubt, recheck all quotations for accuracy.

- Use square brackets if you introduce words of your own into the quotation or make changes to it. (*"And [more] brain research isn't going to define further the matter of 'mind.'"*)

- Use ellipsis marks if you omit material. (*"And brain research isn't going to define . . . the matter of 'mind.'"*)

- If you're quoting a short passage (four lines or less, MLA style; forty words or less, APA style), it should be worked into your text, enclosed by quotation marks. Longer quotations should be set off from the regular text. Begin such a quotation on a new line, indenting every line one inch or ten spaces (MLA) or five to seven spaces (APA). Set-off quotations do not need to be enclosed in quotation marks.

CULTURAL CONTEXTS FOR ARGUMENT

Although some language communities and cultures expect audiences to recognize the sources of important documents and texts, thereby eliminating the need to cite them directly, conventions for writing in North America call for careful attribution of any quoted, paraphrased, or summarized material. When in doubt, explicitly identify your sources.

Paraphrases

Paraphrases involve putting an author's material (including major and minor points, usually in the order they are presented in the original) into *your own words and sentence structures*. Here are some guidelines that can help you paraphrase accurately:

- When you use a paraphrase in your argument, make sure that you identify the source of the paraphrase and that you comment on its significance.
- Make sure you have all the information necessary to create an in-text citation as well as an item in your works-cited or references list. For online sources without page numbers, record the paragraph, screen, or other section number(s) if indicated.
- If you are paraphrasing material that extends over more than one page in the original source, note the placement of page breaks in case you decide to use only part of the paraphrase in your argument.
- Label the paraphrase with a note suggesting where and/or how you intend to use it in your argument.
- Include all main points and any important details from the original source, in the same order in which the author presents them.
- Leave out your own comments, elaborations, or reactions.
- State the meaning in your own words and sentence structures. If you want to include especially memorable or powerful language from the original source, enclose it in quotation marks.
- Recheck to make sure that the words and sentence structures are your own and that they express the author's meaning accurately.

Summaries

A summary is a significantly shortened version of a passage—or even a whole chapter of a work—that captures the main ideas *in your own words*. Unlike a paraphrase, a summary uses just enough information to record the points you want to emphasize. Summaries can be extremely valuable in supporting arguments. Here are some guidelines to help you prepare accurate and helpful summaries:

- When you use a summary in an argument, be sure to identify the source of the summary and add your own comments about why the material in the summary is significant for the argument you are making.

- Make sure you have all the information necessary to create an in-text citation as well as an item in your works-cited or references list. For online sources without page numbers, record the paragraph, screen, or other section number(s) if available.

- If you are summarizing material that extends over more than one page, indicate page breaks in case you decide to use only part of the summary in your argument.

- Label the summary with a note that suggests where and/or how you intend to use it in your argument.

- Include just enough information to recount the main points you want to cite. A summary is usually much shorter than the original.

- Use your own words. If you include any language from the original, enclose it in quotation marks.

- Recheck to make sure that you have captured the author's meaning accurately and that the wording is entirely your own.

Visuals

If a picture is worth a thousand words, then using pictures calls for caution: one picture might overwhelm or undermine the message you are trying to send in your argument. On the other hand, as you've seen in Chapter 15, visuals can have a powerful impact on audiences and can help bring them to understand or accept your arguments. In choosing visuals to include in your argument, make sure that each one makes a strong contribution to your message and that each is appropriate and fair to your subject or topic and your audience.

When you use a visual in your written arguments, treat them as you would any other sources you integrate into your text. Like quotations, paraphrases, and summaries, visuals need to be introduced and commented on in some way. In addition, label (as figures or as tables) and number (Figure 1, Figure 2, and so on) all visuals, provide a caption that includes source information and describes the visual, and cite the source in your bibliography or list of works cited. Keep in mind that even if you create a visual (such as a bar graph) by using information from a source (the results, say, of a Gallup Poll), you must cite the source. If you use a photograph you took yourself, cite it as a personal photograph.

Here is a visual that accompanied the introduction to an argument about bankruptcy that appeared on the front page of the December 15, 2002, *New York Times* Business section. Note that the source of the visual is

FIGURE 21.3 A LAWYER WITH A BINDER OF PAPERWORK INVOLVING THE US AIRWAYS BANKRUPTCY FILING. COMPANIES CAN LOSE CONSIDERABLE VALUE DURING THE CHAPTER 11 PROCESS. (SOURCE: BLOOMBERG NEWS)

listed (Bloomberg News) and that the caption indicates in what way the visual is related to the argument (in this case, the visual depicts bankruptcy papers). If you were going to use this as the first visual in an essay of your own, you would need to include the source, describe the image in relationship to your topic, and head it *Figure 1*. As long as you are using this image in a print text only, you are allowed fair use of it. If you intend to post your argument on the Web, however, or otherwise publish it, you would need to request permission from the copyright owner (see Chapter 20, page 408).

RESPOND●

1. Select one of the essays at the end of Chapters 9 to 13. Then write a brief summary of the essay that includes both direct quotations and paraphrases. Be careful to attribute the ideas properly, even when you paraphrase, and to use signal phrases to introduce quotations.

Trade summaries with a partner, and compare the passages you selected to quote and paraphrase, and the signal phrases you used to introduce them. How do your choices create an ethos for the original author that differs from the one your partner has created? How do the signal phrases shape a reader's sense of the author's position? Which summary best represents the author's argument? Why?

2. Return to the Internet sites you found in exercise 1 of Chapter 20 that discuss free information. Using the criteria in this chapter for evaluating electronic sources, judge each of those sites. Select three that you think are most trustworthy, and write a paragraph summarizing their arguments and recommending them to an audience unfamiliar with the debate.

3. Choose a Web site that you visit frequently. Then, using the guidelines discussed in this chapter, spend some time evaluating its credibility. You might begin by comparing it with Google News or another site that has a reputation for being extremely reliable.

chapter twenty-two

Documenting Sources

What does documenting sources have to do with argument? First, the sources themselves form part of the argument, showing that a writer has done some homework, knows what others have said about the topic, and understands how to use these sources as support for a claim. The list of works cited or references makes an argument, saying, perhaps, "Look at how thoroughly this essay has been researched" or "Note how up-to-date I am!" Even the style of documentation makes an argument, though in a very subtle way. You will note in the instructions that follow, for example, that for a print source the Modern Language Association (MLA) style for a list of works cited requires putting the date of publication at or near the end of an entry, whereas the American Psychological Association (APA) style for a list of references involves putting the date near the beginning. (An exercise at the end of this chapter asks you to consider what argument this difference represents.) And when a documentation style calls for listing only the first author followed by "et al." in citing works by multiple authors, it is subtly arguing that only the first author really matters—or at least that acknowledging the others is less important than keeping citations brief. Pay attention to the fine points of documentation and documentation style, always asking what these elements add (or do not add) to your arguments.

MLA STYLE

FIGURE 22.1   THE *MLA HANDBOOK FOR WRITERS OF RESEARCH PAPERS*

Documentation styles vary from discipline to discipline, with different formats favored in the social sciences and the natural sciences, for example. Widely used in the humanities, the MLA style is fully described in the *MLA Handbook for Writers of Research Papers* (6th edition, 2003). In this discussion, we provide guidelines drawn from the *MLA Handbook* for in-text citations, notes, and entries in the list of works cited.

In-Text Citations

MLA style calls for in-text citations in the body of an argument to document sources of quotations, paraphrases, summaries, and so on. For in-text citations, use a signal phrase to introduce the material, often with the author's name (*As LaDoris Cordell explains . . .*). Keep an in-text citation short, but include enough information for readers to locate the source in the list of works cited. Place the parenthetical citation as near to the relevant material as possible without disrupting the flow of the sentence, as in the following examples.

1. *Author Named in a Signal Phrase*

Ordinarily, use the author's name in a signal phrase—to introduce the material—and cite the page number(s) in parentheses.

> Loomba argues that Caliban's "political colour" is black, given his stage representations, which have varied from animalistic to a kind of missing link (143).

2. Author Named in Parentheses

When you don't mention the author in a signal phrase, include the author's last name before the page number(s) in the parentheses.

> Renaissance visions of "other" worlds, particularly in plays and travel narratives, often accentuated the differences of the Other even when striking similarities to the English existed (Bartels 434).

3. Two or Three Authors

Use all authors' last names.

> Gortner, Hebrun, and Nicolson maintain that "opinion leaders" influence other people in an organization because they are respected, not because they hold high positions (175).

4. Four or More Authors

The MLA allows you to use all authors' last names, or to use only the first author's name with *et al.* (in regular type, not underlined or italicized). Although either format is acceptable when applied consistently throughout a paper, in an argument it may be better to name all authors who contributed to the work.

> Similarly, as Goldberger, Tarule, Clinchy, and Belenky note, their new book builds on their collaborative experiences (xii).

5. Organization as Author

Give the full name of a corporate author if it is brief or a shortened form if it is long.

> In fact, one of the leading foundations in the field of higher education supports the recent proposals for community-run public schools (Carnegie Corporation 45).

6. Unknown Author

Use the full title of the work if it is brief or a shortened form if it is long.

> "Hype," by one analysis, is "an artificially engendered atmosphere of hysteria" ("Today's Marketplace" 51).

7. Author of Two or More Works

When you use two or more works by the same author, include the title of the work or shortened version of it in the citation.

Gardner presents readers with their own silliness through his description of a "pointless, ridiculous monster, crouched in the shadows, stinking of dead men, murdered children, and martyred cows" (Grendel 2).

8. Authors with the Same Last Name

When you use works by two or more authors with the same last name, include each author's first initial in the in-text citation.

Father Divine's teachings focused on eternal life, salvation, and socio-economic progress (R. Washington 17).

9. Multivolume Work

Note the volume number first and then the page number(s), with a colon and one space between them.

Aristotle's "On Plants" is now available in a new translation, edited by Barnes (2: 1252).

10. Literary Work

Because literary works are often available in many different editions, you need to include enough information for readers to locate the passage in any edition. For a prose work such as a novel or play, first cite the page number from the edition you used, followed by a semicolon; then indicate the part or chapter number (114; ch. 3) or act or scene in a play (42; sc. 2). For verse plays, omit the page number and give instead the act, scene, and line numbers, separated by periods.

Before he takes his own life, Othello says he is "one that loved not wisely but too well" (5.2.348).

For a poem, cite the stanza and line numbers. If the poem has only line numbers, use the word line(s) in the first reference (lines 33–34).

On dying, Whitman speculates "All that goes onward and outward, nothing collapses, / And to die is different from what any one supposed, and luckier" (6.129-30).

For a verse play, give only the act, scene, and line numbers, separated by periods.

> As Macbeth begins, the witches greet Banquo as "Lesser than Macbeth, and greater" (1.3.65).

11. Works in an Anthology

For an essay, short story, or other short work within an anthology, use the name of the author of the work, not the editor of the anthology; but use the page number(s) from the anthology.

> In the end, if the black artist accepts any duties at all, that duty is to express the beauty of blackness (Hughes 1271).

12. Sacred Text

To cite a sacred text, such as the Qur'an or the Bible, give the title of the edition you used, the book, and the chapter and verse (or their equivalent), separated by a period. In your text, spell out the names of books. In a parenthetical reference, use an abbreviation for books with names of five or more letters (*Gen.* for *Genesis*).

> He ignored the admonition "Pride goes before destruction, and a haughty spirit before a fall" (New Oxford Annotated Bible, Prov. 16.18).

13. Indirect Source

Use the abbreviation *qtd. in* to indicate that what you are quoting or paraphrasing is quoted (as part of a conversation, interview, letter, or excerpt) in the source you are using.

> As Catherine Belsey states, "to speak is to have access to the language which defines, delimits and locates power" (qtd. in Bartels 453).

14. Two or More Sources in the Same Citation

Separate the information for each source with a semicolon.

> Adefunmi was able to patch up the subsequent holes left in worship by substituting various Yoruba, Dahomean, or Fon customs made available to him through research (Brandon 115-17; Hunt 27).

15. Entire Work or One-Page Article

Include the citation in the text without any page numbers or parentheses.

The relationship between revolutionary innocence and the preservation of an oppressive post-revolutionary regime is one theme Milan Kundera explores in The Book of Laughter and Forgetting.

16. *Work without Page Numbers*

If the work is not paginated but has another kind of numbered section, such as parts or paragraphs, include the name and number(s) of the section(s) you are citing. (For paragraphs, use the abbreviation *par.* or *pars.*; for section, use *sec.*; for part, use *pt.*)

> Zora Neale Hurston is one of the great anthropologists of the twentieth century, according to Kip Hinton (par. 2).

17. *Electronic or Nonprint Source*

Give enough information in a signal phrase or parenthetical citation for readers to locate the source in the list of works cited. Usually give the author or title under which you list the source.

> In his film version of Hamlet, Zefferelli highlights the sexual tension between the prince and his mother.

> Describing children's language acquisition, Pinker explains that "what's innate about language is just a way of paying attention to parental speech" (Johnson, sec. 1).

Explanatory and Bibliographic Notes

The MLA recommends using explanatory notes for information or commentary that does not readily fit into your text but is needed for clarification, further explanation, or justification. In addition, the MLA allows bibliographic notes for citing several sources for one point and for offering thanks to, information about, or evaluation of a source. Use superscript numbers in your text at the end of a sentence to refer readers to the notes, which usually appear as endnotes (with the heading Notes) on a separate page before the list of works cited. Indent the first line of each note five spaces, and double-space all entries.

Text with Superscript Indicating a Note

> Stewart emphasizes the existence of social contacts in Hawthorne's life so that the audience will accept a different Hawthorne, one more attuned to modern times than the figure in Woodberry.[3]

Note

³ Woodberry does, however, show that Hawthorne was often unsociable. He emphasizes the seclusion of Hawthorne's mother, who separated herself from her family after the death of her husband, often even taking meals alone (28). Woodberry seems to imply that Mrs. Hawthorne's isolation rubbed off onto her son.

List of Works Cited

A list of works cited is an alphabetical listing of the sources you cite in your essay. The list appears on a separate page at the end of your argument, after any notes, with the heading *Works Cited* centered an inch from the top of the page; do not underline or italicize it or enclose it in quotation marks. Double-space between the heading and the first entry, and double-space the entire list. (If you are asked to list everything you have read as background—not just the sources you cite—call the list *Works Consulted*.)

The first line of each entry should align on the left; subsequent lines indent one-half inch or five spaces. See page 442 for a sample Works Cited page.

Books

The basic information for a book includes three elements, each followed by a period:

- the author's name, last name first
- the title and subtitle, underlined
- and the publication information, including the city, a shortened form of the publisher's name, and the date.

For a book with multiple authors, only the first author's name is inverted.

1. *One Author*

Castle, Terry. <u>Boss Ladies, Watch Out: Essays on Women, Sex, and Writing</u>. New York: Routledge, 2002.

2. *Two or More Authors*

Appleby, Joyce, Lynn Hunt, and Margaret Jacob. <u>Telling the Truth about History</u>. New York: Norton, 1994.

3. *Organization as Author*

American Horticultural Society. The Fully Illustrated Plant-by-Plant Manual of Practical Techniques. New York: American Horticultural Society and DK Publishing, 1999.

4. *Unknown Author*

National Geographic Atlas of the World. New York: National Geographic, 1999.

5. *Two or More Books by the Same Author*

List the works alphabetically by title.

Lorde, Audre. A Burst of Light. Ithaca: Firebrand, 1988.

---. Sister Outsider. Trumansburg: Crossing, 1984.

6. *Editor*

Rorty, Amelie Oksenberg, ed. Essays on Aristotle's Poetics. Princeton: Princeton UP, 1992.

7. *Author and Editor*

Shakespeare, William. The Tempest. Ed. Frank Kermode. London: Routledge, 1994.

8. *Selection in an Anthology or Chapter in an Edited Book*

Brown, Paul. "'This thing of darkness I acknowledge mine': The Tempest and the Discourse of Colonialism." Political Shakespeare: Essays in Cultural Materialism. Ed. Jonathan Dillimore and Alan Sinfield. Ithaca: Cornell UP, 1985. 48-71.

9. *Two or More Works from the Same Anthology*

Gates, Henry Louis, Jr., and Nellie McKay, eds. The Norton Anthology of African American Literature. New York: Norton, 1997.

Neal, Larry. "The Black Arts Movement." Gates and McKay 1960-72.

Karenga, Maulana. "Black Art: Mute Matter Given Force and Function." Gates and McKay 1973-77.

10. Translation

Zamora, Martha. Frida Kahlo: The Brush of Anguish. Trans. Marilyn Sode Smith. San Francisco: Chronicle, 1990.

11. Edition Other than the First

Lunsford, Andrea, John Ruszkiewicz, and Keith Walters. Everything's an Argument. 3rd ed. New York: Bedford/St.Martin's, 2004.

12. One Volume of a Multivolume Work

Byron, Lord George. Byron's Letters and Journals. Ed. Leslie A. Marchand. Vol. 2. London: J. Murray, 1973-1982.

13. Two or More Volumes of a Multivolume Work

Byron, Lord George. Byron's Letters and Journals. Ed. Leslie A. Marchand. 12 vols. London: J. Murray, 1973-1982.

14. Preface, Foreword, Introduction, or Afterword

Hymes, Dell. Foreword. Beyond Ebonics: Linguistic Pride and Racial Prejudice. By John Baugh. New York: Oxford, 2000. vii-viii.

15. Article in a Reference Work

West, William W. "Memory." Encyclopedia of Rhetoric. Ed. Thomas O. Sloane. New York: Oxford, 2001. 482-93.

"Hero." Merriam-Webster's Collegiate Dictionary. 10th ed. 1996.

16. Book That Is Part of a Series

Moss, Beverly J. A Community Text Arises. Language and Social Processes Ser. 8. Cresskill: Hampton, 2003.

17. Republication

Scott, Walter. Kenilworth. 1821. New York: Dodd, 1996.

18. Government Document

United States. Cong. House Committee on the Judiciary. Impeachment of the President. 40th Cong., 1st sess. H. Rept. 7. Washington: GPO, 1867.

19. Pamphlet

An Answer to the President's Message to the Fiftieth Congress. Philadelphia: Manufacturer's Club of Philadelphia, 1887.

20. Published Proceedings of a Conference

Edwards, Ron, ed. Proceedings of the Third National Folklore Conference. Canberra, Austral.: Australian Folk Trust, 1988.

21. Title within a Title

Tauernier-Courbin, Jacqueline. Ernest Hemingway's A Moveable Feast: The Making of a Myth. Boston: Northeastern UP, 1991.

Periodicals

The basic entry for a periodical includes the following three elements, separated by periods:

- the author's name, last name first
- the article title, in quotation marks
- and the publication information, including the periodical title (underlined), the volume and issue numbers (if any), the date of publication, and the page number(s).

For works with multiple authors, only the first author's name is inverted. Note, too, that the period following the article title goes inside the closing quotation mark.

22. Article in a Journal Paginated by Volume

Anderson, Virginia. "'The Perfect Enemy': Clinton, the Contradictions of Capitalism, and Slaying the Sin Within." Rhetoric Review 21 (2002): 384-400.

23. Article in a Journal Paginated by Issue

Radavich, David. "Man among Men: David Mamet's Homosocial Order." American Drama 1.1 (1991): 46-66.

24. Article in a Monthly Magazine

Wallraff, Barbara. "Word Count." The Atlantic Nov. 2002: 144-45.

25. Article in a Weekly Magazine

Dorfman, Andrea. "A Tree Hugger's Delight." Time 14 Oct. 2002: 58-59.

26. Article in a Newspaper

Friend, Tim. "Scientists Map the Mouse Genome." USA Today 2 Dec. 2002: A1.

27. Editorial or Letter to Editor

Danto, Arthur. "'Elitism' and the N.E.A." Editorial. The Nation 17 Nov. 1997: 6-7.

Judson, Judith. Letter. Washington Post 12 Mar. 2003: A20.

28. Unsigned Article

"Court Rejects the Sale of Medical Marijuana." New York Times 26 Feb. 1998, late ed.: A21.

29. Review

Partner, Peter. "The Dangers of Divinity." Rev. of The Shape of the Holy: Early Islamic Jerusalem, by Oleg Grabar. New York Review of Books 5 Feb. 1998: 27-28.

Electronic Sources

Most of the following models are based on the MLA's guidelines for citing electronic sources in the MLA Handbook (6th edition, 2003), as well as on up-to-date information available at <mla.org/>.

The MLA requires that URLs be enclosed in angle brackets. Also, if a URL will not all fit on one line, it should be broken only after a slash. If a particular URL is extremely complicated, you can instead give the URL for the site's search page, if it exists, or for the site's home page.

The basic MLA entry for most electronic sources should include the following elements:

- name of the author, editor, or compiler
- title of the work, document, or posting
- information for print publication, if any
- information for electronic publication

- date of access
- URL in angle brackets

30. *CD-ROM, Diskette, or Magnetic Tape, Single Issue*

> McPherson, James M., ed. The American Heritage New History of the
> Civil War. CD-ROM. New York: Viking, 1996.

31. *Periodically Revised CD-ROM*

Include the author's name; publication information for the print version of the text (including its title and date of publication); the title of the database; the medium (CD-ROM); the name of the company producing it; and the electronic publication date (month and year, if possible).

> Heyman, Steven. "The Dangerously Exciting Client." Psychotherapy Patient
> 9.1 (1994): 37-46. PsycLIT. CD-ROM. SilverPlatter. Nov. 1996.

32. *Multidisc CD-ROM*

> The 1998 Grolier Multimedia Encyclopedia. CD-ROM. 2 discs. Danbury:
> Grolier Interactive, 1999.

33. *Document from a Web Site*

When possible, include the author's name; title of the document; print publication information; electronic publication information; date of access; and the URL.

> "A History of Women's Writing." The Orlando Project: An Integrated His-
> tory of Women's Writing in the British Isles. 2000. U of Alberta. 14
> Mar. 2003 <http://www.ualberta.ca/ORLANDO/>.

34. *Entire Web Site*

Include the name of the person or group who created the site, if relevant; the title of the site (underlined) or (if there is no title) a description such as *Home page*; the electronic publication date or last update, if available; the name of any institution or organization associated with the site; the date of access; and the URL.

> Bowman, Laurel. Classical Myth: The Ancient Source. Dept. of Greek
> and Roman Studies, U of Victoria. 7 Mar. 2000 <http://web.uvic.ca/
> grs/bowman/myth>.

Mitten, Lisa. <u>The Mascot Issue</u>. 8 Apr. 2002. American Indian Library
Assn. 12 Sept. 2002 <http://www.nativeculture.com/lisamitten/
mascots.html>.

35. Course, Department, or Personal Web Site

Include the Web site's author; name of the site; description of site (such
as *Course home page, Dept. home page,* or *Home page*); dates for the course;
date of publication or last update; name of academic department, if relevant; date of access; and the URL.

Lunsford, Andrea A. "Memory and Media." Course home page. Sept.-
Dec. 2002. Dept. of English, Stanford U. 13 Mar. 2003 <http://
www.stanford.edu/class/english12sc>.

Lunsford, Andrea A. Home page. 15 Mar. 2003 <http://www.stanford.edu/
~lunsfor1/>.

36. Online Book

Begin with the name of the author—or, if only an editor, a compiler, or a
translator is identified, the name of that person followed by *ed., comp.,* or
trans. Then give the title and the name of any editor, compiler, or translator
not listed earlier, preceded by *Ed., Comp.,* or *Trans.* If the online version of
the text has not been published before, give the date of electronic publication and the name of any sponsoring institution or organization. Then give
any publication information (city, publisher, and/or year) for the original
print version that is given in the source; the date of access; and the URL.

Riis, Jacob A. <u>How the Other Half Lives: Studies among the Tenements
of New York</u>. Ed. David Phillips. New York: Scribner's, 1890. 26
Mar. 1998 <http://www.cis.yale.edu/amstud/Inforev/riis/title.html>.

For a poem, essay, or other short work within an online book, include its
title after the author's name. Give the URL of the short work, not of the
book, if they differ.

Dickinson, Emily. "The Grass." <u>Poems: Emily Dickinson</u>. Boston: Roberts
Brothers, 1891. <u>Humanities Text Initiative American Verse Col-
lection</u>. Ed. Nancy Kushigian. 1995. U of Michigan. 9 Oct. 1997
<http://www.planet.net/pkrisxle/emily/poemsOnline.html>.

37. Article in an Online Periodical

Follow the formats for citing articles in print periodicals, but adapt them
as necessary to the online medium. Include the page numbers of the arti-

cle or the total number of pages, paragraphs, parts, or other numbered sections, if any; the date of access; and the URL.

> Johnson, Eric. "The 10,000-Word Question: Using Images on the World-Wide Web." Kairos 4.1 (1999). 20 Mar. 2003 <http://english.ttu.edu/kairos/4.1/>.

> Walsh, Joan. "The Ugly Truth about Republican Racial Politics." Salon 15 Dec. 2002. 3 Jan. 2003 <http://www.salon.com/politics/feature/2002/12/14/race/index_np.html>.

38. Posting to a Discussion Group

Begin with the author's name, the title of the posting, the description *Online posting*, and the date of the posting. For a listserv posting, give the name of the listserv, the date of access, and either the URL of the listserv or (preferably) the URL of an archival version of the posting. If a URL is unavailable, give the email address of the list moderator. For a newsgroup posting, end with the date of access and the name of the newsgroup, in angle brackets.

> "Web Publishing and Censorship." Online posting. 2 Feb. 1997. ACW: Alliance for Computers and Writing Discussion List. 10 Oct. 1997 <http://english.ttu.edu/acw-1/archive.htm>.

> Martin, Jerry. "The IRA & Sinn Fein." Online posting. 31 Mar. 1998. 31 Mar. 1998 <news:soc.culture.irish>.

39. Work from an Online Subscription Service

For a work from an online service to which your library subscribes, list the information about the work, followed by the name of the service, the library, the date of access, and the URL.

> "Breaking the Dieting Habit: Drug Therapy for Eating Disorders." Pschyology Today Mar 1995: 12+. Electric Lib. Green Lib., Stanford, CA. 30 Nov. 2002 <http://www.elibrary.com/>.

If you are citing an article from a subscription service to which you subscribe (such as AOL), use the following model:

> Weeks, W. William. "Beyond the Ark." Nature Conservancy. Mar.-Apr. 1999. America Online. 30 Nov. 2002. Keyword: Ecology.

40. Email Message

Include the writer's name, the subject line, the description *Email to the author* or *Email to [the recipient's name]*, and the date of the message.

> Moller, Marilyn. "Seeing _Crowns_." Email to Beverly Moss. 3 Jan. 2003.

41. Synchronous Communication (MOO, MUD, or IRC)

Include the name of any specific speaker(s) you are citing; a description of the event; its date; the name of the forum; the date of access; and the URL of the posting (with the prefix *telnet:*) or (preferably) of an archival version.

> Patuto, Jeremy, Simon Fennel, and James Goss. The Mytilene debate. 9 May 1996. MiamiMOO. 28 Mar. 1998 <http://moo.cas.muohio.edu>.

42. Online Interview, Work of Art, or Film

Follow the general guidelines for the print version of the source, but also include information on the electronic medium, such as publication information for a CD-ROM or the date of electronic publication, the date of access, and the URL for a Web site.

> McGray, Douglas. Interview with Andrew Marshall. Wired. Feb. 2003. 17 Mar. 2003 <http://www.wired.com/wired/archive/11.02/marshall.html>.

> Aleni, Guilio. K'un-yu t'u-shu. ca. 1620. Vatican, Rome. 28 Mar. 1998 <http://www.ncsa.uiuc.edu/SDG/Experimental/vatican.exhibit/exhibit/full-images/i-rome-to-china/china02.gif>.

> Harry Potter and the Chamber of Secrets. Dir. Chris Columbus. 16 Dec. 2002 <http://movies.go.com/movies/H/harrypotterandthechamberofsecrets_2002/>.

43. FTP (File Transfer Protocol), Telnet, or Gopher Site

Substitute FTP, *telnet*, or *gopher* for *http* at the beginning of the URL.

> Korn, Peter. "How Much Does Breast Cancer Really Cost?" Self Oct. 1994. 5 May 1997 <gopher://nysernet.org:70/00/BCTC/Sources/SELF/94/how-much>.

Other Sources

44. Unpublished Dissertation

Fishman, Jenn. "'The Active Republic of Literature': Performance and Literary Culture in Britain, 1656-1790." Diss. Stanford U, 2003.

45. Published Dissertation

Baum, Bernard. Decentralization of Authority in a Bureaucracy. Diss. U of Chicago. Englewood Cliffs: Prentice-Hall, 1961.

46. Article from a Microform

Sharpe, Lora. "A Quilter's Tribute." Boston Globe 25 Mar. 1989: 13. Newsbank: Social Relations 12 (1989): fiche 6, grids B4-6.

47. Personal and Published Interview

Royster, Jacqueline Jones. Personal interview. 2 Feb. 2003.

Schorr, Daniel. Interview. Weekend Edition. Natl. Public Radio. KQED, San Francisco. 23 Dec. 2002.

48. Letter

Jacobs, Harriet. "Letter to Amy Post." 4 Apr. 1853. Incidents in the Life of a Slave Girl. Ed. Jean Fagan Yellin. Cambridge: Harvard UP, 1987. 234-35.

49. Film

The Lord of the Rings: The Two Towers. Dir. Peter Jackson. Perf. Elijah Wood, Ian McKellan. New Line Cinema, 2002.

50. Television or Radio Program

Box Office Bombshell: Marilyn Monroe. Nar. Peter Graves. Writ. Andy Thomas, Jeff Schefel, and Kevin Burns. Dir. Bill Harris. A&E Biography. Arts and Entertainment Network. 23 Oct. 2002.

51. Sound Recording

Fugees. "Ready or Not." The Score. Sony, 1996.

52. Work of Art or Photograph

Kahlo, Frida. Self-Portrait with Cropped Hair. 1940. Museum of Modern Art, New York.

53. Lecture or Speech

Condoleezza Rice. Baccalaureate Address. Stanford University. 18 June 2002.

54. Performance

Freak. By John Leguizamo. Dir. David Bar Katz. Cort Theater, New York. 7 Mar. 1998.

55. Map or Chart

The Political and Physical World. Map. Washington: Natl. Geographic, 1975.

56. Cartoon

Brodner, Steve. Cartoon. Nation 31 Mar. 2003: 2.

57. Advertisement

Chevy Avalanche. Advertisement. Time 14 Oct. 2002: 104.

On page 441, note the formatting of the first page of a sample essay written in MLA style. On page 442, you will find a sample Works Cited page written for this same student essay.

SAMPLE FIRST PAGE FOR AN ESSAY IN MLA STYLE

Lesk 1

Emily Lesk
Professor Arraéz
Electric Rhetoric
November 15, 2002

Red, White, and Everywhere

America, I have a confession to make: I don't drink Coke. But don't call me a hypocrite just because I am still the proud owner of a bright red shirt that advertises it. Just call me an American.

Even before setting foot in Israel three years ago, I knew exactly where I could find one. The tiny T-shirt shop in the central block of Jerusalem's Ben Yehuda Street did offer other designs, but the one with a bright white "Drink Coca-Cola Classic" written in Hebrew cursive across the chest was what drew in most of the dollar-carrying tourists. While waiting almost twenty minutes for my shirt (depicted in Fig. 1), I watched nearly every customer ahead of me ask for "the Coke shirt, todah rabah [thank you very much]."

At the time, I never thought it strange that I wanted one, too. After having absorbed sixteen years of Coca-Cola propaganda through everything from NBC's Saturday morning cartoon lineup to the concession stand at Camden Yards (the Baltimore Orioles' ballpark), I associated the shirt with singing

Fig. 1. Hebrew Coca-Cola T-shirt. Personal photograph. Despite my dislike for the beverage, I bought this Coca-Cola T-shirt in Israel.

SAMPLE LIST OF WORKS CITED FOR AN ESSAY IN MLA STYLE

```
                                              Lesk  7
                        Works Cited
Coca-Cola Santa pin. Personal photograph by author.
     9 Nov. 2002.
"The Fabulous Fifties." Beverage Industry 87:6
     (1996) 16. 2 Nov. 2002 <http://memory.loc/
     gov.ammem/ccmphtml/indshst.html>.
"Haddon Sundblom." Coca-Cola and Christmas 1999. 2
     Nov. 2002 <http://www.coca-cola.com.ar/
     Coca-colaweb/paginas_ingles/christmas.html>.
Hebrew Coca-Cola T-shirt. Personal photograph by
     author. 8 Nov. 2002.
Ikuta, Yasutoshi, ed. '50s American Magazine Ads.
     Tokyo: Graphic-Sha, 1987.
Library of Congress. Motion Picture, Broadcasting
     and Recorded Sound Division. 5 Nov. 2002
     <http://memory.loc.gov/ammem/ccmphtml/
     index.html>.
Pendergrast, Mark. For God, Country, and Coca-Cola:
     The Unauthorized History of the Great American
     Soft Drink and the Company That Makes It. New
     York: Macmillan, 1993.
```

APA STYLE

The *Publication Manual of the American Psychological Association* (5th edition, 2001) provides comprehensive advice to student and professional writers in the social sciences. Here we draw on the *Publication Manual*'s guidelines to provide an overview of APA style for in-text citations, content notes, and entries in the list of references.

In-Text Citations

APA style calls for in-text citations in the body of an argument to document sources of quotations, paraphrases, summaries, and so on. These in-text citations correspond to full bibliographic entries in the list of references at the end of the text.

1. Author Named in a Signal Phrase

Generally, use the author's name in a signal phrase to introduce the cited material, and place the date, in parentheses, immediately after the author's name. For a quotation, the page number, preceded by *p.*, appears in parentheses after the quotation. For electronic texts or other works without page numbers, paragraph numbers may be used instead, preceded by the ¶ symbol or the abbreviation *para.* For a long, set-off quotation, position the page reference in parentheses two spaces after the punctuation at the end of the quotation.

> According to Brandon (1993), Adefunmi opposed all forms of racism and believed that black nationalism should not be a destructive force.

> As Toobin (2002) demonstrates, Joseph Lieberman unintentionally aided the Republican cause during most of 2002, playing into the hands of the administration and becoming increasingly unwilling "to question the President's motives, because he doesn't like visceral politics" (p. 43).

2. Author Named in Parentheses

When you do not mention the author in a signal phrase, give the name and the date, separated by a comma, in parentheses at the end of the cited material.

> *The Sopranos* has achieved a much wider viewing audience than ever expected, spawning a cookbook and several serious scholarly studies (Franklin, 2002).

3. Two Authors

Use both names in all citations. Use *and* in a signal phrase, but use an ampersand (&) in parentheses.

> Associated with purity and wisdom, Obatala is the creator of human beings, whom he is said to have formed out of clay (Edwards & Mason, 1985).

4. Three to Five Authors

List all the authors' names for the first reference. In subsequent references, use just the first author's name followed by *et al.* (in regular type, not underlined or italicized).

> Lenhoff, Wang, Greenberg, and Bellugi (1997) cite tests that indicate that segments of the left brain hemisphere are not affected by Williams syndrome whereas the right hemisphere is significantly affected.

> Shackelford drew on the study by Lenhoff et al. (1997).

5. Six or More Authors

Use only the first author's name and *et al.* (in regular type, not underlined or italicized) in every citation, including the first.

> As Flower et al. (2003) demonstrate, reading and writing involve both cognitive and social processes.

6. Organization as Author

If the name of an organization or a corporation is long, spell it out the first time, followed by an abbreviation in brackets. In later citations, use the abbreviation only.

> **First Citation**. (Federal Bureau of Investigation [FBI], 2002)

> **Subsequent Citations**. (FBI, 2002)

7. Unknown Author

Use the title or its first few words in a signal phrase or in parentheses (in the example below, a book's title is italicized).

> The school profiles for the county substantiate this trend (*Guide to secondary schools*, 2003).

8. Authors with the Same Last Name

If your list of references includes works by different authors with the same last name, include the authors' initials in each citation.

> G. Jones (1998) conducted the groundbreaking study of retroviruses.

9. Two or More Sources in the Same Citation

List sources by the same author chronologically by publication year. List sources by different authors in alphabetical order by the authors' last names, separated by semicolons.

> While traditional forms of argument are warlike and agonistic, alternative models do exist (Foss & Foss, 1997; Makau, 1999).

10. Specific Parts of a Source

Use abbreviations (*chap.*, *p.*, and so on) in a parenthetical citation to name the part of a work you are citing.

> Pinker (2003, chap. 6) argued that his research yielded the opposite results.

11. Electronic World Wide Web Document

To cite a source found on the Web, use the author's name and date as you would for a print source, then indicate the chapter or figure of the document, as appropriate. If the source's publication date is unknown, use *n.d.* (no date). To document a quotation, include paragraph numbers if page numbers are unavailable.

> Werbach argued convincingly that "Despite the best efforts of legislators, lawyers, and computer programmers, spam has won. Spam is killing email" (2002, p. 1).

12. Email and Other Personal Communication

Cite any personal letters, email messages, electronic postings, telephone conversations, or personal interviews by giving the person's initial(s) and last name, the identification *personal communication*, and the date.

> E. Ashdown (personal communication, March 9, 2003) supported these claims.

Content Notes

The APA recommends using content notes for material that will expand or supplement your argument but otherwise would interrupt the text. Indicate such notes in your text by inserting superscript numerals. Type the notes themselves on a separate page headed *Footnotes*, centered at the top of the page. Double-space all entries. Indent the first line of each note five to seven spaces, and begin subsequent lines at the left margin.

Text with Superscript Indicating a Note

Data related to children's preferences in books were instrumental in designing the questionnaire.[1]

Note

[1] Rudine Sims Bishop and members of the Reading Readiness Research Group provided helpful data.

List of References

The alphabetical list of sources cited in your text is called *References*. (If your instructor asks you to list everything you have read as background — not just the sources you cite — call the list *Bibliography*.) The list of references appears on a separate page or pages at the end of your paper, with the heading *References*, not underlined or italicized, or in quotation marks, centered one inch from the top of the page. Double-space after the heading and begin your first entry. Double-space the entire list.

For print sources, APA style specifies the treatment and placement of four basic elements — author, publication date, title, and publication information. Each element is followed by a period.

- Author: list *all* authors with last name first, and use only initials for first and middle names. Separate the names of multiple authors with commas, and use an ampersand (&) before the last author's name.
- Publication date: enclose the publication date in parentheses. Use only the year for books and journals; use the year, a comma, and the month or month and day for magazines. Do not abbreviate the month.
- Title: italicize titles and subtitles of books and periodicals. Do not enclose titles of articles in quotation marks. For books and articles, cap-

italize only the first word of the title and subtitle and any proper nouns or proper adjectives. Capitalize all major words in a periodical title.

- Publication information: for a book, list the city of publication (and the country or postal abbreviation for the state if the city is unfamiliar) and the publisher's name, dropping *Inc.*, *Co.*, or *Publishers*. For a periodical, follow the periodical title with a comma, the volume number (italicized), the issue number (if provided) in parentheses and followed by a comma, and the inclusive page numbers of the article. For newspaper articles and for articles or chapters in books, include the abbreviation *p.* ("page") or *pp.* ("pages").

The following APA-style examples appear double-spaced and in a "hanging indent" format, in which the first line aligns on the left and the subsequent lines indent one-half inch or five spaces.

Books

1. *One Author*

Rheingold, H. (2002). *Smart mobs: The next social revolution.* Cambridge, MA: Perseus.

2. *Two or More Authors*

Steininger, M., Newell, J. D., & Garcia, L. (1984). *Ethical issues in psychology.* Homewood, IL: Dow Jones-Irwin.

3. *Organization as Author*

Use the word *Author* as the publisher when the organization is both the author and the publisher.

Linguistics Society of America. (2002). *Guidelines for using sign language interpreters.* Washington, DC: Author.

4. *Unknown Author*

National Geographic atlas of the world. (1999). Washington, DC: National Geographic Society.

5. *Book Prepared by an Editor*

Hardy, H. H. (Ed.). (1998). *The proper study of mankind.* New York: Farrar, Straus.

6. Selection in a Book with an Editor

Villanueva, V. (1999). An introduction to social scientific discussions on class. In A. Shepard, J. McMillan, & G. Tate (Eds.), *Coming to Class: Pedagogy and the social class of teachers* (pp. 262-77). Portsmouth, NH: Heinemann.

7. Translation

Perez-Reverte, A. (2002). *The nautical chart* (M. S. Peaden, Trans.). New York: Harvest. (Original work published 2000)

8. Edition Other than the First

Wrightsman, L. (1998). *Psychology and the legal system* (3rd ed.). Newbury Park, CA: Sage.

9. One Volume of a Multivolume Work

Will, J. S. (1921). *Protestantism in France* (Vol. 2). Toronto: University of Toronto Press.

10. Article in a Reference Work

Chernow, B., & Vattasi, G. (Eds.). (1993). Psychomimetic drug. In *The Columbia encyclopedia* (5th ed., p. 2238). New York: Columbia University Press.

If no author is listed, begin with the title.

11. Republication

Sharp, C. (1978). *History of Hartlepool.* Hartlepool, UK: Hartlepool Borough Council. (Original work published 1816)

12. Government Document

U.S. Bureau of the Census. (2001). *Survey of women-owned business enterprises.* Washington, DC: U.S. Government Printing Office.

13. Two or More Works by the Same Author

List the works in chronological order of publication. Repeat the author's name in each entry.

Rose, M. (1984). *Writer's block: The cognitive dimension.* Carbondale, IL: Southern Illinois University Press.

Rose, M. (1995). *Possible lives: The promise of public education in America.* Boston: Houghton Mifflin.

Periodicals

14. Article in a Journal Paginated by Volume

Kirsch, G. E. (2002). Toward an engaged rhetoric of professional practice. *Journal of Advanced Composition, 22,* 414-423.

15. Article in a Journal Paginated by Issue

Carr, S. (2002). The circulation of Blair's *Lectures. Rhetoric Society Quarterly, 32*(4), 75-104.

16. Article in a Monthly Magazine

Dallek, R. (2002, December). The medical ordeals of JFK. *The Atlantic Monthly,* 49-64.

17. Article in a Newspaper

Nagourney, A. (2002, December 16). Gore rules out running in '04. *The New York Times,* pp. A1, A8.

18. Editorial or Letter to the Editor

Sonnenklar, M. (2002, January). Gaza revisited [Letter to the editor]. *Harper's,* 4.

19. Unsigned Article

Guidelines issued on assisted suicide. (1998, March 4). *The New York Times,* p. A15.

20. Review

Richardson, S. (1998, February). [Review of the book *The Secret Family*]. *Discover,* 88.

21. Published Interview

Shor, I. (1997). [Interview with A. Greenbaum]. *Writing on the Edge, 8*(2), 7-20.

22. Two or More Works by the Same Author in the Same Year

List two or more works by the same author published in the same year alphabetically, and place lowercase letters (*a*, *b*, etc.) after the dates.

Murray, F. B. (1983a). Equilibration as cognitive conflict. *Developmental Review, 3*, 54-61.

Murray, F. B. (1983b). Learning and development through social interaction. In L. Liben (Ed.), *Piaget and the foundations of knowledge* (pp. 176-201). Hillsdale, NJ: Erlbaum.

Electronic Sources

The following models are based on the APA's updated guidelines for citing electronic sources posted at the APA Web site <apa.org> as well as in the APA *Publication Manual* (5th edition).

The basic APA entry for most electronic sources should include the following elements:

- name of the author, editor, or compiler
- date of electronic publication or most recent update
- title of the work, document, or posting
- publication information, including the title, volume or issue number, and page numbers
- a retrieval statement that includes date of access, followed by a comma
- URL, with no angle brackets and no closing punctuation

23. World Wide Web Site

To cite a whole site, give the address in a parenthetical reference. To cite a document from a Web site, include information as you would for a print document, followed by a note on its retrieval.

American Psychological Association. (2000). DotComSense: Commonsense ways to protect your privacy and assess online mental health information. Retrieved January 25, 2002, from http://helping .apa.org/dotcomsense/

Mullins, B. (1995). Introduction to Robert Hass. Readings in contemporary poetry at Dia Center for the Arts. Retrieved April 24, 1999, from http://www.diacenter.org/prg/poetry/95-96/intrhass.html

24. Article from an Online Periodical

If the article also appears in a print journal, you don't need a retrieval statement; instead, include the label *[Electronic version]* after the article title. However, if the online article is a revision of the print document (if the format differs or page numbers are not indicated), include the date of access and URL.

> Steedman, M., & Jones, G. P. (2000). Information structure and the syntax-phonology interface [Electronic version]. *Linguistic Inquiry, 31*, 649-689.

> Palmer, K. S. (2000, September 12). In academia, males under a microscope. *The Washington Post.* Retrieved October 23, 2002, from http://www.washingtonpost.com

25. Article or Abstract from a Database (Online or on CD-ROM)

> Hayhoe, G. (2001). The long and winding road: Technology's future. *Technical Communication, 48*(2), 133-145. Retrieved September 22, 2002, from ProQuest database.

> McCall, R. B. (1998). Science and the press: Like oil and water? *American Psychologist, 43*(2), 87-94. Abstract retrieved August 23, 2002, from PsycINFO database (1988-18263-001).

> Pryor, T., & Wiederman, M. W. (1998). Personality features and expressed concerns of adolescents with eating disorders. *Adolescence, 33*, 291-301. Retrieved November 26, 2002, from Electric Library database.

26. Software or Computer Program

> McAfee Office 2000. (Version 2.0) [Computer software]. (1999). Santa Clara, CA: Network Associates.

27. Online Government Document

Cite an online government document as you would a printed government work, adding the date of access and the URL. If you don't find a date, use *n.d.*

> Finn, J. D. (1998, April). *Class size and students at risk: What is known? What is next?* Retrieved September 25, 2002, from United States Department of Education Web site http://www.ed.gov/pubs/ClassSize/title.html

28. *FTP, Telnet, or Gopher Site*

After the retrieval statement, give the address (substituting *ftp*, *telnet*, or *gopher* for *http* at the beginning of the URL) or the path followed to access information, with slashes to indicate menu selections.

> Korn, P. (1994, October). How much does breast cancer really cost? *Self.* Retrieved May 5, 2002, from gopher://nysernet.org:70/00/BCIC/ Sources/SELF/94/how-much

29. *Posting to a Discussion Group*

List an online posting in the references list only if you are able to retrieve the message from a mailing list's archive. Provide the author's name; the date of posting, in parentheses; and the subject line from the posting. Include any information that further identifies the message in square brackets. For a listserv message, end with the retrieval statement, including the name of the list and the URL of the archived message.

> Troike, R. C. (2001, June 21). Buttercups and primroses [Msg 8]. Message posted to the American Dialect Society's ADS-L electronic mailing list, archived at http://listserv.linguistlist.org/archives/ ads-1.html

30. *Newsgroup Posting*

Include the author's name, the date and subject line of the posting, the access date, and the name of the newsgroup.

> Wittenberg, E. (2001, July 11). Gender and the Internet [Msg 4]. Message posted to news://comp.edu.composition

31. *Email Message or Synchronous Communication*

Because the APA stresses that any sources cited in your list of references must be retrievable by your readers, you should not include entries for email messages or synchronous communications (MOOs, MUDs); instead, cite these sources in your text as forms of *personal communication* (see p. 445). And remember that you should not quote from other people's email without asking their permission to do so.

Other Sources

32. Technical or Research Reports and Working Papers

Wilson, K. S. (1986). *Palenque: An interactive multimedia optical disc prototype for children* (Working Paper No. 2). New York: Center for Children and Technology, Bank Street College of Education.

33. Unpublished Paper Presented at a Meeting or Symposium

Welch, K. (2002, March). *Electric rhetoric and screen literacy.* Paper presented at the meeting of the Conference on College Composition and Communication, Chicago.

34. Unpublished Dissertation

Barnett, T. (1997). *Communities in conflict: Composition, racial discourse, and the 60s revolution.* Unpublished doctoral dissertation, Ohio State University, Columbus.

35. Poster Session

Mensching, G. (2002, May). *A simple, effective one-shot for disinterested students.* Poster session presented at the National LOEX Library Instruction Conference, Ann Arbor, MI.

36. Film, Video, or DVD

Jackson, P. (Director). (2002). *The Lord of the Rings: The Two Towers.* [Film]. Los Angeles: New Line Cinema.

37. Television Program, Single Episode

Imperioli, M. (Writer), & Buscemi, S. (Director). (2002, October 20). Everybody hurts [Television series episode]. In D. Chase (Executive Producer), *The Sopranos.* New York: Home Box Office.

38. Sound Recording

Begin with the writer's name, followed by the date of copyright. Give the recording date at the end of the entry (in parentheses, after the period) if it is different from the copyright date.

Ivey, A., Jr., & Sall, R. (1995). Rollin' with my homies [Recorded by Coolio]. On *Clueless* soundtrack [CD]. Hollywood, CA: Capitol Records.

RESPOND •

1. The MLA and APA styles differ in several important ways, both for in-text citations and for lists of sources. You've probably noticed a few: The APA lowercases most words in titles and lists the publication date right after the author's name, whereas the MLA capitalizes most words and puts the publication date at the end of the works-cited entry. More interesting than the details, though, is the reasoning behind the differences. Placing the publication date near the front of a citation, for instance, reveals a special concern for that information in the APA style. Similarly, the MLA's decision to capitalize titles is not arbitrary: that style is preferred in the humanities for a reason.

   Find as many consistent differences between the MLA and APA styles as you can. Then, for each difference, try to discover the reasons these groups organize or present information in that way. The MLA and APA style manuals themselves may be of help. You might also begin by determining which academic disciplines subscribe to the APA style and which to the MLA.

2. Working with another person in your class, look for examples of the following sources: an article in a journal, a book, a film, a song, and a TV show. Then make a bibliography entry for each one, using either MLA or APA style.

GLOSSARY

accidental condition in a definition, an element that helps to explain what is being defined but is not essential to it. An accidental condition in defining a bird might be "ability to fly" because most, but not all, birds can fly. (See also *essential condition* and *sufficient condition*.)

ad hominem **argument** a fallacy of argument in which a writer's claim is answered by irrelevant attacks on his or her character.

analogy an extended comparison between something unfamiliar and something more familiar for the purpose of illuminating or dramatizing the unfamiliar. An analogy might, say, compare nuclear fission (less familiar) to a pool player's opening break (more familiar).

anaphora a figure of speech involving repetition, particularly of the same word at the beginning of several clauses.

antithesis the use of parallel structures to call attention to contrasts or opposites, as in *Some like it hot; some like it cold.*

antonomasia use of a title, epithet, or description in place of a name, as in *Your Honor* for *Judge.*

argument (1) a spoken, written, or visual text that expresses a point of view; (2) the use of evidence and reason to discover some version of the truth, as distinct from *persuasion,* the attempt to change someone else's point of view.

artistic appeal support for an argument that a writer creates based on principles of reason and shared knowledge rather than on facts and evidence. (See also *inartistic appeal.*)

assumption a belief regarded as true, upon which other claims are based.

assumption, cultural a belief regarded as true or commonsensical within a particular culture, such as the belief in individual freedom in American culture.

audience the person or persons to whom an argument is directed.

authority the quality conveyed by a writer who is knowledgeable about his or her subject and confident in that knowledge.

background the information a writer provides to create the context for an argument.

backing in Toulmin argument, the evidence provided to support a *warrant*.

bandwagon appeal a fallacy of argument in which a course of action is recommended on the grounds that everyone else is following it.

begging the question a fallacy of argument in which a claim is based on the very grounds that are in doubt or dispute: *Rita can't be the bicycle thief; she's never stolen anything.*

causal argument an argument that seeks to explain the effect(s) of a cause, the cause(s) of an effect, or a causal chain in which A causes B, B causes C, C causes D, and so on.

ceremonial argument an argument that deals with current values and addresses questions of praise and blame. Also called *epideictic,* ceremonial arguments include eulogies and graduation speeches.

character, appeal based on a strategy in which a writer presents an authoritative or credible self-image to dispose an audience to accept a claim.

claim a statement that asserts a belief or truth. In arguments, most claims require supporting evidence. The claim is a key component in Toulmin argument.

connecting (1) identifying with a writer or reader; or (2) crafting an argument to emphasize where writers and audiences share interests, concerns, or experiences.

connotation the suggestions or associations that surround most words and extend beyond their literal meaning, creating associational effects. *Slender* and *skinny* have similar meanings, for example, but carry different connotations, the former more positive than the latter.

context the entire situation in which a piece of writing takes place, including the writer's purpose(s) for writing; the intended audience; the time and place of writing; the institutional, social, personal, and other influences on the piece of writing; the material conditions of writing (whether it is, for instance, online or on paper, in handwriting or print); and the writer's attitude toward the subject and the audience.

conviction the belief that a claim or course of action is true or reasonable. In a proposal argument, a writer must move an audience beyond conviction to action.

credibility an impression of integrity, honesty, and trustworthiness conveyed by a writer in an argument.

criterion in evaluative arguments, the standard by which something is measured to determine its quality or value.

definition, argument of an argument in which the claim specifies that something does or does not meet the conditions or features set forth in a definition: *Affirmative action is discrimination.*

deliberative argument an argument that deals with action to be taken in the future, focusing on matters of policy. Deliberative arguments include parliamentary debates and campaign platforms.

delivery the presentation of a spoken argument.

dogmatism a fallacy of argument in which a claim is supported on the grounds that it is the only conclusion acceptable within a given community.

either-or choice a fallacy of argument in which a complicated issue is represented as offering only two possible courses of action, one of which is made to seem vastly preferable to the other. *Either-or* choices generally misrepresent complicated arguments by oversimplifying them.

emotional appeal a strategy in which a writer tries to generate specific emotions (such as fear, envy, anger, or pity) in an audience to dispose it to accept a claim.

enthymeme in Toulmin argument, a statement that links a claim to a supporting reason: *The bank will fail* (claim) *because it has lost the support of its largest investors* (reason). In classical rhetoric, an enthymeme is a syllogism with one term understood but not stated: *Socrates is mortal because he is a human being.* (The understood term is: *All human beings are mortal.*)

epideictic argument see *ceremonial argument.*

equivocation a fallacy of argument in which a lie is given the appearance of truth, or in which the truth is misrepresented in deceptive language.

essential condition in a definition, an element that must be part of the definition but, by itself, isn't enough to define the term. An essential condition in defining a bird might be "winged": all birds have wings, yet wings alone do not define a bird since some insects and mammals also have wings. (See also *accidental condition* and *sufficient condition.*)

ethical appeal see *character, appeal based on,* and *ethos.*

ethnographic observation a form of field research involving close and extended observation of a group, event, or phenomenon; careful and detailed note-taking during the observation; analysis of the notes; and interpretation of that analysis.

ethos the self-image a writer creates to define a relationship with readers. In arguments, most writers try to establish an ethos that suggests honesty and credibility.

evaluation, argument of an argument in which the claim specifies that something does or does not meet established criteria: *The Nikon F5 is the most sophisticated 35mm camera currently available.*

evidence material offered to support an argument. See *artistic appeal* and *inartistic appeal.*

example, definition by a definition that operates by identifying individual examples of what is being defined: *Sports car—Corvette, Viper, Miata, Boxster.*

experimental evidence evidence gathered through experimentation; often evidence that can be quantified (for example, a survey of students before and after an election might yield statistical evidence about changes in their attitudes toward the candidates). Experimental evidence is frequently crucial to scientific arguments.

fact, argument of an argument in which the claim can be proved or disproved with specific evidence or testimony: *The winter of 1998 was the warmest on record for the United States.*

fallacy of argument a flaw in the structure of an argument that renders its conclusion invalid or suspect. See *ad hominem argument, bandwagon appeal, begging the question, dogmatism, either-or choice, equivocation, false authority, faulty analogy, faulty causality, hasty generalization, moral equivalence, non sequitur, scare tactic, sentimental appeal,* and *slippery slope.*

false authority a fallacy of argument in which a claim is based on the expertise of someone who lacks appropriate credentials.

faulty analogy a fallacy of argument in which a comparison between two objects or concepts is inaccurate or inconsequential.

faulty causality a fallacy of argument making the unwarranted assumption that because one event follows another, the first event causes the second. Also called *post hoc, ergo propter hoc,* faulty causality forms the basis of many superstitions.

firsthand evidence data—including surveys, observation, personal interviews, etc.—collected and personally examined by the writer. (See also *secondhand evidence*.)

fisking a term invented by Glenn Reynolds to describe a line-by-line refutation, usually online, of an argument that the writer finds inaccurate or rhetorically suspect.

flashpoint see *fallacy of argument*.

forensic argument an argument that deals with actions that have occurred in the past. Sometimes called judicial arguments, forensic arguments include legal cases involving judgments of guilt or innocence.

formal definition a definition that identifies something first by the general class to which it belongs *(genus)* and then by the characteristics that distinguish it from other members of that class *(species)*: *Baseball is a game* (genus) *played on a diamond by opposing teams of nine players who score runs by circling bases after striking a ball with a bat* (species).

genus in a definition, the general class to which an object or concept belongs: *baseball is a sport; green is a color.*

grounds in Toulmin argument, the evidence provided to support a claim or reason, or *enthymeme.*

hard evidence support for an argument using facts, statistics, testimony, or other evidence the writer finds.

hasty generalization a fallacy of argument in which an inference is drawn from insufficient data.

hyperbole use of overstatement for special effect.

hypothesis an expectation for the findings of one's research or the conclusion to one's argument. Hypotheses must be tested against evidence, counterarguments, and so on.

immediate reason the cause that leads directly to an effect, such as an automobile accident that results in an injury to the driver. (See also *necessary reason* and *sufficient reason*.)

inartistic appeal support for an argument using facts, statistics, eyewitness testimony, or other evidence the writer finds. (See also *artistic appeal*.)

intended readers the actual, real-life people whom a writer consciously wants to address in a piece of writing.

invention the process of finding and creating arguments to support a claim.

inverted word order moving grammatical elements of a sentence out of their usual order (subject-verb-object/complement) for special effect, as in *Tired I was; sleepy I was not.*

invitational argument a term used by Sonja Foss to describe arguments that are aimed not at vanquishing an opponent but at inviting others to collaborate in exploring mutually satisfying ways to solve problems.

invoked readers the readers directly addressed or implied in a text, which may include some that the writer did not consciously intend to reach. An argument that refers to *those who have experienced a major trauma*, for example, invokes all readers who have undergone this experience.

irony use of language that suggests a meaning in contrast to the literal meaning of the words.

line of argument a strategy or approach used in an argument. Argumentative strategies include appeals to the heart (emotional appeals), to values, to character (ethical appeals), and to facts and reason (logical appeals).

logical appeal a strategy in which a writer uses facts, evidence, and reason to make audience members accept a claim.

metaphor a figure of speech that makes a comparison, as in *The ship was a beacon of hope.*

moral equivalence a fallacy of argument in which no distinction is made between serious issues, problems, or failings and much less important ones.

necessary reason a cause that must be present for an effect to occur; for example, infection with a particular virus is a necessary reason for the development of AIDS. (See also *immediate reason* and *sufficient reason*.)

non sequitur a fallacy of argument in which claims, reasons, or warrants fail to connect logically; one point does not follow from another. *If you're really my friend, you'll lend me five hundred dollars.*

operational definition a definition that identifies an object by what it does or by the conditions that create it: *A line is the shortest distance between two points.*

parallelism use of similar grammatical structures or forms for pleasing effect: *in the classroom, on the playground, and at the mall.*

parody a form of humor in which a writer transforms something familiar into a different form to make a comic point.

pathos, appeal to see *emotional appeal.*

persuasion the act of seeking to change someone else's point of view.

precedents actions or decisions in the past that have established a pattern or model for subsequent actions. Precedents are particularly important in legal cases.

prejudices irrational beliefs, usually based on inadequate or outdated information.

premise a statement or position regarded as true and upon which other claims are based.

propaganda an argument advancing a point of view without regard to reason, fairness, or truth.

proposal argument an argument in which a claim is made in favor of or opposing a specific course of action: *Sport utility vehicles should have to meet the same fuel economy standards as passenger cars.*

purpose the goal of an argument. Purposes include entertaining, informing, convincing, exploring, and deciding, among others.

qualifiers words or phrases that limit the scope of a claim: *usually; in a few cases; under these circumstances.*

qualitative argument an argument of evaluation that relies on nonnumerical criteria supported by reason, tradition, precedent, or logic.

quantitative argument an argument of evaluation that relies on criteria that can be measured, counted, or demonstrated objectively.

reason in writing, a statement that expands a claim by offering evidence to support it. The reason may be a statement of fact or another claim. In Toulmin argument, a *reason* is attached to a *claim* by a *warrant*, a statement that establishes the logical connection between claim and supporting reason.

rebuttal an answer that challenges or refutes a specific claim or charge. Rebuttals may also be offered by writers who anticipate objections to the claims or evidence they offer.

rebuttal, conditions of in Toulmin argument, potential objections to an argument. Writers need to anticipate such conditions in shaping their arguments.

reversed structures a figure of speech that involves the inversion of clauses: *What is good in your writing is not original; what is original is not good.*

rhetoric the art of persuasion. Western rhetoric originated in ancient Greece as a discipline to prepare citizens for arguing cases in court.

rhetorical analysis an examination of how well the components of an argument work together to persuade or move an audience.

rhetorical questions questions posed to raise an issue or create an effect rather than to get a response: *You may well wonder, "What's in a name?"*

ridicule humor, usually mean-spirited, directed at a particular target.

Rogerian argument an approach to argumentation that is based on the principle, articulated by psychotherapist Carl Rogers, that audiences respond best when they do not feel threatened. Rogerian argument stresses trust and urges those who disagree to find common ground.

satire a form of humor in which a writer uses wit to expose—and possibly correct—human failings.

scare tactic a fallacy of argument presenting an issue in terms of exaggerated threats or dangers.

scheme a figure of speech that involves a special arrangement of words, such as inversion.

secondhand evidence any information taken from outside sources, including library research and online sources. (See also *firsthand evidence*.)

sentimental appeal a fallacy of argument in which an appeal is based on excessive emotion.

simile a comparison that uses *like* or *as*: *My love is like a red, red rose* or *I wandered lonely as a cloud.*

slippery slope a fallacy of argument exaggerating the possibility that a relatively inconsequential action or choice today will have serious adverse consequences in the future.

species in a definition, the particular features that distinguish one member of a *genus* from another: *Baseball is a sport* (genus) *played on a diamond by teams of nine players* (species).

spin a kind of political advocacy that makes any fact or event, however unfavorable, serve a political purpose.

stance the writer's attitude toward the topic and the audience.

stasis theory in classical rhetoric, a method for coming up with appropriate arguments by determining the nature of a given situation: *a question of fact; of definition; of quality; or of policy.*

sufficient condition in a definition, an element or set of elements adequate to define a term. A sufficient condition in defining God, for example, might be "supreme being" or "first cause." No other conditions are necessary, though many might be made. (See also *accidental condition* and *essential condition.*)

sufficient reason a cause that alone is enough to produce a particular effect; for example, a particular level of smoke in the air will set off a smoke alarm. (See also *immediate reason* and *necessary reason.*)

syllogism in formal logic, a structure of deductive logic in which correctly formed major and minor premises lead to a necessary conclusion:

Major premise	All human beings are mortal.
Minor premise	Socrates is a human being.
Conclusion	Socrates is mortal.

testimony a personal experience or observation used to support an argument.

thesis a sentence that succinctly states a writer's main point.

Toulmin argument a method of informal logic first described by Stephen Toulmin in *The Uses of Argument* (1958). Toulmin argument describes the key components of an argument as the *claim, reason, warrant, backing,* and *grounds.*

trope a figure of speech that involves a change in the usual meaning or signification of words, such as *metaphor, simile,* and *analogy.*

understatement a figure of speech that makes a weaker statement than a situation seems to call for. It can lead to powerful or to humorous effects.

values, appeal to a strategy in which a writer invokes shared principles and traditions of a society as a reason for accepting a claim.

warrant in Toulmin argument, the statement (expressed or implied) that establishes the logical connection between a claim and its supporting reason.

Claim	Don't eat that mushroom;
Reason	it's poisonous.
Warrant	What is poisonous should not be eaten.

ACKNOWLEDGMENTS

Chapter-Opening Art

Barbie doll: the first Barbie doll produced in 1959, Barbie Doll Museum, Palo Alto. Photo © Neema Frederic/CORBIS; Seal of the President/United States. Photo Joseph Sohm/Photo Researchers. White Dove: Photo © Roger Tidman/CORBIS; 4×4 on Road: Photo Getty Images/Antonio M. Rosario.

Texts

Dave Barry. "How to Vote in One Easy Step: Use Chisel, Tablet." Excerpt from *The Miami Herald*, September 13, 2002. Copyright © 2002 Dave Barry and The Miami Herald. Reprinted by permission of the author.

Derek Bok. "Protecting Freedom of Expression at Harvard." First published in the *Boston Globe*, May 25, 1991. Reprinted with permission of the author.

Damien Cave. "Does MP3 file trading hurt the music industry?" From *Salon.com*, August 23, 2002. Copyright © 2002. Reprinted with the permission of Salon.com. www.salon.com.

Dana Cloud. "Modified Pledge of Allegiance." Originally published in *The Daily Texan*, July 1, 2002. © 2002. Reprinted by permission of the author.

Jessica Cohen. "Grade A: The Market for a Yale Woman's Eggs." Short excerpt from *Atlantic Monthly*, December 2002, pp. 74, 78. Copyright © 2002. Reprinted by permission of the author.

Michelle Cottle. "Turning Boys into Girls." From *The Washington Monthly*, May 1998. Copyright by Washington Monthly Publishing, LLC, 733 15th St. NW, Suite 520, Washington, DC 20005. (202) 393-5155. Web site: www.washingtonmonthly.com.

Catherine Crier. Excerpt from Introduction in *The Case Against Lawyers* by Catherine Crier. Copyright © 2002 by Catherine Crier. Reprinted with permission of Broadway Books, a division of Random House, Inc.

Craig R. Dean. Excerpt from "Legalize Gay Marriage." From *The New York Times*. © 1991 by The New York Times Company. Reprinted by permission.

Alan Dershowitz. "Testing Speech Codes." From *Boston Globe Index*. Copyright © 2002 by Globe Newspaper Company (MA). Reproduced with permission of Globe Newspaper Company (MA) in the format of Textbook via Copyright Clearance Company.

James Fallows. Excerpts from "The Fifty-First State?" Originally published in *The Atlantic Monthly*, November 2002, p. 53. Copyright © 2002. Reprinted by permission of the author.

Peter Ferrara. Excerpt from "What is An American" by Peter Ferrara. Originally published in *National Review Online*, September 25, 2001. Reprinted with the permission of the author.

Nick Gillespie. "Happy Birthday, MTV." From *Reason* Magazine, August/September 2001. Copyright © 2003 by Reason Foundation, 3415 S. Sepulveda Blvd. #400, Los Angeles, CA 90034. Reprinted with permission. www.reason.com.

Chester Himes. "Hot Day, Hot Night." Copyright © 1969 by Estate of Chester Himes. Originally published as *Blind Man with a Pistol*. Now in print in Vintage trade paperback. Permission granted by Rosyln Targ Literary Agency, Inc.

Langston Hughes. "Harlem—A Dream Deferred." From *Collected Poems* by Langston Hughes. Copyright © 1994 by the Estate of Langston Hughes. Reprinted by permission of Alfred A. Knopf, a division of Random House, Inc.

Pizzello/AP/WW; Fig. 7.1, Sam Mircovich/AP/WW; Fig. 7.3, © 2003 USA TODAY. Reprinted by permission. Usatoday.com; Fig. 9.1, InstaPundit.com; Fig. 10.2, Chris Pizzello/AP/WW; Fig. 10.3, courtesy, American Honda Models; Fig. 10.4, Scott Frances/ESTP Photographics; Fig. 11.3, Seth Perlman/AP/WW; Fig. 12.1, courtesy, Americans for the Arts; pg. 256, Bedford/St. Martin's photo; Figs. 13.1, 13.2, reprinted with permission of *The Onion*, © 2001, © 1998 by Onion, Inc. www.theonion.com; pg. 265, reprinted by permission from American Family Life Assurance of Columbus (AFLAC), Columbus, Ga.; Fig. 13.3, Todd Nienkerk, TEXAS TRAVESTY, The University of Texas at Austin; Fig. 14.1, photo by Carl Van Vechten/The Granger Collection; Fig. 14.2, *Doonesbury* © G. B. Trudeau. Reprinted with permission of Universal Press Syndicate. All rights reserved; Fig. 14.3, Ric Feld/AP/WW; Fig. 14.4, Reprinted by permission of *The Ironic Times*; Fig. 15.1, courtesy, Mercedes-Benz, USA; Fig. 15.2, courtesy, Viking/Penguin Publishing Co./Coral Graphics, Inc.; Fig. 15.3, "The Chinese Horse" Lascaux Caves, France/Art Resource; Fig. 15.4, Paul Schutzer, LIFE Magazine, TIMEPIX/Getty Images; Fig. 15.5, Bridget Besaw Gorman/AP/WW; Fig. 15.6, Joe Rosenthal/AP/WW; Fig. 15.7, Marty Lederhandler/AP/WW; Fig. 15.9, © 2003 Benetton Group S.P.A.; Fig. 15.10, courtesy, United Nations World Food Programme, www.wfp.org; Fig. 15.11 (a), AP/WW, (b), courtesy, McDonald's Corp., ©, courtesy BMW of North America; Fig. 15.12, Reprinted with permission of Dennis Tyler; Fig. 15.13, Reprinted with permission of Dennis Tyler; Fig. 15.15, Reprinted by permission of Google; Fig. 15.18, J. Scott Applewhite/AP/WW; Fig. 15.19, NASA/AP/WW; Fig. 15.21, courtesy, Brown Lenox Co. Ltd.; Fig. 16.1, Reprinted with permission of Patrick Ruffini; Fig. 16.2, Reprinted by permission of Jerlynn Merritt; Fig. 16.3, copyright © 2003 The American Society for the Prevention of Cruelty to Animals. Reprinted with permission of ASPCA. All rights reserved; Fig. 16.4, reprinted by permission of the Foundation for Individual Rights in Education; Fig. 16.5, Reprinted by permission of Google; Fig. 17.1, AP/WW; Fig. 17.2, © 20th Century Fox/Photofest; Fig. 17.3, Andrew Dalmau/EFE/AP/WW; Fig. 17.4, AP/WW; Fig. 18.1, Michael Caulfield/AP/WW; Fig. 18.2, the Federation of Gay Games, Inc.; Fig. 19.1, Ed Sirrs/Retna; Fig. 19.2, courtesy, World Wildlife Fund; Fig. 19.3, © Jimmy Margulies. Reprinted by permission; Fig. 20.1, courtesy, U.S. Copyright Office; Fig. 20.2, © Garry Trudeau. Reprinted with permission of Universal Press Syndicate. All rights reserved; Fig. 20.3, Janet Hostetter/AP/WW; Fig. 21.1, © 2003 PEOPLE Magazine, photo: Craig DeCristo/L2 Agency, (inset) Matt Jones, (top) Ramey Photo, (cent.) Gary Caspry/Reuters, (bot.) Lester Cohen/WireImage; Fig. 21.2, courtesy, ZYZZYVA, San Francisco; Fig. 21.3, Jack Kutz/Image Works; Fig. 21.4, Dennis Brack/Bloomberg News/Landov; Fig. 22.1, courtesy, The Modern Library Assn.; Fig. 22.2, © 2001 by the American Psychological Association. Courtesy, Naylor Design. Reprinted with permission.

INDEX